Equipment and Motor Vehicle Leasing and Hiring Law and Practice

AUSTRALIA
LBC Information Services
Sydney

CANADA and USA
Carswell
Toronto ● Ontario

NEW ZEALAND
Brooker's
Auckland

SINGAPORE and MALAYSIA
Thomson Information (S.E. Asia)
Singapore

Equipment and Motor Vehicle Leasing and Hiring Law and Practice

Iwan Davies
LL.B. (Cantab.), LL.M., Ph.D. (Wales)
Barrister and Reader in Law
University of Wales

FIRST EDITION

LONDON
SWEET & MAXWELL
1997

Published in 1997 by
Sweet & Maxwell Limited of
100 Avenue Road, London NW3 3PF
Typeset by LBJ Enterprises Ltd, Aldermaston and Chilcompton.
Printed and bound by Butler and Tanner Ltd, Frome and London.

No natural forests were destroyed to make this product;
only farmed timber was used and replanted

British Library Cataloguing in Publication Data

A CIP catalogue record for this book
is available from the British Library

ISBN 0421-535-008

Preface

The purpose of this book is to provide a guide to the law of leasing and hiring of goods with particular emphasis on motor vehicles. Core concepts are identified and the focus of the work is to examine the common law and statutory framework which defines the equipment leasing context. In this respect there is no legal distinction between the expression "lease" and "hire" in respect of the organisational framework of bailment and these terms are used interchangeably throughout this book. At the same time it is not the purpose of this work to consider in detail the taxation regime which relates to the leasing of equipment as this has been dealt with in other specialist texts.

The leasing transaction is of great commercial importance and large amounts of capital is ventured on the basis of its validity. In the precedents section I have tried to identify the most common precedents which are appropriate to the equipment leasing context and by doing so I have attempted to avoid duplication. Nevertheless, it has to be acknowledged that the leasing industry is a vibrant one and its overwhelming characteristic is that of innovation.

It is a pleasure for me to record my gratitude to Mr Michael Cronin who is both a mentor and friend. Further, I should like to acknowledge the support of Mrs Margaret Waldren, Head of Operations at the Finance and Leasing Association whose enthusiasm for all things leasing knows no bounds! As always I am grateful to Messrs Walter Rainbird, Jeff Evans and Kris Thorne for their consideration during the writing of this book. Finally, I should like to record my gratitude to my wife and also our children, Elidir and Osian, who are constant source of joy.

Iwan Davies
Iscoed Chambers
86 St Helen's Road
Swansea

February, 1997

Contents

PART 1
COMMERCIAL AND LEGAL CONTEXT

Chapter

PART 2
ENTERING INTO AGREEMENT

PART 3
WRONGFUL DEALINGS IN LEASED ASSETS AND THIRD PARTY CONFLICTS

PART 4
INSOLVENCY AND INTERNATIONAL LEASING

PART 5
SELECTED PRECEDENTS AND APPENDICES

Precedent

Appendix

Table of Cases

Table of Statutes

Table of Statutory Instruments

Table of Abbreviations

CCA 1974	Consumer Credit Act 1974
CPA 1987	Consumer Protection Act 1987
FA 1889	Factors Act 1889
FTA 1973	Fair Trading Act 1973
SGA 1979	Sale of Goods Act 1979
SGSA 1982	Supply of Goods and Services Act 1982
SOGIT 1973	Supply of Goods (Implied Terms) Act 1973
TDA 1968	Trade Descriptions Act 1968
UCC	Uniform Commercial Code
UCTA 1977	Unfair Contract Terms Act 1977

Part 1

Commercial and Legal Context

Chapter 1

Introduction

Development

The essence of a lease, whether of goods or land, is to allow the lessee to acquire possession without paying the full capital cost. At the same time the lessor can receive a return on its investment while retaining the title and security in the goods or land. The lease is by no means a new phenomenon and historical evidence suggests its widespread use by the ancient Sumerians circa 5000 B.C. Indeed, Claes-Olof Livijn has chronicled the many incidents of leasing techniques with the aim of showing that it is a "natural, inevitable and eternal alternative to outright ownership".[1] In England and Wales, however, despite the fact that the Statute of Wales 1284 declared that the action of covenant was available for leases of movable property as well as land, it was only in the wake of the industrial revolution that the leasing of equipment became particularly prevalent.

On both sides of the Atlantic, financial leasing was a forerunner to the burgeoning twentieth century personal credit business which grew with the motor car industry and other consumer durables. In the nineteenth century, entrepreneurs would lease coal wagons to collieries, whilst the idea of using the contract of hire as a disguised contract of sale was common among the costermongers in the East End of London who would hire their barrows on a weekly basis extending over many years. Eventually the hire-purchase technique was developed mainly for consumer finance as a direct result of nineteenth-century bills of sale legislation inhibiting chattel mortgages by individuals.[2]

The leasing of business and industrial equipment has developed during the last quarter of the twentieth century as a popular and viable alternative to other methods of financing capital acquisition. This is a world-wide phenomenon which explains why UNIDROIT embarked on a programme of preparing uniform rules on leasing contracts, which culminated in the UNIDROIT Convention on International Financial Leasing 1988. Indeed the volume of leasing business in the United Kingdom continues to rise, and the value of new plant and equipment, including motor vehicles, leased in 1995 by the national association of United Kingdom lessors, the Finance and Leasing Association, was in excess of £17 billion. There is no doubt that fiscal stimulus to leasing in

[1] See Livijn, *Leasing 5000 Years* (1984).
[2] See below.

3

the United Kingdom accounted for much of its growth during the early years of the 1980s. It is not the purpose of this book to consider the taxation regime relating to the leasing of equipment, as this is the focus of other specialist texts.[3] This work is concerned to examine the common law and statutory framework which defines the equipment leasing context. In this respect it should be noted that there is no legal distinction between the expression "lease" and "hire" and these terms are used interchangeably throughout this book.

Of course, whilst there are many forms of lease contract, they all share one common characteristic which is that of title retention by the lessor. This is so even though the lessee may have selected the equipment from a manufacturer or a vendor. Juridically, such contracts provide for the bailment of the asset leased and, in addition to the contractual position between the parties, rights and obligations arise by virtue of the *fact* of bailment. At the outset, however, the most obvious characteristic of the hire contract needs to be explored, namely, the ostensible ownership problem that arises out of the fact of the hirer's possession of the equipment and the lessor's right of ownership in respect of it. The reservation of a proprietary interest (*jus in re aliena*) by the financier as owner is a real right which goes to the core of a successful pursuit for security in the equipment.

Historical Growth:
The Ostensible Ownership Problem

Introduction

The growth of non-possessory security interests in chattels was dealt a severe blow in *Twyne*'s case[4] which, in conjunction with English bankruptcy legislation, articulated a simple rule, namely, in order to obtain priority over an asset in respect of third parties, it was not only necessary to receive consent of the prior owner but also possession of the chattel. Although a "possession only" rule has the virtue of simplicity, this is bought at considerable indirect costs as can be illustrated with stock-in-trade financing. The reason for this is that the creditor wants only a *contingent* right to take collateral at a specified time, namely on default. The difficulty is that a possession-based system cannot accommodate the split of rights between two parties. Even if the ostensible ownership problem is "cured" by the lender taking possession, this in itself creates ostensible owernship problems since the focus shifts away from the creditors of the debtor to the creditors of the lender.

[3.] See Sadler, Reisbach, Thomas, *Equipment Leasing* (1993); Wainman, *Leasing* (2nd ed., 1995).
[4.] *Coke Att.-Gen. v. Twyne* (1601) K.B. 76 E.R. 809 (Star Chamber).

The traditional method adopted by the common law in curing the ostensible ownership problem posed by a creditor being out of possession is through public filing. The filing of a security interest is seen as an alternative to the taking of possession of the secured property by the secured party. The modern history of the recognition and regulation of non-possessory security interests in the common law countries commenced with the English Bills of Sale Act 1854 which introduced a system of publicity. The basic statute now in force replacing the earlier legislation is the Bills of Sale Act 1878. However, a bill of sale is not necessarily a document creating a security, for example there may be an absolute bill of sale. The 1878 Act governs absolute bills of sale and also regulates security bills, except in so far as they are inconsistent with the Bills of Sale Act (1878) Amendment Act 1882 which was aimed at the unscrupulous practice of moneylenders in enforcing their security.

Absolute Bills of Sale

Absolute bills of sale constitute an out-and-out transfer of ownership. Whilst the 1878 Act imposes requirements as to the contents of such a bill, no statutory form is prescribed although registration is necessary so as to cure the ostensible ownership problem of the grantor remaining in possession. An immediate effect of this was to make bills of sale more attractive to creditors, since security was preserved even following the grantor's bankruptcy.[5] Not surprisingly, during the period 1877–1880 the number of bills registered increased dramatically. Often the interest rates charged were oppressive, and the nature of the security taken covered both present and future chattels. It was especially the unscrupulous practice of moneylenders enforcing their security that led to the Bills of Sale Act (1878) Amendment Act 1882, which laid down a prescribed form to which all security bills had to conform and authorised powers of repossession by the grantee except for specified cause.

It is doubtful whether the Bills of Sale Acts 1854–1891 have any place in a modern personal property law regime. Indeed, Kay L.J. remarked in *Tuck v. Southern Counties Deposit Bank*,[6] soon after the passing of the 1882 Act, that it was necessary to tread very warily whenever a matter fell within the purview of the law of bills of sale. The main problem is the divergent "objectives" of such legislation so that the Bills of Sale Act (1878) Amendment Act 1882 has two contradictory purposes: first, protecting third-party creditors from being deceived by a secret transaction between the parties to a bill of sale; secondly, protecting the grantor from the excesses of the grantee. These divergent objectives are incapable, as a matter of legal logic, of producing integrated legislation.[7]

[5.] The significance of the 1878 Act was that it took properly registered absolute bills out of the reputed ownership provision of bankruptcy: Bills of Sale Act 1878, s. 20.

[6.] (1889) 42 Ch.D. 471 at 476.

[7.] For a detailed discussion as to the formal requirements and exclusions in bills of sale, see 4(1) *Halsbury's Laws* (4th edn., Reissue) (Bills of Sale).

Security Bills of Sale

The legislation

All documents recording legal or equitable interests in personal chattels and licenses to take possession as security are covered by the legislation. Section 4 of the Bills of Sale Act 1878 provides:

> "The expression "bill of sale" shall include bills of sale, assignments, transfers, declarations of trust without transfer, inventories of goods with receipt thereto attached, or receipts for purchase moneys of goods, and other assurances of personal chattels . . ."

It would appear that the legislation only bites where the document itself is intended as part of the contract which purports to effect a proprietary transfer at law or in equity. If the title passes by oral agreement, then the bill is not registrable since the legislation strikes at documents as distinct from transactions. Where there is an invoice or receipt, this does not constitute a bill of sale if property has passed independent of the document. It is otherwise if the payment of the price was made conditional upon the giving of a receipt.[8]

At the outset it should be emphasised that where an arrangement is a sham in the sense that it was designed to avoid the bills of sale legislation, the documents will almost invariably fail to accord with the prescribed statutory form. It is otherwise where the purpose of the finance documentation and procedures is designed to create a valid security bill of sale. The primary object of the 1882 Act was to restrict and regulate the taking of bills of sale by moneylenders and, therefore, has more in common with the Moneylenders Acts than with the preceding Bills of Sale Acts 1854 and 1878. The form and contents of security bills of sale are exceedingly technical which has promoted their lack of use. The principal requirements of a security bill of sale are as follows:

1. The grantee's right of seizure is confined under section 7 to five specified causes, namely: (a) if the grantor makes default in payment of the sum or sums secured by the bill at the time therein provided for payment, or in the performance of any covenant or agreement contained in the bill and necessary for maintaining the security; (b) if the grantor becomes a bankrupt or suffers the goods or any of them to be distrained for rent, rates or taxes; (c) if the grantor fraudulently either removes or suffers the goods or any of them to be removed from the premises; (d) if the grantor does not, without reasonable excuse, upon demand in writing by the grantee, produce to him his last receipts for rent, rates and taxes; and (e) if execution is levied

---

[8] *Ramsey v. Margrett* [1894] 2 Q.B. 18 at 24, *per* Lord Esher M.R.

against the grantor's goods under any judgment at law. It is further provided, in section 13 of the 1882 Act, that any goods seized must remain on the premises where they were seized and must not be removed or sold until five days after the date of seizure. This gives the grantor time to apply to the court to restrain the grantor from either selling or removing the goods.

2. A brief and simple bill of sale is set out in the 1882 Act which provides for the statement of the consideration and terms of payment as well as setting out the statutory grounds of seizure and specifying the property comprised in the bill. Failure to comply with the prescribed form makes the bill absolutely void in respect of the personal chattels comprised in it.[9]

3. Under the 1878 Act, an absolute bill of sale is not totally void if it is unregistered, that is, it is valid as between grantor and grantee. In contrast, under the 1882 Act an unregistered security bill is absolutely void. Registration must be renewed before the expiration of five years from the prior registration of renewal.[10] Section 8 of the 1882 Act requires registration to be made within seven days after the making of a security bill of sale, or, when made out of England, within seven days after it would have arrived in England if posted immediately upon execution. During the seven days' period the bill is valid; if it is not duly registered, its avoidance is retrospective so that an execution by a third party during the seven days is effective. The procedure for registration is mainly set out in section 10(2) and (3) of the 1878 Act and the place of registration is the Bills of Sale Department at the Central Office of the Royal Courts of Justice. Section 11 of the 1882 Act directs the registrar to transmit copies of the bills of sale to the registrar of the county court, in whose district the chattels are placed, whenever either the residence of the grantor himself or the place of the chattel lie outside the London bankruptcy district. In addition to the bill of sale, the following documents have to be registered:

    (i)   Every schedule or inventory annexed to or referred to in the bill of sale, for example, a collateral agreement.[11]
    (ii) A true copy of the bill of sale (including attestation provided by one or more credible witnesses by virtue of sections 8 and 10 of the 1882 Act) and of the schedule and inventory.
    (iii) An affidavit proving the time and execution of the bill of sale and its due execution and attestation. This affidavit must also contain a description of the residence and

---

[9.] Bills of Sale Act (1878) Amendment Act 1882, s. 9.
[10.] Bills of Sale Act 1878, s. 11.
[11.] Bills of Sale Act 1878, s. 10.

occupation of the grantor and of every attesting witness. The object is that third parties may make all necessary inquiries to protect themselves before advancing money, or supplying goods on credit, to the grantor.

(iv) All bills of sale given in consideration of a sum of less than £30 were made absolutely void by virtue of section 12 of the 1882 Act.

Security bills of sale and third party purchasers

The effect of failure to abide by the statutory form is that the bill of sale, as a security bill of sale, will be void and, in the case of non-registration, absolutely void even against the mortgagor. It follows, for example, that in a sale and leaseback sham[12] where the mortgagor has disposed of for example a vehicle to a third party, that third party will acquire a good title because the mortgagor is still the owner at the time he disposed of it to the third party.[13] One consequence of a bill of sale being void is that the instrument is totally void as a contract of loan as well as regards the chattels comprised in the so-called bill. Thus, the lender can only recover money had and received and will then only be able to recover a reasonable rate of interest based upon the incontrovertible benefit to the mortgagor. As a personal remedy, this is of little value on the bankruptcy of the mortgagor of the so-called bill of sale.

The rules fixing priority with security bills of sale can in no sense be described as coherent. As between competing bills of sale priority is determined by the order of registration, but where the prior bill of sale was an absolute one which remains valid between mortgagor and mortgagee even if unregistered, this will leave no title in the mortgagor, so he ceases to be the owner for the purposes of section 5 of the 1882 Act.[14] True ownership for the purposes of section 5 of the 1882 Act includes ownership at law or equity and beneficial ownership therefore is sufficient. Section 10 of the 1882 Act fixes priority between registered bills of sale by order of registration, but at the same time does not purport to make registration the equivalent of actual notice to all the world. Consequently there is no requirement to search the register, so that compliance with the statutory form for security bills of sale through registration does not constitute constructive notice. It follows that a registered bill of sale will not prevail against third parties who obtain a title from the mortgagor in the ordinary course of the mortgagor's business on the basis of ostensible or implied authority, that is, by leaving the mortgagor in possession, the mortgagee of the bill is deemed to impliedly authorise the carrying on of the ordinary course of business of the mortgagor. In the case of a private disposition, the mortgagor of a

---

[12.] See below.

[13.] *Polsky v. S. and A. Services* [1851] 1 All E.R. 185; affd. [1951] All E.R. 1062, C.A.

[14.] See *Tuck v. Southern Counties Deposit Bank* (1889) 42 Ch.D. 471, C.A.

security bill of sale who afterwards disposes of the goods does not do so as a seller thereby triggering section 8 of the Factors Act 1889 and section 24 of the Sale of Goods Act 1979 (the seller in possession provision), because a security bill of sale is not a contract of sale as between the mortgagor and mortgagee, that is, the grantor of a security bill is a mortgagor in possession so that the innocent purchaser provisions do not apply. This phenomenon is considered further in Chapter 6, below.

Avoidance of security bills of sale

It is conventional wisdom that the House of Lords in *McEntire v. Crossley Bros.*[15] decided that hire-purchase agreements are not within the definition of bills of sale. The Bills of Sale Acts contain nothing which prevent parties entering into a contract, the legal effect of which is to leave the title wholly in the vendor and to let the intending purchaser into possession as a bailee for use with a possessory title only until he exercises his option. Indeed, the legal distinction drawn between hire-purchase and a security bill of sale can be simply stated: in the case of the former, the owner temporarily gives up possession, whereas in the case of a security bill of sale, the owner parts with ownership. As Lord Herschell L.C. put it in *McEntire*[16]: "The Bills of Sale Act relates to assurances or assignments or rights to seize given or conferred by the person who owns the property".

Whilst the distinction drawn may be simply stated, in fact there is a close almost symbiotic relationship between a sale transaction and a bill of sale (chattel mortgage). A chattel mortgage resembles a sale in that general property, in the sense of legal title, passes to the creditor, but whereas in a sale it passes absolutely[17] in a mortgage the mortgagor is entitled to redeem. The problem of sham arises where the transfer of property is expressed in unconditional terms whereas, in fact, it is intended to operate as a security. The two statutory provisions which echo each other here are section 62(4) of the Sale of Goods Act 1979, which expressly excludes from its application "a transaction in the form of a contract of sale which is intended to operate by way of security", and the Bills of Sale Act 1882, which strikes at documents purporting to grant security over goods where the grantor retains possession and declares void such a document which has not been duly registered. The distinction between the two is especially acute in Scotland, as there is no equivalent to the bill of sale, and it is only the Sale of Goods Act 1979 which allows for the transfer of ownership of goods without delivery.[18] The determining issue is whether the so-called "owner" is really the

---

[15] [1895] A.C. 457.
[16] *Ibid.* at 461.
[17] Sale of Goods Act 1979, s. 2(1).
[18] See *Robertson v. Hall's Trustee* (1896) 34 R. 120, Ct. Sess.; *Armour v. Thyssen Edelstahlwerke AG* [1991] A.C. 339.

owner of the goods or whether he is a sham owner purporting to let the goods to the person who is the real owner.

Even though the courts insist that the Acts are not evaded by a sham transaction, the court cannot impeach genuine transactions whose effect is to escape the legislation, because this is viewed as a legitimate option for the parties. The point becomes clear in Lord Esher M.R.'s judgment in *Re Watson, ex p. Official Receiver*[19] when his Lordship said:

> "I do not deny that people may evade an Act of Parliament if they can, but, if they attempt to do so by putting forward documents which affect to be one thing when they really mean something different, and which are not true descriptions of what the parties to them are really doing, the court will go through the documents in order to arrive at the truth".

Indeed much of the case law has been concerned with methods of *avoiding* the application of bills of sale legislation, especially in the sale and leaseback scenario where the seller retains possession. Here the courts have adopted a true intention test, determined by the principal document and any collateral or oral evidence, to ascertain whether there has been a genuine composite transaction, that is, a sale complete with an agreement or option to repurchase the goods. In fact, the distinctions drawn in the cases based upon the true intentions of the parties are difficult to state, because very often the parties will intend both to sell the goods and raise money on the security of the goods. The common theme is to avoid the scope of the bills of sale legislation in view of the attraction of hire-purchase and leasing as financing mechanisms.

The Doctrine of Sham: Sale and Leaseback of Equipment

Determination of the legal nature of the transaction

In determining the question of sale or security for a loan the courts will determine the legal nature of the transaction. Typically there are two routes employed.[20] The first route is the so-called "external" one where the courts scrutinise the document with a view to eliciting whether it is a sham, that is where it conceals the true nature of the agreement between the parties. The second route is the "internal" one which involves a scrutiny of the terms of the agreement in order to conclude as a matter of law whether it constitutes a security interest as distinct from a sale.

The issue of sham and security expresses itself, in the equipment leasing context, in sale and leaseback transactions. This is a perfectly legitimate mechanism and is a way of raising finance in relation to

---

[19.] (1890) 25 Q.B.D. 27 at 29.
[20.] See Staughton L.J. in *Welsh Development Agency v. Export Finance Co. Ltd* [1992] B.C.C. 270.

equipment, for example, where the putative lessee enters into a sale transaction with the supplier because of long-standing economies of communication existing between them or perhaps because the lessee, for commercial reasons, wishes to conceal from its creditors that it is utilising a leasing facility. There are of course tax difficulties with such transactions, in particular an equipment lessor seeking to claim capital allowances must consider to what extent his claim may be restricted by statutory anti-avoidance provisions, especially section 75 of the Capital Allowances Act 1990. A typical example of an anti-avoidance provision is section 75(3) of the Act which restricts the writing down allowance which can be claimed where the lessor has obtained an assignment of the benefit of a contract under which ownership of machinery or plant may or will pass on the performance of the contract. An obvious way of obviating the difficulties is through novation of the relevant sale contract as this will ensure that section 75(3) will not apply at all.[21]

The sale and leaseback mechanism

Scrutiny of the transaction. The courts will scrutinise the transaction to ensure that the transfer of ownership is a reality and not a disguised mortgage, for example where it is purely a financing mechanism and the seller/lessee still retains an interest in the goods. It is a widely established legitimate practice that where the lessee acts as the undisclosed principal of the lessor in acquiring the equipment from the supplier and then sells it and leases it back from the lessor, this is not treated as a chattel mortgage so long as there is an outright transfer of title to the lessor. Thus in *Re Watson, ex p. Official Receiver in Bankruptcy*,[22] Mary Watson sold her furniture to a financier and hired it back under a hire-purchase agreement which empowered the financier to seize the furniture on default. This was held to be a loan on the security of the furniture because it was not Mary Watson's intention to give the financier absolute title to the furniture. As Lord Esher M.R. pointed out the documentation "affect to be one thing when they really mean something quite different, and which are not true descriptions of what the parties to them are really doing".[23] The crucial issue is whether the parties intended to avoid the application of the bills of sale legislation and, with this in mind, executed documents whose purpose was to conceal the true nature of the transaction entered into between them. In

---

[21.] For a full discussion on the condition of entitlement to capital allowances and anti-avoidance provisions, see Sadler, Reisbach, Thomas, *Equipment Leasing* (1994), Pt. 2.
[22.] (1890) 25 Q.B.D. 27.
[23.] *Ibid.* at 37. See also *Kingsley v. Sterling Industrial Securities Ltd* [1966] 1 All E.R. 414; [1967] 2 Q.B. 747, C.A.; *Stoneleigh Finance Ltd v. Phillips* [1965] 1 All E.R. 513; [1965] 2 Q.B. 537; *North Central Wagon Finance Co. Ltd v. Brailsford* [1962] 1 All E.R. 502; *Polsky v. S. & A. Services* [1951] 1 All E.R. 185 (affd. [1951] 1 All E.R. 1062).

Re George Inglefield Ltd[24] Romer L.J. explained the essential differences between a genuine sale and leaseback from a charge in the following terms.[25]

> "In a transaction of sale the vendor is not entitled to get back the subject-matter of the sale by returning to the purchaser the money that has passed between them. In the case of a mortgage or charge the mortgagor is entitled, until he has been foreclosed, to get back the subject-matter of the mortgage or charge by returning to the mortgagee the money that has passed between them. The second essential difference is that if the mortgagee realises the subject-matter of the mortgage for a sum more than sufficient to repay him, with interest and the costs, the money that has passed between him and the mortgagor he has to account to the mortgagor for the surplus. If the purchaser sells the subject-matter of the purchase, and realises a profit, of course he has not got to account to the vendor for the profit. Thirdly, if the mortgagee realises the mortgage property for a sum that is insufficient to repay him the money that he has paid to the mortgagor, together with interest and costs, then the mortgagee is entitled to recover from the mortgagor the balance of the money ... If the purchaser were to resell the purchased property at a price which was insufficient to recoup him the money that he has paid to the vendor, of course he would not be entitled to recover the balance from the vendor".

This approach is particularly significant in the context of a sophisticated lease structure, where rentals has been assigned to a third-party funder of the lessor.[26]

An obvious indication of a sham would be where the purchase price was fixed by reference not to the value of the goods or a genuine price but to the sum required to discharge the seller's liability on another transaction, or where the agreement contains oppressive powers unlikely to be found in a genuine agreement, or where no cash had in fact passed between the parties.[27] There are many variations of the sale and leaseback theme and the main ones will now be considered.

Where there is a sale followed by a lease to the seller's nominee who does not take delivery of the goods. In this context section 24 of the Sale of Goods Act 1979 would appear to be pertinent, because in any subsequent disposition of the goods the seller's continuity in *de facto* possession would pass a good title to a bona fide third-party purchaser.[28] However, it would appear to be the case that if the finance company was ignorant of the true position the lease will be upheld as valid as against the seller and hirer.[29]

[24.] [1933] Ch. 1.
[25.] *Ibid.* at 26–27.
[26.] See below.
[27.] See *Polsky v. S. and A. Services* [1951] 1 All E.R. 185 (affd. [1951] 1 All E.R. 1062).
[28.] See *Gamer's Motor Centre (Newcastle) Pty Ltd v Natwest Wholesale Australia Pty Ltd* (1987) 163 C.L.R. 236; *Forsythe International (U.K.) Ltd v. Silver Shipping Co. Ltd* [1994] 1 All E.R. 851.
[29.] *Snook v. London West Riding Investments Ltd* [1967] 1 All E.R. 518.

Where there has been a sale by the ostensible owner to the finance company followed by a hiring to the true owner. The hiring transaction will be upheld, as the true owner will be estopped from denying the dealer's right to sell in this circumstance.[30] Where, however, the finance company is aware of the true facts, the transaction will be treated as a bill of sale and will probably be void for non-registration,[31] although, since the consideration will have failed, the finance company will have an action for money had and received against the seller in this circumstance.

Refinancing arrangement. A refinancing arrangement is where the true owner sells to the dealer with a view to raising finance and the latter then disposes of the equipment to the finance house who leases it back to the original owner. Under this arrangement the position of the finance company would appear to be secure from the perspective of sham, since it will be one step removed from the original owner. This will be the case even though the finance company was aware that the purpose of the transaction was to enable the original owner to obtain funds, so long as there was a genuine sale and re-hiring.[32] In *Stoneleigh Finance Ltd*, the Court of Appeal upheld an indirect sale and leaseback arrangement through a sale to an intermediate party. As Davies L.J. explained in that case[33]:

> "A sale of goods by A to B followed by a hiring back of the goods by B to A is not, if the parties genuinely intend the transactions to be effective, a bill of sale or otherwise invalid . . . Still less is it so if the transaction takes the form of a sale by A to B, a sale by B to C, and a subsequent hiring by C to A."

An entrustment principle? The DTI Consultation Paper *Transfer of Title: Sections 21 to 26 of the Sale of Goods Act 1979*[34] recommended the extension of the entrustment principle in English commercial law, that is, where the owner of goods has entrusted those goods to, or acquiesced in their possession by, another person, then an innocent purchaser of those goods should acquire a good title. In effect this proposal would, if implemented, involve a statutory extension of the common law estoppel doctrine which, in the context of chattels, has traditionally stressed the need for a representation either by words or by conduct.[35] The emphasis upon wilful conduct has meant that the common law doctrine does not go very far in entrustment cases, since it is well settled that mere possession of a chattel does not *by itself* convey a title to dispose of it. Indeed this provided the legal rationale for the financing of equipment

---

[30] *Eastern Distributors Ltd v. Goldring* [1957] 2 Q.B. 600.
[31] *North Central Wagon Finance Co. Ltd v. Brailsford* [1962] 1 All E.R. 502.
[32] See *Stoneleigh Finance Ltd v. Phillips* [1965] 2 Q.B. 537. *Cf. Yorkshire Wagon Co. v. Maclure* (1882) 21 Ch.D. 309.
[33] [1965] 2 Q.B. 537 at 569–570.
[34] January 1994.
[35] See Chap. 6, below.

through title retention mechanisms in the common law world, especially hire-purchase and lease mechanisms. As such, the extension of the simple entrustment principle suggested by the DTI would inevitably impact upon especially motor vehicle financing in England, not least because it would tend to make wrongful dispositions too easy for the seller and too safe for the impudent buyer. At the same time, it could compromise the relatively new motor vehicle financing techniques which fund the depreciation rather than the acquisition of ownership of the vehicle.

In fact the approach adopted by Professor Diamond in another DTI Report,[36] and which has for many years influenced the debate over reform of personal property security interests not only in England but also recently in Australia and New Zealand, recommended the setting up of a comprehensive security register with the establishment of a notice filing system accompanied by a first to file priority rule. The model here is that seen in the United States of America with Article Nine of the Uniform Commercial Code and also the various Personal Property Security Acts seen in most Canadian Provinces. Such a radical approach was rejected by the British Government on the basis of complexity, cost and lack of commercial support. Even so, it is unlikely that the new regime envisaged for company charges under the Companies Act 1989 will reach fruition. In the light of the current uncertainty with the company charges scheme, it would be contrary to principle to penalise a creditor supplying goods on the basis of a retention of title clause, including a lease mechanism, merely because of the potential policy rejection of the lack of an efficient system of notification.

Economic Substance and Triumph of Legal Form

As has already been discussed, hire-purchase and conditional sale transactions do not come within the bills of sale legislation, because there is no assurance, assignment or license to seize.[37] The reason is that the legal title of the creditor is vested in him independently of the hire-purchase or conditional sale document.[38] Quite simply, although possession is delivered to the debtor, property remains in the creditor as owner and does not pass until all the instalments have been paid. In the case of a lease transaction, such a conclusion is bolstered by the fact that property remains with the lessor as legal owner throughout the term of the lease, notwithstanding the fact that the lessee enjoys the benefit of

---

[36.] *A Review of Security Interests in Property* (1989).

[37.] See *McEntire v. Crossley Bros Ltd* [1895] A.C. 547.

[38.] *Manchester, Sheffield and Lincolnshire Rly Co. v. North Central Wagon Co.* (1888) 13 App. Cas. 554.

possession and use of the equipment for most, if not all, of its economic life. The issue in English law is not that of economic substance but rather one of legal form.

It is the policy of the courts in England, where there is security with recourse to property which can be effected by means other than a transaction of loan or charge, not to treat it as registrable under section 395 of the Companies Act 1985. This is so even though the exact economic effect might be carried out through a transaction which in form was registrable as a security interest in the goods. As Staughton L.J. put it in *Welsh Development Agency v. Export Finance Co. Ltd*[39]:

> ". . . statute law in this country when it enacts rules to be applied to a particular transaction is in general referring to the legal nature of a transaction and not its economic effect."

This phenomenon can be illustrated in the context of retention of title clauses, and similar considerations can apply to leases where, for example, the lessor employs at the end of the primary lease term the lessee as his agent to dispose of the asset and to retain most of the proceeds of sale.[40] In *Welsh Development Agency v. Export Finance Co. Ltd* (1992) the facts revolved around a company, Parrot Ltd, in which the Welsh Development Agency was a principal shareholder. The company, by a debenture dated in October 1985, charged its book debts and other property and assets in favour of the WDA. By May 1989, the company was insolvent and the WDA appointed receivers under the debenture. The WDA claimed that by virtue of its charge, it was entitled to receive payment of all debts owed by overseas buyers in relation to goods exported to them by Parrot. However, the defendant (EXFINCO) claimed that it was entitled to the debts on the basis of its agreement with Parrot, namely, that the selling of goods by Parrot was done on the basis of an agency relationship for EXFINCO. The merits of the scheme for EXFINCO were as follows: first, debts due under the contracts to sell goods to overseas buyers would never have been the property of Parrot but belonged to EXFINCO as undisclosed principal so they would, therefore, not be subject to any prior floating charge over Parrot's debt or property; secondly, such a transaction would be a sale and not a secured borrowing and, as a result, the transaction would involve "off balance sheet" accounting.

At first instance it was held that the transaction amounted in substance to a charge and was void for non-registration. This judgment was reversed by the Court of Appeal, which upheld the arrangement as a genuine agency agreement. This was so despite the fact that the parties had constructed the agreement in such a way as to avoid all contact between the financier and the overseas buyer. Furthermore, the manu-facturer's mandate to sell on behalf of the financier was limited to goods

[39.] [1992] BCC 148 at 158.
[40.] See Chap. 2, below.

that complied with the sale contract, including the (then) statutory implied terms of merchantable quality and fitness for purpose. This ensured that there would be no recourse against the financier for breach of contract. Nevertheless, the Court of Appeal held that an agent's authority to bind an undisclosed principal must have existed when the agent made the contract ostensibly as principal. As a matter of legal form the arrangement was categorised as a sale and not a charge on the debts. As the Privy Council noted in *Chow Yoong Hong v. Choong Fah Rubber Manufactory*[41]: "There are many ways of raising cash besides borrowing. One is by selling book debts . . .". In contrast in *Curtain Dream v. Churchill Merchandising*,[42] there was an agreement for the sale of stock by a company to a finance company and for resale of the stock to the company on terms reserving title in the stock to the finance company, which it was held constituted a charge on the basis of the company's entitlement to redeem by repurchasing the stock.

Financing assignments of rentals may be important in the context of complex lease structures where a head lessor requires financing in order to fund his lease arrangements. This was the position with Atlantic Computer Systems plc who were at one time the largest lessors of computer equipment in the world. Computer equipment, by its very nature, is obsolescent on installation and the Atlantic system enabled the customer to trade-in the equipment and replace it with the latest state-of-the-art equipment. Essentially, Atlantic gave its customers the opportunity to trade-in during the currency of its seven year lease, and Atlantic undertook to settle the lessee's obligations providing that the replacement equipment was again leased through Atlantic. In order to fund the lease, Atlantic entered into hire-purchase arrangements with its funders in respect of the lease rentals. One such funder was Orion Finance Ltd, who would accept the assignment of the rents due to Atlantic from approved customers in satisfaction of the instalments payable by Atlantic under the hire-purchase agreements. An agreement of this kind was known as a "non-recourse agreement" which entailed that Orion would bear the risk that the customer might be unable to meet the rental payments under the lease and would have no recourse against Atlantic for the hire-purchase instalments in the event of the customer's default. Another type of agreement was a limited recourse arrangement where Atlantic was to remain responsible to pay the instalments. It was held by the Court of Appeal in *Orion Finance Ltd v. Crown Financial Management Ltd*[43] that a hire-purchase agreement coupled with a non-recourse charge of the lease rentals to secure the payment of the instalments of hire was a charge on book debts and was void for non-registration. As Millett L.J. pointed out:

"Atlantic expressly undertakes an obligation to pay the hire instalments, even if the obligation is satisfied by the assignment; the assignment purports to be

---

[41.] [1962] A.C. 209 at 216.
[42.] [1990] BCC 341.
[43.] Unreported, December 21, 1995 (C.A.).

security for payment of the instalments as well as the means for paying them. There is nothing in the documentation which is inconsistent with the intention of the parties being to create a charge, and I would construe the documentation in conformity with that intention."

It is essential, therefore, to distinguish between form and function. This theme is pursued further in the next chapter where various lease structures are examined.

Chapter 2

Equipment Leasing

Definitions and Structures

Introduction

The leasing facilities provided by the instalment credit industry in the United Kingdom consists of two principal types, namely, finance leases and operating leases. Although somewhat similar, the basic distinction between them relates to the leasing company's ability to recover fully the cost of the equipment through the contracted lease rentals. In the United Kingdom the distinction is specifically recognised for accounting purposes and may also be important in respect of the liability of the lessor in respect of the equipment delivered to the lessee. However, it is important not to be dogmatic in this context in respect of non-lease structures because any distinction drawn between the finance lease and for example, hire purchase is more apparent than real. Since both represent periodic payment transactions inextricably linked to the economic cost of the equipment plus the cost of money, it is difficult to determine which part of the total payments made is principal and which is interest. This is an aspect of the triumph of legal form which is a consistent and continuing theme in English law.[1]

The Operating Lease

The operating lease is the standard contract of hire of plant and machinery, that is where the hirer rents the equipment for a period which is less than its useful life and for hire payments totalling less than the purchase cost of the item. Reliance is placed on the realisation of a residual value on disposal or re-leasing of the equipment. The owner-lessee will be intimately concerned with the maintenance, insurance and taxing of the equipment, but these costs will figure in the rental rate. Such an arrangement enables a hirer to operate on a small capital base where the equipment involving high capital cost is required temporarily or for a fluctuating time, thereby achieving an efficient utilisation of investment capital. In addition, it enables a hirer, where the equipment is new and unproven, great flexibility without incurring the risks of obsolescence whilst giving a manufacturer-lessor the opportunity, through servicing the equipment on the customer's premises, of

[1] See Chap. 1 at pp. 14–17, above.

customer-orientated research and product development which may facilitate future sales or leases. Servicing and maintaining such equipment by the lessor may be more economically efficient for the hirer, since the lessor will build up vast experience in maintenance as well as enjoying economies of sale. Furthermore, where the lessor carries out the functions of handling, licensing and registration of, for example, vehicles on a volume basis, administrative costs may be dramatically cut.

The Finance Lease

The finance agreement is one where the primary period rentals are sufficient for the lessor to recover the cost of the equipment, financing costs, overhead expenses and also to earn a return on the investment in the lease. The primary period usually approximates to between 50 and 75 per cent of the estimated useful life of the equipment and at the end of this period, the lessee may continue to use the equipment in return for a nominal rent. Potential obsolescence before the end of the equipment's useful life is taken into account by the lessor, where the terms are so arranged that the lessee is indirectly paying for this.[2] The following would appear to be the main characteristics of a finance lease:

1. The duration of the lease is likely to cover a substantial part of the asset's useful life.

2. Terms protecting the lessor's investment in the lease on early termination.

3. Terms allocating repair, maintenance and insurance liability on the lessee.

4. The risks of ownership such as malfunction, loss, destruction and obsolescence lie with lessee.

5. Supplier selected by lessee.

6. Amortised acquisition costs to be recovered by lessor together with financing costs with residual value enuring to the benefit of the lessee.

Under the finance lease both the lessor and the lessee enjoy the "benefits" and "burdens" of ownership. At the end of the finance lease term the lessee will enjoy 95 to 99 per cent of the residual value of the equipment but will not enjoy an option to purchase, at least in the United Kingdom, since the lessee is still essentially selling its own tax depreciation to the lessor. At the same time, the lessor is exposed to both benefits and burdens because the term itself involves a risk, for example, if rental terms diminish or increase. This is particularly pertinent in the

[2] See Chap. 3, below.

case of long-term leases (over five years) where the residual value at the end is small. Even if the lessor can retain the surplus realised by resale of the asset at the end of the lease term, it is obvious that because the opportunity and risk associated with the equipment can be separated from those associated with the use or possession of the goods, this would suggest that there is no tenable economic distinction between a lease and a security interest.

In recent years the finance lease has been recognised as constituting a unique and asset-based financing device. Significantly, at the private international law level, UNIDROIT recognises the *sui generis* characteristic of the finance leasing transaction. Indeed, the Convention on International Financial Leasing attempts to reflect the economic reality of the transaction, as evidenced by the parties in their respective contracts, so as to facilitate the removal of certain legal impediments to the international financial leasing of equipment.[3] In a similar vein, Article 2A of the American Uniform Commercial Code (UCC) recognises a finance lease as a unique kind of lease which is defined in section 103(1) of the UCC as follows:

> " 'Finance lease' means a lease in which (i) the lessor does not select, manufacture or supply the goods, (ii) the lessor acquires the goods or the right to possession and use of the goods in connection with the lease, and (iii) either the lessee receives a copy of the contract evidencing the lesssor's purchase of the goods on or before signing the lease contract, or the lessee's approval of the contract evidencing the lessor's purchase of the goods is a condition to effectiveness of the lease contract."

A finance lease is unique because of the *control* that the lessee exercises in the selection, acquisition by the lessor, and approval of the equipment subject to the lease. This can be illustrated by reference to the standard terms and conditions of a typical finance lease where the onus is firmly placed on the supplier and the lessee.[4]

A variation of the finance lease which is seen in the United States of America is the equipment trust. Under this arrangement the equipment is purchased by a trustee who obtains finance by the sale of equipment trust certificates which are issued to financial institutions or a syndicate of banks in relation to a particular project. The trustee leases the equipment to the buyer and holds the benefit of the lease and the equipment on trust for the holders of the certificates. This United States phenomenon has not yet mirrored itself in the United Kingdom as it is mainly a tax-driven vehicle.

The Operating Lease and Finance Lease Distinguished

Even though the distinction between a finance lease and an operating lease is relatively easy to draw in abstract, sometimes the distinction will

[3] See UNIDROIT *News Bulletin*, Nos. 75, 76, October 1988.
[4] See Chap. 3, pp. 50–56, below.

become blurred, for example, in the case of a leased computer for a five-year primary period which can be returned or traded-in at any time (subject to a minimum payment clause) and which will probably be re-leased to another lessee on termination.[5] The resolution of this problem may well depend on the attitude of the lessee. If he sees leasing as an alternative to buying the property, this will tend towards the finance lease, whereas an operating lease will arise when the lessee does not consider buying the property as a viable alternative. The distinction between the two types of lease will be important as it goes to the root of the question of the lessor's liability for defective equipment.

The distinction between the two different types of lease is often characterised as one of a conflict between a "true" or operating lease, and a "security" or finance lease. This reference to a finance lease is concerned with the ostensible ownership problem where there is a separation of ownership and possession.[6] The argument here is that a person wishing to take a non-possessory property interest should bear the burden of "curing" the ostensible ownership problem through a notice mechanism. It is important to adopt a balanced approach. A distinction can be drawn between leases and conditional sales which represent in economic terms a security interest, in particular where the leases are of short duration which do not look to the ultimate acquisition of the goods by the lessee. In this context, application to the true lease of the remedies traditionally associated with the conditional sale would do violence to the contract rights of the parties. Nonetheless, the question of public notice still remains and this was one of the main criticisms of the DTI Consultation Paper on *Transfer of Title* (1994), which blandly recommended the adoption of an entrustment principle in English law[7] which would have effectively destroyed the lessor's interest in the goods against innocent third parties, with no means of protection being given to the finance lessor through a notice mechanism. In contrast, Professor Diamond recommended[8] that a notice filing mechanism similar to the American Model under the Uniform Commercial Code should be adopted in England and there should be a requirement to file, subject to a *de minimis* period of three years, all finance lease transactions.

The distinction between a finance lease and an operating lease is a troublesome one. One possible approach, which could be adopted in distinguishing, could be to concentrate upon the nature of the items leased as being indicative of the type of lease and these have been identified as follows:

[5] *Re Atlantic Computers Systems* [1992] Ch. 505.
[6] See Chap. 1, pp. 4–14, above.
[7] See Chap. 1, pp. 13–14, above.
[8] See the DTI Report, *A Review of Security Interests in Property* (1989) para. 9.7.15.

Operating Lease:

Character of asset	Example
Long lasting	Containers
Simple	Trainers
Legally identifiable	Motor homes
Not of small value	Light aircraft
Not prone to obsolescence	
Easy to insure	

Finance Lease:

Character of asset	Example
Sophisticated	Computers
Fragile	Electronic machines
Complicated	Motor vehicles
Difficult to identify	Large commercial aircraft
Doubtful residual value	Technological machinery
Difficult to insure	Office equipment
Prone to obsolescence	

Grey Areas

Agricultural machinery
Ships
Small commercial aircraft
Cars

As can be seen from the above list, asset leasing covers a wide spectrum of activities, and it is simplistic and potentially misleading to classify all leases under just two headings. Indeed some hire facilities combine the characteristics of both, for example, contract hire.

Contract Hire

Contract hire has been developed especially within the motor industry as a means of providing motor vehicles on a fleet basis. Both the user and the owner intend that the vehicle must be returned to the owner at the end of a defined period of hire, usually between 12 and 36 months. Finance for the fleet is provided by a finance house, under a hire arrangement, and there will normally be an undertaking from the dealer to repurchase the vehicle from the finance house on expiry of the hiring period at an agreed price. Often the hirer will enter into a separate maintenance contract with the dealer/supplier of the vehicle.

Hire-Purchase and Conditional Sale

The twentieth century conceptual basis for the financing of goods in England draws upon the ingenuity of Victorian commercial lawyers in the seminal decision of *Helby v. Matthews*.[9] In this case it was held that a hirer with an option but not an obligation to purchase, because he could return the goods at any time, was not a person who had "bought or agreed to buy goods" and could not, therefore, confer a good title on a purchaser by virtue of section 9 of the Factors Act 1889.[10] As a matter of legal form a distinction is drawn between a hire-purchase transaction and a sale, even though the rentals payable by the hirer are equivalent, or substantially equivalent, to the purchase price before a nominal option to purchase was payable.[11] This is an aspect of the triumph of legal form in England.

Finance Leases and Hire-Purchase: An Accounting Perspective

The economic symmetry between finance leases and hire-purchase contracts is reflected in accounting treatment. This approach is based on the view that the right to the use of property under a hire-purchase contract and a lease is an economic resource. Prior to the introduction of the Statements of Standard Accounting Practice, SSAP 21 (1984), it was not necessary for lessees to disclose their obligation to make future rental payments under a finance lease on their balance sheets. As such this gave lessees a means of obtaining off-balance sheet financing and prejudiced the "true and fair" concept of accounts. SSAP 21 states that a finance lease should be recorded on the balance sheet of a lessee as an asset and as an obligation to pay future rentals. The rationale for this is that the lessee typically has the right to use the asset for substantially the whole of its useful economic life, which is for most practical purposes equivalent to legal ownership. As with hire-purchase transactions the accounting treatment is governed by the perceived position of the lessee in economic terms rather than on the strict basis of the legal relationship between the lessor and lessee. This is now also significant in the light of the 1996 Budget where the general approach adopted by the Chancellor of the Exchequer was for the tax treatment of leases to be more closely aligned with the accounting treatment.

A distinction is still drawn between financing and operating hire-purchase and lease contracts. In this respect SSAP 21 defines a finance lease in the following terms:

"*A finance lease* is a lease that transfers substantially all the risks and rewards of ownership of an asset to the lessee. It should be presumed that such a transfer of risks and rewards occurs if at the inception of a lease the present value of the minimum lease payments, including any initial payment, amounts to substantially all (normally 90 per cent or more) of the fair value of

[9] [1891] A.C. 471.
[10] *Cf. Lee v. Butler* [1893] 2 Q.B. 269.
[11] See Chap. 6, below.

the leased asset. The present value should be calculated by using the interest rate implicit in the lease . . . If the fair value of the asset is not determinable an estimate thereof should be used.

Notwithstanding the fact that a lease meets the conditions in para. 15, the presumption that it should be classified as a finance lease may in exceptional circumstances be rebutted if it can be clearly demonstrated that the lease in question does not transfer substantially all the risks and rewards of ownership (other than legal title) to the lessee."[12]

In the spring of 1994 the Accounting Standards Board issued its Financial Reporting Standard (FRS 5) on the reporting of the substance of transactions and one of the points that emerges is that the 90 per cent rule is clearly rebuttable, and that the acid test for reportability in the lessee's accounts is the commercial reality, that is where substantially all the risks and rewards of ownership have passed to the lessee. From this there are clear implications for the classification of leases and also for the reporting in appropriate cases of operating leases by lessees.

The Financial Reporting Standards Report (FRS 5) identifies the following features which gives rise to difficulty in the classification of leases:

1. The existence of rights to terminate or extend the lease or purchase the asset on terms which are arguably not a "bargain".

2. Leases marketed in conjunction with maintenance contracts subject to a single charge for both leasing and maintenance—the allocation of the overall charge between leasing and maintenance (in the lessee's accounts) can affect whether the lease element falls within the 90 per cent test, but correct identification of the maintenance element can be problematic.

3. Break options and renewal clauses—leases may contain complex provisions regarding these such that it is difficult to assess at the beginning of the lease which options the lessee will exercise (and therefore what in fact is the likely amount of the minimum lease payments)—even though the parties may in practice have a clear understanding on this.

4. Rights to exchange equipment—where the lessee effectively has the ability to exchange the leased equipment for new or upgraded equipment, this may (depending on the terms) have the effect of transferring the risk of obsolescence to the lessor, and thus call into question the classification between finance lease and operating lease.

5. Residual benefits—because the 90 per cent test is based on the present value of relevant amounts, the report considers that it does not properly take into account the volatility of residual

---

[12] *Accounting for Leases and Hire Purchase Contracts*, SSAP 21 (1984) paras. 15, 16.

values nor (insofar as these will generally be largely retained by the lessee) the potential upside of residual benefits.

6. Control over remarketing of second-hand equipment by manufacturer/supplier—an unquantified benefit for lessee.

7. Purchase and sale options for lessee.

8. Arrangements involving the "slicing" of residual value risk, under which risk a certain amount is taken by the lessee and risk below a certain amount by the lessor.

Leasing and Credit Enhancement

Introduction

In the case of big ticket leasing, which involves the acquisition of very expensive assets, the lessor may require an advancement of capital from a third-party lender (funder). This is sometimes referred to as a leveraged lease, because the funding provided by the lender gives leverage to the lessor's purchasing power and on smaller deals enables the lessor to increase the volume of its business. There are various ways in which the leveraged element is structured, but typically it involves the lessor (borrower) in a non-recourse loan where the rentals constitute the security. In this scenario the lender will normally take a charge over the equipment leased and also the rentals. There are therefore two charges which must be registered and if not registered will be void against the liquidator and creditors of the lessor, namely, under section 396(1)(c) of the Companies Act 1985, "a charge created or evidenced by an instrument which, if executed by an individual, would require registration as a bill of sale" and also under section 396(1)(e) "a charge on book debts of the company".

Fixed and Floating Charge Dichotomy over Book Debts

In order to enhance its position the lender may seek a fixed charge over the book debts to which the funding relates. A specific charge is not deferred in priority to preferential creditors in the event of receivership or liquidation. Furthermore, a registered specific charge over present and future book debts retains the priority of the chargee against a subsequent absolute assignment of the debt for example, to a factoring company. In contrast, registration of a floating charge will only provide constructive notice of the existence of the charge and not of a restrictive clause such as automatic crystallisation within its contents. The main difficulty is determining whether or not a specific charge is in reality a disguised floating charge, where there is a charge over future and present rent streams from hire-purchase and equipment lease agreements.

The courts have taken an enabling approach to the creation of a fixed charge over such rental streams, even though the chargor was free to use the cash proceeds for the ordinary purposes of its business. Thus in *Re Atlantic Computer Systems plc*[13] it was held that there was a fixed charge in the property assigned, since this was confined to rights which arose under specific existing contracts of sublease.[14] Even so as a matter of consistency with the case law on disguised floating charges it is likely that the unencumbered use of cash proceeds by the chargor will be indicative of the creation of a floating charge.[15] In the Court of Appeal in *Re Yorkshire Woolcombers' Association Ltd*,[16] Romer L.J. referred to the three characteristics of a floating charge, namely, a charge on a class of present and future assets changing in the ordinary course of business from time to time. In the context of book debts the issue is whether the chargor can carry on its business in the ordinary way. Thus in *Re Brightlife*,[17] in a charge purporting to be a fixed charge which included negative restrictions against the chargor dealing with its book debts, otherwise than in the ordinary course of getting them in and realising them, it was held that this constituted a floating charge. The significant feature of the charge was that the chargor was free to collect its debts and pay the proceeds into its bank account. Similarly in *Re Pearl Maintenance Services Ltd*[18] an expressed specific charge over present and future book debts was held to be a floating charge, as there was no relevant provision in the charge restricting the freedom of the chargor to realise the book debts and use them in the ordinary course of business. This was not a convertible charge with consent.[19]

It was the element of control relating to money proceeds that convinced the court at first instance in *Royal Trust Bank v. National Westminster Bank* (1995) that the nature of the charge was a fixed one over present and future hire-purchase and lease agreements deposited with the bank from time to time. The control provisions were as follows:

1. The assignment by the chargor to the bank of the right to receive all rentals and other payments due or to become due to hold absolutely for the bank.

[13.] [1992] Ch. 505.

[14.] See also *Re Atlantic Medical Ltd* [1992] B.C.C. 653.

[15.] See, *e.g. Mercantile Bank of India Ltd v. Chartered Bank of India, Australia and China, and Strauss and Co. Ltd (in liquidation)* [1937] 1 All E.R. 231. *Cf. Siebe Gorman and Co. Ltd v. Barclays Bank Ltd* [1979] 2 Lloyd's Rep. 142; *Re Keenan Bros Ltd* [1985] I.R. 401, Sup. Ct. of Ireland; *Re A Company (No. 005009 of 1987), ex p. Capp* [1989] B.C.L.C. 13; *William Gaskell Group Ltd v. Highley (Nos 1, 2, 3)* [1979] Lloyd's Rep. 142; *Royal Trust Bank v. National Westminster Bank* [1995] B.C.C. 128.

[16.] [1903] 2 Ch. 284.

[17.] [1987] Ch. 200.

[18.] [1995] BCC 657.

[19.] See *Re New Bullas Trading Ltd* [1994] BCC 36.

2. First fixed charge over present or future equipment subject to hire-purchase or lease agreements.

3. Negative restrictive covenant in respect of the charged property.

4. A requirement to maintain a minimum level of cover of receivables due under the agreements being at least 140 per cent of the principal amount of the secured debt.

5. Company to collect all sums due under the agreements as agent for the bank.

6. If required by the bank at any time, the company should open an account with the bank designated as a rental income collection account, pay the money proceeds of the agreements into that account and notify debtors to pay directly to the bank.

7. The company should be allowed to make withdrawals from the designated account only with the prior written consent of the bank.

The company paid the collection proceeds into its account with a second bank and used the money for its own business purposes. Subsequently the bank chargee notified the second bank by letter that it had a fixed charge over the moneys paid into the account and this was held to be for the sole benefit of the bank chargee.[20] At first instance it was held that upon the true construction of the fixed charge the company did not have the right to use the proceeds of the charged receivables, in the ordinary course of its business, free from the Bank's security interest. In the Court of Appeal,[20a] whilst it was conceded that the nature of the charge was a fixed one it was held that upon the true construction of the charge, the company was at all material times at liberty to deal with the sums collected as its owner and was not a trustee of the sums. The clear implication of the Court of Appeal's decision is that it calls into question any purported fixed charge over income streams deriving from equipment leases and instalment credit agreements which are not in existence at the time when the fixed charge is created, unless the charge obliges the chargor to pay the proceeds of the income streams into an account over which the chargor does not have control.

Leveraged Leases and Guarantees

This usually accompanies "big ticket" deals where the lessor is partly financed by a bank loan to buy the equipment and the bank takes the credit risk of the lessee. It may be that the lessor is a specially formed

---

[20] For a comprehensive discussion of disguised floating charges in the context of book debts, see W.J. Gough *Company Charges* (2nd ed. 1996), Chap. 22.
[20a] Unreported, April 30, 1996 (C.A.).

company which acquires the equipment for a specific project. We have already referred to the facilitating bank taking a security over the equipment itself and also the book debts. There may be a chain of leases and it is normal to assign the benefit of the sublease(s) rental(s) to the intermediate lessee as security for the lessee's obligations under the head lease or alternatively to the bank as collateral security for the loan.

In the case of project finance, it is conventional practice for part of the capital to be provided by bank loans and another part by a finance lease of the plant and/or equipment where the main lending bank for the project issues a guarantee to the lessor which relates to the lessee's ability to pay. The nature of such a guarantee is by way of a standby letter of credit or first demand type, that is, it is drawable on a statement to the effect that the lessee is in default and stating the amount payable. Where a financial institution issues a "guarantee" which matures on virtually any evidence of default, this cannot be characterised as a guarantee, in the strict legal sense, as it is an independent primary obligation, that is, it is not an accessory guarantee in the sense that the surety's obligations spring out of those of the principal debtor and the liability of the surety is coterminous with that of the principal debtor.

In the case of a demand guarantee, the bank must pay the beneficiary on first demand. In order to protect itself against such an eventually, the lessee will normally indemnify the bank guarantor and as security will assign its rights under the lease to the bank. Significantly this will include the right to terminate the lease following the default of the lessee. In addition the bank may take a mortgage over the equipment from the lessor by way of collateral security for the liabilities of the lessee to the bank under the reimbursement indemnity. The difficulty with this is that lessors are reluctant to provide for such security, not least because it will not cover other indemnities provided by the lessee to the lessor, notably taxes imposed on the lessor or other owner liabilities imposed upon the lessor, for example, in relation to product liability caused by defective equipment. Interestingly, in a conventional security scenario, where the bank guarantee would be provided for a loan of mortgaged equipment the guarantor would then be subrogated to the rights of the creditor/lessor in respect of the equipment. It is unlikely that subrogation would permit the bank guarantor on payment to take over the lessor's beneficial ownership of the equipment leased, as the principle would be confined to the lessor's rights as against the lessee. Of course the lessor could agree to transfer ownership in the equipment to the bank guarantor, although this is unlikely since the former will be unsure as to whether the lessee's indemnities to it as to potential liability on the equipment have been discharged.[21]

Financing Assignments

There are two broad categories: first, those where the rental stream is to be diverted to the financier at inception, so that notice of assignment

[21.] See Wood, *Title Finance, Derivatives, Securitisations, Set-Off and Netting* (1995) pp. 3–6.

must be given to the lessee; and secondly, those where the rental stream is to continue to flow to the original lessor and is only to be diverted if there is a default by the lessor under the financing.[22] In any event the new lessor will wish to preserve the "liquidity" of the lease, by expressly stating that it reserves the right at any time during the lease term to effect an outright assignment of its rights or transfer of its rights and obligations.

The Proprietary Basis of Equipment Leasing

Title Structures and Leasing of Equipment

Introduction

Where equipment is sold subject to a continuing lease, the transfer to the lessor is usually initiated through novation. Under this arrangement the lessor will enter into a private sale agreement with the purchaser of the equipment and at the same time will ask the lessee to sign a three-party novation with the lessor and the purchaser (the new lessor) under which the purchaser takes over all the official lessor's rights and obligations and releasing the original lessor from further obligations. It may be that the original lessor may want to include a clause preserving accrued rights and obligations between it and the lessee for the portion of the lease prior to the sale. Where the original lessor is seeking funding only, then a head-lease structure may ensue, whereby the funder becomes the owner of the equipment, purchasing it from the supplier and subsequently letting it out on lease or hire-purchase to the leasing company and granting the latter permission to enter into sub-lease arrangements. These arrangements will be governed by a master agreement which, since it involves a sale to the funder, will not constitute, as a matter of legal form, a security agreement. Of course incidental to the master agreement there may be security elements, for example, if the head-lessor takes a charge over the book debts of the intermediate lessee to the end-user lessee. In the course of time the head-lessor may terminate the head-lease, perhaps due to the insolvency of the inter-mediate lessee, and in this way the rentals due will be payable to the head-lessor as owner of the equipment and not as a chargee of the sub-rentals. It is, therefore, important to include such a power of termination within the master agreement.[23]

[22.] *Orion Finance Ltd v. Crown Financial Management Ltd* (C.A. unreported) December 21, 1995. See Chap. 1, above.

[23.] *Central Transport Rental Group plc v. Darwen Leasing Ltd* (Q.B.D.) (Commercial Court unreported) October 5, 1995. Even a contingent right to possession in the head-lessor gives rise to proprietary interests. Compare *Melluish (Inspector of Taxes) v. BMI (No. 3) Ltd* [1995] 4 All E.R. 453. This case is discussed in Chap. 9, below.

A substantial and vexed issue concerns the relationship between the end-user and the head-lessor, because prima facie there is no privity of contract between them. It is necessary to examine this issue in greater detail, especially if the covenants between the lessee and sub-lessee (end-user) are different from those between the lessee and the head-lessor (funder). In turn this invites scrutiny of the nature of the lessee's interest in the equipment.

Categorisation of the lessee's interest under an equipment lease and that of the hirer under a hire-purchase contract

It is important to categorise exactly the nature of the lessee's interest in the equipment for the following reasons:

1. On sale is the purchaser bound by the terms and conditions of the lease contract between the lessor and lessee?

2. If the under-lessor became insolvent damages would be an inadequate remedy and the hirer in possession would thereby be seeking to retain the hired goods. The issue can be stated as follows: Is the nature of the lessee's interest a proprietary one thereby enabling him to retain possession of the goods for the hire period on payment of the hire charges?

3. The buyer of the equipment may have bought this at a discount in view of the fact of the lease and it would be, in principle, inequitable to allow him to evict the lessee if he knew all along that he was there.

Before considering these thorny issues it is important to draw a distinction between an equipment lease and a hire-purchase contract. The latter is a form of delayed sale and the option to purchase is a real right, albeit one which is personal to the hirer. If the hirer is in default, but the hire-purchase arrangement still subsists, the option to purchase belongs *exclusively* to the hirer. Consequently, if payment is made by a third party which clears the debt, full title is only vested in the hirer.[24] It follows that the party discharging the debt can only rely upon a personal enforcement of the debt assigned to him by the original bailor. As Lord Denning pointed out in *Bennett v. Griffin Finance*[25]:

"The hirer has the contractual right to buy the car on paying the settlement figure. No one else has that right. The hirer alone is entitled to pay it and acquire the title to the car. If anyone else pays it, he must be paying it on the hirer's behalf, for otherwise he would be acting unlawfully. No third person can be allowed to assert that he paid it and become the owner himself: for that would be to take advantage of his own wrong. The only permissible

[24.] See *Snook v. London and West Riding Investments Ltd* [1967] 2 Q.B. 796.
[25.] [1967] 2 Q.B. 46 at 49–50.

31

conclusion is that, when the settlement figure is paid, the car becomes the property of the hirer. And it is for the hirer then to dispose of it as he pleases or has agreed."

If the hire-purchase agreement has been terminated, then the option to purchase will re-vest in the original owner (the finance company). This is significant where a hirer under a hire-purchase agreement wrongfully purports to sell the goods by representing himself as the owner.[26]

Head-Lessor versus Sub-Lessee Conflicts

The enforceability of non-possessory covenants

The case of *De Mattos v Gibson*[27] is often cited as authority for the proposition that where the purchaser of a chattel has actual notice of a covenant over a chattel this will bind him. This was the approach adopted by Knight Bruce L.J. in interlocutory proceedings against a mortgagee of a vessel who had notice of a charterparty entered into by the mortgagor with the plaintiff and who was threatening to foreclose the mortgage for non-payment, irrespective of the burden of the charterparty. Knight Bruce L.J. held:

"Reason and justice seem to prescribe that at least as a general rule where a man, by gift or purchase, acquires property from another with knowledge of a previous contract, lawfully and for valuable consideration made by him with a third person, to use and employ the property for a particular purpose in a specified manner, then the acquirer shall not, to the material damage of the third person, in opposition to the contract and inconsistently with it, use and employ the property in a manner not allowable to the giver or seller." [28]

In the substantive hearing it was Lord Chelmsford's view, but with no authority cited, that a transferee taking property with actual notice of a pre-existing covenant prevented the latter from engaging in any positive acts which might interfere with its performance. The main problem with this approach is that it is antithetical to the doctrine of privity which was at its infancy at the time of the decision. Moreover, Knight Bruce L.J. held that the principle was equally applicable to movable and immovable property drawing upon *Tulk v. Moxhay*.[29] However, this decision has been severely qualified in relation to land: first, only covenants which were restrictive in nature would be enforced, that is, positive covenants are not enforced against successors[30]; secondly, the

---

[26.] See Chap. 6, below.

[27.] (1859) 4 De G. & J. 276. For an excellent discussion, see *Interests in Goods* (eds Palmer, McKendrick, 1993) Chap. 1. Swadling, *The Proprietary Effect of a Hire of Goods*.

[28.] *Ibid.* at 276.

[29.] (1848) 2 Ph. 774.

[30.] See *Hayward v. Brunswick Permanent Benefit Building Society* (1881) 8 Q.B.D. 407.

covenant would be enforced only where the covenantee retained land for the benefit of which the covenant was taken. This restriction in part reflects the rationale of *Tulk v. Moxhay* where Lord Cottenham L.C. said that the covenant should be enforced so as to safeguard the sale of land into lots because "it would be impossible for an owner of land to sell part of it without incurring the risk of tendering what he retains worthless."[31] Clearly this last qualification cannot apply to personalty and the *De Mattos* doctrine would seem, therefore, to be heavily qualified not least by the way in which the doctrine has developed in relation to land but also by the privity doctrine. Indeed this conclusion led Scrutton L.J. to hold in *Barker v. Strickney*[32] that the principle expounded by Knight Bruce L.J. was redundant in the case of personalty.

Despite this the *De Mattos* principle was applied by the Judicial Committee of the Privy Council in *Lord Strathcona Steamship Co. v. Dominion Coal Co.*[33] where a ship built to the specifications of charterers under a charterparty who entered into a contract with the owner Lord Curzon Co. for a charter for 10 successive seasons, was sold several times and was eventually sold to the Lord Strachcona Steamship Co., who refused to perform the charter. Lord Shaw, who gave judgment for the Board, held the purchaser bound by the charter obligation on the following basis:

> "If a man acquires from another rights in a ship which is already under charter the ship to be used for a particular purpose and not inconsistently with it, then he appears to be plainly in the position of a constructive trustee with obligations which a court of equity will not permit him to violate."[34]

The requirement of the convenantee holding a dominant tenement and a servient tenement to be held by the covenantor was accepted by the Privy Council, but Lord Shaw overcame the difficulty by saying that, whilst the buyers owned the ship and the charterers had no proprietary rights in her, during the continuance of the charterparty the charterers had a "plain interest" in her so long as the vessel was fit to go to sea. Subsequent decisions have found it impossible to determine the juridical rationale for this interest.[35] Furthermore, the language of constructive trusteeship used by Lord Shaw is inherently vague and cannot provide support for a general doctrine of the running of covenants with chattels, because it must pre-suppose some undertaking by the purchaser/owner that he will abide by the covenant. Clearly trust language here is inappropriate, but the result may be justified if the privity rule is reformed notably if third-party beneficiaries can sue on the contract.[36]

[31.] See *London County Council v. Allen* [1914] 3 K.B. 642; *Clore v. Theatrical Properties Ltd* [1936] 3 All E.R. 483.

[32.] [1919] 1 K.B. 121.

[33.] [1926] A.C. 108.

[34.] *Ibid.* at 125.

[35.] See *Port Line v. Ben Line Steamers* [1958] 2 K.B. 146.

[36.] See the *Law Commission Report No. 242, Privity of Contract: Contracts for the Benefit of Third Parties* (1996).

It is sometimes argued that the *De Mattos* principle is the equitable analogue of *Lumley v. Gye*,[37] the tort of inducing a breach of contract. This was the approach adopted by Browne-Wilkinson J. in *Swiss Bank Corp v. Lloyds Bank Ltd* [38] who maintained that *De Mattos* was good law in that it represented the counterpart in equity of the tort of knowing interference with contractual rights. Undoubtedly an analogy may be drawn with the two decisions, not least that in both cases the defendant had actual rather than constructive knowledge of the other party's rights. However, the analogy is misleading because a distinction can be drawn between *directly* affecting contractual relations and acting in a way which incidentally (even if this is inevitable) affects contractual relations. In *Lumley v. Gye*, the defendant knowingly and directly interfered with the contract of engagement entered into by the opera singer with a rival establishment. In *De Mattos*, the mortgagee, through the exercise of his rights, may have caused the breach of contract by the shipowner to the charterparty, but this was incidental only to the exercise of his rights, that is he was not a party to the breach. In this way, *De Mattos* can hardly be described as the equitable equivalent of the tort of inducing breach of contract.

The lessee's right to possession: a proprietary interest?

One approach is to say that, by virtue of the sub-lessee's *de facto* possession of the equipment, the latter has a proprietary interest in the goods.[39] In this vein Professor Goode states:

> "The doctrine of estates does not apply to chattels so that the sub-lease does not automatically come to an end with the cessation of the head lease, for the sub-lessee's interest in the equipment is not carved out of the head lease but is an independent interest derived from possession."[40]

This approach begs the question whether the sub-lessee's right to possession is based upon his contractual arrangement and if the basis of the proprietary interest is contract (the basis of the right to possession) this cannot bind a third party with a superior title since relativity of title is the basis of English personal property law. At the same time the basis of the sub-lessee's right as against the intermediate lessee/lessor is not to disturb the former's quiet possession in the equipment. However, the purchaser and substitute lessor or head-lessor make no such promise to the lessee and should, therefore, be able to recover possession of the equipment. If this were not the case it would undermine the fact that the law of property allows obligations to be imposed irrespective of consent. Whilst there may be contractual restrictions *inter se* this does not bind

[37.] (1853) 2 E. & B. 216.
[38.] [1979] Ch. 548.
[39.] See Holdsworth (1993) 49 L.Q.R. 576.
[40.] Goode, *Commercial Law* (2nd ed. 1995), pp. 791–792, n. 40.

the owner from transferring an unencumbered title in a sale to a third party irrespective of notice.[41] Sometimes it is argued that the contract itself is a proprietary right and that the lessor, who has already conferred possession or an immediate right of possession upon a hirer, cannot subsequently confer a superior right of possession upon a third party, that is *nemo dat quod non habet*.[42] It would follow from this that possession coupled with contract would mean that these rights could not be pre-empted by a subsequent dispossee. Such an analysis is not the common law *nemo dat* rule but rather the Civilian concept of *possession vaut titre*.[43] The application of such a principle would destroy the concept of good faith purchase as well as the distinction drawn in English law between legal and equitable proprietary rights.

In any case the nature of the sub-lessee's possession as a bailee is not necessarily helpful in establishing a proprietary right. Whilst a pledge gives the bailee a special property interest in the chattel which will bind a third party, this arises out of the nature of the transaction, that is a bailment of personal property to secure an obligation of the bailor. The question of principle remains, namely, should the promise to allow the bailee possession for a certain term, supported by consideration, bind a purchaser of goods from the bailor? In the case of a gratuitous bailment the determination of the bailment by the bailor is incontrovertible: a mere promise supported by consideration does not alter the position, and the doctrine of privity of contract ensures that the bailor's promise will only bind himself.

The interference of the head-lessor: the relevance of tort

English law has dealt with wrongful interference with goods from the perspective of the law of tort rather than property law. This can be demonstrated in the case of detinue which, although it has now been statutorily abolished, the scope of conversion has been simultaneously expanded[44] to cover the case where detinue historically would be available but conversion would not. Detinue developed into a particular remedy of the bailor against his bailee for the return of his goods, that is where the defendant had obtained these goods with the consent of the plaintiff. The juridical rationale for this was the "special property interest" in the hirer where detinue was available against the bailor for breach of the bailment arrangement. However, the term "special property" must be understood in the context of relativity of title, and it refers to the position *qua* the bailor (*inter se*) rather than any absolute concept good against the whole world.[45] Therefore, whilst a pledgee has a special

---

[41.] See *King v. David Allen Billposting Ltd* [1916] 2 A.C. 54.

[42.] See Thornley (1974) 13 J.S.P.T.L. 150 at 151.

[43.] See Chap. 6, below.

[44.] See Torts (Interference with Goods) Act 1977, s. 2(2).

[45.] See Sale of Goods Act 1979, s. 61(1), which draws a distinction between general and special property.

property interest in the absence of the exceptions to *nemo dat* applying,[46] there is no suggestion that the pledge will bind the owner with a paramount title. Nevertheless, it will bind a successor in title to the pledgor by virtue of ancient law.[47] The difficulty is that possessory rights straddle the boundary between property and contract law.

The basis of the bailee's special property is that the bailor is estopped from denying the bailee's right to possession.[48] But the estoppel, whilst binding the parties, has no operation outside this arrangement. Certainly as far as the availability of trespass was concerned, this tort is grounded upon the need to protect possession and the title of the plaintiff is not relevant to the action in the absence of a *jus tertii*. At common law a wrongdoer could not raise against a plaintiff in actual possession of the goods a plea of *jus tertii* that the true owner of the goods was a person other than the plaintiff. Thus in *Wilson v. Lombank Ltd*[49] the plaintiff had bought a car from a person with no right to sell it in circumstances which did not fall within any of the exceptions to the *nemo dat* rule, and was able to bring a successful action against the defendant for the full value of the car where the defendant's servant had taken the car in the mistaken but honest belief that it belonged to his employers. Now the Torts (Interference with Goods) Act 1977 deals with this situation and avoids potential double liability claims as the Act apportions damages between the claimants[50] or, where one claimant sues for and recovers damages for the full value of the goods, requires him to account to any other person having a right to claim.[51]

The availability of trespass has no bearing on the existence of a proprietary right in the goods. Whilst an owner of goods will have an action, more generally if at the material time the owner did not have possession or an immediate right to possession the action is confined to the injury done to his reversionary interest in the goods.[52] Similarly in the case of conversion, the owner of the goods cannot, unless there is a threat to his reversionary interest, sue where he has hired the goods to another. However, in *International Factors Ltd v. Rodriguez*[53] the Court of Appeal held that a mere equitable owner with no prior possession of the chattels could bring on action for conversion. By a factoring agreement the plaintiffs had purchased debts owing to a company of which the defendant was a director. The agreement provided that in the event of assigned debts being paid to the company, it would hold them in trust for the plaintiffs and immediately hand them over to them. In breach of the agreement four cheques sent to the company in respect of the

---

[46.] See Chap. 6, below.
[47.] *Franklin v. Neate* (1844) 13 M. & W. 481.
[48.] See *Biddle v. Bond* (1865) 6 B. & S. 225.
[49.] [1963] 1 W.L.R. 1294.
[50.] See Torts (Interference with Goods) Act 1977, s. 7(1), (2).
[51.] *Ibid.* s. 7(3).
[52.] See *France v. Parkinson* [1934] 1 W.L.R. 581.
[53.] [1979] Q.B. 315.

assigned debts were paid into the company's bank account on instructions from the defendant. The Court of Appeal upheld Judge Newey, at first instance, that the defendant was liable in conversion on the basis that the plaintiffs had an equitable title to the goods and an immediate right to possession. Significantly Buckley L.J. held that contractual rights were sufficient to maintain the action. Even so, it cannot be the case that conversion protects ownership because as Clerk and Lindsell have pointed out[54]:

> "Any person having a right to the possession of goods may bring trover in respect of the conversion of them and allege them to be his property."

Had the *International Factors* case been decided solely on the issue of mere equitable ownership, it is doubtful that the decision could survive in the light of the House of Lords treatment in *Leigh and Sullivan Ltd v. Aliakman Shipping Co. Ltd, the Aliakman*[55] where the House of Lords upheld the principle that a claimant who sues for negligence in respect of the loss of or damage to goods must demonstrate either the legal ownership of, or some possessory title to, those goods at the time of the loss or damage.

The head-lessor and the tort of inducing breach of contract

A purchaser of equipment subject to a lease contract, if he has *actual knowledge* of the existence of the lease, will be liable for the tort of inducing a breach irrespective of whether he induced the purchaser to sell.[56] The lessee's remedy would be to sue for damages—he would have no rights in respect of the chattel itself. If the lessee learnt of the sale before it took place, then he could seek an injunction against the vendor to restrain the breach and against the purchaser for inducing the breach. In this way the tort may provide some protection for the lessee against the purchaser for inducing the breach.

The sub-lessee and specific performance

If in the contract of the sale of the lease, the purchaser (head-lessor) had covenanted not to interfere with the sub-lessee/lessee, then the seller (intermediate lessee or lessor) himself may be persuaded to bring an action for breach of contract. Furthermore the seller/covenantee may be able to require the covenantor to specifically perform his obligations. It may then be argued that this is an equitable proprietary right which will bind all third parties with the exception of a purchaser in good faith without notice of a legal title in the chattel. Such an approach was

[54.] *Torts* (ed. R.W.M. Dias, 16th ed., 1989) p. 1246.
[55.] [1986] 1 A.C. 785.
[56.] See *Torquay Hotel Co. v. Cousins* [1969] 2 Ch. 106.

adopted by Sir Nicholas Browne-Wilkinson V.-C. in *Bristol Airport plc v. Powdrill*.[57] In this case the lessee company of a number of aircraft was indebted to several airports in respect of unpaid airport charges. The company was subject to an administration order.[58] By virtue of section 11(3) of the Insolvency Act 1986, no steps can be taken over an insolvent company's property except with the leave of the court or the consent of the administrator. The airport authorities purported to detain the aircraft under section 88 of the Civil Aviation Act 1982 which also empowered them to sell the aircraft to recover these charges where the operator was in default. It was argued that as lessees they did not have "property" in the aircraft and so did not require leave to seize the aircraft. This approach was rejected by Sir Nicholas Browne-Wilkinson V.-C.[59]:

> "I have no doubt that a court would order specific performance of a contract to lease an aircraft since each aircraft has unique features peculiar to itself. Accordingly in my judgment the "lessee" has at least an equitable right of some kind in the aircraft which falls within the statutory definition as being some 'description of interest ... arising out of or incidental to' that aircraft."[60]

The definition of "property" in section 436 of the Insolvency Act 1986 is very wide indeed and in that sense the decision is unimpeachable. However, the point of principle is whether Sir Nicholas Browne-Wilkinson's more broad statement can be correct:

> "The basic equitable principle is that if, under a contract, A has certain rights over property as against the legal owner, which rights are specifically enforceable in equity, A has an equitable interest in such property."[61]

This begs the question as to whether the lessee does at law have a proprietary interest. If this is not the case then the application of the maxim "Equity regards as done that which ought to be done" has little meaning because the executory proprietary interest is merely illusory. The allusion to specific performance being available to protect proprietary rights is in any case outmoded because the sole criterion now for the application of specific performance is the inadequacy of damages.[62] Merely because an equitable remedy is available this does not indicate whether the rights being enforced are personal or proprietary in effect. What is clear is that both common law and equitable remedies protect

---

[57.] [1990] Ch. 744.
[58.] Insolvency Act 1986, s. 8.
[59.] [1990] Ch. 744 at 759.
[60.] *Cf. Australian Provincial Assurance Co. Ltd v. Coroneo* (1938) 38 S.R. (N.S.W.) 700, where Jordon C.J. at 714–715 held that the hirer's interest is merely possessory and refused to draw any parallel with leasehold interests in land.
[61.] *Ibid.* at 759.
[62.] See *Beswick v. Beswick* [1968] A.C. 58.

proprietary and personal rights. In this respect, it is essential to examine precisely the nature of the right which is being protected. It is necessary to adopt this approach in order to avoid the error of Lord Denning in *Errington v. Errington and Woods*[63] when his Lordship held that a mere contractual license has an equitable proprietary effect binding third-party purchasers, other than a bona fide purchaser without notice of a legal estate. It took over 25 years to correct this error in *Ashburn Anstalt v. Arnold*[64] where the Court of Appeal held that a contractual licence to occupy land did not create, either in law or equity, a property right. Merely because a contractual right is given to possess land, this does not determine the issue of the proprietary nature of that right.

The mere fact that a covenantee has a right to possession of the subject-matter of the contract is neutral in respect of the question of whether he has a proprietary right. As Diplock J. pointed out in *Port Line Ltd v. Ben Line Steamers Ltd*,[65] the projection of a pre-existing contract relationship upon a subsequent purchaser of the subject-matter of that contract cannot be achieved simply by showing that the plaintiff had a contractual right and that he stood to lose financially if performance of the contract were rendered impossible by the refusal of a non-party to be governed by its terms. The analogy of land law demonstrates that contractual licenses are personal rights notwithstanding that they may be specifically enforceable.[66] The list of proprietary interests works on a *numerus clausus* principle, that is a finite principle, and the issue is whether the rights of the hirer/lessee of goods should be admitted to that list as is the lessee of land. Whilst historically the tests of property rights have been predominantly judge-made,[67] it may be that the creation of new property rights should, as a matter of principle, rest with Parliament. There are obvious policy issues involved in categorising the interest of a hirer as being proprietary in character. Significantly in *Swiss Bank Corp. v. Lloyds Bank Ltd*,[68] Browne-Wilkinson J. expressly rejected the analogy of land law, in the context of covenants running with chattels, on the basis that this had caused conceptual confusion.

The Head-Lessor and the Sub-Lessee: a Sub-Bailment on Terms?

The case law has developed an important exception to the general privity problem as between the head-lessor as principal bailor and the

[63.] [1952] 1 K.B. 290.
[64.] [1989] 1 Ch. 1.
[65.] [1958] 2 Q.B. 146.
[66.] *Cf.* the constructive trust approach adopted by the Court of Appeal in *Binions v. Evans* [1972] Ch. 359.
[67.] See *Tulk v. Moxhay* (1848) 2 Ph. 774.
[68.] [1979] Ch. 548; rev. on facts [1982] A.C. 584.

sub-lessee. In *Morris v. C.W. Martin and Sons Ltd*[69] the issue was considered at length by Lord Denning and he drew an analogy with the law of liens, that is, if a bailee acting with the bailor's authority deals with the goods entrusted to him in such a way as to confer a lien on a third party, that lien binds not only the bailee, but also the bailor.[70] Thus it was held that the principal bailor is bound by the terms of the sub-bailment if he consented, expressly or impliedly, to the goods being sub-bailed on those terms. Lord Denning in *Morris*[71] said that: "the owner is bound by the conditions [contained in the contract between the principal bailee and the sub-bailee] if he has expressly or impliedly consented to the bailee making a sub-bailment containing those conditions, but not otherwise." Of course the overall commercial context has to be considered in determining whether the bailor's consent can be implied in relation to the sub-bailment terms. In this respect *Morris* is important in that it lays down two propositions: first, that the sub-bailee owes the principal bailor all the duties of a bailee; secondly, the sub-bailee is entitled to rely on his exemption clauses. Whilst the original basis for these propositions was not clear, nonetheless there has been a steady stream of judicial authority since *Morris* which has endorsed them.[72]

The judicial basis of *Morris* was considered more recently by the Privy Council in *The Owners of Cargo lately on Board the Vessel K.H. Enterprise v. The Owners of the Vessel Pioneer Container; The Pioneer Container.*[73] The facts were that the plaintiff's goods were being carried from Taiwan to Hong Kong in the K.H. Enterprise, a sister ship of the Pioneer Container, when she collided with another ship and sank. The plaintiffs commenced proceedings in Hong Kong claiming damages for the loss of the cargo. The defendant shipowners applied for a stay of proceedings relying on an exclusive jurisdiction clause in their bills of lading under which claims were to be determined in Taiwan, where in fact they would now be time-barred. There was no doubt that some of the plaintiffs had contracted directly with the shipowners for the carriage of goods and they were undoubtedly bound by the clause. However, others had entrusted their goods to other carriers who had sub-contracted the carriage to the shipowners who acted therefore as sub-bailees. It was held in the Court of Appeal in Hong Kong and the Privy Council that the exclusive jurisdiction clause could be relied upon, following the principles laid down in *Morris*, because the plaintiffs had expressly or impliedly authorised the sub-bailment of their goods to the shipowners bill of lading which included the exclusive jurisdiction clause. Indeed in view of the fact that a shipowner may be exposed to many claims by

[69.] [1996] 1 Q.B. 716.
[70.] See *Tappenden v. Artus* [1964] 2 Q.B. 185.
[71.] [1996] 1 Q.B. 716 at 719.
[72.] See, *e.g. The Kapetan Markos N.L. (No. 2)* [1987] 2 Lloyd's Rep. 321; *The Captain Gregos (No. 2)* [1990] 2 Lloyd's Rep. 395.
[73.] [1994] 2 A.C. 324.

cargo-owners, their Lordships considered that the incorporation of such a clause in the sub-bailment was rational, in that it allowed orderly disposition of disputes within a single jurisdiction.

In the *Pioneer Container* case Lord Goff of Chieveley held that contrary to the dicta in at least one case it was not necessary to base the proposition on that of estoppel.[74] The main difficulty with the estoppel analysis is identifying its application—is it to deal with the issue of whether the exemption clauses are terms of the bailment between the principal bailor and the sub-bailee or does it go to the issue of the terms' enforceability? Of course estoppel will be relevant if there were recourse to the doctrine of ostensible authority under the law of agency. If, however, the agency analysis is at the root of *Morris*, it should still be possible in certain circumstances for the sub-bailee to rely on the protection of the sub-bailment even though the terms were not actually authorised by the principal bailor, for example, if the principal bailee had apparent authority to bail the goods on terms of the sub-bailment. Whilst the Privy Council in the *Pioneer Container* case accepted that agency analysis could provide the rationale, nonetheless Lord Goff also appears to suggest that the rationale is to be found in the specific development in the law of bailment itself, that is, it is in effect a *sui generis* rule of convenience which does not depend upon agreement.[75] In *Johnson Matthey Ltd v. Constantine Terminals Ltd*[76] it was further held that a sub-bailee will be protected even by the terms of an unauthorised sub-bailment, in the absence of apparent authority, so long as the principal bailor ratifies it. As such this would be an exception to the rule that undisclosed principals cannot ratify.[77] There is nothing anomalous in this, because it can be presumed in the sub-bailment context that the principal bailee is not dealing with his own property and that it can, therefore, be presumed that he intended to act for the principal bailor.[78]

One of the major difficulties with the so-called *Matthey* doctrine has been the extravagance of its ambit in as much as it holds that a bailor is bound by the terms of the sub-bailment regardless of consent. Insofar as *Matthey* stands for this proposition, this has now been subject to disapproval by the Privy Council although technically it has not been overruled. Lord Goff gave the following reasons why the *Matthey* doctrine could not be accepted by the Board. First, it was antithetical to the nature of the relationship between the bailor and the sub-bailee, which is based upon the voluntary taking of the former's goods so that the bailor can bring a cause of action against the sub-bailee for breach of a duty of care, and does not need to rely on the terms of the sub-bailment itself. Where the sub-bailment is authorised, the relationship

[74.] *Cf. The Kapetan Markos (No. 2)* [1987] 2 Lloyd's Rep. 321 at 336, 340.
[75.] See also *Dresser U.K. Ltd v. Falcongate Freight Management Ltd* [1992] 2 All E.R. 450.
[76.] [1976] 2 Lloyd's Rep. 215.
[77.] *Keighley Maxted and Co. v. Durant* [1901] A.C. 240.
[78.] See Bell, *Modern Law of Personal Property in England and Ireland*, p. 135.

between the principal bailor and the sub-bailee is that of bailor and bailee, that is there exists a collateral bailment. Under this collateral bailment the sub-bailee is subject to the same standard of care as under the sub-bailment itself—there is no question of the nature of this bailment being regarded as gratuitous. It was held in the Privy Council, following the approach of Professor Palmer,[79] that the bailee's voluntary taking into his possession of the property of another creates the bailment. However, this unilateral relationship can be varied by agreement, for example, qualifying terms with the consent of the bailor. Even so the basis of the sub-bailee's duties rests upon his voluntary assumption of possession and not his bailment of contract. In a profound sense the *Pioneer Container* case does reveal a shift in the juridical basis of the law of bailment from contract to status.[80] A second reason adopted by Lord Goff was that if *Matthey* was to prevail there would be no limit to what the bailor would have to accept. The basis of the *Morris* doctrine is consent.

In summary, the decision of the Privy Council is that a sub-bailee can only rely on a term of the sub-bailment where the principal bailor has expressly or impliedly consented to that term or if the principal bailee has ostensible authority to include the term in the sub-bailment. In so far as this approach prejudices the position of the sub-bailee, the latter has recourse against the principal bailee through suing for breach of warranty of authority. The significance of the *Pioneer Container* case is the decisive rejection of the *Matthey* decision. Whilst there are dicta in the *Pioneer Container* case which allude to the unsatisfactory state of the doctrine of privity of contract in English law, nonetheless the reform of the law anticipated in the Law Commission Report[81] confined its recommendations for reform to the issue of a benefit imposed on a third party. It would appear that the decision of the *Pioneer Container* case will represent the common law position, even after prospective reform is instituted.

One problem that emerges from the *Pioneer Container* case concerns the position of a sub-bailee who is unaware of the existence of the principal bailor and thinks that the goods entrusted to him belong to the principal bailee. Although this was not strictly in point, the Privy Council did consider this issue and indicated that the sub-bailee would not owe the principal bailor the duties of a bailee, because the sub-bailee could not be said to have voluntarily taken the principal bailor's goods into his possession.[82]

[79.] *Bailment* (2nd ed., 1991) pp. 31 *et seq.*
[80.] See Bell, "Case and Comment" [1995] L.M.C.L.Q. 177 at 181.
[81.] Law Commission Report No. 242, *Privity of Contract: Contracts for the Benefit of Third Parties* (1996).
[82.] *Cf.* the Court of Appeal decision in *Award v. Pillai* [1982] R.T.R. 266, where it was held that the sub-bailee owes the undisclosed owner of the goods a duty of care in tort.

Part 2

Entering into Agreement

Chapter 3

The Lessor–Lessee Relationship

Introduction

Whilst equipment leasing covers a wide spectrum of assets and the agreements will generally reflect the different commercial purposes for various commercial arrangements, nonetheless the basic core of the terms of all hiring agreements are similar. In this respect all leases will reflect the need to govern the relationship between the lessor and the lessee: the agreement to hire; payment of rentals; allocation of responsibilities in relation to the asset; termination. In addition to this central core, there may be other embellishments including a maintenance provision, an obligation imposed upon third parties to buy back the goods (typically motor dealers). The lease itself may also include certain costs and taxation assumptions all of which have to be accommodated in the lease agreement. The function of the express terms in the lease contract is to govern the relationship between the lessor and lessee in such a way as to protect the lessor's investment, first, in relation to the goods themselves and, secondly, in relation to the rental stream. This is especially the case with the finance lease, because after delivery of the leased asset generally the finance lessor is required to do nothing further and it is up to the lessee to carry out the expressed terms. It is otherwise in the case of operating leases where the lessor will often assume responsibility for maintenance and taxation and also the provision of operators of the equipment, for example, in the case of the time-charter of a ship, the crew.

This chapter will focus upon the common terms of all equipment leases. However, before considering what are the most commonly used contractual obligations it is necessary to briefly consider pre-lease procedures.

Pre-Lease Considerations

Introduction

There may be a long lead in time in respect of the lease of sophisticated equipment. In this situation the lessee will usually have ordered the equipment and will only subsequently consider the issue of financing it. There is nothing unreasonable in this approach, because where the actual projected delivery time is remote it is unlikely that prospective lessors will quote rates so far in the future. The following information will be required by the lessor in determining issues of risk and acceptability of a lease proposal.

The Nature of the Equipment

The nature of the equipment is important for the purposes of capital allowances. In addition if the equipment is to be physically attached to premises so as to become fixtures, it will usually be necessary for the lessee to obtain an undertaking from his landlord or mortgagee acknowledging the lessor's interest in the equipment and his right to remove it in the circumstances stipulated for in the lease. Where the lessee owns the premises to which the plant is to be attached, the lessor will normally seek a covenant from the lessee not to mortgage the property without having first obtained such an undertaking from the mortgagor.[1] In the case of software leases including the programming part of data processing, it will be necessary for the lessor to ensure that the range of services needed to support the hardware, including the various licenses, will be turned over to the lessor on the lessee's default. The lessor will need to be satisfied that he can grant to or procure the necessary rights for the lessee for the use of the software and recover its value if the lease is terminated prematurely. This is usually achieved by the software owner granting a license to the lessor with the right to assign the benefit of the license to a purchaser from him. This gives the lessor control over the hire equipment and software, but will also visit at least implied obligations and liability upon the lessee in respect of these.

In relation to the leasing of films and other literary artistic and musical works, it will be necessary for the lessor to ensure copyright protection. This will also be the case in relation to software and other computer programs. There are no particular problems relevant to hiring as opposed to other dealings in goods in relation to securing intellectual property rights and detailed consideration of these is beyond the scope of this book.

Identification of the Equipment

Identification of the equipment is linked with the expected date for delivery which is crucial, as it determines the period from which lease payments must be made and, from the lessor's perspective, the tax year for claiming allowances and the basis upon which tax and interest rate assumptions have to be made. Where delivery has been delayed or progress payments are required in respect of the construction of equipment and the lessor has paid in advance or made progress

---

[1.] See Chap. 9, below.

payments, it is usual for the lessor to seek an indemnity from the lessee to provide against the possibility of non-delivery.

Interesting problems arise in the situation where the equipment in question, perhaps, through fraudulent behaviour on the part of the lessee, turns out to be non-existent. Such a phenomenon is illustrated in *Associated Japanese Bank (International) Ltd v. Crédit du Nord SA*,[2] where the facts involved the sale to the plaintiffs and leaseback of non-existent machines. The defendants separately agreed with the plaintiffs to guarantee the seller's obligations under the leaseback agreement and, following the default of the (now) lessee it was discovered that the machines did not exist. It was held that the machines constituted the principal security of the defendants as guarantors and, since these did not exist, the guarantee contract was void *ab initio* for common mistake at common law.[3] As a consequence, the plaintiff's claim under the guarantee agreement failed. The reason for this is that the guarantee is an accessory contract in the sense that the surety's obligations spring out of those of the principal debtor, and the liability of the surety is coterminous with that of the principal debtor.

Risk Management

The credit risk assumed by the financier in the case of an equipment lease or a hire-purchase agreement where no initial deposit is paid is somewhat similar. Inquiries to obtain the same kinds of information as to the credit standing of the lessee and hirer will therefore be necessary. This will usually encompass such matters as the nature of the lessee's business, its latest financial accounts, an assessment of the quality of its management and future prospects in the market place. At the same time the lessor will usually seek to protect its position in relation to the asset itself by requiring the lessee to insure it. Both the lessor as owner and the lessee have an insurable interest in the equipment. The insurable interest of a lessee in equipment is similar to that of a purchaser in equipment that is purchased and the lessee will wish to arrange insurance on the same basis. Insurance cover is normally sought in respect of physical loss or damage to the equipment and in respect of possible legal liability from third party claims relating to its use.

Certain risks are normally excluded from insurance policies, although cover can sometimes be arranged by indorsement or by the issue of a separate policy. The use of leased equipment for an illegal purpose, or its operation by an unqualified operator, may invalidate the policy. Nonetheless, the lessor will be protected in these circumstances if the policy covers its interest and contains, for the lessor's benefit, a "breach of warranty" clause stating that the insurance provided under the policy is

[2.] [1989] 1 W.L.R. 255.
[3.] See *Couturier v. Hastie* (1856) 5 H.L. Cas. 673.
[4.] See Chap. 13, below.

not invalidated by any act or omission on the part of the lessee or his servants or agents. Some types of risks are completely uninsurable, for example, criminal liabilities, nuclear detonations and the insolvency of the insurer.

It is usual for the amount of insurance cover to be provided for liability purposes to be stipulated by the lessor. Even so, neither a lessor nor a lessee is under any statutory obligation specifically to insure leased equipment. However, in the case of motor vehicles, section 143 of the Road Traffic Act 1988 renders it unlawful for a person to use, or permit any other person to use, a motor vehicle on a road unless the use of the vehicle is insured against liability in respect of death or of personal injury to third parties. The effect of this is to make a lessor criminally liable if the vehicles are permitted to be used without such insurance and, possibly, also liable for damages awarded against the uninsured lessee of the vehicle to the extent that the lessee is unable to satisfy any claim. In order to avoid such liability the lessor will seek to include a provision in the leasing agreement prohibiting the lessee from using the vehicle without cover satisfying the statutory requirements, thereby, making any such use without the lessor's permission and, as a consequence, outside the scope of section 143 of the 1988 Act.

Acquisition of the Leased Asset

The legal structures are governed by whether the leasing facility is in place prior either to the ordering or the delivery of the equipment. In the case of the finance lease it will be the lessee who selects the equipment and also the principal supply terms with the dealer/supplier.

Where the Lease Facility is in Place before Ordering

Where the lease facility is in place before ordering, the acquisition of the asset can be effectuated as follows:

1. Direct purchase by the lessor so there is no privity of contract between the lessee and the dealer/supplier.[5]

2. The lessee to act as an agent on behalf of the lessor in accordance with its terms. In this respect the agency might be restricted to the placement of a specific order on behalf of the lessor who, as a disclosed principal, will be responsible to paying the supplier directly. In the alternative, the lessee may make payment to the supplier and obtain reimbursement from the lessor where the latter is an undisclosed principal.[6] Under both instances, the

[5] See Chap. 5, below.
[6] See Chap. 5, below.

agency arrangement will usually be governed by a memorandum or agreement which will normally include:

    (a) the description of the goods or nature of the goods including specification;

    (b) limit on the price of the goods;

    (c) specification of delivery date;

    (d) acknowledgement that the lessee is to accept delivery of the goods from the supplier on behalf of the lessor;

    (e) a recital that upon acceptance by the lessee, the goods become subject to the leasing agreement;

    (f) where the agency agreement covers payment to the supplier, undertakings by the lessee to pay invoices on their due dates and also by the lessor to reimburse the lessee according to their agreement.

Where the Lease Facility is not in Place before Ordering

The introduction of the lessor to the purchased equipment may come about in the following ways:

1. **Assignment.** The difficulty with the mechanism of assignment is that allowances granted to the lessor may be compromised. The supplier will still have a right of action against the lessee under the contract should the lessor default on his obligations. Furthermore there are *ad valorem* tax repercussions to this mechanism.[7]

2. **Novation.** Under novation the original purchase order is cancelled and is replaced by a new and identical order. This contrasts with assignment where merely the rights of the lessee are transferred to the lessor. Novation is the only method by which the original obligor can be effectively replaced by another: A, B and C must make a new contract by which in consideration of A (the supplier) releasing B (the potential lessee) from his obligation, C (the lessor) agrees to assume responsibility for its performance. It would appear that it will be necessary for the lessor and supplier to contract on the same terms with the lessor paying for the cost of the equipment. Thus, any similar sums already paid by the lessee will have to be returned, and this will clearly show that the debt between the lessee and supplier has been extinguished so providing consideration for the arrangement. Seemingly, therefore, any exclusion clause governing the first agreement, for example relating to sections 12 to 15 of the Sale of Goods Act 1979, will have to be included in the novation as well.

[7.] See Chap. 4, below.

Where the Lease Facility is not in Place by the Time of Delivery

Where the invoicing of the equipment has taken place between the supplier and the prospective lessee then in this circumstance equipment leasing finance may be arranged on a sale and leaseback basis.[8] It is normal in such circumstances for the lessee to sign a delivery note acknowledging that the leased assets are accepted and in good condition, which has obvious evidentiary repercussions.

Where the Lease Facility is in Place but the Character of the Lessee Changes as a Result of Statutory Intervention

Statutory novation was the mechanism used as part of the privatisation initiative of the Conservative Government in order to transfer liabilities in respect of equipment leases. This was imposed upon finance lessors who might not otherwise have accepted the change of lessee, on the basis that the original assumption of risk made will have materially altered as a result of the change of status to, for example, in the case of the National Health Service, a health authority being replaced by a hospital trust which could theoretically face bankruptcy. Even so section 96(1A) of the National Health Service and Community Care Act 1990 provides for transfer of property which includes:

> "(b) any other asset leased or hired from a third party or in which a third party has an interest,
> the transfer shall be binding on the third party notwithstanding that, apart from this subsection, it would have required his consent or concurrence."

The Core Terms of an Equipment Lease Agreement

Introduction

Much depends upon the commercial context and the requirements of the lessee and the practices of the lessor. Typically in the case of finance leases of plant and machinery, the issue of delivery of the equipment is not dealt with except insofar as the inclusion of a provision to the effect that the hiring commences on delivery. It is otherwise where the lessor funds the construction of the equipment, where the lease will contain detailed provisions relating to the period up to and including delivery whereby the lessor will seek indemnities against the lessee for a failure

---

[8.] See Chap. 2, above.

by the supplier to deliver or, alternatively, delivery to a satisfactory standard.

Whilst finance leases have not become standard form documents, the following would appear to represent the normal structure and legal logic of the transaction.

The Lessor's Covenants

1. Definition, including all accessories and replacements and renewals of parts of the equipment.

2. Title of the equipment is retained by the lessor notwithstanding incorporation into land or any other chattel. The lessor will usually preserve the express right to assign its rights to another financier/purchaser. This is perfected usually by issuing a notice of assignment to the lessee and will typically want the lessee to issue an acknowledgement dealing with the following:

    (a) The financier (new lessor) is entitled to cure any breaches of the lease by the lessor within a grace period (usually 14 days).

    (b) A direct lease be entered into between the new lessor and lessee which will enable it to take the benefit or a "hell or high water" clause.

    (c) The lessee has not received any prior notice of assignment.

    In any assignment the new lessor will want the benefit of any indemnities and also insurance.

    As an alternative mechanism, the prospective new lessor may seek novation of the original lease. In this respect, the novation agreement will make consequential amendments to the terms of the lease to reflect the identity of the new lessor. It is usual for the new lessor to require further representations and warranties from the lessee namely:

    (i) There are no current disputes between the lessee and lessor.

    (ii) The lessee has not paid all rent or any other amounts in advance.

    (iii) If the lessee possesses a purchase option or option to extend or terminate the lease terms, it has not given any notice of exercise of those options.

    (iv) That the lessee has not entered into any agreement to sub-lease the equipment.

    (v) That the equipment is not damaged or has not suffered any unrepaired damage.

3. Terms of the agreement. Finance leases generally provide that the leased assets are hired to one lessee for an agreed fixed or

primary period of hire during which time the lessee will, by payment of the rentals agreed during this period, pay the cost of the leased asset to the lessor together with the profit which the lessor expects to make from the transaction. It is common for there to be a secondary period of hire which will equate to the remainder of the useful life of the equipment usually at a nominal rent. In contrast, operating leases, whilst having a fixed period of hire, may not normally be capable of extension of the hire period because, for example, a buy-back scheme may have been negotiated with the dealer or the manufacturer of the product. Clearly in some types of hire on a short-term basis, fixed-term hire will not be appropriate.

The Lessee's Covenants

1. To pay rentals. Punctual payment is usually included as an essential term of the lease. In sophisticated lease transactions payments may be declining during the term (step payments) or increasing (balloon payments) to reflect the lessee's financial requirements. In addition there may be rental variation provisions dealing with the lessor's funding of the leased assets which will take into account tax allowance(s) and also money cost variations as interest rates fluctuate.

2. To maintain and repair the leased asset. In finance leases the repairing obligation is linked with the maintenance obligation and is the responsibility of the lessee. In the case of an operating lease the maintenance obligation will not be the responsibility of the lessee, although the latter will be responsible for the condition of the leased asset on re-delivery.

   The standard of maintenance and repair is that necessary to ensure that the leased assets may be lawfully, safely and efficiently used during the period of hire. At common law the hirer as a bailee for mutual advantage must take reasonable care of the chattel and must use reasonable skill in its management. The burden of proving that the appropriate degree of care has been taken rests with the hirer.[9] It will be a defence for the hirer to show that it was not his neglect or mismanagement that caused or contributed to the loss.[10] A distinction should be drawn between neglect and fair wear and tear. Clearly the equipment at the end of the term will be subject to fair wear and tear which may be important to the lessor for the purposes of claiming capital allowances. Sometimes the lease contract will place the obligation to repair the leased asset in the insurance clause, the

---

[9] *Port Swettenham Authority v. T.W.Wu and Co.* [1979] A.C. 580.
[10] See N.E. Palmer, *Bailment* (2nd ed., 1991) p. 1264.

---

proceeds of insurance being applied directly to their repair. If the equipment is not repairable, then the insurers will treat the claim as a total loss in which case the lease will terminate and any shortfall in recovery will have to be made up by the lessee. If a total loss has not occurred but the equipment is not capable of repair to their former condition, the lessor's asset will have been reduced in value and it will be necessary to reduce the financial liability of the lessee in respect of those assets. In these circumstances the lease may provide that the equipment should be repaired from the lessee's own resources, the insurance proceeds being paid to the lessor in reduction of future rentals.

3. To bear the cost of all taxes, expenses and outgoings relating to the leased assets including their operational use and their acquisition. This clause should cover all costs including licence fees for software for equipment. In addition the costs involved (if any) in dismantling the equipment at the end of the term should also be included.

4. Lawful use of the equipment. It is essential that the leased assets are operated safely by the lessee and that the lessee is made responsible for this in accordance with the Health and Safety at Work etc. Act 1974 and related legislation. It is worth noting that in certain circumstances, for example, if unexcised fuel is used in leased commercial vehicles, the lessor as owner will incur liability for the unlawful use of the leased asset.[11]

5. The insurance obligation. There are normally two aspects to this: first, insurance against material damage; secondly, insurance for third-party risks. Typically the following general requirements will be included in the insurance clause of a leasing agreement.

    (a) The policy will be effected in the joint names of the lessor and lessee or at least the interest of the lessor will be noted on the insurance policy. The lessor may also require the lessee to assign all rights and interest in the insurances to the lessor and to warrant that the lessee will not assign, charge or pledge the policies to any third party.
    (b) Any payment made under the policy in pursuance of a claim should be made directly to the lessor or, in the case of a liability claim, will be applied directly for the satisfaction of that claim.
    (c) Evidence of payment should be sent to the lessor or be available on request.
    (d) The policy to be effectuated with an insurer approved by the lessor.

[11.] See Chap. 6, below.

(e) The policy will provide that it may not be cancelled or materially modified until a specified time after prior written notice of intended cancellation or modification has been given to the lessor.

(f) No other insurance will be effected by the lessee if a claim under such insurance could result in the operation of any average clause in the policy taken out by the lessee in accordance with the provisions of the leasing agreement.

The insurance clause will also need to accommodate the situation of underpayment in respect of the lessor's interest in the equipment. Where there is overpayment, perhaps due to any consequential losses suffered by the lessee which is recovered, the lessor will have to account to the lessee in this respect. In the case of excess proceeds relating to the value of the equipment, these proceeds will be apportioned according to the terms of the lease for sharing proceeds at the end of the lease term.

6. To indemnify the lessor against the obsolescence and other risks of the leased asset. Since the lessee has chosen the asset, this indemnity is intended to reflect as far as possible that any liability or loss affecting the lessor as the result of the transaction is passed on to the lessee. A further extension of this is the taxation indemnity clause, which is maintained despite variation in taxation allowances which is particularly significant in respect of long-term equipment leases. The lessor's net rate of return is maintained by adjusting the rentals as the lease term continues.

7. To maintain possession of the goods and not to underlet or mortgage them or create any lien over them. This is the provision protecting the lessor from third party rights. A lessee may seek the lessor's consent to an assignment or transfer clause which consent is not to be unreasonably withheld. However, the lessor is unlikely to agree to this since it will have made a detailed appraisal of the current lessee's creditworthiness and will wish to retain complete discretion in reviewing whether or not to consent to assignment. In deciding whether or not to permit assignment the following considerations are relevant:

(a) The assignee must be in possession of the necessary licences and approvals for the operation of the equipment.

(b) All security issued to support the original lessee's payments under the lease should be re-issued to reflect the identity of the new lessee.[12]

(c) All rights and obligation under the lease should be transferred to the new lessee usually through a novation.

(d) Any default by the lessee should be cured before assignment.

[12.] See Chap. 13, below.

---

8. To ensure that the lessor's rights in the leased assets are not prejudiced by their becoming a fixture or accessories. In this situation the lessor can protect its position by means of a waiver by the landlord.[13]

9. To re-deliver at the end of the term. There may be detailed provisions as to storage at the lessee's premises at the end of the term until arrangements have been made for disposal. The provisions dealing with the disposal of leased assets at the end of the period are often contained in a side-letter. Provisions are sometimes made for the lessee to act as the lessor's agent for disposal with most of the sale proceeds being rebated to the lessee (usually 95–98 per cent). Some of the sale proceeds are retained by the lessor in order to avoid an argument based on sham that this is in fact a disguised hire-purchase agreement. Whilst sale negotiations take place, the lease agreement will regulate the storage and insurance obligations of the lessee.

10. Termination by the hirer. This will be subject to the payment by the lessee of the balance of the lessor's interest in the leased asset and is common in operating leases. It is less common where the scale of the transaction in finance leases increases, where the lessor will seek to ensure that early termination does not occur since having identified a financing opportunity the lessor will wish to exploit it for the entire term by avoiding discount for early termination.

11. Termination by lessor. This is usually linked with default in payment or breach of the terms of the lease or insolvency or act of insolvency of the lessee. A typical clause will deal with re-possession rights and/or damages. Where the equipment is highly specialised and there is no obvious second-hand market, a provision is usually included for stipulated loss values which are applied at specified periods during the hiring. The efficacy of such minimum payment clauses are considered later.[14]

12. Lessee's right to renew for a further term. This is the secondary period of rental in a finance lease.

13. Variation clauses. These are formal provisions which deal with fluctuations in the cost of money or changes in tax liability or concessions.

14. A clause prescribing the governing law of the agreement and method for serving notices.

15. In the case of an agreement regulated by the Consumer Credit Act 1974, additional terms are incorporated in order to ensure compliance.

[13] See Chap. 9, below.
[14] See pp. 101–113, below.

Summary of The Primary Obligations of Lessee/Hirer

1. To pay the agreed rental.
2. To take reasonable care of the equipment during the term. The concomitant of this is that the hirer can escape liability if it can be shown that any damage was not done due to the negligence of the hirer.[15]
3. To use the equipment within the range of purposes for which it was let.
4. To return the equipment at the end of the term.
5. To pay any costs involved in the return of the equipment.

In an attempt to bolster the primary obligations of the lessee/hirer in particular in relation to the payment of rentals a guarantee perhaps by way of an indemnity might be bought from a third party.[15a]

The Obligations of the Lessor

Contractual Privity and Finance Leasing

Introduction

Due to the interrelated nature of the finance leasing transaction, it is clear that any breach of the supply agreement between the supplier and the lessor will ultimately affect the lessee who has chosen the equipment and has contracted for its use and possession. In many cases, it may be that a breach of the supply agreement by the supplier will, in turn, result in a breach of the leasing agreement as well. Inevitably the question arises as to whether the lessor, as primarily a financier, should be responsible for any defects? Significantly under Article 2A of the American Uniform Commercial Code, the lessee in a finance lease, as distinguished from other leases, does not benefit from warranties against "infringement",[16] or implied warranties of merchantability (satisfactory quality) or fitness for purpose.[17] The finance lessee must shoulder the risk of loss,[18] and has irrevocable independent obligations upon acceptance of the equipment[19] entailing that he may not revoke acceptance of the equipment under the same circumstances as other leases.[20]

[15.] *British Crane Hire Corps Ltd v. Ipswich Plant Hire Ltd* [1975] Q.B. 303.
[15a.] See *Chitty on Contracts* (27th ed.) Chap. 42.
[16.] UCC, Art. 2A (211).
[17.] *Ibid*. Art. 2A (212), (213).
[18.] *Ibid*. Art. 2A (219).
[19.] *Ibid*. Art. 2A (407).
[20.] *Ibid*. Art. 2A (517).

Undoubtedly, the justification for this approach is the recognition of the economic reality underlying the transaction which is, in large measure, echoed in the UNIDROIT Convention on International Financial Leasing, carried out in Ottawa on May 28, 1988.

The tripartite nature of the finance lease transaction introduces complex legal problems. The financing lessor is the intermediary who concludes a contract with the client and another contract with the supplier; it would seem that no contract is directly created between the client and the supplier. It cannot be that the supplier and client are total strangers since the object of the contract is for the use of the client and, in any case, it may be that the supplier was chosen by the client who laid down detailed specifications for the object sold. The interrelated nature of the contracts makes it impossible to treat each contract separately or to view the contracts as one transaction between the supplier and the lessee. By treating the transaction as two independent contracts, this permits the supplier and the lessor to modify the supply agreement without notifying the lessee. Since the finance lessee will have negotiated the technical aspects of the supply agreement and will ultimately use the goods and be directly affected by their specifications, no changes should be made without the lessee's consent. This consent requirement flows from the principle that neither the lessee nor the lessor should act to jeopardise the rights of the other.

Most domestic lease transactions are structured to minimise the privity problem posed in a finance leasing context. Typically, the lease agreement may assign to the lessee those warranties created in the supply agreement. However, this will not give the lessee adequate protection since it does not address those warranties given to the lessee in the supplier-lessee negotiations. Nonetheless, any such undertaking made by the supplier to the lessee during negotiations could be construed as an express warranty which will bind the supplier under a collateral contract, the consideration for which being the lessee entering into the main agreement.[21] The lessee, as the assignee of the warranties, may be limited to damages suffered by the lessor due to the supplier's breach, rather than recovering for its own loss. The difficulty here is that the interests of the lessor and the lessee are not the same, nor are the damages suffered by each. In the case of a delay in delivery when payment is conditional upon delivery, the loss or damage to the lessor may be minimal. On the other hand, the lessee may have suffered huge consequential losses. The question is not of transferring rights from the lessor to the lessee, but of giving the lessee an independent cause of action against the supplier. Significantly, in the absence of agreement, some United States' courts have allowed a direct action against the supplier on the basis of the latter's strict liability, the lessor being regarded as merely performing a financing function.[22]

[21.] *Shanklin Pier Ltd v. Detel Products Ltd* [1951] 2 K.B. 854.
[22.] See *Citicorp Leasing Inc. v. Allied Institutional Distributors Inc.* 454 F.Supp 511 (1977); *Atlas Industries Inc. v. National Cash Register Co.* 531 P 2d 41 (1975).

In England, it is unlikely that the identity of object and the connection in fact between the lessee and the supplier will triumph over the principle of contractual privity. The privity doctrine is still entrenched and is applied, albeit reluctantly by the courts, as seen in Lord Scarman's approach in *Woodar Investment Development Ltd v. Wimpey Construction U.K. Ltd*[23]:

> "I respectfully agree with Lord Reid that the denial by English Law of a *ius quaesitum tertio* calls for reconsideration . . . If the opportunity arises, I hope the House will reconsider *Tweddle v. Atkinson*[24] and the other cases which stand guard over the unjust rule."

Many of the arguments used to justify privity are especially spurious in the finance leasing context. In this respect, privity is sometimes justified on the basis that the promisor would otherwise be subject to a double performance liability. This is not problematic in finance leasing because there is only *one* promise and, once it is enforced by the promisee or the third party, the promisor will have realised his liability. It is sometimes argued that third-party intervention would inhibit or disallow the original parties from varying or rescinding their contract, but what is objectionable in this if this is indeed what the original parties bargained for? Furthermore, there is nothing gratuitous about the position of the third party, since the lessor in the finance lease will have paid for the promise and the lessee will have relied upon this by entering into the lease contract.

The general rule remains in English law that a third party cannot enforce a contract made for his benefit. It is for this reason that the Law Commission[25] have recommended a legislative initiative enabling a third party to sue on a contract made for his benefit where it is the intention of the contracting parties that he be given enforceable rights. This would appear to apply directly to the finance leasing scenario. However, the problem of remoteness and the lessee's consequential losses as a result of the supplier's breach will still remain. These issues were not addressed by the Law Commission, where the focus of the discussion was confined to the *nature* of the rights created in favour of a third party. The Law Commission recommended that third party rights extend to: "(1) a right to all remedies given by the courts for breach of contract (and with the standard rules applicable to those remedies applying by analogy) that would have been available to the third party had he been a party to the contract . . . and (2) a right to take advantage of a promised exclusion or restriction of the promisor's rights as if the third party were a party to the contract."[26]

---

[23] [1980] 1 W.L.R. 277 at 300. See also *Darlington B.C. v. Wiltshier Northern Ltd (Lowes and ors, third parties)* [CA] [1995] 3 All E.R. 895.

[24] (1861) 1 B. & S. 393.

[25] *Privity of Contracts: Contracts for the Benefit of Third Parties* (Law Com. No. 242, 1996). See draft Bill, Contracts (Rights of Third Parties) clause 1.

[26] *Ibid.* para. 3.32 and draft Bill, clauses 1(4) and 1(5).

The damages recoverable by the lessee may be wholly inadequate even if the Law Commission's proposals are implemented in relation to consequential losses. These losses will only be recoverable if they fall within the reasonable anticipation of the defendant in the light of circumstances known to him. Thus, the lessee will have to prove that the supplier had knowledge of any special contract entered into by the lessee, that it was reasonably foreseeable and that such a contract would be lost as a result of the breach. In practice, this will be a difficult burden to displace. Of course, where the finance lessor is suing under the supply contract, the loss will be limited to the rentals withheld under the leasing agreement as a result of the supplier's breach. On the other hand it could be argued under the present law that the finance lessor as assignor could recover substantial damages on behalf of the lessee as assignee through the trust mechanism. Where a contract constitutes one party a trustee of the other party's promise to confer a benefit on a third party, the trustees can personally recover damages to represent the loss of the benefit on behalf of the third party.[26a]

The position in tort

The doctrine of privity of contract only means that a non-contracting party cannot bring an action on the contract; it does not exclude a successful action being brought in tort. In *Junior Books Ltd v. Veitchi Co. Ltd*,[27] the House of Lords awarded damages for the misperformance of a construction sub-contract to a pursuer company which was not party to the contract, by allowing it an action in negligence against the defaulting sub-contractor. Lord Roskill's speech in that case represents the recent high-water mark of the development of the tort of negligence in relation to recovery for economic loss. His Lordship considered the pursuer's claim as one based on pure economic loss and not physical damage. Through the application of Lord Wilberforce's two-stage test in *Anns v. Merton London Borough Council*,[28] it was held that there was sufficient "proximity" between the parties to give rise to a duty of care which, on breach, allowed the non-contracting party to sue for losses, including economic benefit. Undoubtedly, the implications of this case for the law of contracts and product liability were staggering. This explains why *Anns* was expressly overruled by the House of Lords in *Murphy v. Brentwood District Council*.[29]

Subsequent case law has restricted *Junior Books Ltd v.Veitchi Co. Ltd* either as being a case confined to its own facts or, on the basis that the

---

[26a.] See *Lloyd's v. Harper* (1880) 16 Ch.D. 290; *Darlington B.C. v. Wiltshier Northern Ltd (Lowes and ors, third parties)* [CA] [1995] 3 All E.R. 895.

[27.] [1983] 1 A.C. 520.

[28.] [1978] A.C. 728.

[29.] [1991] 1 A.C. 398.

pursuer had suffered damage to its property.[30] The settled position would now appear to be that whereas a manufacturer may be liable in tort for injury to persons or damage to property caused by a defective chattel, in the absence of a contract, no liability arises in tort to purchasers of a chattel who suffer economic loss because it is defective in *quality*. The damage to property versus defective quality issue is a thorny one as can be illustrated in the case of *Simaan General Contracting Co. v. Pilkington Glass Ltd (No. 2)*. The plaintiffs were the main contractors of a building erected in Abu Dhabi for which the plans and specifications required double-glazed units of green glass to be incorporated into curtain walling. The supply and erection of this was sub-contracted to an Italian company Feal which, as required by the terms of the sub-contract, ordered the glass panels from the defendant. The glass supplied was not of a uniform colour and the building owner withheld payment from Simaan until the panels were replaced. In the Court of Appeal, it was held that in the absence of a contract between the main contractor and the glass supplier, the main contractor could not sue the glass supplier directly for economic loss. Reference was made to the way *Junior Books Ltd v. Veitchi Co. Ltd* had been interpreted in subsequent decisions as involving damage to property. Even though there had been in *Simaan* a failure to comply with the description, merchantability and fitness for purpose conditions under the Sale of Goods Act 1979, this was not considered to constitute damage to *property*. As Bingham L.J. held[31]:

> "There is in my view no physical damage in this case. The units are as good as ever they were and will not deteriorate . . . What we have here are not, in my view, defects but failures to comply with Sale of Goods Act conditions . . . It would, I think, be an abuse of language to describe these units as damaged."

The significance of this analysis, in the context of finance leasing goes to the question of acceptance of the goods by the lessee as well as the lessor's duty to supply goods of the correct specification.

In *Junior Books* the existence of the contract put the plaintiff and the defendant in the closest possible degree of proximity to one another. The issue of proximity must be significant in the finance leasing context, due to the level of control and involvement by the lessee in choosing the equipment. Indeed it may be persuasively argued that the supplier should be deemed to have assumed responsibility for the equipment in

---

[30.] See *Governors of the Peabody Donation Fund v. Sir Lindsay Parkinson and Co. Ltd* [1985] A.C. 210; *Candlewood Navigation Corp. Ltd v. Mitsui OSK Lines Ltd* [1986] A.C. 1; *Leigh & Sillavan Ltd v. Aliakmon Shipping Co. Ltd* [1986] A.C. 785; *D and F Estates Ltd v. Church Commissioners for England* [1989] A.C. 177; *Simaan General Contracting Co. v. Pilkington Glass Ltd (No. 2)* [1988] Q.B. 758; *Greater Nottingham Cooperative Society Ltd v. Cementation Piling and Foundations Ltd* [1989] Q.B. 71; *Pacific Associates Inc. v. Baxter* [1990] 1 Q.B. 993.

[31.] [1988] Q.B. 758 at 781, 782.

respect of the lessee. Moreover, the emphasis is now upon the concept of assumption of responsibility.[32] In *Henderson v. Merritt Syndicates*[33] the defendant underwriting agent and the plaintiff "Names" were remote parties in a chain of contracts, but Lord Goff still held the defendants had assumed responsibility towards the plaintiffs because of the close relationship between "Names" and underwriting agents on the Lloyd's market. His Lordship acknowledged that in analogous cases in the building context, such as *Simaan*, there would normally not be a sufficiently close relationship between remote parties on a contractual chain to support a finding of assumption of responsibility between them. It would appear then that if assumption of responsibility is the proper basis of liability for purely economic loss, there may be recovery in tort for purely economic loss so long as there is a close relationship between the parties. Indeed such a conclusion derives from principles laid down in *Hedley Byrne v. Heller.* [34]

Ultimately a contractual solution, such as that anticipated under the recommendations of the Law Commission Report (No. 242) is preferable as this would allow the finance lessee to sue upon the supply contract. A contractual solution has the following advantages in the context of finance leasing: first, the choice-orientated approach adopted in contract seems more appropriate than the locus of the "accident" tort approach; secondly, the measure of damages in contract ensures full expectation loss; thirdly, great problems would arise if one relationship is subject to one limitation period rule and the other relationship subject to another. Furthermore, the privity rule can be criticised on the grounds of economic efficiency. If the finance lessor wishes to provide the lessee with an enforceable benefit from a contract with the supplier, the lessor must first contract with the supplier and then the latter must contract with the lessee who must provide some nominal consideration. The supplier will be required to perform in the same way in any case, but extra transactional costs are incurred.

The Statutory Implied Terms

Introduction

Prior to the Supply of Goods and Services Act 1982 (the SGSA 1982) there was some degree of uncertainty as to what precisely the owner's obligations under a contract of hire were. In some cases the liability was said to be "strict" in the Sale of Goods sense[35] whilst in other cases the liability was said to simply be founded on negligence.[36] There was a

---

[32.] See *White v. Jones* [1995] 2 W.L.R. 187.
[33.] [1994] 3 W.L.R. 761.
[34.] [1964] A.C. 465.
[35.] *Hyman v. Nye* (1881) 6 Q.B.D. 685.
[36.] *Jones v. Page* (1867) 15 L.T. 619.

further line of authority which comprised of a *via media* between the above two approaches.[37] The English position has been clarified by the general assimilation into all contracts of supply, including hire, of the implied terms found in the Sale of Goods Act 1979 (the SGA 1979).[38] It is appropriate to consider these implied terms and assess their impact upon lessors of equipment including finance lessors.

Quiet possession and title

The quiet possession guarantee. In the case of contracts of hire the only issue relates to quiet possession as there is no implied term that the goods are free from encumbrances and charges found in the SGA 1979 and other contracts of supply. Section 7(2) of the SGSA 1982 states:

> "(2) In a contract for the hire of goods there is also an implied warranty that the bailee will enjoy quiet possession of the goods for the period of the bailment except so far as the possession may be disturbed by the owner or other person entitled to the benefit of any charge or encumbrance disclosed or known to the bailee before the contract is made."

In the case of a lease, the lessor impliedly warrants that the hirer will enjoy uninterrupted use and enjoyment of the goods for the period of the hire. This may prove problematical for a sub-lessee where the intermediary lessor had no right to sub-lease the goods. Use of the goods by the sub-lessee might amount to conversion, but if the action is brought by the finance lessor after the subsidiary hiring term expired, it will be difficult to establish that such action creates an incursion upon the subsidiary hirer's quiet possession.

It may be considered that the lack of an implied term that the goods are free from any charges or encumbrances will therefore operate to the

---

[37.] See *Implied Terms in Contracts for the Supply of Goods* (Law Com. No. 95, 1979) paras. 74 *et seq.*

[38.] The contracts concerned under the definition of hire of goods are set out in the SGSA 1982, s. 6, as follows:

"(1) In this Act [in its application to England and Wales and Northern Ireland] a "contract for the hire of goods" means a contract under which one person bails or agrees to bail goods to another by way of hire, other than an excepted contract.

(2) For the purposes of this section an excepted contract means any of the following:

(a) a hire-purchase agreement;

(b) a contract under which goods are (or are to be) bailed in exchange for trading stamps on their redemption.

(3) For the purposes of this Act [in its application to England and Wales and Northern Ireland] a contract is a contract for the hire of goods whether or not services are also provided or to be provided under the contract, and (subject to subsection (2) above) whatever is the nature of the consideration for the bailment or agreement to bail by way of hire."

disadvantage of the hirer, because he may be prevented from effectively exercising a contractual power to sub-lease because of a subsequent discovery of a charge or encumbrance. The hirer is not assisted either by the common law which has not as yet recognised the existence of such an implied term.

The general property guarantee. In the case of contracts for bailment, section 7(1) of the SGSA 1982 provides that there is an implied condition that the bailor has a right to bail the goods and not necessarily that he is the owner of the goods. With regard to hire purchase, section 8(1) of the Supply of Goods (Implied Terms) Act 1973 (the SOGIT 1973)[39] provides that there is an implied condition that the creditor-owner will have the right to sell the goods *when* the property is to pass. An important distinction may be drawn here with the contract of sale where, following *Rowland v. Divall*,[40] a buyer can reject the goods, notwithstanding long use, if his seller had no right to sell at the time of delivery. Nevertheless, the reasoning adopted in *Rowland v. Divall* is that the *purpose* of a sale transaction is to transfer a perfect title, which is not the case with a hire contract nor with hire-purchase at least until the time when the property is to pass. In this respect the question relates to whether an initial defective title can be cured.[41]

Where the lessor of equipment never had a right to transfer possession of the goods, on the basis of the reasoning in *Rowland v. Divall* (1923), the rentals paid even after long use are likely to be recoverable. The justification for such an approach being that whilst the hirer has enjoyed the use of the goods hired, that use has not been at the expense of the lessor but at the expense of the true owner of the goods. In any case, as a matter of principle, a hirer cannot be compelled to pay rent to a lessor who is not the owner of the goods.[42] In this respect, it is necessary to distinguish seizure by a third party claiming a title paramount from seizure by an encumbrancer. Where the goods are seized by a party claiming under a title paramount, this will bring the agreement to an end and damages will be assessed on the usual principles, including a duty on the part of the hirer to mitigate, for example by accepting replacement equipment.

In the case of all chattel leases, the lessor will be able to exclude liability for breach of either or both of the terms implied in section 7 of the SGSA 1982 provided that he can show that the relevant exclusion clause is reasonable under section 7(4) of the Unfair Contract Terms Act 1977 (the UCTA 1977).[43]

[39.] As substituted by the Consumer Credit Act 1974, Sched. 4.
[40.] [1923] 2 K.B. 500.
[41.] See *Barber v. NWS Bank plc* [1996] 1 All E.R. 906.
[42.] See *N.E.* Palmer *Bailment* (2nd ed., 1991) p. 1217.
[43.] See pp. 77–83, below.

Conformity to description

Section 13(1) of SGA 1979 lays down that:

> "Where there is a contract for the sale of goods by description, there is an implied condition that the goods shall correspond with the description."

This undertaking can also be found in the case of a bailment[44] as well as in a hire-purchase arrangement.[45] Further, a sale or hire or hire purchase can be by description even though the buyer or hirer has seen the goods and had selected them.[46]

If goods are sold by description, that is by prescribing the characteristics they are to possess, then, as Salmond J. pointed out in *Taylor v. Combined Buyers Ltd,*[47] every element of the description, whether it relates to number, quality, kind, state, should in theory form part of the description. The reasoning here is that such goods are only capable of being identified through defining their characteristics. This phenomenon is particularly prevalent in the case of unascertained future goods, where a strict approach is often evidenced. As Lord Blackburn said in *Bowes v. Shand*[48]: "If the description of the article tendered is different in any respect it is not the article bargained for and the other party is not bound to take it." The leading case is *Arcos Ltd v. EA Ronaasen and Son*[49] where the buyers agreed to buy a quantity of staves of half an inch thickness for making cement barrels. Only five per cent of the staves were of the correct thickness but the rest were nearly all less than nine-sixteenths of an inch thick. It was found as a fact by the arbitrator that the goods "were commercially within and merchantable under the contract specification". Despite this, the House of Lords rejected any concept of commercial equivalence so that Lord Atkin held[50]:

> "It was contended that in all commercial contracts the question was whether there was 'substantial' compliance with the contract: there must always be some margin and it is for the tribunal of fact to determine whether the margin is exceeded or not. I cannot agree. If the written contract specifies conditions of weight, measurement and the like, those conditions must be complied with. A ton does not mean about a ton, or a yard about a yard. Still less when you descend to minute measurements does half an inch mean about half an inch. If the seller wants a margin he must, and in my experience does, stipulate for it . . .

---

[44] SGSA 1982, s. 8(1), (2).
[45] SOGIT 1973, s. 9(1) (as substituted: see n. 39, above).
[46] SGA 1979, s. 13(3); SOGIT 1973, s. 9(2); SGSA 1982, ss. 3(4), 8(4).
[47] [1924] N.Z.L.R. 627.
[48] (1877) 2 App. Cas. 455 at 460.
[49] [1933] A.C. 470.
[50] *Ibid.* at 479–480. See also *Re Moore and Co. and Landauer and Co.* [1921] 2 K.B. 319.

No doubt there may be microscopic deviations which businessmen and therefore lawyers will ignore . . . But, apart from this consideration, the right view is that the conditions of the contract must be strictly performed."

In the light of the excessive technicality seen here, it is little wonder that Lord Wilberforce in *Reardon Smith Line Ltd*[51] and the House of Lords in *Ashington Piggeries*[52] proposed giving a narrower scope to section 13, confining it to matters of identification. As Lord Diplock said in *Ashington Piggeries*[53]:

"The 'description' by which unascertained goods are sold is, in my view, confined to those words in the contract which were intended by the parties to identify the kind of goods which were to be supplied. It is open to the parties to use a description as broad or as narrow as they choose. But ultimately the test is whether the buyer could fairly and reasonably refuse to accept the physical goods proffered to him on the ground that their failure to correspond with what was said about them made them goods of a different kind from those he had agreed to buy. The key to s. 13 is identification."

The problem with this approach is that it begs the question concerning the nature of identification in unascertained future goods.

Although Lord Wilberforce in *Reardon Smith Lines* called for a review of cases based upon excessive technicality, his Lordship's views are *obiter*, but it would appear that section 15A(1) of the SGA 1979 (as amended) has dealt with the mischief alluded to, that is, a non-consumer buyer can no longer avoid an improvident bargain by merely relying upon a technical breach of section 13. This is also the position in contracts of hire-purchase and hire.[54] However, it is otherwise where the commercial context as defined by the contract requires strict compliance. Indeed in *Moralice (London) Ltd v. E.D. and F. Man*[55] it was held that where the price is payable by means of a banker's commercial credit against the shipping documents, the *de minimis* maxim has no application as between the seller and the bank.

The buyer or hirer must contract to buy or hire the goods by description. If there is no reliance then, notwithstanding the fact that the goods were offered for sale by description, the buyer has bought the goods on other terms. Even so, proof of reliance is not difficult especially in view of section 13(3) of the SGA 1979, section 8(4) of the SGSA 1982, and section 9(2) of the SOGIT 1973, which provides that ordinary articles of commerce as specific goods are expressly included in the definition of sale or hire or hire-purchase by description. In *Harlingdon and Leinster Enterprises Ltd v. Christopher Hull Fine Art Ltd*,[56] the Court of

---

[51.] *Reardon Smith Line Ltd v. Hansen Tangen* [1976] 1 W.L.R. 989.
[52.] *Ashington Piggeries Ltd v. Christopher Hill Ltd* [1972] A.C. 441.
[53.] *Ibid.* at 503–504.
[54.] SOGIT 1973, s. 11A, SGSA 1982, s. 10A.
[55.] [1954] 2 Lloyd's Rep. 526.
[56.] [1991] 1 Q.B. 564.

Appeal considered the issue of reliance on description and it is worth dwelling upon the facts. The defendants were art dealers who carried on business from a London gallery owned and controlled by the principal of the defendants, Mr Christopher Hull. In 1984, Mr Hull was asked to sell two oil paintings which had been described in a 1980 auction catalogue as being by Gabriele Munter, an artist of the German expressionist school. Mr Hull specialised in young contemporary British artists and had no training, experience or knowledge which would have enabled him to conclude from an examination of the pictures whether they were by Munter. He took the paintings to Christie's who expressed interest in them and, at the same time, he contacted the plaintiffs who carried on business as art dealers at a London gallery specialising in the German expressionist school. He told the plaintiffs that he had two paintings by Munter for sale and accordingly an employee of the plaintiffs visited the defendants' gallery to view the paintings. Mr Hull made it clear that he did not know very much about the paintings and that he was not an expert in them. The plaintiffs' employee agreed to buy one of the paintings for £6,000 without asking any questions about the provenance of the painting, or making any further inquiries about it. The invoice for the painting described it as being by Munter, but it was later discovered to be a forgery. The plaintiffs claimed repayment of the purchase price on the basis that the contract was for the sale of goods by description within section 13(1) of the SGA 1979 and could, therefore, be avoided on the grounds of misdescription.

The judgment for the majority in the Court of Appeal (Stuart Smith L.J. dissenting) was given by Nourse L.J. who held that there had not been a sale "by" description. In this respect considerable reliance was placed upon Lord Diplock's *dictum* in *Gill and Duffus SA v. Berger and Co. Inc.*[57]:

> ". . . while 'description' itself is an ordinary English word, the Act contains no definition of what it means when it speaks in that section of a contract for the sale of goods being a sale '*by* description'. One must look to the contract as a whole to identify the kind of goods that the seller was agreeing to sell and the buyer to buy . . . where, as in the instant case, the sale (to use the words of s. 13) is '*by* sample as well as *by* description', characteristics of the goods which would be apparent on reasonable examination of the sample are unlikely to have been intended by the parties to form part of the 'description' *by* which the goods were sold, even though such characteristics are mentioned in references in the contract to the goods that are its subject matter." (Lord Diplock's emphasis at 394.)

The conclusion arrived at was that the requirement "by description" had to be determined by reference to the contract as a whole, that is, whether the characteristics had become terms in the contract. Moreover, where there was no reliance upon the description, it was unlikely that this

[57.] [1984] A.C. 382.

could be considered to be an essential term in the contract. Since Mr Hull had made it plain that he was not qualified to give an opinion about the painting's authorship, the plaintiff's employee must have realised that in proceeding with the purchase he was relying on his own skill and judgment.

The issue of reliance has been considered more recently by the Court of Appeal in *Don Commercials Ltd v. Lancaster Trucks Ltd*.[58] This case concerned a sale to the plaintiffs of a second-hand consignment of tractor units taken by the defendants in part-exchange as part of a deal with a third-party purchaser. The tractor units were inspected by the plaintiff's managing director and a dispute subsequently arose in relation to one unit which was described in the invoice as "Make - DAF Model FTG 2800. Reg. No. B30 ANO". At first instance it was found that:

"B30 was a pig in a poke. It was a FTG 2800 in appearance but its engine, although of the same size and internal bore and stroke, was from a much older four-wheel vehicle and was not one usually inter-cooled. Its torque characteristics were different. It developed less brake horsepower. The B30 was not a FTG 2800 as such. It could do the work that FTG 2800 could do, but its performance was different. There is no suggestion that the defendant knew this. The defendant was in the habit of buying from a customer which it valued called Canute, the condition of whose vehicles was less than the best."

In the Court of Appeal, Balcombe L.J. cited with approval Slade L.J.'s dictum in *Harlingdon* (above) where he said:

"While some judicial dicta seem to support the view that there can be no sale by description unless there is actual reliance on the description by the purchaser, I am not sure that this is strictly correct in principle. If a party to a contract wishes to claim relief in respect of a misrepresentation as to a matter which did not constitute a term of the contract, his claim will fail unless he is able to show that he relied on this representation in entering into the contract; in general, however, if a party wishes to claim relief in respect of a breach of a term of a contract (whether it be a condition or warranty) he need prove no actual reliance. Nevertheless, where a question arises as to whether a sale of goods was one by description, the presence or absence of reliance on the description may be very relevant in so far as it throws light on the intention of the parties at the time of the contract. If there was no such reliance by the purchaser, this may be powerful evidence that the parties did not contemplate that the authenticity of the description should constitute a term of the contract—in other words, that they contemplated that the purchaser would be buying the goods as they were. If, on the other hand, there was such reliance (as in *Varley v. Whipp*,[59] where the purchaser had never seen the goods) this may be equally powerful evidence that it was contemplated by both parties that the correctness of the description would be a term of the contract (so as to bring it within section 13(1)."[60]

[58.] 1984, unreported.
[59.] [1900] 1 Q.B. 513.
[60.] [1991] 1 Q.B. 564 at 584.

The test applied by Balcombe L.J. was that of reliance based upon an objective assessment of what the parties said and did in the circumstances of the case. In this regard the material factors were as follows:

(a) both parties were motor dealers;
(b) the tractors had been inspected by the plaintiff's managing director before making an offer and indeed the offer made was less than the provisional figure negotiated in the light of the defects found at the inspection;
(c) the terms of the invoice included the specific phrase "sold as seen no warranty given or implied".

In the light of the above factors, it was held that from an objective standpoint the parties could not have intended that the authenticity of the description, that is that the tractor was a FTG 2800, should be a term in the contract. This would undoubtedly be the position in a finance leasing context.

Exclusion of description requirement

In the *Harlingdon Ltd* case it was argued, at first instance, that there was an actual usage or custom in the London art market which excluded the application of section 13 of the SGA 1979. Although section 6(2)(a) of the UCTA 1977[61] provides that "as against a person dealing as consumer", obligations arising from an undertaking as to compliance with description cannot be excluded or restricted, the definition of "dealing as a consumer" in section 12 of the UCTA 1977 excludes a person who makes the contract "in the course of a business". In this case the clause is subject to the test of reasonableness which is discussed in greater detail below. There is no reason to suppose that in *Harlingdon Ltd* such an exclusion clause would not have been maintained, especially since it would hardly be likely to deter art experts from using their skills in the market place to discover masterpieces. Moreover, it is the present position that art-expert buyers, in the absence of fraud or a fiduciary relationship, have no obligation to disclose information relating to the true identity of a painting.

Any clause excluding or limiting contractual description will have to be construed in the light of common law. Obviously, if the contract goods are unascertained, an attempt to exclude all undertakings as to description would destroy the certainty of subject-matter in the contract. It is otherwise where the attempt is made to exclude liability for trivial breaches as in *Arcos Ltd v. E.A. Ronaasen and Son* (1933). In *Harlingdon* and *Don Commercials*, the decisions of the Court of Appeal that section 13(1) of the SGA 1979 cannot apply because of the absence of a sale "by description", avoided the need for the parties to exclude the term under

---

[61.] As amended by SGA 1979, Sched. 2, para. 19.

section 6 of the UCTA 1977 and thus expose themselves to the "reasonableness" test. It would appear, therefore that section 6 of the UCTA 1977 can be undermined simply by framing the matter of description into the general law of express contractual terms.

Undertakings as to quality

Introduction. The SGA 1979, the SOGIT 1973 and the SGSA 1982 imply conditions as to fitness and quality. No other warranties or conditions to such effect may be implied except in so far as they may be annexed to the contract by custom or trade usage.[62] The usage must fulfil all the normal tests of a custom and it will become part of the contract so long as it is reconcilable with the terms of the contract.[63] As such, this subsection is an illustration of the general rule that the intention of the parties with respect to a contract must be gleaned in the light of the surrounding circumstances. However, the normal rule applicable is that of *caveat emptor*, which is reflected in section 14(1) of the SGA 1979:

"Except as provided by this section and s. 15 below and subject to any other enactment, there is no implied condition or warranty about the quality or fitness for any particular purpose of goods supplied under a contract of sale."

This approach is also mirrored in section 10(1) of the SOGIT 1973 and sections 4(1) and 9(1) of the SGSA 1982.
Before considering the implied terms of quality and fitness for purpose, some common themes applicable to both must first be discussed.

The supply must be in the course of a business. Both the quality and fitness for purpose warranties apply only where the bailor bails the goods in the course of a business. In commercial dealings this will always be the case, even in the situation of an initial leasing or hiring of equipment by a lessor. As Dillon L.J. pointed out in *R and B Customs Brokers Co. Ltd v. United Dominions Trust Ltd*[64]:

". . . there are some transactions which are clearly integral parts of the businesses concerned, and these should be held to have been carried out in the course of those businesses: this would cover, apart from much else, the instance of a one-off adventure in the nature of trade, where the transaction itself would constitute a trade or business."

A significant exception to the supply in the course of a business is where a private supplier chooses to use a business agent to find a client. In this respect, section 14(5) of the SGA 1979 provides:

"The preceding provisions of this section apply to a sale by a person who in the course of a business is acting as agent for another as they apply to a sale

---

[62.] SGA 1979, s. 14(4); s. 10(4) SOGIT 1973; SGSA 1982, ss. 4(7), 9(7).
[63.] *Peter Darlington Partners Ltd v. Gosho Co. Ltd* [1964] 1 Lloyd's Rep. 149.
[64.] [1988] 1 W.L.R. 321 at 330–331.

by a principal in the course of a business, except where that other is not selling in the course of a business and either the buyer knows that fact or reasonable steps are taken to bring it to the notice of the buyer before the contract is made."

A similar provision can also be found in hire and hire-purchase transactions.[65] Liability is anticipated except where the seller is not in fact selling in the course of a business and prior to contracting the transferee knows this fact, or reasonable steps have been taken to bring it to his notice. Where this is not done the ordinary agency rules apply, so that an undisclosed principal may be sued by a buyer, typically where the agent acting in the ordinary course of business employed to dispose of an asset becomes insolvent. Thus in *Boyter v. Thompson*,[66] the seller instructed agents to sell on his behalf a cabin cruiser under a brokerage and agency agreement. The buyer bought the boat thinking it was owned by the agents; he was not told that the agents were acting as such nor did he know the name of the owner nor that the owner was not selling in the course of a business. The boat proved to be unseaworthy and was unfit for the purpose for which it was purchased, and in the House of Lords the seller contended that he could not be sued under section 14(5) of the SGA 1979 because that subsection rendered an agent liable if he was acting for an undisclosed principal, with the result that it was the agents and not the seller who were liable for breach of contract to the buyer. This was rejected and Lord Jauncey, who, giving the judgment on behalf of the House of Lords, held[67]:

"In my view subs. (5) is applicable to any sale by an agent on behalf of a principal whether disclosed or undisclosed, where circumstances giving rise to the exception do not exist. When the subsection applies the normal common law rules of principal and agent also apply. There having been in this case no attempt to bring to the notice of the respondent the fact that the appellant was not selling in the course of business it follows that the respondent was entitled to claim damages from the appellant in reliance on the provisions of s. 14(2), (3) and (5)."

The implied terms as to quality extend to the goods supplied. The undertakings as to quality extend not only to the contract goods but also to other goods supplied under the contract, for example, a defective bottle in the case of a supply of ginger beer,[68] or mineral water.[69] The reference in these cases is to section 61 of the SGA 1979 (section 18 of the SGSA 1982) where the definition of "quality of goods" covers "their state or condition".

---

[65] SOGIT 1973, s. 10(5); SGSA 1982, ss. 4(8), 9(8).
[66] [1995] 3 All E.R. 135.
[67] *Ibid.* at 138.
[68] *Morrelli v. Fitch and Gibbons* [1928] 2 K.B. 638.
[69] *Geddling v. March* [1920] 1 K.B. 668.

The protection conferred by the implied terms as to quality also applies to labels and instructions accompanying the product.[70] At first instance, in *Wormell v. R.H.M. Agriculture (East) Ltd*,[71] it was held that accompanying written instructions were "goods supplied under the contract". However, this was not relied on by the Court of Appeal who reversed the decision on the facts.

The implied obligation of satisfactory quality

Introduction. The Sale of Goods (Amendment) Act 1994 (c.32) implemented the recommendations of the Law Commissions set out in their Reports, *the Sale and Supply of Goods*,[72] and introduced an implied obligation of satisfactory quality. In fact the Law Commissions Reports recommended an "acceptable quality" standard, but this was changed to "satisfactory quality" in the amending Act on the basis, first, that it was a higher standard, and secondly, there would have been the possibility of confusion between the concept of acceptance for the purposes of cutting off rejection, and the idea of acceptable quality as a standard. It would appear that there is considerable scope for a new body of case law to emerge if the courts treat this new terminology as a legislative signal to adopt a more purposive application of the quality test. The introduction of the "satisfactory quality" standard applies to other contracts under which goods are supplied, namely, section 10 of the SOGIT 1973 (hire purchase), sections 4, 9 of the SGSA 1982 (supply contracts and hire).

The satisfactory quality test. The inclusion of a purposive adjective "satisfactory" means that the equipment must meet a standard that a reasonable person would consider to be satisfactory. It is not the hirer or buyer's expectations that are relevant, which could allow the standard to decline because of inertia by the hirer or buyer and could furthermore allow the supplier to establish that goods of a particular type could reasonably be expected to have a number of defects on delivery.

Under section 14(2B) of the SGA 1979 and section 10(2B) of the SOGIT 1973 there is a wide list included in determining the issue of satisfactory quality. This list is absent from the SGSA 1982 but it will presumably be persuasive in determining the issue of quality and this is confirmed in section 18(3) of that Act. The durability requirement is the one which will particularly affect hire of goods. There is no doubt that the requirement of durability applies to contracts of supply, including hire and hire-purchase, and it bears in this context the same meaning as for contracts of sale. As the Law Commission pointed out[73]:

"It does not mean that throughout the period of the hiring the goods must necessarily remain in the same condition as when they were supplied. Exactly

[70.] See *Niblett Ltd v. Confectioners' Materials Co. Ltd* [1921] 3 K.B. 387.
[71.] [1986] 1 W.L.R. 336.
[72.] (1987) Law Com. No. 160; Law Com. No. 164.
[73.] (1987) Law Com. No. 160, para. 3.70.

how durable the goods must be will depend on all the circumstances. However, the length of the period of hire and type of hiring involved may well be relevant."

In this respect the Law Commission approach mirrored that adopted by the Court of Appeal in *UCB Leasing Ltd v. Holtom*.[74]

Clearly, hiring a car for three years and a suit for one evening will sound in different levels of durability; it is natural to expect signs of wear and tear after several months in the case of a motor vehicle, which will require servicing and perhaps the replacing of parts. Even so, in the case of contract hire of motor vehicles the requirement of durability for the whole contract period is often expressly incorporated in the contract where, of course, the hirer pays extra rental for facilities such as servicing and the provision for a replacement vehicle.

Excepted defects. There is no condition as to satisfactory quality where defects have been drawn to the buyer's attention before the contract is made, or if the defects should have been obvious from examination. Thus section 9(3) of the SGSA 1982[75] provides:

"(3) The condition implied by subsection (2) above does not extend to any matter making the quality of goods unsatisfactory—

   (a) which is specifically drawn to the bailee's attention before the contract is made,

   (b) where the bailee examines the goods before the contract is made, which that examination ought to reveal, or

   (c) where the goods are bailed by reference to a sample, which would have been apparent on a reasonable examination of the sample."

Proviso (a). It is difficult to understand the defence under proviso (a) of section 9(3) of the SGSA 1982, because it is already included within the statutory definition of satisfactory quality as it will affect the description under which the goods are bailed. The requirement that the defects be disclosed to the bailee is one of degree and it is probable that some positive act of drawing attention seems to be required.

Proviso (b). There is no requirement that the bailee examines the goods. At common law the merchantability undertaking was excluded by the mere opportunity for pre-contract examination, which is retained in the case of bailment by sample. Under the amended section 9(3)(b) of the SGSA 1982, the crucial issue is what defects the examination actually carried out ought to have revealed. The standard applied here is objective, based upon the reasonable man in the bailee's position, ignoring any peculiar idiosyncrasies of the bailee. In a lease context the

---

[74.] [1987] R.T.R. 362.
[75.] Replicated in SGA 1979, s. 14(2C); SOGIT 1973, s. 10(2C).

lessee will normally be under a contractual obligation to examine the goods and undertake that the goods are acceptable. The fact that the hirer has inspected the chattel beforehand will be relevant in indicating that the agreement was to hire the chattel subject to all the defects and characteristics that were evident upon an inspection of the kind that had been made.

Proviso (c). The purpose of a sample is to give the potential bailee an opportunity of examining it so that he can decide whether or not it is suitable. Under the previous law there appeared to be nothing to prevent the bailee still relying upon the implied term that goods had to be merchantable. This new provision ensures that a sale by sample will now prevail over section 9(2) as amended.

The implied obligation of fitness for purpose

Introduction. The implied condition of satisfactory quality is supplemented by the fitness for purpose requirement found in sections 9(4)–(5) of the SGSA 1982 which provide:

> "(4)   Subsection (5) below applies where, under a contract for the hire of goods, the bailor bails goods in the course of a business and the bailee, expressly or by implication, makes known—
>
> > (a)   to the bailor in the course of negotiations conducted by him in relation to the making of the contract, or
> >
> > (b)   to a credit-broker in the course of negotiations conducted by that broker in relation to goods sold by him to the bailor before forming the subject matter of the contract,
>
> any particular purpose for which the goods are being bailed.
>
> (5)   In that case there is (subject to subsection (6) below) an implied condition that the goods supplied under the contract are reasonably fit for that purpose, whether or not that is a purpose for which such goods are commonly supplied."

Similar obligations can be found under section 14(3) of the SGA 1979 and also other supply contracts.[76] It would seem that two factors are especially relevant: First, knowledge on the part of the bailor, seller, transferor or their agent of the purpose for which the goods are sought; secondly, reliance upon the skill or judgment of the bailor, seller or transferor.

The question of knowledge. The problem of ascribing to the lessor knowledge of the purpose for which goods were intended is complicated by the fact that the goods may sometimes have more than one purpose.

[76.] SOGIT 1973, s. 10(3); SGSA 1982, s. 4(3).

The overlap with the satisfactory quality provision is obvious and often the two will coincide. However, section 9(4) of the SGSA 1982 comes into its own where the purpose in question is not a common one, especially since the bailee will probably, in the case of a finance lease,[76a] have expressly notified the lessor of the purpose he had in mind. Indeed this would form part of the finance lessor's credit assessment of the lessee. Furthermore, under section 9(4)(b) where a particular purpose is communicated to a credit-broker, the bailor is deemed to have knowledge of that purpose. This is meant to solve the common law problem where a particular purpose is made known by especially a consumer to a dealer who may not have had ostensible or actual authority to receive such communication.[77] Such liability seems inappropriate as between commercial concerns bargaining at arm's length, since it distorts the leasing transaction, and the finance lessor would be forced to shift its cost of insurance onto the lessee, thereby increasing the cost of leasing to him. This is recognised under section 9(6) of the SGSA 1982 which provides:

> "(6) Subsection (5) above does not apply where the circumstances show that the bailee does not rely, or that it is unreasonable for him to rely, on the skill or judgment of the bailor or credit-broker."

The question of reliance. It is not enough that the bailor knows of the particular purpose of the goods supplied, the bailee, as mentioned above, must also have relied upon the credit-broker or bailor's skill and judgment at the date of the contract. It is for the bailor to prove that there was no reasonable reliance, but this should not prove to be problematical at least in the finance lease context. In *Teheran-Europe Co. Ltd v. Belton (S.T.) Ltd*,[78] the facts involved the sale of machinery to a Persian company and it was held that there was no reliance on the seller's skill or judgment since the seller was ignorant of the foreign market where the goods were destined for resale.

The mere fact that the bailee has inspected the goods beforehand does not necessarily preclude reliance. Certainly, undertakings in the contract that the bailee has not relied upon the bailor's skill and judgment will not be conclusive, especially in consumer hire where section 7 of the UCTA 1977 precludes contracting-out of the implied condition of fitness. Of course, it is still a matter of degree as the contract may be concluded specifically on the basis of non-reliance but even if this is the case, the obligation of satisfactory quality will still remain. This will be

---

[76a.] The normal implication is that the goods will be fit for the purpose for which the goods would ordinarily be used and there can be no breach of the implied condition of fitness where the failure of the goods to meet the intended purpose arises out of an idiosyncrasy unknown to the supplier. See *Slater and others v. Finning Ltd* [1996] 3 All E.R. 398.

[77.] See Chap. 4, below.

[78.] [1968] 2 Q.B. 545.

significant in the finance leasing context since it may not be considered unjust to expect the finance lessor to accept some responsibility for the quality of the goods, since the lessor has chosen the lease form as a financing venture.[79]

Hiring by sample

Section 10 of the SGSA 1982 and section 11 of the SOGIT 1973 imply a requirement of correspondence with sample equivalent to section 15 of the SGA 1979. This provision is not likely to have much practical importance in the commercial asset leasing context and it is not proposed to deal with it in detail. It is sufficient to say that the law developed in relation to sale of goods will obviously be relevant.[80]

Other implied terms

The statutory undertakings discussed above are perhaps the best known examples of the implied terms recognised in the common law and have been codified as such. Nevertheless section 9(7) of the SGSA 1982 provides[80a]:

> "(7) An implied condition or warranty about quality or fitness for a particular purpose may be annexed by usage to a contract for the hire of goods."

The general rules apply that the usage or custom must be reasonable, universally accepted by the particular trade, certain, not unlawful and not inconsistent with the express or implied terms of the contract. An example of terms routinely implied in the context of hire is the obligation to deliver the goods in substantially the same condition as they were when inspected by the hirer. In the case of hire-purchase contracts, the supply of documentation, including a log book or registration document, has been considered necessary.[81] The bailee's implied duties normally include not to convert the goods nor to deviate in the case of a carrier's obligation to follow his stipulated route. Different standards of care are applicable to the various types of bailment recognised in the seminal case of *Coggs v. Bernard*.[82]

Contracting out of Implied Terms

The Unfair Contract Terms Act 1977

Scope of the Act. Far-reaching controls on attempts to exclude contractual and tortious liability were introduced by the UCTA 1977. Section 6

[79.] See below.
[80.] See Davies, *Sale and Supply of Goods* (2nd ed., 1996).
[80a.] SOGIT 1973 s. 10(4).
[81.] *Bentworth Finance Ltd v. Lubert* [1968] 1 Q.B. 680.
[82.] (1703) 2 Ld. Raym. 909.

THE LESSOR-LESSEE RELATIONSHIP

contains certain special provisions which relate to the statutory implied terms in contracts of sale, and section 7 (as amended by the SGSA 1982) contains analogous provisions with regard to other contracts for the transfer of goods. Section 7 provides:

"7.—(1) Where the possession or ownership of goods passes under or in pursuance of a contract not governed by the law of sale of goods or hire-purchase, subsections (2) to (4) below apply as regard the effect (if any) to be given to contract terms excluding or restricting liability for breach of obligation arising by implication of law from the nature of the contract.

(2) As against a person dealing as a consumer, liability in respect of the goods' correspondence with description or sample, or their quality or fitness for any particular purpose, cannot be excluded or restricted by reference to any such term.

(3) As against a person dealing otherwise than as consumer, that liability can be excluded or restricted by reference to such a term, but only in so far as the term satisfies the requirement of reasonableness.

[(3A) Liability for breach of the obligations arising under section 2 of the Supply of Goods and Services Act 1982 (implied terms about title, etc. in certain contracts for the transfer of the property in goods) cannot be excluded or restricted by references to any such term.]

(4) Liability in respect of—

(a) the right to transfer ownership of the goods, or give possession; or

(b) the assurance of quiet possession to a person taking goods in pursuance of the contract,

cannot [(in a case to which subsection (3A) above does not apply)] be excluded or restricted by reference to any term except in so far as the term satisfies the requirement of reasonableness."

It is therefore essential to distinguish between consumer and non-consumer transactions.

Dealing as consumer. Whether a person acts in the course of a business is a key element in establishing whether a person "deals as consumer". Section 12(1) of the UCTA 1977 provides as follows:

"(1) A party to a contract 'deals as consumer' in relation to another party if—

(a) he neither makes the contract in the course of a business; nor holds himself out as doing so; and

(b) the other party does make the contract in the course of a business; and

(c) in the case of a contract governed by the law of sale of goods or hire-purchase, or by section 7 of this Act, the goods passing under or in pursuance of the contract are of a type ordinarily supplied for private use or consumption."

The Court of Appeal in *R. & B. Custom Brokers Co. Ltd v. United Dominions Trust Ltd*,[83] applied the criteria identified in cases under the Trade Description Act 1968 including *Davies v. Sumner*[84] in resolving this question. It was held that a private company which was buying a car for a director did not acquire the vehicle "in the course of a business". The acquisition of a car for the private and business use of a director was not considered by both members of the Court of Appeal (Neill and Dillon L.JJ.) to be an integral part of the company's business. Furthermore, there was an insufficient degree of regularity to make the purchase of the car by the plaintiffs something which was done in the course of their business.

The requirement that the goods must be of a type ordinarily supplied for private use or consumption is obviously problematic. This is illustrated by the facts in *R. & B. Customs Brokers*, where a car can be used both for business and private use. It is surely a matter of degree whether the goods are "ordinarily" supplied for private use, but section 12(3) of the UCTA 1977 provides that the onus is upon the supplier to prove that the buyer is not a consumer. The two special cases in section 12(2) should also be noted, namely, a buyer is not to be treated as a consumer where he buys at auction, nor where the sale is by competitive tender. In the case of a commercial agent who sells on behalf of an undisclosed principal who is a consumer, the sale is made by the agent in the course of a business and will be fully regulated by the UCTA 1977. It is unlikely that section 9(8) of the SGSA 1982 affects the liability of an agent in this respect because this relates only to section 9(8) of *that* Act, so the consequence would appear to be that the agent will be liable notwithstanding that he is acting for a private bailor.[85]

Exemption clauses affected by the UCTA 1977

Scope. The UCTA not only limits clauses which purport expressly to exclude or restrict liability but also deals with clauses which have this effect, such as excluding a particular remedy, for example, set-off,[86] or alternatively imposing a short-time period during which claims must be brought. In addition section 10 states that a term excluding or restricting liability which is contained in a separate contract, rather than in the contract giving rise to the liability, is ineffective in so far as it attempts to take away a right to enforce a liability which under the Act cannot be excluded or restricted.

The ambit of the UCTA 1977 over exclusion clauses includes attempts to disclaim, by notice, liability in tort for negligence. Thus section 2(1) of UCTA 1977 nullifies contractual provisions and notices excluding or restricting liability for negligence resulting in death or injury. Where a

[83.] [1988] 1 W.L.R. 321.
[84.] [1984] 1 W.L.R. 1301.
[85.] See *Boyster v. Thomson* [1995] 3 All E.R. 135.
[86.] *Stewart Gill Ltd v. Horatio Myer and Co. Ltd* [1992] Q.B. 600.

party to a contract deals as consumer or on the other's written standard terms of business,[87] that other cannot by reference to a contract term limit, exclude or restrict his liability,[88] and this applies to terms and notices.[89] In determining what is meant by "written standard terms" it is not necessary that all the terms may be altered by the other party so that it can be considered a particularised or individual contract.

The requirement of reasonableness. Part I of the UCTA 1977 permits a party to restrict or exclude liability, by reference to the requirement of reasonableness, in the following cases:

1. Neglect damage to property (section 2(2));

2. Standard form contracts (section 3(2));

3. Indemnity clauses (section 4(1));

4. Implied terms in supply contracts (sections 6, 7);

5. Misrepresentation (section 3 of Misrepresentation Act 1967, as amended by the UCTA 1977).

Except for criterion 1., the requirement of reasonableness can only be invoked outside a consumer context.

The reasonableness test is set out in section 11 with further guidelines provided in Schedule 2 to the UCTA 1977. Section 11(1) of the 1977 Act states:

"In relation to a contract term, the requirement of reasonableness for the purposes of this Part of the Act, section 3 of the Misrepresentation Act 1967 and section 3 of the Misrepresentation Act (Northern Ireland) 1967 is that the term shall have been a fair and reasonable one to be included having regard to the circumstances which were, or ought reasonably to have been, known to or in the contemplation of the parties when the contract was made."

The onus lies on the party relying on the exclusion clause to show that it is reasonable.[90]

Some guidance as to the requirements of reasonableness has emerged from the House of Lords in *George Mitchell (Chesterhall) Ltd v. Finney Lock Seeds Ltd.*[91] Care should be taken here because it was the wording of the SOGIT 1973 which was considered, and although this is substantially similar to the 1977 Act, it differs in some respects. Hence the 1973 Act provides that exclusion clauses are void "to the extent that" they did not comply with reasonableness, whereas, under the UCTA 1977, a term

---

[87.] *McCrone v. Boots Farm Sales Ltd* 1981 S.L.T. 103.
[88.] UCTA 1977, ss. 3(1), 13(1).
[89.] UCTA 1977, s. 13(2).
[90.] UCTA 1977, s. 11(5).
[91.] [1983] 2 A.C. 803.

shall not be effective "except *in so far* as the term satisfies the requirement of reasonableness". Although the House of Lords did not give a concluded opinion, the inclination of the judgments was that the Court could not use the test to limit a plaintiff to a proportion of his losses. It would seem that the change made under the UCTA 1977 does not affect this point. A second guideline which emerges from this decision is that the application of the reasonableness test is not merely the exercise of a discretion, but is a decision. Accordingly, a first-instance decision will only be reversed on appeal if it proceeded on some erroneous principle or was plainly and obviously wrong. Given this approach, it is likely that inconsistency will continue to be a feature of cases decided under the reasonableness test of the UCTA 1977.

The 1977 Act also deals with clauses exempting a party to a contract from liability for misrepresentation. Under section 8 of UCTA 1977, section 3 of the Misrepresentation Act 1967 is replaced by the following:

> "3.—If a contract contains a term which would exclude or restrict—
>
> (a) any liability to which a party to a contract may be subject by reason of any misrepresentation made by him before the contract was made; or
>
> (b) any remedy available to another party to the contract by reason of such a misrepresentation,
>
> that term shall be of no effect except in so far as it satisfies the requirement of reasonableness as stated in s. 11(1) of the Unfair Contract Terms Act 1977; and it is for those claiming that the term satisfies that requirement to show that it does."

No guidelines are given for the interpretation of section 8 except that the term to be included must have been a fair and reasonable one having regard to the circumstances which were, or ought reasonably to have been, known to or in the contemplation of the parties when the contract was made.[92] In *Howard Marine and Dredging Co. Ltd v. A. Ogden and Sons (Excavations) Ltd,*[93] a case decided under section 3 of the 1967 Act, Lord Denning considered the following factors to be relevant: the parties were of equal bargaining position, the representation made was innocent, and in any case the plaintiffs had failed to prove that they had reasonable grounds for believing the truth of the statement.

The question of reasonableness is determined as between the actual parties. This allows a court to adjust its decision according to the other party involved. Such a phenomenon may be illustrated further by the facts in *Phillips Products v. Hamstead Plant Hire,*[94] which involved the hire of a crane and driver. As a consequence of the driver's negligence, damage was caused to the plaintiff's factory, but the conditions of hire excluded such liability. This exclusion clause was considered to be

---

[92.] UCTA 1977, s. 11(1).
[93.] [1978] Q.B. 574.
[94.] (1985) 4 Tr. L. 98.

unreasonable on the basis of the following factors. First, the hire period was short and the plaintiffs therefore had little time to arrange insurance. Secondly, the plaintiffs were not regular hirers of such equipment. The result might have been otherwise had the hirers received previous notice of their obligation to insure which, of course, invites scrutiny of the issue relating to incorporation of terms.[95]

Some propositions do emerge from the case law. First, the court will take into consideration the whole of the exclusion clause in determining the question of reasonableness. The rationale here is that section 11(1) states that the time for assessing the reasonableness of the clause is the time at which the contract is made, and at this point it will not be known which part of it will be relied upon by the defendant. Secondly, the courts do not have the power to sever the unreasonable parts of an exclusion clause leaving the reasonable parts in force.[96] The significance of this for drafting exclusion clauses is clear—the different elements of the clause should be set out in sub-clauses so that a failure of one part will not invalidate the clause as a whole.

Statutory guidelines. Supplementary guidelines to the reasonableness test are included in Schedule 2 to the 1977 Act. These guidelines are similar to those in the original 1973 Act and apply to sale and supply contracts by virtue of section 11(2) of the UCTA 1977. Even so, the guidelines have been used in other cases as factors to be considered where the statute applies.[97] These guidelines, although not exhaustive of the factors to be considered, include the following:

(a) the strength of the bargaining positions of the parties relative to each other, taking into account (among other things) alternative means by which the customer's requirements could have been met;

(b) whether the customer received an inducement to agree to the term, or in accepting it had an opportunity of entering into a similar contract with other persons, but without having to accept a similar term;

(c) whether the customer knew or ought reasonably to have known of the existence and extent of the term (having regard, among other things, to any custom of the trade and any previous course of dealing between the parties);

(d) where the term excludes or restricts any relevant liability if some condition is not complied with, whether it was reasonable at the time of the contract to expect that compliance with that condition would be practicable;

[95.] See *Olley v. Marlborough Court* [1949] 1 K.B. 532.
[96.] See *Steward Gill Ltd v. Horatio Myer and Co. Ltd* [1992] Q.B. 600.
[97.] See *Woodman v. Photo Trade Processing Ltd* reported by Lawson in (1981) 131 New L.J. 933 at 935.

    (e)   whether the goods were manufactured, processed or adapted to the special order of the customer.

If one party freely consents to a clause, a court is unlikely to hold it unreasonable. Paragraphs (a)–(c) and perhaps (d) of Schedule 2 reflect this fact. Clearly a pertinent factor in the determination of the free consent issue, is whether one party has exercised superior bargaining strength to impose terms on the other. The central theme of the House of Lords decision in *Photo Production Ltd v. Securicor Transport Ltd*,[98] is that the parties' arrangements will stand if there is no inequality. In this respect, alternative courses of action available to the party will be relevant. This is significant in the finance leasing context because leasing contracts are notoriously flexible and may be modified to cover any particular asset or lessee's conditions. Furthermore, where there are many leasing companies as well as other means of raising finance, it would appear that at least the guidelines for the application of the reasonableness test under Schedule 2 of UCTA 1977 are satisfied.

The application of the UCTA 1977 to leases of commercial equipment

Introduction. The structure of supply contracts, especially finance leasing arrangements, poses specific problems in the application of the UCTA 1977. This phenomenon can be illustrated in *W. Photoprint Ltd v. Forward Trust Group Ltd*.[99] In this case, the parties over a period of years had made over 80 hire-purchase or leasing agreements with each other in relation to all types of goods and equipment for Photoprint's business. As such, the defendant had provided the plaintiff with a financial facility up to a certain limit. The equipment was never supplied directly by the defendant who would customarily buy them from a supplier and then lease them or make a hire-purchase contract with the plaintiff. In 1988, the plaintiff company decided that it needed a new processor. The operations director learnt from the second defendant that they would soon be marketing a new advanced type of processor. In view of the enhanced capabilities of the processor and the satisfactory experience with the processors previously supplied by the second defendants, he decided that the processor on offer was an obvious choice. He relied solely on a brochure supplied by, and telephone conversations with, the second defendants, whose representative informed him that he had not seen the machine either and was relying on American colleagues for his information.

    The plaintiff company ordered the processor and entered into a hire-purchase agreement with the first defendants. The machine never worked satisfactorily and it was accepted that it was not of merchantable quality and not reasonably fit for the purpose for which it was required.

[98.] [1980] A.C. 827.
[99.] (1993) 12 Tr. L.R. 146.

The plaintiff company purported to terminate the agreement on this basis, the processor was removed by the second defendants who returned the price to the first defendants, who in turn subsequently credited the plaintiff company with the same amount. The plaintiff company's claim was for substantial consequential losses. The first defendants sought to rely on a clause in the hire-purchase agreement as being reasonable and effectively excluding any such liability.

The plaintiff had signed the relevant agreement with Forward Trust adjacent to a statement to the effect that the terms and conditions had been read, and that attention had been drawn to the exclusion clause. It was common ground that the agreement was subject to section 10(2) of the SOGIT 1973 implying a condition of merchantable quality and that it was on written standard terms and therefore fell within the provision of section 3(1) of the UCTA 1977. Nevertheless the defendant argued, relying on the exclusion clause, that the goods were not let "subject to any undertaking express or implied whether statutory or otherwise" and that section 10 never became any part of its contractual obligations because the exclusion clause defined the extent of the liability that it was assuming. This argument was not specifically addressed by the plaintiffs and, as a matter of principle, it is difficult to maintain since the obligation is already imposed by the 1973 Act and is inconsistent with this statutory obligation that it should be excluded.

More recently in *Lease Management Services Ltd v. Purnell Secretarial Services*,[1] a clause purporting to exclude the liability of a finance house "in respect of any conditions, warranty or representation relating to the suitability or fitness of the equipment for any purpose for which it may be required" was rejected. The purpose of the defendant acquiring the goods (a photocopier) was to produce paper plates. This was a fundamental term in the contract and the exclusion clause would have enabled the plaintiff to disregard any express warranty made. The Court of Appeal rejected the general proposition that an exclusion clause will be reasonable in a hire or hire-purchase contract where the finance company does not inspect the goods or participate in antecedent negotiations.

Examination of the goods and estoppel. It was acknowledged in the *Photoprint* case that the plaintiff had not examined the goods, even though they had signed an undertaking to this effect. In *Lowe v. Lombank*[2] a similar clause was held to have raised an estoppel but even if it did, Forward Trust in the *Photoprint* case would have been precluded from relying upon this by virtue of the rule that estoppel cannot be invoked to deprive a party of his statutory rights.[3]

The reasonableness provision. It was held in the *Photoprint* case that the clause which was made expressly subject to the requirement of reasonableness was not uncertain on the basis that, as a matter of law, it either

[1] (1994) Tr. L.R. 337, C.A.
[2] [1960] 1 W.L.R. 196.
[3] *Campbell Discount Ltd v. Gall* [1961] 2 All E.R. 104.

applied or did not. In addition there was no doubt that the clause had been incorporated into the contract because the plaintiff had signed the agreement alongside the clause drawing attention to the disputed clause. In applying the reasonableness test in respect of the guidelines in Schedule 2, the following factors emerged in this case:

1. The plaintiff would have been able to enter a similar contract with another party without the disputed term. But if the plaintiff had asked for the exclusion clause to be removed it was probable that Forward Trust would have acceded provided that the plaintiff paid for the insurance needed to cover Forward Trust's exposure to risk.

2. The plaintiff had chosen the machine.

3. The plaintiff was very familiar with hire-purchase and leasing arrangements; this was not a case of the plaintiff being sent by the supplier to a captive finance company.

4. The plaintiff could have financed the acquisition of the machine in other ways.

5. Whilst as a matter of fact the machine required a two-weeks' settling in period for it to be assessed, the argument of the plaintiff that it was unfair to allow Forward Trust to exclude liability when the plaintiff itself could not assess the machine was dismissed on the basis that this problem was not in the contemplation of the parties when the contract was made. Further, there was the declaration in the contract that the plaintiffs had examined the machine and found it satisfactory and they had relied on their own skill and judgment. It was held that Forward Trust had satisfied the burden of proof placed on them and had shown that the exclusion clause was a fair and reasonable one.

The Unfair Terms in Consumer Contracts Regulations 1994

The Unfair Terms in Consumer Contracts Directive was adopted by the European Union on 5 April, 1993.[4] The mischief of the new legislation is to protect consumers within the European Union and is viewed as a necessary element in the creation of the internal market. The Directive has been introduced by statutory instrument[5] leaving the UCTA 1977 untouched. This saved on parliamentary time and also the risk of failing

---

[4.] [1993] O.J. L.95/29. See *Implementation of the E.C. Directive on Unfair Terms in Consumer Contracts (93/13; A Consultative Document* (DTI, October 1993) and *Implementation of the E.C. Directive on Unfair Terms in Consumer Contracts (93/13; A Further Consultation Document* (DTI, September 1994).

[5.] S.I. 1994 No. 3159.

to integrate the new measure fully with the preceding law. It was argued that the UCTA 1977 and the Directive should be aligned by introducing a common test of fairness, but this was not pursued because the two tests are not the same and nor is the nature of the contractual terms which they cover. In particular, the Directive regulates only terms in consumer contracts and is not limited to exclusion contracts, whilst the UCTA 1977 deals mainly with exclusion clauses and does extend to contracts other than non-negotiated consumer contracts.

Scope of the Regulations

Introduction. The Regulations are limited to contracts between a consumer and a seller or supplier of goods or services. The preamble of the Directive explains that its scope does not include *inter alia* contracts of employment, contracts relating to succession rights, contracts relating to rights under family law, and contracts relating to the incorporation and organisation of companies or partnership agreements. Contracts regulated by international conventions are also excluded, by virtue of Article 1(2). Notwithstanding these exclusions, the Directive is still broader in scope than the UCTA 1977 with respect to contracts which created or transfer an interest in land, contracts involving the transfer of securities and also contracts of insurance.

Seller and supplier. Regulation 2(1) defines a "seller" as a "person who sells goods" and "supplier" as a "person who supplies goods or services" and "in making a contract to which these Regulations apply, is acting for purposes relating to his business".

Consumer. This is defined in regulation 2(1) to mean a "natural person who, in making a contract to which these Regulations apply, is acting for purposes which are outside his business". This is a more expansive definition than that seen under the UCTA 1977 since it extends protection to small business persons for activities which are incidental to their business. Furthermore, the fact that the consumer is a buyer by auction or by competitive tender is irrelevant for the purposes of the Regulations, unlike the UCTA 1977 definitions.

Terms not individually negotiated. The Regulations apply only to terms which have not been individually negotiated, the rationale for this as set out in regulation 3(3) being that the consumer is unable to influence the substance of such a term. In theory it may be possible to differentiate sharply between terms which have and terms which have not been individually negotiated, but in practice the delineation may not be so easy. However, a substance test is included, notably, where part of a term or an entire term has been individually negotiated the application of the Directive to the rest of the contract shall not be excluded if, on an overall assessment of the contract, it appears that it is a pre-formulated standard contract. But what happens if the supplier offers alternatives from a pool of standard terms? It could be argued that although these terms have been pre-drafted as a mechanism for cutting down trans-actional costs, nonetheless they have been individually negotiated in the sense that they have been selected by the consumer. In this context the burden of proof is crucial, and by virtue of regulation 3(5) the seller/supplier who relies upon the argument that a standard term has been individually negotiated has to prove that this is the case.

Good faith and the Regulations. In determining good faith the preamble of the Directive, which is reproduced in Schedule 2 to the Regulations, states:

> "[I]n making an assessment of good faith, particular regard should be had to the strength of the bargaining positions of the parties, whether the consumer had an inducement to agree to the term and whether goods or services were sold or supplied to the special order of the consumer . . . the requirement of good faith may be satisfied by the seller or supplier where he deals fairly and equitably with the other party whose legitimate interests he has to take into account."

There are some familiar concepts here—the strength of the bargaining positions of the parties,[6] the issue of inducement offered to the con-sumer[7] and whether the goods are made to the special order of the consumer.[8] Whilst there is not specific reference to reasonableness as part of the general concept of good faith, nevertheless the preamble does refer to good faith as involving an overall evaluation of the different interests involved.

The balancing issue is at the heart of the unfairness concept so that regulation 4(1) refers to "significant imbalance in the parties' rights and obligations under the contract to the detriment of the consumer". This phrase lacks precision as it assumes that there is parity between contracts and that this is the norm. The difficulty is that whilst there may be significant imbalance this does not necessarily make the contract unreasonable. However, there is no concept of a duty to trade fairly, as the Regulations are not concerned with unfairness arising out of the mere difference in bargaining strength—it is the abuse of this power which has been targeted. In determining what is meant by "significant imbalance", regulation 4(2) refers to "the nature of the goods or service for which the contract was concluded" (typically new or secondhand goods) and also the surrounding circumstances. The broad context of bargain is maintained and a result not far distant from that arrived at using the more familiar English concept of reasonableness is achieved.

Price and subject-matter. Regulation 3(2) provides that whilst terms which directly describe the main subject matter of the contract or the price/

[6.] UCTA 1977, Sched. 2, para. (a).
[7.] UCTA 1988, Sched. 2, para. (b).
[8.] UCTA 1977, Sched. 2, para. (c).

ratio quality are not subject to the test of fairness, they are subject to the requirement of intelligibility and, therefore, will be relevant in making an overall assessment of the fairness of the terms.

The plain language provision. Regulation 6 provides that terms offered to consumers in writing must always be expressed in "plain, intelligible language" and that clauses will be read *contra proferentem*. The burden of proof rests upon sellers and suppliers as to the issue of intelligibility, and the interpretation most favourable to the consumer will prevail. This provision will impact upon the development of the fundamental breach doctrine in the wake of *Photo Production v. Securicor Transport*[9] by resurrecting the *contra proferentem* approach to exclusion clauses.[10]

Unfair terms: the indicative list. As we have seen, Schedule 2 of the Regulations lists four indicia in making an assessment of good faith. Schedule 3, which implements the Annex in the Directive, contains a list of 17 types of terms which are held to be unfair if they have certain objects or effects. What we have here is an attempt at compromise between the *method* of civil and common law—the latter tends to use a broad test applied in each case whereas the former tends to more finite rules. Even so from a common law perspective the structure is not alien, because sections 6 and 7 of the UCTA 1977 list types of contracts where obligations cannot be excluded, whereas in other types of contract the criterion of reasonableness applies. In any case the Annex in the Directive is not prescriptive, it is merely indicative and is by definition non-exhaustive.

The Annex is a valuable guide to practitioners as to the types of contractual terms that are likely to be deemed to be unfair. Many are in any case included in the UCTA 1977, for example, excluding or limiting liability for death or personal injury, inappropriately relying upon limitation clauses which purport to restrict or exclude the consumer's legal rights if the supplier fails to satisfy their contractual obligation. Example (b) in the Annex has already been recognised in the UCTA 1977, where a right of set-off was considered to be an exclusion of liability so that under the Directive the seller or supplier should not, in appropriate cases, be able to contract out of the consumer's right to set-off debts owed by the seller or supplier against any claim that the consumer may have against that party. Other examples include permitting retention of deposits in the event of default or penalty clauses, that is, requiring any consumer who defaults to pay "a proportionately high sum in compensation". This should be read in the context of example (f) in the Annex which refers to unilateral dissolution and retention of sums provisions, typically where in a contract of hire the supplier can dissolve the contract at any time but the consumer must guarantee a

---

[9] [1980] A.C. 827.
[10] See *Hollier v. Rambler Motors AMC Ltd* [1972] 1 Q.B. 71.

fixed term. It would appear, therefore, that a seller or supplier will only be allowed to rely upon such terms where the contract provides the consumer with an identical right to dissolve the contract on a discretionary basis. Somewhat curiously, while provision is made for clauses which permit the seller to retain sums paid for services not yet supplied by him, no provision is made for the return of sums paid for associated goods that have not been supplied to the consumer.

Other examples in the Annex refer to the need for reasonable notice periods for termination in contracts of indeterminate duration unless there are serious grounds for termination, but no examples of this are provided. One significant innovation relates to unilateral extension of fixed duration contracts, typically, hire contracts. It would appear from this that the supplier must remind the consumer of his right to non-renewal of the hire contract, and the Directive introduces a test of fairness into the renewal period and also into the time given under the contract for the customer to make up his mind whether to renew. The most important indicative term of unfairness in the Directive relates to unseen terms, so that example (i) in the Annex provides that the consumer must have a "real opportunity of becoming acquainted" with the terms of the contract. It may be inferred, therefore, that the consumer must be afforded a realistic chance of understanding the implications of what he is binding himself to and, of course, this goes to the intelligibility of the terms.

Remedies Regulation 5(1) provides that an unfair term in a contract concluded with a consumer by a seller or supplier shall not be binding on the consumer. Regulation 5(2) states that the contract shall continue to bind the parties provided that it is capable of continuing in existence without the unfair terms. This is an issue of severance and the applicability of the blue pencil test. It is foreseeable that there will be some incongruity here especially where, for example, a standard form has been challenged by an appropriate organisation but an individual opts to continue with the contract.

Regulation 7 is an important safeguard in that it provides that an E.C. consumer does not lose protection simply because of a choice of law clause making the applicable law that of a non-E.C. state.

The relationship of the Regulations and UCTA 1977

The Regulations do not merely duplicate control over exclusion clauses with the UCTA 1977, rather they regulate the balance of obligations with respect to subsidiary terms. Significantly, the Regulations can provide the basis for a challenge to the obligations of the parties (including price) where these are formulated obscurely, because of the requirement of plain and unambiguous language. However, in general the Regulations do not provide a means of challenge merely on the grounds of unfair price. The differences between the provisions of the Regulations and the UCTA 1977 are as follows:

1. The UCTA 1977 envisages the possibility of a company being a "consumer" when it enters into a contract outside its line of business (section 12(1)(a)), whereas the Regulations confine "consumers" to natural persons. Even so, the UCTA 1977 cuts down the definition of consumer by excluding contracts involving the supply of goods not ordinarily supplied for private use or consumption and sales by auction. It is possible under the Regulations that a small business trading as a natural person or partnership can count as a consumer if the goods purchased or acquired, though normally only used in business, are not the kind of goods usually purchased or acquired by that particular business.

2. The scope of the UCTA 1977 is limited to control over terms which exclude or restrict liability, but the Act gives an extended meaning to exemption clauses so that it covers terms which entitle the party apparently in breach to render a contractual performance substantially different from that expected of him. The courts have been inventive in their approach to exclusion clauses, leading some commentators to call for more clarity in the definition of obligations which come within the scope of the legislation. In particular the inclusion of clauses which define liability as part of the formal definition of an exclusion clause, that is, the approach taken is that if there would be an obligation and liability in the absence of the clause, then the clause is brought within section 13(1) of the UCTA 1977.[11] Even the extended meaning of an exemption clause does not detract from the fact that UCTA 1977 is narrower in scope than the Directive as it refers to terms in general and not a particular category of terms.

3. Whereas the UCTA 1977 can deal with limitation of damages clauses and also related issues which seek to extend defences, for example, elimination of a right of set-off,[12] it does not reach the whole range of remedies, whereas these do fall within the Regulations.

Strict Liability and the Lessor of Equipment

An outstanding issue is whether liability, especially against a finance lessor, can be envisaged in the absence of proof of negligence through the application of strict liability in respect of the equipment leased. The Consumer Protection Act 1987 (the CPA 1987), in seeking to implement

---

[11.] See *Phillips Products Ltd v. Hyland* [1987] 2 All E.R. 620; *Smith v. Eric S. Bush* [1989] 2 All E.R. 514; *Johnstone v. Bloomsbury Health Authority* [1991] 2 All E.R. 293.

[12.] *Stewart Gill Ltd v. Horatio Myer and Co. Ltd* [1992] 2 All E.R. 257.

the E.C. Directive on Product Liability 1985,[13] aims to make producers and certain others involved in the chain of distribution liable for death, personal injury or specified property damage resulting from unsafe products. The Act is primarily aimed at "producers", which means manufacturers, persons who win or abstract substances as well as persons who carry out an industrial or other process on products not manufactured. There are two other categories of persons similarly civilly liable; first, anyone who has held himself out to be the producer of the product; and secondly, anyone who, in the course of business, has imported the product into any State in the European Community from any place outside the Community. In addition to the "primary defendants", the Act makes *certain* suppliers liable to the plaintiff. Any person who supplied a defective product, not necessarily to the plaintiff, may be liable to the plaintiff if he fails to identify one or more of the primary defendants or his own supplier after receiving a request from the plaintiff. Supply, for both primary and substitute defendants, embraces selling, hiring out, lending, hire-purchase, prizes and gifts, contracts for work and materials. However, where a finance company acquired goods from a dealer and finances their provision to a customer by means of a hire-purchase or leasing agreement, the person supplying under the Act will be the dealer so that the finance lessor would appear to be exempt.[14]

The general approach is that a supplier is not liable under Part I of the CPA 1987 for defective goods, but he may be liable in contract or negligence, or perhaps be criminally liable under Part II. However, section 2(3) of the CPA 1987 enables the persons injured to hold an effective supplier liable where, for example, the product is anonymous. The CPA 1987 specifically provides in section 4 for defences available with respect to "the person proceeded against" for defects supplied. One such defence under section 4(1)(b) is "that the person proceeded against did not at any time supply the product to another". The "no supply" defence has been used by taxi firms as a means of escaping liability under the Act. The reasoning here is that section 46(9) provides that ships, aircraft and motor vehicles do not count as being "supplied" for the purposes of the Act if the arrangement with the customer is solely to provide transport services "for a particular period or for particular voyages, flights or journeys".

Under Part II of the CPA 1987 "consumer goods" must comply with the general safety requirement. Under the general safety requirement, retailers are criminally liable if they knowingly expose an unsafe product for sale, whereas in civil law, under the product liability regime, retailers are liable to third party-victims only if they present themselves as the producer or cannot identify the person who supplied them with the

[13.] E.C. Directive 85/374. For a comprehensive discussion dealing with consumer elements see Wright C., *Product Liability—The Law and Its Implications for Risk Management* (1989). See also European Product Liabilities (eds Kelly, Attree 2nd ed. 1997).
[14.] CPA 1987, s. 46(2).

product. Liability is confined to "consumer goods" intended for private use supplied in the course of a business. Finance lessors are not treated as suppliers for liability purposes.[15] Furthermore the General Product Safety Regulations 1994[16] would also not apply as these Regulations are aimed at producers or distributors and finance lessors are not covered by the definition, presumably because it is unlikely that they can formally affect the safety of the product. There is no doubt that in some spheres finance lessors are held to be strictly liable as owners of equipment. Under section 153 of the Merchant Shipping Act 1995, strict liability is imposed upon tanker owners (lessors) where oil pollution is caused or where there is a "relevant threat of contamination".[17] Indeed, it is worth noting the policy factors which often underlie the imposition of strict liability in order to assess the position of the finance lessor in this regard.

In a functional sense the finance lessor considers itself to be a supplier of *money* rather than a product. The essence of the transaction to the lessor is that its investment will be "paid out" in full by the end of the lease term. This financial role is recognised both in Article 2A of the UCC and the UNIDROIT rules which tolerate even "hell or high water" clauses under which the lessee agrees to pay rentals to the lessor whatever happens, and regardless of whether the goods prove to be defective. The crucial point is the time at which the promise to pay becomes enforceable which, in the case of the lease, is upon the lessee's acceptance of the goods. We shall now consider this question further.

The Lessor's Duty to Deliver and the Lessee's Duty to Accept Delivery

In large measure the complexity of the law is due to the multiplicity of the remedies available to the hirer. Of particular significance is the right of the hirer to reject the equipment tendered and rescind on the grounds of defective performance. However, this right may be lost where the hirer has accepted the goods as this will be treated as an election to affirm the contract.

Acceptance in Contracts of Supply

Introduction

The SGSA 1982 does not purport to regulate the exercise of the transferee's remedies. The issue concerning the loss of the right to reject

---

15. CPA 1987, s. 46(2).
16. S.I. 1994 No. 2328.
17. Merchant Shipping Act 1995, s. 153(2). A statutory action *in rem* against the ship itself is available in respect of "damage done by a ship" under s. 21(4)(b)(i) of the Supreme Court Act 1981.

is determined by the common law, although there is no substantial divergence from the position under the SGA 1979. There is no doubt that the right to reject lapses after a reasonable time in contracts of hire purchase.[18] At one time it was argued that in the case of a contract of hire purchase, the supplier must supply goods which remain fit to be used throughout the period of hire on the basis of the theory of continuous breach. This approach was firmly scotched by the Court of Appeal in *UCB Leasing Ltd v. Holtom*.[19]

The question of acceptance in contracts of hire-purchase is construed widely, the courts taking into account factors such as the conduct of the hirer, attempts at repairs, negotiations for a settlement and the discovery of latent defects. Thus in *Porter v. General Guarantee Corp.*,[20] the plaintiff acquired a secondhand car from the defendants, a finance company, under a hire agreement dated January 26, 1980. The agreement was negotiated by third-party dealers who had been informed by the plaintiff that he wished to use the car as a taxi. They informed him that it would be suitable for such use. On delivery, the car was found to be defective in many respects. Repairs, negotiations and inspections continued over a period of two months with the plaintiff continuing to use the vehicle. Finally, the contract was repudiated on March 20. On the question of whether the plaintiff has lost his right to repudiate by continuing to use the car when he was aware of the defects, Kilner Brown J. stated[21]:

"I think it was reasonable to continue negotiation to see whether or not the third party would pay for the work done at the plaintiff's behest and on his own terms. If he was unreasonable in his demands this does not go to affirmation."

The plaintiff was allowed to reject the car, the judge indicating that he would be liable for an outstanding instalment under the agreement representing his use of the car over a month during which he was in a position to repudiate. Undoubtedly, following this case, the relevant factor determining the affirmation issue is that of knowledge of the defect and lack of satisfaction with the product. This can be summarised by Lord Denning's approach in *Farnworth Finance Facilities v. Attryde*[22] where, despite the concession that the hirer had used the motor cycle (the object of the hire-purchase contract) for four months and had ridden it for 4,000 miles, it was held[23]:

"A man only affirms a contract when he knows of the defects and by his conduct elects to go on with the contract despite them. In this case the hirer

---

[18.] *Jackson v. Chrysler Acceptances Ltd* [1978] R.T.R. 474.
[19.] [1987] R.T.R. 362.
[20.] [1992] R.T.R. 384.
[21.] *Ibid.* at 394.
[22.] [1970] 1 W.L.R. 1053.
[23.] *Ibid.* at 1059.

complained from the beginning of the defects and sent the machine back for them to be remedied . . . But the defects were never satisfactorily remedied . . . The hirer was entitled to say then: "I am not going on with this machine any longer. I have tried it long enough.' After all it was a contract of hiring. The machine was not his until the three years had been completed . . ."

It would appear that where the goods contain a latent defect the customer is better off in a non-sale case since he does not lose his right to terminate until he becomes aware of the defect.[23a]

In *Woodchester Equipment Leasing Ltd v. Marie*,[24] a drinks vending machine was installed at the defendant's hairdressing salon, but there was a hire agreement between the plaintiff finance company and the defendant which had come about following a sale by the suppliers of the equipment which was then leased back to the defendant. The vending machine was faulty although it was still held to be merchantable by the Court of Appeal, so the defendant was confined to setting-off a sum of money representing her damages against the sum which would other-wise have been the plaintiff's entitlement. As Russell L.J. found:

"The equipment was still in the possession of the defendant and still being used no doubt to her advantage, albeit a limited advantage, for a considerable period of time after defects first came to the notice of the defendant."

In some situations where there is a breach which goes to the root of the contract the damages awarded to the defendant may be sufficient to extinguish its liability to the plaintiff. The case in point here is *UCB Leasing Ltd v. Holtom (trading as David Holtom and Co.)*[25] which involved the purchase by the plaintiff of a new Alfa Romeo car which was then hired out to the defendant for the term of 37 months. From the date of delivery the car proved to be troublesome and there were many failures and defects. The car was returned for repair from time to time, but the root cause of the problems was not detected. After three months, the hirer, who had on previous occasions complained, ceased to pay the hire charges and expressed great dissatisfaction with the car. Even so, he still used the car occasionally during daylight because then its defective electrical system was not problematical! By the time the car was returned to the lessor it had done 8,000 miles and seven months had elapsed since the hiring began. At first instance it was held that the defect was so serious as to be a breach of a fundamental term. The argument followed that the hirer, once the agreement was brought to an end (as it was) by the leasing company in consequence of the failure of the hirer to pay instalments, was entitled to contend that but for the fundamental defect he would, for the rest of the period of the agreement, have had to hire an alternative vehicle, hypothetically at the same cost to

[23a] *Cf. Bernstein v. Pamsons Motors (Golders Green) Ltd* [1987] 2 All E.R. 220.
[24] 1993, C.A., unreported.
[25] [1987] R.T.R. 362.

him. The Court of Appeal found the claim by the hiring company in respect of a long period after the vehicle was returned to them was extinguished by the notional loss occasioned to the hirer.

No recommendation was made by the Law Commission[26] to harmonise sale and supply contracts in respect of acceptance, and a distinction was drawn between hire contracts and sale. In the case of the former, there is a continuing relationship between the parties and in a very real sense in operational leases the goods belong to the owner who may have a continuing obligation to repair and replace hired goods. Furthermore, in hire there is a convenient method of valuing use and enjoyment of the goods, namely the hire charge itself. In the case of sale no principles on the use and enjoyment of goods have emerged. Even so, it could be argued that leasing and hire-purchase are devices established to finance the acquisition of goods and a distinction drawn with sale is purely a matter of legal form. However, the Law Commission pointed out[27]:

> "It is true that hire purchase is a device for financing what in the end will amount to a sale. We are, however, not persuaded that this means that the acceptance rule of sale contracts should also apply to hire purchase. A pattern of rights and duties has grown up and we do not think this pattern should be disturbed unless there are compelling reasons to do so."

The opportunity of curing a defective tender is lost where the hirer has accepted the goods or is deemed to have accepted them, because there is no concept of revocation of acceptance in English law. Of course, if the lessor offers to substitute performance and the lessee rejects, this conduct will go to the issue of mitigation of loss. Furthermore, if the lessor in an operational lease proceeds to repair the equipment or agrees to do so, the parties may be held to this on the basis of either a collateral agreement or estoppel. Interestingly under the 1985 UNIDROIT draft Rules on International Finance Leasing a limited "right to cure" was recognised in the sense that, by virtue of article 19(2), the lessor and supplier were given an additional period of time to substitute a conforming tender. This has been replaced under the Convention, and the lessor's right to cure a failure in performance is now expressed to be exercisable on the same conditions and in the same manner as if the lessee had agreed to buy the equipment from the lessor under the terms of the supply agreement.[28] The balance is still firmly tilted in favour of the lessor as the supplier of the finance because, after acceptance of the goods, the lessee has no right to withhold rentals for non-conforming delivery.

[26.] See n. 72, above.

[27.] *Ibid.* para. 5.4.6.

[28.] UNIDROIT Convention on *International Financial Leasing* (1988), Art. 12(1), (2).

A right to "cure" a defective tender?

Defective performance does not necessarily mean that the contract is terminated for breach. Indeed the common law rule is that the defaulting party enjoys the right to cure a defective performance.[29] However the right to cure is circumscribed by the time permitted for performance in the contract which, of course, presupposes what is the appropriate time period. In addition, there are some subsidiary issues, namely, whether damages are available to the aggrieved party in respect of any consequential loss due to the original tender and also whether a right to cure subsists in the absence of a rejection by the aggrieved party of the original tender. It should be noted that the right to cure does not mean substitution unless this conforms with contractual stipulations relating to the description of the goods ordered.

A distinction should be drawn between contractual terms which are conditions as distinct from warranties, as there is authority that a substitute tender must be accepted where there is a breach of warranty, the aggrieved party's appropriate remedy being damages for breach of warranty.[30] In a sense this coheres with an important public policy issue, which is that of promoting performance of contracts. This is the rationale underlying section 15A of the SGA 1979, section 11A SOGIT 1973, sections 5(A), 10(A) of the SGSA 1982 (as amended) in that they provide a check on the right to withdraw from a *commercial* contract by reference to the concept of reasonableness.

The loss of the so-called right to cure

Time limits. In the absence of repudiation, the defaulting party has until the expiration of the period of time permitted for performance under the contract to cure the defective performance or, in the absence of a time period being stipulated in the contract, within a reasonable time. It follows that where time is of the essence then defective performance means that no right to cure can emerge, simply because the condition precedent of the buyer or hirer's liability (payment) cannot be triggered since a subsequent tender or delivery will be out of time. Where time is not of the essence, whilst the buyer or hirer will have the right to damages for delay, the fact of delay will not entitle the aggrieved party to terminate the contract.[31] In this situation the issue revolves around the time period for curing the defect—is it a reasonable time or a time after which the delay amounts to a substantial failure in performance or a delay which can be considered to go to the root of the contract? These tests can lead to different results, for example, a delay may be unreasonable in the context of how hard the aggrieved party has pressed for performance but it may not rob him of substantially the whole benefit of the contract.

[29] *Motor Oil Hellas (Corinth) Refineries SA v. Shipping Corp of India; The Kanchenjunga* [1990] 1 Lloyd's Rep. 391.
[30] *ERG Petroli SpA v. Vitol SA; The Ballenita* [1992] 2 Lloyd's Rep. 355.
[31] *Raineri v. Miles* [1981] A.C. 1050.

In *McDougall v. Aeromarine of Emsworth Ltd*[32] there was a clause in a contract to build a yacht which provided that the seller would use his "best endeavours" to build it by a certain time but this could not be guaranteed. It was held by Diplock J. (as he then was) that this clause placed on the sellers a duty to deliver within a reasonable time. However, it should be noted that whilst ultimately in this case the time was not fixed, nevertheless the seller did give an undertaking to use his "best endeavours" to get the yacht ready by a certain date and the reasonableness test used would appear therefore to be appropriate. It is significant that the issue of reasonableness was measured in terms of the purpose of the contract which was to use the yacht during the yachting season and the buyer terminated at a time when he could be described as having substantially lost this benefit. On the other hand, there are other cases where it has been held that the aggrieved party can only terminate where the delay is so long that it goes to the root of the contract.[33]

Where no term is specified in the contract, the court will imply a term that performance must be within a reasonable time. The issue then is whether failure to cure within a reasonable time amounts to repudiatory breach as distinct from merely entitling the buyer to damages. As a matter of consistency, where time is stipulated in the contract the supplier is only entitled to cure the defect until such time as the acquirer is deprived of substantially the whole benefit under the contract.

Curing defective tender beyond the contract period: waiver. Where the hirer waives the time for performance, then he is bound to accept substitute performance and the aggrieved party cannot terminate on the expiration of the original contract date. Of course, the aggrieved party may revert to the strict position and make time of the essence either by extending the time for performance by fixed periods[34] or, alternatively, by fixing time by reference to the concept of reasonableness.

Consequential loss from original defective tender. When a financier as owner (lessor) tenders a defective performance which is rejected, the lessor is treated as if he has not tendered at all. It follows therefore that the lessor does not commit a breach of contract in making an initial defective tender which is then subsequently cured. As Cockburn C.J. said in *Frost v. Knight*[35]:

> "The promisee has an inchoate right to the performance of the bargain, which becomes complete when the time for performance has arrived. In the meantime he has a right to have the contract kept open as a subsisting and effective contract."

[32.] [1958] 1 W.L.R. 1126.
[33.] *Hong Kong Fir Shipping Co. Ltd. v. Kawasaki Kisen Kaisha Ltd* [1962] 2 Q.B. 26.
[34.] See *Nichimen Corp. v. Gatoil Overseas Inc.* [1987] 2 Lloyd's Rep. 46 at 53.
[35.] [1872] L.R. 7 Ex. 111 at 114.

It follows from this that since there has been no breach of contract there can then be no action for damages in contract, for example, for consequential losses that may have been incurred as a result of the abortive first delivery. Typically such losses could be storage expenses incurred in anticipation of a satisfactory first delivery. The dilemma is to identify a judicial rationale for compensating for consequential losses. One approach could be to do so on the basis of implying a collateral term not to make an invalid tender and that a breach of this duty sound in damages. An alternative approach is that the first tender could be treated as a non-repudiatory breach.

A so-called "right to cure" promotes the performance of a hire contract and minimises waste in the sense that if the wrongdoer can cure the defective performance the hirer is adequately compensated, and any expenditure incurred will not therefore be thrown away. A significant consideration is that such a right prevents parties from escaping improvident bargains, for example, by giving one party the excuse of terminating for a technical breach in order to avoid an improvident bargain. Moreover, it can be argued that a right to cure accords with commercial reality, in that the hirer will normally seek a fresh tender of the goods and that a right to cure coheres with what the parties would have agreed to in any case. At the same time the right to cure is a valuable self-help remedy in that it throws the risk of the contract performance back on the party in breach, that is, he must cure his performance or be left with termination of the contract and damages for breach.

The Action for Damages

Introduction

A hirer may have at his disposal an action for damages available against his supplier or third party for breach of the supply contract, or for some collateral contract otherwise concluded. As an alternative, there is no reason why the hirer should not be able to treat the collateral warranty as a misrepresentation and rescind the contract. Where there has been a fraudulent misrepresentation, the supplier will be liable in tort for deceit. For negligent misrepresentation, damages are available at common law when the misrepresentation results in physical injury, or where there was a breach of a fiduciary duty, or of a duty created by a special relationship.[36] A right to damages is now expressly provided by section 2(1) of the Misrepresentation Act 1967.

Breach of contract

General rule. The general rule is that the measure of damages constitutes the difference between the rentals or price paid, or if it is lower, the

---

[36] *Hedley Byrne and Co. Ltd. v. Heller and Partners Ltd* [1994] A.C. 465.

market value of what was contracted for, and the market value of what was obtained. In the supply of goods context, the conventional scenarios for the action for damages for breach may take one of two forms: first, an action for damages for non-delivery; and secondly, an action founded on a breach of a term(s) in the contract of hire.

Non-delivery. In the case of a simple contract of hire or hire-purchase, the measure of damages for failure to deliver should be the difference between the contract hire or hire-purchase rate and the market rate for such transaction. As a matter of consistency in logic, this should also be the case where a hirer lawfully terminates the contract and rescinds.

Breach. Where the hirer has accepted delivery but has subsequently rejected on the basis of continuous breach, it was held in *Yeoman Credit Ltd v. Apps*[37] that the hirer can recover by way of damages the reasonable sum necessary to repair the object bailed. Of course, this is open to the objection that the measure of damages relates to breach of warranty rather than rescission. The theoretical incongruity here in no small measure contributed to the demise of the continuous breach doctrine,[38] so the measure of damages is confined where the hirer affirms the contract following a reasonable opportunity to discover the defect.

Defects in title. Defects in title has already been discussed.[39] The hirer will be able to recover any payment made on the basis of total failure of consideration.[40] The transferee may also recover any consequential losses which the supplier ought reasonably have contemplated would flow as a result of the breach.

Delay in delivery. Where time is of the essence, late delivery is treated as a breach of condition. The effect of this is that where a late tender is made, the hirer's lawful rejection makes the case one of non-delivery. In the case of a delay in delivery which the transferee cannot rescind, the action for damages is akin to a breach of warranty. As such, the contract continues and this has an impact on the transferee's duty to mitigate his loss. Thus, in the case where goods are bought for resale, where there is an available market value, the prima facie measure for damages is the amount by which the market value at the contractual time for delivery exceeds the market value at the actual time of delivery. Contracts of hire or hire-purchase contain a prohibition of sale by the hirer so there is, by definition, no available market. This will also be the case where goods are bought for use, and the measure of damages here relates to the deprivation of the use of the asset for the period of delay. It follows that where the asset is of an income-producing kind, the transferee should be

[37] [1962] 2 Q.B. 508.
[38] See *UCB Leasing Ltd v. Holtom* [1987] R.T.R. 362.
[39] See pp. 62–63, above.
[40] *Rowland v. Divall* [1923] 2 K.B. 500.

able to recover for the loss of profit that the transferor could reasonably have contemplated as flowing from the breach.[41] Of course, the transferee is under a duty to mitigate his loss where he can, for example, by hiring substitute goods pending delivery.

Defects in quality. In the case of contracts of hire, the measure of damages should be the difference between the warranted hire rate and the amount which the hired goods could command in their actual state. With contracts of hire-purchase, an allowance should be made for the option to purchase and account should be taken of the possibility that the hiring may be determined. No general rule can be laid down, but in *Charterhouse Credit Co. Ltd v. Tolly*,[42] Upjohn L.J. suggested that in the absence of the owner terminating the hire-purchase contract, the hirer would have been entitled to the amount required to put the vehicle in a proper state of repair as well as damages for loss of use.

Remedies under Lease and Hire Contracts

The law may not be satisfactory especially from the lessor's point of view since the case law turns on two unrelated principles of law: (1) a lease of chattels is analogous to the lease of real property and, therefore, attracts some of the principles of landlord and tenant; and (2) the rule against penalties developed in contract law applies.

Remedies Available to the Lessor while Keeping the Lease on Foot

There is no doubt that the lessor may, upon default, leave the equipment in the possession of the lessee and recover the rental payment as it falls due. In addition, damages will be available for a specific breach of the contract, such as a failure to insure the equipment or maintain it. At least two other approaches are available to the finance lessor.

Acceleration clauses

The lease contract may provide for rental payments being called up in full upon the lessee's default. Sometimes the agreement will provide for automatic acceleration of liability on the occurrence of stated events. Such an approach is likely to prove inflexible in practice, so creditors will often take power to accelerate indebtedness on default only after notice has been given to the lessee. Where there is a "true" lease, such a

---

[41.] See *Victoria Laundry (Windsor) Ltd v. Newman Industries Ltd* [1949] 2 Q.B. 528.
[42.] [1963] 2 Q.B. 683.

clause can be considered foreign to the lessor/lessee relationship because, unlike a defaulting buyer or borrower, a lessee is generally not obliged under the rules of damages to pay a specific predetermined sum to the lessor. Although the lessor will be entitled to damages for breach of contract, there is no certainty that those damages will be assessed to be the equivalent of all rental payments owing under the lease (discounted for early payment and also realisation of the chattel).

Under a finance lease where the lessor has no interest in the return of the asset, an acceleration clause is not foreign to the lease transaction. Indeed, an acceleration clause can be considered a natural and necessary part of the financing aspect of the transaction. It is obvious, in this circumstance, that the lessee is contractually obligated to make rental payments equivalent to the instalment purchase price of the chattel. The term of the lease dealing with default will provide for acceleration of all unpaid lease payments since it is the only way to guarantee the lessor recovery of its capital and a return on its investment. No question of penalty can arise in a contract where there is a stipulation that the entire rent be immediately due, but the lessor agrees to accept payment of it by instalments, *debitum in praesenti solvendum in futuro*, although two Australian cases have demonstrated the difficulty of drafting such a clause.[43] It has been held that an entitlement to this rent is fundamentally inconsistent with an early right to repossession, on the basis that entitlement to the entire rent is consistent only with an affirmation of the contract of hire, whereas entitlement to repossession is consistent only with its termination. Following on from this, there is no doubt that where the acceleration clause is combined with a right of repossession this will invite scrutiny on the basis of the court's jurisdiction to grant a hirer equitable relief from forfeiture.[44]

An acceleration clause, even in the case of a regulated consumer credit agreement, is not considered void as being a restriction on the statutory right of the debtor to terminate the contract.[45] This is because the sum payable under such a clause may be considered a "final payment" for the purposes of section 99(1) of the CCA 1974 which states:

> "At any time before the final payment by the debtor under a regulated hire-purchase or regulated conditional sale agreement falls due, the debtor shall be entitled to terminate the agreement by giving notice to any person entitled or authorised to receive sums payable under the agreement."

It should be noted that under a regulated consumer-credit agreement, section 93 of the CCA 1974 protects the debtor against default interest, that is an increase in the rate of interest on default, and he is also granted the benefit of a seven-day notice period.[46]

---

43. See *O'Dea v. Allstates Leasing Systems (W.A.) Pty Ltd* (1983) 57 A.L.J.R. 172; *Amev-UDC Finance Ltd (formerly United Dominions Corp. Ltd) v. Austin and Anr* (1986) 60 A.L.J.R. 74.
44. See pp. 109–113, below.
45. *Wadham Stringer Finance Ltd v. Meaney* [1981] 1 W.L.R. 39.
46. CCA 1974, ss. 76(1)(a), 87(1)(b).

Sub-leasing

Where the lessee has defaulted in his agreement with the lessor, in an attempt to sustain the lease and also to fulfil the duty imposed by the law of contract to mitigate the loss, the lessor may act as agent of the lessee and assign or sub-lease the equipment. Such an act by the finance lessor may be regarded as inconsistent with the continued existence of the lease, thereby releasing the lessee from his obligations under it and leaving the finance lessor with recovery only for breaches occurring before the date of release.[47] However, in *Highway Properties Ltd v. Kelly Douglas and Co. Ltd*,[48] the Supreme Court of Canada showed that as dealings in commercial property developed, maintaining a theoretically pure approach to leases as executed contracts conflict with practical reality, because once the tenant abandons the premises, the landlord can very easily resume possession and mitigate the losses. As Laskin C.J. held[49]:

> "It is no longer sensible to pretend that a commercial lease, such as the one before this court, is simply a conveyance and not also a contract. It is equally untenable to persist in denying resort to the full armoury of remedies ordinarily available to redress repudiation of covenants, merely because the covenants may be associated with an estate in land. Finally, there is merit here as in other situations in avoiding multiplicity of actions that may otherwise be a concomitant of insistence that a landlord engage in stalemate litigation against a repudiating tenant."

This judgment represents Laskin C.J.'s attempt to bring property concepts into line with contract principles.[50] Such a reconciliation is both fairer and more efficient for society, in the sense that a productive use will be made of the property, promoting activity and minimising waste. In repudiating the purported distinction between damages for breach of leases and damages for breach of other contracts, the *Highway Properties* case echoed the sentiments expressed in an American legal commentary written within the first quarter of the twentieth century[51]:

> "Long after the realities of feudal tenure have vanished and a new system based upon a theory of contractual obligation has in general taken its place, the old theory of obligations springing from the relation of lord and tenant survives. The courts have neglected the caution of Mr Justice Holmes, 'that continuity with the past is only a necessity and not a duty'. If one turns from a decision upon the conditions implied upon a contract for the sale of goods

---

[47.] See *Total Oil Great Britain Ltd v. Thompson Garages (Biggin Hill) Ltd* [1972] 1 Q.B. 318.

[48.] (1971) 17 D.L.R. (3d) 710.

[49.] *Ibid.* at 721.

[50.] See also *Progressive Mailing House Pty Ltd v. Tabali Pty Ltd* (1985) 57 A.L.R. 609.

[51.] (1924–5) 23 Mich. L.R. 211 at 221–222.

in instalments to one upon the obligation of the parties to a lease, one changes from the terms and ideas of the 20th century to those of the 16th. The notion of 'privity of estate' and its attendant rights and duties appears as quaint and startling as a modern infantryman with a crossbow."

If this approach were adopted in the context of finance leasing, the lessor's contractual rights under the lease would be protected. Consequently, a claim for any loss resulting from the sub-letting such as the difference in the rent received, could be recovered.

Remedies Available where the Lease is not Kept on Foot

Self-help

The possibility of repossession of the equipment by the lessor is predicated upon the idea that the equipment is worth more than the costs involved with repossession. It may be possible for the finance lessor to insure against depreciation in the residual value of the equipment at the end of the lease term. Following a failure by the hirer or lessee to return the goods after a request by the owner, the latter is entitled to use reasonable force to recover the goods. Of course, the question of what constitutes reasonable force is a matter of degree so that if unreasonable force is used, this will amount to an assault.[52] Moreover, there is the criminal offence of unlawful harassment of debtors.[53]

One alternative to recaption is repossession through court action on the basis of the hirer or lessee's neglect, or refusal to return the goods which is adverse to the owner's right to immediate possession. The forms of judgment available where goods are wrongfully detained can be found in section 3 of the Torts (Interference with Goods) Act 1977.[54] In exercising self-help the lessor will have to consider the position of third-party interests especially landlords, mortgagees, third-party acquirers and lien holders. Prudence would, therefore, dictate that it will be necessary for a lessor to determine in *advance* of funding what impact the various third-party positions may have upon the collateral.

Repudiation and termination

Introduction. Where the lessee acts in such a way as to renounce his future obligations under the lease and the lessor accepts this repudiation, the agreement will be terminated. The classic statement of principle is as follows[55]:

"Any act or disposition which is wholly repugnant to or as it were an absolute disclaimer of the holding as bailee, reverts the bailor's right to possession, and

[52.] *Dyer v. Munday* [1895] 1 Q.B. 742.
[53.] See Chap. 12, below.
[54.] See Chap. 11, below.
[55.] Pollock and Wright, *Possession in the Common Law* (1888) p. 132.

therefore also his immediate right to maintain trover or detinue even where the bailment is for a term or is otherwise not revocable at will . . ."

A failure to pay the agreed rental is a breach of contract which entitles the owner to sue for damages. Normally, a single lapse will not amount to repudiation, but where there is a persistent refusal, or where the agreement specifically provides for termination in this event, it will amount to repudiation of the contract. Here the lessor can claim damages in respect of loss of profit on further rentals to which it would have been entitled had the leasing run its full course.[56] Mitigation of damages will be a difficult factor where the leased chattel is unique. The rentals are discounted in order to allow for acceleration of payments. In the case of hire-purchase, no account is taken of the hirer's right to terminate, which would militate against recovery of the whole hire-purchase price.[57] As against the hirer or his assignee, the courts have restricted the supplier to the outstanding balance of the hire-purchase price. Of course in principle where the agreement has been terminated, the supplier should be entitled to the full value of the goods. The explanation here is that the hire-purchase rule is *sui generis*.[58]

The effects of a repudiatory breach. One of the only English cases dealing with the effect of repudiation in a finance lease is *Lombard North Central Plc v. Butterworth*.[59] It is worth dwelling upon the facts. The plaintiffs, a finance company, leased a computer to the defendant for a period of five years on payment of an initial sum of £584.05 and 19 subsequent quarterly instalments of the same amount. Clause 2(a) of the agreement made punctual payment of each instalment the essence of the agreement, and failure to make such payments entitled the plaintiffs to terminate the agreement. Clause 6 of the agreement provided that following termination, the plaintiffs were entitled to all arrears of instalments and all future instalments which would have fallen due had the agreement not been terminated. When the sixth instalment was six weeks overdue, the plaintiffs terminated the agreement and, having recovered possession of the computer, sold it for only £172.88. The plaintiffs brought an action against the defendant claiming the sixth unpaid instalment and the 13 future instalments, or alternatively, damages for breach of contract. Before the Court of Appeal, the defendant contended that he ought not to be held liable for more than the amount due and unpaid at the date of termination. The argument employed was that clause 6 of the agreement created a penalty and that the defendant's conduct had not

---

[56.] *Yeoman Credit Co. v. Waragowski* [1961] 1 W.L.R. 1124; *Yeoman Credit Co. v. McLean* [1962] 1 W.L.R. 1312; *Overstone v. Shipway* [1962] 1 W.L.R. 117.

[57.] See *Union Transport Finance Ltd v. British Car Auctions Ltd* [1978] 2 All E.R. 385.

[58.] *Belsize Motor Supply Co. v. Cox* [1914] 1 K.B. 244; *Belvoir Finance Co. Ltd v. Stapleton* [1971] 1 Q.B. 210.

[59.] [1987] Q.B. 527.

amounted to a repudiation. The plaintiffs argued that clause 2(a) of the agreement entitled them to treat default in one payment as a repudiation of the agreement, thereby enabling them to recover their loss in respect of the whole transaction.

The lessor succeeded in the Court of Appeal and recovered for its loss of bargain under the general law of damages, irrespective of the fact that the liquidated damages provision could be struck down as a penalty. This conclusion was arrived at by the Court of Appeal somewhat reluctantly because, as Nicholls L.J. pointed out, there was "no practical difference" between the terms of the contract in this case and the previous decision of the Court of Appeal in *Financings Ltd v. Baldock.*[60] In the latter case, an owner had terminated a hire-purchase agreement under an express provision entitling him to terminate for non-payment of hire. It was held that he was, in the absence of repudiation, entitled to no more than the amount of the hire unpaid at the time of termination. As Nicholls L.J. said in *Lombard North Central*[61]:

> "There is no practical difference between (1) an agreement containing such a power [for termination] and (2) an agreement containing a provision to the effect that time for payment of each instalment is of the essence so that any breach will go to the root of the contract. The difference between these two agreements is one of drafting form and wholly without substance. *Yet under an agreement drafted in the first form, the owner's damages claim arising on his exercise of the power of termination is confined to damages for breaches up to the date of termination, whereas under an agreement drafted in the second form the owner's damages claim, arising on his acceptance of an identical breach as a repudiation of the agreement will extend to damages for loss of the whole transaction.*"

The reluctance of the learned judge in this case fails to take fully into account the following matters. First, merely because the parties refer to a term (time in this case) as a condition, this is not necessarily determinative of the question in so far as it describes the legal nature of the breach. Secondly, a finance lease is a financing venture where payment schedules go to the root of the contract because the lessor looks primarily towards the rental stream rather than repossession of the asset. Thus, in this case there was a considerable risk of obsolescence, which is not so prevalent in the normal hire-purchase transaction involving consumer durables.

Where the breach is not deemed repudiatory, the courts have in the context of hire-purchase transactions taken into account the existence of the right to terminate as seen in *Financings Ltd v. Baldock* (1963). In this case, Lord Denning enunciated a new general principle of law[62]:

> "I see no difference in this respect between the letting of a vehicle on hire and the letting of land on a lease. If a lessor under a proviso for re-entry, re-

[60.] [1963] 2 Q.B. 104; 2 W.L.R. 359.
[61.] [1987] Q.B. 527 at 546. Emphasis added.
[62.] [1963] 2 Q.B. 104 at 110–111.

enters on the ground of non-payment of rent or of disrepair, he gets the arrears of rent up to the date of re-entry and damages for want of repair at that date, but he does not get damages for loss of rent thereafter or for breaches of repair thereafter."

What was awarded to the owner in the *Baldock* case having "unreasonably terminated the agreement" was the two instalments of rent in arrears plus interest. The major objection to this is the failure to recognise that the lease in real property is both a conveyance and a contract, and usually a minimum payment clause (indemnity) will govern termination of an agreement. More recently in *UCB Leasing Ltd v Holtom*,[63] the Court of Appeal refused to follow the approach of Holroyd Pearce L.J. in *Yeoman Credit v. Apps*.[64] In that case his Lordship held that if the hirer affirms the contract but the goods subsequently remain unfit, the continuing breach entitles the hirer to reject the goods. In *UCB Leasing Ltd*, the hirer did not reject the car until he had had it for seven months, and the court held that he had affirmed the contract by virtue of a lapse of a reasonable period of time. The owners were held entitled to all instalments due until rejection. The Court of Appeal applied *Financings Ltd v. Baldock* (1963), namely, that the hirer by returning the car had not repudiated the agreement and the owners were, therefore, not entitled to payment in respect of the future instalments that had not fallen due before the owner's termination of the agreement. Interestingly, Balcombe L.J. in *UCB Leasing Ltd* pointed out that since the owner had made payment on time the essence of the contract, the owners were entitled to treat the contract as repudiated and, following *Lombard North Central* (1987), were entitled to compensation for loss of future instalments, subject to the hirer's counterclaim for damages.[65]

In *Amev U.D.C. v. Austin*,[66] the Australian High Court pointed out that there was nothing objectionable about an indemnity clause which anticipated the recovery of actual loss on early termination. Nevertheless, the majority held that where the indemnity clause was penal, it was not for the courts to rewrite the stipulation so as to limit it to what could be recovered as an indemnity. The court held that the lessor's claim should be limited to loss flowing from the breach, which did not include loss of bargain where there was no repudiation. Such an approach is unduly restrictive in a finance leasing context because as Dawson J., dissenting, said in that case[67]:

"For my part I am unable to see why the intention of the parties concerning payment of compensation upon termination would be disregarded merely

[63] [1987] R.T.R. 362.
[64] [1962] 2 Q.B. 508.
[65] See *Charterhouse Credit Co. Ltd v. Tolly* [1963] 2 Q.B. 683.
[66] (1986) 60 A.L.J.R. 74.
[67] *Ibid*. at 761–762.

because the provision which they make fails as a penalty. Just as actual loss is recoverable upon breach, even where there is a stipulation which is unenforceable as a penalty, there is no reason to my mind why actual loss should not be recoverable upon termination in the same circumstances."

Significantly, in *Robophone Facilities Ltd v. Blank*,[68] Diplock L.J. suggested that a liquidated damages clause could properly include compensation for a loss which would normally be too remote. Such an argument is attractive in a non-consumer case such as *Lombard North Central* (1987), since businessmen should be expected to understand the terms offered in the contract of supply. Furthermore, the finance lessor's loss is easily calculable. It is significant that Article 11(3) of the UNIDROIT Convention on International Financial Leasing (1988) provides that compensation on termination of the leasing agreement is to be enforceable between the parties unless it is disproportionate to that fixed by Article 11(2)(b), namely "such compensation will place the lessor in the position in which it would have been had the lessee performed the leasing agreement in accordance with its terms, except in so far as the lessor has failed to take all reasonable steps to mitigate loss."

Lawful termination

The basic function of a termination clause is as a self-help mechanism, that is it provides a means of termination which depends on proof of nothing more than that an event within the scope of the clause has occurred. Furthermore the clause will purport to deal with the consequences of termination, notably, by providing for payment of specific sums by the lessee on default. The approach of the common law, based upon the presumed intention of the parties, is that terms regulating rights and liabilities (liquidated damages and exclusion clauses extending to events following termination) as well as terms in respect of which there is an *accrued* right to receive performance are enforceable after termination. The function of the termination clause is to crystallise the parties' rights so that if the contract stipulates for the payment of periodical sums, such as a lessee's rental payments, and payments were due at the time of termination, these will normally be recoverable on the basis of an accrued right.[69] Deposit payments are probably also recoverable on the basis of accrued rights.

The difficulty with termination clauses which provide for minimum stipulated sums concerns the meaning of a genuine pre-estimate of loss. In addition, to what extent is it possible to accommodate the doctrine of penalties, especially in the context of finance leasing transactions, bearing in mind the theoretical underpinnings of contract law? Occasionally, the agreement will represent neither, especially since both English and Australian courts have affirmed that a term will not be

[68] [1966] 1 W.L.R. 1428.
[69] *Brooks v. Beirnstein* [1909] 1 K.B. 98.

characterised as a penalty clause if it is expressed to take effect upon an event other than a breach of contract by the hirer. In *Bridge v. Campbell Discount Co. Ltd*,[70] the House of Lords was divided on this question and Denning L.J. pointed out that equity, by this method, commits itself to an "absurd paradox" appearing to grant relief only on breach of contract. Nevertheless, more recently, this reluctance has been overturned by the House of Lords in *Export Credit Guarantee Department v. Universal Oil Products Co*.[71] The reasoning here is that it has never been the function of the courts to relieve a party from a contract on the mere ground that it proves to be onerous or imprudent.

One important effect of the above approach is that it allows a skilled legal draftsman to avoid the rule against penalties. Ironically, a lessee who honours his obligations by terminating the agreement in a manner prescribed by the contract will be in a worse position than an irresponsible lessee who breaks the contract, and whose liability will be avoided because of the rule relating to penalties. Be that as it may, any attempt by a finance lessor to circumscribe the rule against penalties through mechanistically invoking an acceleration clause, and then proceeding to terminate the lease for default in payment of the accelerated rentals, is unlikely to succeed before the courts. Such conduct is similar to sharp practice making it inequitable to allow the finance lessor to retain the benefit of its full legal rights without allowing the lessee a *locus poenitentiae* under the rules against forfeiture.[72] On the other hand, the exercise by the lessor of a contractual power of termination for breach is enforceable.[73]

Penalty clauses

In an attempt to protect its investment on the lessee's default, the finance lessor may invoke a "minimum payment" clause. One of the main difficulties here concerns the genuineness of the pre-estimate of loss. Care has to be taken in drafting an adeemed repudiation clause so as to realistically limit the acts of default, that would be deemed to constitute a repudiation, to such matters as go to the root of the contract. Since finance leases will often contain a long list of events of default, for example failure to insure or to repair, these very contractual provisions may run afoul of the rule against penalties. The courts may not consider all of these breaches of contract as being sufficiently serious so as to amount to repudiation by the lessee. Even so, the penalty clause will remain enforceable up to the amount of loss suffered, that is, the plaintiff's actual loss.[74]

A minimum payment clause designed to confer upon the creditor a right to damages for loss of future instalments after termination will be

---

[70.] [1962] A.C. 600.
[71.] [1983] 1 W.L.R. 339.
[72.] See *Barton Thompson and Co. Ltd v. Stapling Machines Co.* [1966] Ch.D. 499.
[73.] As to the position following the insolvency of the hirer, see Chap. 13, below.
[74.] See *Jobson v. Johnson* [1989] 1 All E.R. 621.

penal and unenforceable. Damages for future rentals will only be available following repudiatory breach.[75] All the relevant English cases to date have concerned minimum payment clauses with no realistic provision being made for the value of the repossessed equipment or for the acceleration of rentals. In *Bridge v. Campbell Discount Co.*,[76] a clause which provided that a sum equalling to two-thirds of the hire-Purchase price together with expenses incurred by the owner should be payable, was considered not to be a genuine pre-estimate of liquidated damages. In spite of this, it is clear from the judgments given in the House of Lords that had the default clause been properly drawn as a genuine pre-estimate of damages, it would have been enforceable. Even so, such an ideal has proved elusive in subsequent cases. Thus in *Anglo-Auto Finance Co. Ltd v. James*,[77] the Court of Appeal considered a minimum payment clause, which required payment of all moneys in arrears and a sum equal to the amount by which the hire-purchase price (less the deposit and monthly instalments already paid) exceeded the net amount realised by the sale of the vehicle, to be penal. The judgments seem to indicate that, since in the *Bridge* case two-thirds of the hire-purchase price recoverable under the minimum payment clause was held to be penal, a clause providing for 100 per cent of the purchase price had to be penal. Unfortunately, the judgments fail to take account of one essential difference: the clause in *Auto Finance* provided for the resale price of the car being deducted from the hire-purchase price in computing the damages, but admittedly, it did fail to take into account a discount for acceleration of payment resulting from the disposal of the repossessed goods. Only in this latter sense could the clause be considered penal. As a matter of principle, there is nothing oppressive in a clause enabling the owner to place upon the lessee the risk of any deficiency resulting from repossession and resale from the discounted hire-purchase price, except where the deficiency is increased as a result of the owner's negligence.

An example before the High Court of Australia of a liquidated damages clause being upheld can be seen in *Esanda Finance Corp. v. Plessnig*.[78] In this case, the hire-purchase agreement provided that if the hirer made default in any payment under the agreement, the owner would be entitled to retake possession of the goods, whereupon the hiring would terminate and the owner would be entitled to recover, as liquidated damages, an amount equal to the total rent payable under the agreement, less the deposit, any rentals paid, the value of the goods being the best wholesale price reasonably obtainable for them at the time of repossession, and a rebate of charges. This case confirms the possibility of drafting effective liquidated damages provisions that will not be struck down as penal.

In order to successfully draft a remedy clause, an allowance will have to be given to the lessee both for the value of the equipment repossessed

---

[75.] See *Yeoman Credit Ltd v. Waragowski* [1961] 1 W.L.R. 1124.
[76.] [1962] A.C. 600.
[77.] [1963] 1 W.L.R. 1042.
[78.] (1988) 166 C.L.R. 131.

and also for the accelerated payments given to the lessor. The difference between computing the owner's loss under a hire-purchase agreement and that incurred under a finance lease is that in the case of the former the full net proceeds of sale must be brought into account, whereas in the case of the finance lease the owner would in any event have regained the goods at the end of the period. The finance lessor's potential gain, for which it will have to give allowance if the clause is not to be struck down as penal, will not equal the full proceeds of sale, but the amount by which this exceeds what would have been the value of the goods at the end of the hiring period. A useful summary of the damages formula is:

(a) any past-due rentals; plus

(b) interest or delay damages; plus the present value of the future rent stream; plus

(c) the value of any insurance, maintenance and tax liabilities assumed by the lessee; plus

(d) the present value of the end-of-term residual value, adjusted for any loss due to abusive use; plus

(e) the additional costs and expenses of realisation.

There may be problems in determining the appropriate discount rate applicable. To the extent that the above formulation makes prior estimation of the loss by the lessor very difficult to assess, the court might favour a "broad brush" approach. In *Robophone Facilities Ltd v. Blank*,[79] it was held that a clause providing for the pre-estimate of damages involving the repudiation of an operating lease of telephone-answering equipment was not a penalty, even though it was not precise, because it was "reasonably close" to the actual loss likely to be occasioned to the plaintiffs so far as it was capable of prediction. The clause required payment as liquidated damages of 50 per cent of the gross rents which would have been payable, and this was estimated to lie within a range of 47–58 per cent of the gross rents for the unexpired term of the contract. Such a provision was commended by the court for its sound business sense, in that it attempted to avoid the uncertainty of proving in a court the actual loss sustained. As Lord Diplock said[80]:

" . . . the more difficult it is likely to prove and assess the loss which a party will suffer in the event of a breach, the greater the advantages to both parties of fixing by the terms of the contract itself an easily ascertainable sum to be paid in that event. Not only does it enable the parties to know in advance what their position will be if a breach occurs and so avoid litigation at all, but, if litigation cannot be avoided, it eliminates what may be the very heavy

[79.] [1966] 1 W.L.R. 1428.
[80.] *Ibid*. at 1447.

legal costs of proving the loss actually sustained which would have to be paid by the unsuccessful party . . ."

In applying the discount rate, credit should be given to the finance lessor for initial expenses incurred in setting up the transaction in the first instance. Of course, these initial expenses will figure prominently in the first few payments of the lease. In this respect it would seem that a rebate on a straight apportionment may not do justice to the lessee, that is to treat the finance charged evenly over the period of the lease.

Equitable relief against forfeiture

Equity's jurisdiction to relieve against forfeiture of a lease in realty is well known. More problematical are other commercial transactions where the subject-matter of the forfeiture is an interest in personal property. In *Stockloser v. Johnson*[81] the plaintiff agreed to buy plant and machinery from the defendant and the contract provided that if any instalment paid under the contract was in default for more than 28 days then the defendant was given the right to rescind the contract, forfeit the instalments already paid and recover possession of the plant and machinery. The plaintiff brought an action for the return of all the instalments paid on the basis that their retention constituted a penalty and that he was entitled to equitable relief. On the facts the Court of Appeal refused him relief, although both Somerwell and Denning L.JJ. thought that in appropriate circumstances relief could be given, first, if the sum forfeited was out of all proportion to the damage; and secondly, that it would be unconscionable for the seller to retain the money. However, Romer L.J. in a strong dissenting opinion disagreed on the basis that whilst equity had always granted relief against fraud, undue influence or breach of a fiduciary relationship, it had never interfered with improvident bargains.

An expansive approach can be seen in some of the cases relating to equitable relief against forfeiture in personalty. Indeed in *Shiloh Spinners Ltd v. Harding*,[82] Lord Simon of Glaisdale maintained that equity has an unlimited and unfettered jurisdiction to relieve against contractual forfeiture and penalties, that is whilst the court may impose internal constraints to the exercise of its jurisdiction these are merely self-imposed. Nevertheless in subsequent cases, the courts have shown a marked unwillingness to apply equity's jurisdiction to commercial contracts and in *Scandinavian Trading Tanker Co. AB v. Flota Petrolera*

[81.] [1954] 1 Q.B. 476.
[82.] [1973] A.C. 691. See also *Mardorf Peach and Co. Ltd v. Attica Sea Carriers Corp. of Liberia; The Laconia; Afovos Shipping Co. SA v. R Pagnan and F Lli; The Afocos* [1980] 2 Lloyd's Rep. 469. An expansive view can also be seen in the majority judgments in the High Court of Australia in *Stern v. McArthur* (1988) 165 C.L.R. 489. See Goff and Jones, *The Law of Restitution* (4th ed., 1993), pp. 433–438.

Ecuatoriana; The Scaptrade,[83] Lord Diplock went so far as to say that Lord Simon's dictum in *Shiloh Spinners* was in fact a "beguiling heresy".[84] The scope of equity's jurisdiction was considered by Lord Diplock, and in his view it arose historically in the context of contracts involving the transfer of proprietary or possessory rights and that the insertion of the right to forfeit was essentially to secure the payment of money, for example, where the forfeiture clause was to secure the payment of rent due under a lease. The thrust of the reasoning of the House of Lords was that a time-charter (as opposed to a charter by demise) transferred to the charterers no interest in or right to possession of the vessel in question. On the contrary, it fell to be classified as a contract for services to be rendered to the charterer by the shipowner through the use of the vessel by the shipowners' own servants, acting in accordance with the directions contained in the charterparty. As such, it constituted a class of contract which historically had been denied the remedy of specific performance. Thus, to prohibit the shipowners from exercising their right of withdrawal of the vessel (by invoking an equitable jurisdiction to relieve from such forfeiture) would be to afford relief directly contrary to established principle which had consistently disclaimed any jurisdiction to grant specific performance in such a class of contract. On this basis, therefore, a time-charter fell to be distinguished from a lease of land. In this respect this was a case of advance hire payments and that as such this did not constitute a penalty.

The House of Lords decision in the *Scaptrade* case was followed in *Sport International Bussum BV v. Inter-Footwear Ltd*[85] where Lord Templeman said that there were recognised equitable boundaries and one such boundary related to claims for relief arising from the termination of contractual licences. In the Court of Appeal it was held that the availability of equitable relief was confined to cases where the subject-matter of the forfeiture was an interest in land. Indeed the Court of Appeal approach evinced a marked reluctance to enlarge equity's jurisdiction in commercial contracts outside realty on the basis of the importance of certainty in commercial transactions. However, a more expansive approach was adopted in *BICC plc v. Burndy Corp. and Another*,[86] where it was held that although relief was only available in respect of proprietary or possessory rights, this was not restricted to land but also extended to interests in personal property (in this case patent rights). Even so, the fact that forfeiture arises under a commercial contract is relevant as a matter of policy, especially the certainty issue, as to whether relief should be ordered. Nevertheless, in *Nutting v. Baldwin*[87] it was held that a provision under the rules of an association, formed for the purpose of co-ordinating and financing the prosecution of claims by

83. [1983] 2 A.C. 694.
84. *Ibid.* at 700.
85. [1984] 1 W.L.R. 776, H.L.
86. [1985] Ch. 232.
87. [1995] 2 All E.R. 321.

Lloyd's Names in respect of Lloyd's syndicates which provided that a member who failed to pay an additional subscription would be debarred from sharing in recoveries, was prima facie a forfeiture. The nature of the members interest was proprietary in nature in the form of a beneficial interest under the trust set up to share the fruits of recovery. Even so it was held that this was not a proper case where relief should be ordered because as Rattee J. said[88]:

"To allow a member who has not undertaken his share of the risk by paying his subscriptions on time to come in after the litigation has been successfully concluded, so that there is no longer any risk, and still share in the fruits of the litigation on payment of his overdue subscription would, in my judgment, undermine rather than attain the object of the forfeiture provision against which relief is sought, and indeed one of the fundamental objectives of the constitution of the association. This being so, whatever the individual circumstances of the defendants, and whatever the reasons for their default, it would in principle be wrong for the court to grant relief against forfeiture. However hard the result may bear on individual defaulting members they must, in my judgment, be held to the arrangement constituted by the rules of the association to which they expressly agreed when they signed their application to join the association."

It is now established that there is equitable jurisdiction to relieve against forfeiture of personal property,[89] and the issue is the extent of equity's jurisdiction in this context. This was considered in the case of *Goker v. NWS Bank plc*,[90] where it was held in the Court of Appeal that although the Court has jurisdiction to provide relief to the hirer of a chattel from forfeiture, such relief will only be exercised in exceptional circumstances, notably, where the vendor would not be significantly prejudiced by the granting of relief. In this case, the buyer purchased a car under a hire-purchase agreement on terms that he would pay a deposit of £10,000 and the balance of the purchase price (£35,000) in monthly instalments over 34 months. The buyer failed to meet the instalments and the finance company retook possession of the car. The buyer argued that if relief was not granted, the finance company stood to make an unexpected windfall if, in addition to retaining the sums already paid, they were able to dispose of the car and keep the proceeds. This submission was rejected on the basis that to oblige the owner to give up his contractual rights would be to visit upon the owner a greater risk than that contemplated when the contract was made. Furthermore, it was held that a necessary pre-condition to relief was readiness and willingness to pay off the arrears within the specified time and since the buyer had persistently failed to meet his obligation then it was inappropriate to grant relief in the light of these facts.

[88] *Ibid.* at 328–329.
[89] See, *e.g. Jobson v. Johnson* [1989] 1 All E.R. 621, where the issue involved the rule of shares in a football club where the vendors retained no legal or equitable interest in the shares.
[90] (1990) T.L.R. 393.

In *Transag Haulage (In Administrative Receivership) v. Leyland Daf Finance*,[91] it was held by Knox J. that in deciding whether to grant relief from forfeiture in respect of an option to purchase under a hire-purchase contract, the court would take into account whether the hirer had committed defaults in instalments payments, whether the grant of relief would cause financial loss to the owner, and whether the refusal of relief would result in a substantial windfall profit to the owner and cause the hirer a disproportionate loss. In this case the court granted relief against forfeiture and *Goker* was distinguished on the following bases: first, in *Goker* the windfall was 22 per cent in terms of realisation of assets whereas in *Leyland Daf* the windfall was 30 per cent; secondly, in *Goker* the hirer had been in repeated default and the granting of equitable relief in that case would have visited upon the owner a greater risk than that contemplated when the contract was made. In summary it would appear that equitable relief is available in commercial equipment lease contracts but only in exceptional cases, and the burden is upon the party in breach strictly to demonstrate that it would be unconscionable to retain the payment. Of course this is in addition to the well-recognised jurisdiction in equity to relieve against the payment of penalties. The classic dictum of Lord Wilberforce in *Shiloh Spinners* would appear to represent the current state of the law when his Lordship said[92]:

".. . it remains true today that equity expects men to carry out their bargains and will not let them buy their way out by uncovenanted payment. But it is consistent with these principles that we should reaffirm the right of courts of equity in appropriate and limited cases to relieve against forfeiture for breach of covenant or condition *where the primary object of the bargain is to secure a stated result which can effectively be attained when the matter comes before production of that result.* The word "appropriate" involves consideration of the conduct of the applicant for relief, in particular whether his default was wilful, of the gravity of the breaches, and of the disparity between the value of the property of which forfeiture is claimed as compared with the damage caused by the breach."

It should be noted that there has been statutory interference in relation to regulated consumer-hire agreements so that section 132(1) of the CCA 1974 provides:

"Where the owner under a regulated consumer hire agreement recovers possession of goods to which the agreement relates otherwise than by action, the hirer may apply to the court for an order that—

(a) the whole or part of any sum paid by the hirer to the owner in respect of the goods shall be repaid, and

(b) the obligation to pay the whole or part of any sum owed by the hirer to the owner in respect of the goods shall cease.

[91.] [1994] 2 B.C.L.C. 88.
[92.] [1973] A.C. 691 at 723. Emphasis added.

and if it appears to the court just to do so, having regard to the extent of the enjoyment of the goods by the hirer, the court shall grant the application in full or in part."

Similar powers are also conferred on the court in the case of where an owner brings an action for repossession as distinct from recapture of the goods.[93] It is important to note that the court has a discretion whether or not to grant relief, but in exercising this the court will not resort to outside formulae based, for example, upon the interest and administrative costs incurred by lessors but will consider solely the statutory test "the extent of the enjoyment of the goods by the hirer".[94] The court may not therefore make an order under this section merely because the owner on repossession sells the goods at a price which, when added with the hirer's payments, exceeds the original value of the owner's "investment" in the goods. The issue is whether the hirer's payment far exceeded the value to him of the use of the property by the date of termination of the agreement.[95]

It would appear that a genuine pre-estimate of loss on repudiatory breach will be upheld by the court as being just. Thus, in *Automotive Financial Services Ltd v. Henderson* (1992) the facts involved the lease by the plaintiffs of a car to the defendants for a period of 36 months under a regulated consumer-hire agreement. The original value of the car was £8,144. After six months the defendants refused to make further payments and returned the car having by that time paid a total of £2,150 in rentals. The plaintiffs terminated the agreement and sold the car for £6,000. The sheriff's court upheld an additional claim for £3,840 being the sum due from them on termination as liquidated damages. This sum represented the rentals in arrears plus the future rentals payable less a discount.

Sub-letting of the goods

The difficulties involved in quantifying damages will often lead the draftsman of the finance lease to include a right to sub-lease in the main leasing contract. This right to sub-lease will prima facie be limited to the duration of the main leasing agreement, unless the sub-hirer can establish that the finance lessor held out the lessee as being the owner, or as being authorised to sub-let for a period not limited to the main hiring agreement. Such a conclusion is unlikely in the light of the fact that the courts, at least in hire-purchase cases, have consistently held that the owner is not estopped from denying the hirer's authority to sell by mere delivery of possession, unless there is some representation which can be spelled out from the owner's conduct.[96] It normally follows

---

[93.] CCA 1974, s. 132(2).
[94.] See *Automotive Financial Services Ltd v. Henderson* 1992 S.L.T. (Sh.Ct.) 63.
[95.] *Galbraith v. Mitchenall Estates Ltd* [1965] Q.B. 473.
[96.] *Lloyds and Scottish Finance Ltd v. Williamson* [1965] 1 W.L.R. 404.

that the termination of the main leasing agreement will automatically terminate the sub-lease. Indeed, if the sub-hirer refuses to deliver up possession he may be sued for "wrongful interference" by virtue of section 3 of the Torts (Interference with Goods) Act 1977.

Clearly, the finance lessor will be interested in continuing the sub-lease on the insolvency of the lessee. The alternative of repossession will be costly, and full recovery of damages under a minimum payment clause or otherwise may be impossible where there are insufficient funds. The lessor will often release the goods on different terms to those in the original lease in order to satisfy the needs of the new lessee. Determining the fair market value of the lease in order to award market price damages will be extremely difficult when the only evidence of the secondary market value is the release itself. Some leases set forth the anticipated value of the goods at given periods during the lease and provide that the lessee should have a credit against future rentals for the depreciation saved by early cancellation. If the figures in these schedules represent bona fide approximations of the actual values, such clauses should be upheld.

The assignment of the benefit of the lease, for example the rights of the lessee under the sub-lease including the right to terminate or to accept termination by the sub-lessee, will only bind the lessee's liquidator if it was made before the commencement of the compulsory winding-up of the company.[97] Such an assignment to the finance lessor of the sub-rentals due could be categorised as a charge of the lessee's book debts which will be void as against the liquidator unless registered.[98]

Leasing and the Consumer Credit Act 1974

Introduction

It is necessary to briefly consider the impact of the Consumer Credit Act 1974 (the CCA 1974). Detailed discussion of the elaborate administration and legal provisions as they relate to seeking business, the form and content of the regulated agreement, withdrawal from the agreement, are beyond the scope of this book.[99] In any case, both the Government and the Office of Fair Trading agree that all business hiring and lending should be removed from the Act as part of the deregulation initiative.[1] One consequence of this would be that such lending would be freed from the tight controls currently imposed on the form and contents of credit. The suggestion is that the exemption from regulation would

---

[97.] *Cf. Re Atlantic Computers Systems plc* [1992] Ch. 505. See Chap. 13, below.
[98.] Companies Act 1985, s. 396(1)(e).
[99.] See Harding *Consumer Credit and Consumer Hire Law: A Practical Guide* (1995).
[1.] See *Releasing Enterprise* (Cmnd. 512). A draft Order to this effect was laid before Parliament on January 27, 1997.

apply where the debtor of hirer holds himself out as requiring the goods or facilities wholly or predominantly for business purposes. It is suggested that deregulation in this sphere could provide sole traders and partnerships with access to finance or facilities, the availability of which is currently deterred or constrained by lenders' and lessors' unwillingness or reluctance to make regulated agreements.

The Ambit of the Consumer Credit Act 1974

The CCA 1974 applies to regulated credit agreements. In order to satisfy this, four conditons must be satisfied:

1. The transaction must have been entered into on or after April 1, 1977.[2]

2. The debtor must be an individual, not a company.[3]

3. The amount of credit given must not exceed £15,000.[4] The credit here denotes not the total amount the debtor has to pay but the element of financial accommodation. The relevant formula would appear to be:

    Credit = Total price — any deposit payable (s. 189(1) + the total charge for credit (s. 9(4)).

    In seeking to define what items are to be included as part of the total charge for credit, section 20 emphasises that what matters is the cost to the debtor rather than the net return to the lender.[5] In the case of hire-purchase transactions, hire rent is treated as credit by virtue of section 9(3) of the CCA 1974.[6]

4. It must not be an exempt transaction. A number of agreements otherwise falling within the ambit of the CCA 1974 are exempted under section 16 of the Act. Most of these relate to mortgages of land and are of no concern here. However, two types of exempt agreements are of significance. The first is in relation to debtor-creditor-supplier agreements where the amount owed is to be paid off in a few instalments. Thus, the Consumer Credit (Exempt Agreements) Order 1980[7] (as amended) which implements section 16(5)(a) of the CCA 1974, provides, in the case of

---

[2.] Consumer Credit Act 1974 (Commencement No. 2) Order 1977, S.I. 1977 No. 325.
[3.] CCA 1974, s. 8(1).
[4.] Consumer Credit (Increase of Monetary Limits) Order 1983, S.I. 1983 No. 1878.
[5.] See Directive 90/88 and also Consumer Credit (Total Charge for Credit) Regulations 1980, S.I. 1980 No. 1, Pt. 2 (as amended).
[6.] See CCA 1974, Sched. 2, Example 10.
[7.] S.I. 1980 No. 52.

fixed-sum credit, that the agreement is exempt if no more than four payments are involved, whereas, in the case of running-account credit, exemption is provided if full settlement is made at the end of each period of account. The same statutory instrument implements section 16(5)(b) which exempts debtor-creditor agreements on the basis of the rate of interest charged. Following on from this, a debtor-creditor agreement will be exempted if the annual percentage rate does not exceed the higher of either 13 per cent or one per cent more than the base rates of lending banks.

Termination of Regulated Consumer Hire Agreements

The 1974 Act is concerned with consumer hire agreements, which consist of agreements made by a person with an individual for the bailment of goods which is not a hire-purchase agreement, and is capable of subsisting for more than three months. "Individual" is defined in section 189(1) as including "a partnership or other unincorporated body of persons not consisting entirely of bodies corporate". It follows that the CCA 1974 applies wherever the debtor is not a body corporate and would presumably apply to an unincorporated club, or charity, or trade union, or small business. Significantly the Government decided to amend the Act to take small businesses outside its ambit.[8] In any case, very many commercial leasing arrangements will usually involve sums over £15,000 which is outside the current credit limit for the application of the CCA 1974.[9]

Some treatment of the Act is required in relation to the exercise by the lessor of any remedies under the lease contract. The exercise of the creditor's remedies are covered by the Act irrespective of the different forms of hiring agreement, for example, leasing, hire, contract hire, or rental, and any distinctions between them are regarded as purely functional and having little legal significance. Thus, a provision in the lease that the full balance shall immediately become payable is covered by section 76 of the Act which requires seven days' notice in the prescribed form to be given by the owner to the hirer. By virtue of section 87(1), service of a default notice in accordance with section 88 is necessary before the owner can become entitled, following a breach by the debtor or hirer, to terminate the agreement or to demand earlier payment of any sum and recover the goods.

One of the most worrying aspects of the CCA 1974, from the equipment lessor's point of view, could have been the provision in section 101(1) enabling the hirer under a regulated consumer-hire agreement to terminate the agreement by giving notice after 18 months.

[8] (1987) 42 CC5/24.
[9] Consumer Credit (Increase of Monetary Limits) Order 1983, S.I. 1983 No. 1878, Art. 8(2).

debtor may seek relief from the courts, where a time order may be granted in situations considered by the court to be just. In the case of hire-purchase and conditional-sale agreements, a time order can reschedule all remaining instalments so that it will not be confined to those instalments which have fallen due.[23] Additionally, the court may make a transfer order dividing the goods between the debtor and the creditor. Section 133 contains special rules to compensate the creditor for having to accept the return of used goods.

The consumer credit agreement may contain provisions relating to termination on death or insolvency. In these situations, the general rule still pertains so that no action can be taken without the giving of seven days' notice.[24] The position on death is that the creditor must obtain a court order before taking action, but no action may be taken if the agreement is fully secured. Unfortunately, the distinction between fully secured and partly secured or unsecured is not defined under the Act. Section 189 defines "security" as follows:

"'security', in relation to an actual or prospective consumer credit agreement or consumer hire agreement, or any linked transaction, means a mortgage, charge, pledge, bond, debenture, indemnity, guarantee, bill, note or other right provided by the debtor or hirer, or at his request (express or implied), to secure the carrying out of the obligations of the debtor or hirer under the agreement . . ."

It is difficult to determine from this whether a hire-purchase contract constitutes a "fully secured" agreement. Although the creditor in this circumstance has the right to the return of his goods, has this right been "provided by the debtor"? It would appear that an agreement is "fully secured" if the debtor gives the creditor the right to take possession of the goods upon the termination of the agreement.

Section 93 of the CCA 1974 prevents a debtor under a regulated consumer credit agreement from being obliged to pay interest on sums which, in breach of the agreement, are unpaid by him at a rate exceeding the rate payable on the principal apart from any default.[25] However, section 93(b) provides that interest may be charged on interest due but unpaid at a rate not exceeding the rate payable on the principal apart from any default. It should be noted that a provision to the effect that on default of making one instalment the whole amount of the principal and interest unpaid becomes accelerated, these are not sums which are unpaid in breach of the agreement and therefore the interest may be increased on them. Of course this does not prevent such an acceleration of payment and interest as being categorised as a penalty.[26] Nonetheless the provision for rebate on early settlement under section 94 of the CCA

[23.] CCA 1974, s. 130(2).
[24.] CCA 1974, s. 76.
[25.] CCA 1974, s. 93(a).
[26.] See *Wadham Stringer Finance Ltd v. Meaney* [1981] 1 W.L.R. 39.

1974 and especially the "rule of 78" made pursuant to the Consumer Credit (Rebate on Early Settlement) Regulations[27] may prevent it from being penal.[28] Furthermore, outside of the CCA 1974 context, there is no reason in principle why a contractual provision, the effect of which is to increase the consideration payable under an executory contract upon the happening of a default, should be struck down as a penalty if the increase could in the circumstances be explained as commercially justifiable, provided that its dominant purpose was not to deter the other party from breach; that is where "the dominant function was *in terrorem* the borrower".[29]

Repossession

Repossession, as the most dramatic illustration of self-help exercised by the creditor, is rigorously controlled by the CCA 1974 with regard to regulated hire or hire-purchase or conditional-sale agreements. Thus section 92(1) provides:

> "Except under an order of the court, the creditor or owner shall not be entitled to enter any premises to take possession of goods subject to a regulated hire purchase agreement, regulated conditional sale agreement or regulated consumer hire agreement."

Further protection is afforded under such an agreement where the debtor has paid one-third or more of the total price of the goods where this is relevant. Following this circumstance, the goods are considered to be "protected goods", and can only be repossessed by an order of the court. In determining the one-third rule, special provision is made under section 90(2) for compulsory installation charges so that one-third of the total price is construed for this purpose as the aggregate of the installation charge and one-third of the remainder of the total price. Special provision is also seen in the case of successive linked agreements so that where the first agreement falls within section 90, both the old and new goods will fall within this section regardless of any amount paid.

A severe sanction attaches to wrongful repossession; the agreement is terminated under section 91 of the CCA 1974 and the debtor can recover all the money he had paid out under it. However, "protected goods" status is lost if the debtor has exercised his right of termination under section 90(5), or has consented to repossession at the time of recaption.[30] To be effective, the debtor should be informed what his rights would be if he refused consent.[31] If the debtor has abandoned the goods, the

---

[27.] S.I. 1983 No. 1562.
[28.] See *Forward Trust plc v. Robinson* [1987] C.C.L.R. 10.
[29.] See *Lordsvale Finance plc v. Bank of Zambia* [1996] 2 All E.R. 156.
[30.] *Cf.* CCA 1974, s. 173(3).
[31.] *Chartered Trust v. Pitcher* [1987] R.T.R. 72.

creditor can seize them without contravening section 90 because he will not have seized them "from the debtor". This can be illustrated in *Bentinck v. Cromwell Engineering Co.*,[32] a case under the equivalent provision of section 90 in the Hire-Purchase Act 1965. In this case the debtor, after having paid the deposit and a few instalments, badly damaged the vehicle in question and the credit payments fell into arrears. The car was left in a garage, but the debtor did not give orders to repair it. The finance company traced the car and sought to contact the debtor who had by then disappeared. After nine months, the finance company took the car and it was held that it had been abandoned by the debtor. It should be noted that the protection of possession anticipated under section 90 is limited to the debtor, or his assignee, or authorised bailee, since the goods will be deemed to be in the debtor's possession. It follows that such protection does not extend to a sub-buyer.[33]

It is worth noting the powerful effect of section 132 of the CCA 1974. This enables the court to order total or partial repayment of rentals to the hirer and release the hirer from all or part of any future liability under the agreement in any case where the hirer repossesses the goods, or obtains an order for their return, whether this results from termination by the owner for the hirer's default or termination by the hirer himself. In addition, the court has a wide discretion as to time orders under sections 129 and 130 of the CCA 1974, where no limitation is imposed on the court in allowing time for repayment by the hirer so long as the time does not go beyond the contract period of hire.

Extortionate agreements

Extortionate agreements lies at the very heart of the CCA 1974. Indeed, sections 137–140, apply whether or not the agreement is regulated for the purposes of the Act. The court is empowered, on application by the debtor or surety, to reopen an extortionate credit agreement and the burden of proving the contrary is placed upon the creditor.[34] The jurisdiction may only be invoked with regard to a credit agreement which is defined in section 137(2)(a) as "any agreement between an individual (the "debtor") and any other person (the "creditor") by which the creditor provides the debtor with credit of any amount". It is obvious from this that consumer hire agreements will be excluded.

There is no means of comparing rental charges under regulated consumer hire agreements equivalent to the APR in relation to credit agreements. There is also no statutory limit upon the rental charges

---

[32.] [1971] 1 Q.B. 324.
[33.] See *Bentinck v. Cromwell Engineering Co.* [1971] 1 Q.B. 324.
[34.] CCA 1974, s. 171(7).

corresponding to the extortionate credit bargain provisions found in section 139(2) of the Act.[35]

[35.] CCA 1974, s. 139(2) provides as follows:

"In reopening the agreement, the court may, for the purpose of relieving the debtor or a surety from payment of any sum in excess of that fairly due and reasonable, by order—

(a) direct accounts to be taken, or (in Scotland) an accounting to be made between any persons;

(b) set aside the whole or part of any obligation imposed on the debtor or surety by the credit bargain or any related agreement;

(c) require the creditor to repay the whole or part of any sum paid under the credit bargain or any related agreement by the debtor or a surety, whether paid to the creditor or any other person;

(d) direct the return to the surety of any property provided for the purposes of the security; or

(e) alter the terms of the credit agreement or any security instrument."

An order may be made under the above irrespective of the fact that it places "a burden on the creditor in respect of an advantage unfairly enjoyed by another person who is a party to a linked transaction" (s. 139(3)).

Chapter 4

Finance House and Dealer Legal Relations

Given the level of dealer defaults, in terms of their obligations to the finance houses and also the level of dealer insolvencies, it is surprising that there are relatively few reported cases. The main legal relationships will now be considered.

Contractual Relationship

Introduction

The relationship between the dealer and the finance lessor is one of seller and buyer, and it follows that the agreement will be regulated by the Sale of Goods Act 1979 (the SGA 1979). The supply arrangements in the case of on-going contractual commitments will be supplemented by provisions in a master agreement, notably, a form of guarantee or indemnity. The master agreement will make the raising of an invoice a compulsory method of trade between the dealer and the finance company, that is, the invoice will constitute an offer for sale to the finance house. The object of the master agreement is to set out the terms and conditions on which the finance company is prepared to accept hire-purchase and lease transactions introduced by the dealer. Typically the agreement will stipulate the range of goods by reference to type and cost which the finance house is prepared to accept, although it will always reserve the right not to accept the goods. The master agreement will set out the way in which a dealer is to present a transaction, for example, by raising an invoice in a certain form. There may also be provisions to the effect that the dealer is not to make any representations to the prospective hirer on behalf of the finance company, and that there is no power to vary the standard terms and conditions of the agreement. Furthermore, the master agreement will lay down the limits of collection of money on its behalf by limiting this (usually) to the deposit payable.

The Application of the Sale of Goods Act 1979

Acceptance of goods by the finance house

The implied terms have been discussed elsewhere.[1] In this context the problem lies with the peculiar position of the finance house and also the

---

[1] See Chap. 3, above.

bar to rejection of the goods, because it is not the practice of finance houses to examine goods which they buy for letting out on hire or hire-purchase. Acceptance is an interrelating rule to the right of examination of the goods provided by section 34 of the SGA 1979, but in the absence of this the SGA 1979 specifies three types of conduct as constituting acceptance, namely, (1) express acceptance, (2) lapse of time; or (3) inconsistent act with the ownership of the seller. It is only in the latter case that problems have emerged.

It is difficult to understand what is meant by an act "inconsistent with the ownership of the seller". If the property has passed to the buyer, this can only mean an act which is inconsistent with the reversionary interest of the seller.[2] The commonest example here would be sub-sale by the buyer.[3] However, it is important not to be dogmatic as it is difficult to see how the original seller's reversionary interest would be prejudiced, even on sub-sale, where the sub-buyer rejected the goods. Essentially, it is a question of fact to be decided in each case as to what sort of use the buyer has made of the goods, and then relating this to the seller's continuing reversionary interest, for example, by pledging or hiring out or mortgaging the goods. In *E. Hardy and Co. v. Hillerns and Fowler*,[4] it was held in the Court of Appeal that there was an act inconsistent with the seller's ownership when the buyers took delivery of part of a cargo and sent it to the sub-buyers. As a matter of principle, it is questionable whether the buyer should have lost his right to reject in this situation as he could have restored the goods to the seller.

There are two main strands of authority. The first relates to where the buyer has destroyed, damaged or used the goods or incorporated them into another product so that they could not be returned to the seller in good order. The second strand is where the buyer has acted in such a way as to show that he did not intend to reject the goods, notably by delivering them to a third party following a sub-sale. The SGA 1979 as amended deals with the latter and in the same way acceptance is not deemed to have taken place simply by virtue of asking or agreeing to a repair of goods. Section 35(6) provides:

> "The buyer is not by virtue of this section deemed to have accepted the goods merely because—
>
> (a) he asks for, or agrees to, their repair by or under an arrangement with the seller, or
>
> (b) the goods are delivered to another under a sub-sale or other disposition."

In this way an informal cure mechanism can be found in the amended SGA.

---

[2] *Kwei Tek Chao v. British Traders and Shippers Ltd* [1954] 2 Q.B. 459.
[3] See *Graanhandel T. Vink v. European Grain* [1989] 2 Lloyd's Rep. 531.
[4] [1993] 2 K.B. 490.

If the buyer is unable to restore the goods in substantially the same condition as when they were delivered, this can be considered inconsistent with the interest of the seller. Moreover, if the goods are damaged, albeit accidentally by the buyer, he will be precluded from rejecting the goods on the basis that *restitutio in integrum* is not possible which, as a common law bar to rejection, is specifically preserved by section 62(2) of the SGA 1979. On the other hand, where the goods are damaged without the fault of either the seller or buyer, the latter does have a prima facie right to reject. The issue is one of risk, and it would seem, following *Head v. Tattersall*,[5] that the risk of loss in this circumstance falls on the seller.

Express warranties or representations by dealer

The implied terms under the SGA 1979 will be supplemented by express terms in the master agreement or in the dealer's offer for sale, notably, the information with respect to the goods, and also the lessee or hirer, is true and that all legal formalities have been fully observed. Often the dealer will make representations in relation to the goods, the object of the sale, and it is a question of fact whether such a representation has become a term in the contract. Problems have arisen where the dealer has made false representations in relation to the deposit paid for the goods or about the goods themselves, notably the age and condition of them which, of course, will go to the issue of description.[5a]

The representation as a statement of fact which induced the finance house into the financing contract is not strictly speaking a promise. As such, the falsity of the representation cannot, in the absence of a collateral contract, give rise to an action for damages for breach of contract. Where a misrepresentation is fraudulent at common law, then damages may be recovered in the tort of deceit. The aim of, and award of, damages in deceit is to put the plaintiff in the position which he would have been in had the tort not been committed.[6] In addition, all damage directly flowing from the fraudulent inducement will be recoverable, and although such damage need not be foreseeable it must have been directly caused by this deceit.[6a] In the case of negligent misrepresentation, at common law damages are awarded which put the plaintiff in the position he would have been in had the tort not been committed. The representor will be liable for all losses which are a reasonably foreseeable consequence of the misrepresentation.[7] If the representee has also been at fault, then the damages payable may be reduced on the grounds of contributory negligence.[8]

[5] (1871) L.R. 7 Ex. 7.
[5a] See Chap. 3 at pp. 64–69, above.
[6] *Doyle v. Olby* [1969] 2 Q.B. 158.
[6a] *Smith New Court Securities Ltd v. Scrimgeour Vickers (Asset Management) Ltd* [1996] 4 All E.R. 769.
[7] *The Wagon Mound (No. 1)* A.C. 388.
[8] Law Reform (Contributory Negligence) Act 1945, s. 1; *Gran Gelato Ltd v. Richcliff (Group) Ltd* [1992] Ch. 560.

Historically it is notoriously difficult to prove fraudulent misrepresentation.[9] In *Hedley Byrne and Co. Ltd v. Heller and Partners*,[10] the House of Lords recognised that there could be liability in tort for negligent misrepresentation dependent upon the establishment of a duty of care between the parties. Where the negligent misrepresentation induces a contract between the parties, it will probably be more advantageous to proceed under the Misrepresentation Act 1967 which allows rescission even if the misrepresentation has become a term of the contract (section 1(a)) and notwithstanding that the contract has been fully performed (section 1(b)). Moreover, the 1967 Act reverses the onus of proof upon the maker of a non-fraudulent misrepresentation to disprove the negligence,[11] and such a misrepresentation cannot be excluded or limited except in so far as this is reasonable.[12]

Section 2(1) and (2) of the Misrepresentation Act 1967 also make provision for the recovery of damages for misrepresentation. The measure of damages under section 2(1) is to put the plaintiff in the position which he would have been in had the representation not been made. Damages are assessed as if the representor had been fraudulent[13] so that the remoteness rules applicable are those pertaining to the tort of deceit, not the tort of negligence. It has also been held that damages payable under section 2(1) may be reduced on the basis of the representee's contributory negligence.[14] This approach does seem somewhat incongruous since in *Royscot* it was held that the appropriate analogy was with the tort of deceit, where contributory negligence does not apply.[15] However, it is worth noting that even in respect of the tort of deceit the issue of causation is relevant and the plaintiff will have to take reasonable steps to mitigate his loss once the fraud is discovered.[16]

It is worth elaborating upon the facts of *Royscot Trust* in greater detail. The plaintiff finance company was induced to enter into a hire-purchase transaction with Mr Rogerson as a result of a misrepresentation by the defendant car dealers. As the defendants knew, it was the plaintiffs' policy not to enter into a hire-purchase transaction unless 20 per cent of the purchase price of a car was paid to the dealer by the customer. Mr Rogerson agreed with the defendants to put down a deposit of £1,200 on a car, the price of which was £7,600; but that produced a deposit of only some 16 per cent of the purchase price. So the defendants falsely stated

---

[9] See *Derry v. Peek* (1889) 14 App. Cas. 337; *Thomas Witter Ltd v. TBP Industries Ltd* [1996] 2 All E.R. 573.

[10] [1964] A.C. 465.

[11] Misrepresentation Act 1967, s. 2(1).

[12] Misrepresentation Act 1967, s. 3.

[13] See *Royscot Trust Ltd v. Rogerson* [1991] 2 Q.B. 297.

[14] See *Gran Gelato Ltd v. Richcliff (Group) Ltd* [1992] Ch. 560.

[15] See *Alliance and Leicester Building Society v. Edgestop Ltd* [1994] 2 All E.R. 38.

[16] See *Smith New Court Securities Ltd v. Scrimgeour Vickers (Asset Management) Ltd and Another* (1996) *ibid*.

that the price of the car was £8,000 and that Mr Rogerson had paid a deposit of £1,600; thus producing the required 20 per cent deposit. Somewhat surprisingly there was no allegation that the defendants were guilty of fraud in making these amendments and the case proceeded on the basis that the defendants had not been fraudulent. The court held that the action of Mr Rogerson in dishonestly selling the car was a direct result of the defendants' misrepresentation, in the sense that there was no break in the chain of causation between the misrepresentation and the loss. The plaintiffs were therefore entitled to recover damages of £3,625, namely the difference between the £6,400 they advanced to Mr Rogerson and the instalments of £2,775 they received from him before his default. The practical effect of this decision is that it reduces the significance of the tort of deceit because the same measure of damages is available under section 2(1), where it is not necessary to prove deceit and neither is it even necessary to prove that the representor was negligent.

At common law the traditional rule was that damages were not available for innocent misrepresentations. This strict approach has been mitigated by section 2(2) of the Misrepresentation Act 1967, so that courts now have a discretion to award damages in lieu of rescission. It provides:

"Where a person has entered into a contract after a misrepresentation has been made to him otherwise than fraudulently, and he would be entitled, by reason of the misrepresentation, to rescind the contract, then it if is claimed, in any proceedings arising out of the contract, that the contract ought to be or has been rescinded, the court or arbitrator may declare the contract subsisting and award damages in lieu of rescission, if of the opinion that it would be equitable to do so, having regard to the nature of the misrepresentation and the loss that would be caused by it if the contract were upheld, as well as to the loss that rescission would cause to the other party."

The power to award damages under section 2(2) does not, however, depend on the right to rescind still being extant but on the plaintiff having had such a right in the past. The fact that rescission is no *longer* a viable remedy is no bar to the award of damages under section 2(2).[17] The right to rescind will be lost where *restitutio in integrum* is impossible either through lapse of time[18] or, more likely, an innocent third-party interest would be adversely affected, in this case that of the hirer.

The principal weakness of the rescission remedy and the statutory alternative of damages in lieu of rescission, is that they do not provide for consequential loss, for example, profits on resale. Even though equity together with rescission gives an indemnity, this is limited in scope to cover only expenditure *necessarily* incurred as a result of entering into the contract.[19] In order to get full compensation the buyer will have to

[17.] *Thomas Witter Ltd v. TBP Industries Ltd* (see n.9, above).
[18.] See *Leaf v. International Galleries* [1950] 2 K.B. 86.
[19.] *Whittington v. Seale-Hayne* (1900) 82 L.T. 49.

look to tort, as in the case of fraudulent misrepresentation, or sue for breach of contract. It would seem from this that the issue of whether the representation has become a term of the contract cannot be avoided, especially if the buyer seeks compensation for loss of profits since expectation damages are linked to breach of contract.[20] Even so, it should be noted that section 2(3) of the 1967 Act provides that damages may be awarded under section 2(2) against a person who is also liable under section 2(1) "but where he is so liable any award under the said subsection (2) shall be taken into account in assessing his liability under the said subsection (1)". It would follow from this that the award of damages under section 2(2) is meant to be less than that under section 2(1). A possible rationale for this is that the deceit rule of remoteness governs section 2(1) whilst damages are limited by the more restrictive contract rule of remoteness under section 2(2). It would appear, therefore, that an innocent misrepresentation under section 2(2) would limit liability to the amount by which the actual value was less than the price, while in the case of a negligent misrepresentation there would, in addition, be liability for consequential loss under section 2(1).

Recourse to Dealer Provisions in Supply Contracts

Introduction

Typically a recourse provision is where the master agreement provides for recourse against the dealer for loss suffered under the leasing arrangement. Such a recourse provision may also be included in a distinct document where big ticket deals are concerned, that is, in relation to specific contracts relating to specific items of equipment. There are two types of recourse provision: first, a buy-back obligation; secondly, an indemnity by the dealer for the loss sustained by the finance house for a failure by the lessee to pay the minimum amount due.

Buy-back obligations

The main difficulty with the repurchase obligation for the finance house is the necessity of re-delivering the equipment to the dealer—or at least there must be an undertaking from the finance house that the goods are both in existence and are capable of being recovered otherwise the transaction will fail for lack of consideration.[21] Furthermore, time is an important issue as the finance company may be deemed to have waived its right to force the repurchase obligation if it has held on to the goods for an unreasonable length of time following repossession.[22] If the dealer

[20.] See *William Sindall v. Cambridgeshire C.C.* [1994] 1 W.L.R. 1016.
[21.] See *Watling Trust Ltd v. Briffault Range Co. Ltd* [1938] 1 All E.R. 525.
[22.] See *United Dominion Trust (Commercial) Ltd v. Eagle Aircraft Services Ltd* [1968] 1 All E.R. 104.

is under an obligation, by virtue of the recourse obligation, to repossess the equipment, he recovers possession of them as agent of the finance company and not as seller under the original contract of sale, and he cannot therefore pass a good title in them as a *seller* in possession.[23]

Guarantee by way of indemnity for loss

A guarantee by way of indemnity for loss is one of the most common forms of recourse clause, that is, the finance house will have recourse against the dealer in the event of hirer or lessee default or failure for any reason to complete the agreement. Upon making the payment the dealer will then be subrogated to the rights of the finance house under the agreement. The finance company has no duty to the dealer in respect of the goods beyond that owed by a creditor to a guarantor so that if without the fault of the finance company the goods have been lost or destroyed no question of failure of consideration arises. It is otherwise, of course, if, as a matter of contract, there is an unqualified obligation on the finance house to hand over the goods. As such, much depends upon the wording of the recourse agreement. A breach of contract by the finance house will not normally entitle the dealer to disclaim liability, although damages suffered can be set-off against any claim made by the finance house. If the equipment subject to the lease is destroyed whilst being in the lessee's possession, it is likely that the lessor's inability to deliver the equipment will sound in damages, but these will only be nominal. This is because of the nature of the indemnity, which is an underwriting risk and will relate to individual transactions. In this situation the dealer recourse arrangement is framed in terms of an indemnity against loss rather than, for example, guaranteeing the obligations of the lessee. One important consequence of this is that the extent of the dealer's liability is not limited to a particular lessee in respect of whom the indemnity is given. Furthermore, since the basis of the dealer's liability is on the happening of an event (non-payment) which has taken place, it is not open to the dealer to claim that the amount outstanding is a penalty and neither is it necessary for the finance house to have given credit for the proceeds of sale of the repossessed goods (in the absence of a contrary agreement), because the nature of this indemnity is structured in such a way to cover the loss suffered in the transaction.

Terms in Favour of Dealer

The terms in favour of dealers, broadly relate to authorising the dealer to deliver the goods to the lessee and also guarantee payment by the finance house. Normally the dealer is deemed to be the finance house's agent in terms of acceptance of any deposit paid, as the finance house will merely advance the balance.

[23] Sale of Goods Act 1979, s. 24.

The lessee as the financier's agent

This may be the case where there is an established commercial relationship between the lessee and the financier. The extent of the lessee's authority will be determined by the terms of the agreement, although, of course, the finance house will be bound by the principle of apparent authority and in this situation the finance house will be entitled to be indemnified against any loss or expenses it has incurred. Since the agency is disclosed, title in the equipment will pass directly to the lessor (financier).

Purchase by lessee as apparent principal

The undisclosed principal rules developed in agency law will apply and, as a consequence, there is apparently no limit to the lessee's powers. Furthermore title to the equipment will pass to the lessee on the basis of estoppel or mercantile agency and the latter will, therefore, have the *power* but not the *right* to pass title in the equipment.[24] In this situation the lessee will acquire ownership in the equipment from the dealer and in order for this to be transferred to the finance house as principal, three conditions must be fulfilled: first, the equipment must be identified; secondly, the lessee as agent must intend to pass title; and thirdly, there must be an act of unconditional appropriation, that is, a confirmation of the agent's mandate which will occur where the lessee has formerly executed the equipment lease. If there is a coalition between all the three elements identified above, there is no moment in time where the lessee's ownership is unencumbered so that the effect of the sale to the agent is to feed title in the equipment simultaneously to the finance house. As a result there should be no potential exposure to the agent's bankruptcy.

The capacity in which the lessee as agent acts depends upon the agreement between them. Normally the mandate to transfer title will be based upon an agency duty,[25] and, as such, the agent will have a lien on the equipment for any commission or expenses incurred.[26] If the agent fails to deliver, then the finance house will have a claim for breach of duty to the extent of the loss suffered.[27]

Novation

Novation has been discussed in Chapter 3, above.

Where the dealer takes equipment in part-exchange

The dealer does not hold the part-exchange goods as an agent of the finance company. The nature of the transaction is a sale of the part-

[24.] *Cf. Barber v. NWS Bank plc* [1996] 1 All E.R. 906.
[25.] See *Ireland v. Livingstone* (1872) L.R. 5 H.L. 395.
[26.] See Sale of Goods Act 1979, s. 38(2).
[27.] See *Cassaboglou v. Gibb* (1883) 11 Q.B.D. 797.

exchange goods to the dealer for the amount of the allowance, and the latter may pay over this amount or part of it to the prospective lessee as a mechanism for releasing capital in the equipment. On the other hand, the dealer may hold this sum as part of the deposit or pre-payments necessary under the lease agreement. From the finance companies perspective the dealer is holding a cash sum. This point emerges graphically in Lord Upjohn's dictum in *Branwhite v. Worcester Works Finance Ltd*[28] when his Lordship said in relation to the part-exchange transaction in that case:

> "Then the parties negotiated about the price of the car to be taken in part exchange. The hirer wants to get as much for his old car as he can; the dealer wants to obtain a price which will ensure to him, so far as he can, a reasonable profit when he resells it. They are both negotiating as principals and settling the price which the dealer will in account pay the hirer for the car. What has the finance company to do with this transaction? Absolutely nothing at all. In many cases (whether that was the truth in this case or not the evidence does not disclose, for the simple reason that the finance company called no evidence) the finance company will be in complete ignorance whether the sum stated in the proposal for the hire-purchase finance as the initial instalment of hire-rent is in fact represented by a motor car taken in part exchange or by a cash deposit or partly the one and partly the other."

If the prospective lessee fails to deliver the equipment, the conventional position is that prior to delivery there has been no sale of the equipment because all the dealer has done in offering to take in part exchange is to give the prospective lessee the option to pay the deposit or part of it by part exchange of goods.

Where the lease transaction does not materialise, the narrow legal issue centres around liability in respect of the part-exchange goods especially if they have been delivered to the dealer. Much will depend upon the intention of the parties. There are three possibilities:

1. **Unconditional sale:** this would not link the part-exchange element with the entry into the lease and in this respect the dealer would be obliged to pay over the agreed cash sum to the owner.

2. **The equipment lease as a condition precedent:** the effect of this is that if the lease does not materialise then the condition necessary to trigger the sale to the dealer has not been effected. If there has been a disposition by the dealer of the goods, it is likely that title will pass to a third party by virtue of the fact that the dealer will be categorised as someone who has "agreed to buy goods" for the purposes of section 9 of the Factors Act 1889 and section 25(1) of the Sale of Goods Act 1979. If there is no time limit stipulated for the entry into the lease agreement, it is

[28.] [1969] 1 A.C. 552 at 561.

probable that the court would infer that the part-exchange contract was only intended to remain operative on the basis that the condition precedent would be fulfilled within a reasonable time.

3. **Sale of goods and a condition subsequent:** this provides an option for the previous owner to recover the goods if the lease contract fails to materialise. This is a contractual option and does not have any proprietary consequences as to third parties because the dealer will be free to deal with the part-exchange goods until rescission.

Block Discounting

Introduction

Block discounting is a financing technique which allows a dealer to unfreeze capital tied up in hire agreements or other types of deferred payment including hire purchase. The mechanism allows the dealer to offer for sale, usually in pursuance of a master agreement, to a finance company block finance agreements. Included in this offer for sale will be a schedule setting out the agreements and also showing the balance outstanding on each agreement, including the time remaining on each of them. The finance company, on the basis of risk assessment, would acquire the agreements remitting a percentage of the total outstanding under the agreements minus a discount. In addition the finance company will keep a significant percentage (25 per cent) by way of security which it will release to the dealer on collection. A block discounting arrangement can be with notice or without, the latter being a form of confidential invoice discounting. In this latter situation there is no formal assignment, which has the advantage of avoiding *ad valorem* stamp duty (the agreement to assign is executory), although there will normally be in the master agreement a power of attorney in the finance company's favour whereby the dealer appoints the finance house as the dealer's attorney for the purpose of executing any necessary assignment in the name of the dealer.

A block discounting arrangement is not without dangers for the finance house, especially if on a confidential basis where there has been no notification the finance house is "trumped" by a subsequent assignee.[29] It is for this reason that the master agreement will usually seek an indemnity from the dealer for any losses and also any other security which the dealer can offer. This is important because whilst the dealer will collect the rentals due as agent for the finance house, the obligation to account is not related to specific transactions but to the

---

[29.] *Dearle v. Hall* (1828) 2 Russ. 1.

block and is usually accommodated by a series of bills of exchange for equal amounts at specific intervals. The guarantee by way of indemnity is only triggered when the bills have matured and have not been honoured. In addition, if the hirer terminates the agreement either on default or by exercising his right to terminate, for example under the Consumer Credit Act 1974, in this situation the master agreement will usually include an undertaking on the part of the dealer to make good any deficiency which arises.

Block Discounting: the Legal Structure

The sale of receivables

The fact that the nature of the transaction, from an economic functionalist position, can be analysed as a loan is not relevant, because English law treats absolute title financing as a legitimate option available to the parties.[30] Thus the mere fact that the dealer is responsible for the debtor's default through a recourse provision in the master agreement does not convert the transaction into a loan with the consequence of being a registerable charge on the book debts under the Companies Act 1985.[31] The mere fact that there is a right of recourse should not affect the categorisation of the transaction as a sale, because the assignor's liability is not to repay an advance but rather to pay a sum in discharge of a recourse obligation.

The master agreement will usually include provisions relating to the quality of the underlying goods and also freedom from encumbrances. In addition certain warranties and representations will be implied, notably that if the finance agreement records a payment by way of deposit or advanced rental then this has in fact been made and a failure here will sound in the tort of deceit or negligent misrepresentation.[32]

The dealer as agent for rentals

Until the debtor has notice of the assignment he can fully discharge his obligations by paying the dealer directly. The dealer will owe all of the usual duties of an agent to his principal, in particular good faith, and also a duty to account. Such a duty will usually be bolstered by making the dealer under the master agreement a guarantor of the payments due whilst at the same time indemnifying the finance company against any loss it may have suffered as a result of early termination of, for example, the contract of hire.

Title in the goods of assigned receivables

In the case of an assignment of contract hire receivables, normally the dealer's title in the goods will also be assigned to the financier. We have

[30.] See Chap. 1 above.
[31.] See *Olds Discount Ltd v. John Playfair Ltd* [1938] 3 All E.R. 275; *Chow Yoong Hong v. Choong Fah Rubber Manufacturing* [1962] A.C. 209.
[32.] See *Royscot Trust* (n. 13, above).

already discussed the legal structures of the supplier-lessor relationship in Chapter 3, above. There are, however, more elaborate structures which include an element of leverage, that is, where the original lessor in search of funding approaches another financial institution which becomes the owner of the equipment under a master lease agreement. Normally, the funder will reinforce its rights by taking a charge over the sub-leases rental streams and such a charge will be registerable under section 395 of the Companies Act 1985. A failure to register this charge will make it void as against the liquidator and creditors of the original (now intermediate) lessor. If the head-lessor under such a leveraged structure terminates the head lease, this does not affect the sub-lease because the doctrine of estates does not apply to chattels[33] as it is an independent interest of the head-lease derived from possession. As a result, under this situation the head-lessor will collect the future rent stream as an owner of the equipment and not as a chargee of the rentals so that a failure to register a charge on the book debts would not be fatal.

Amount of Receivables

Restricted to specified rentals

This will be specifically the case in a contract hire scenario where the rental agreements for a substantial part of the agreement (say 30 out of 36 months) will be discounted. This has the advantage of not placing the obligation of the disposal of the equipment at the end of the term upon the finance house, and also the benefit of the agreement as a whole remains with the dealer and the assignment represents an equitable assignment of part of the debt. Since the assignment operates in equity, it is prudent to include a power of attorney in the master agreement in order to ensure that the dealer's name can be joined in all proceedings against the hirer under the rental agreement in question.

Individual assignment

This is where the dealer acts as a commission agent by introducing the finance house directly to the customer. The dealer will collect any advance payments as an agent of the finance house and will seek approval from the financier before adopting the transaction. The result of such an arrangement is that the supplier for the purposes of the Consumer Credit Act 1974 and also the Sale of Goods Act 1979 is the financier. Since title in the equipment has passed to the financier, the dealer cannot replace the equipment without committing the tort of conversion. However, where this mechanism is used in rental agreements of goods of small value, like white goods, a common provision in the master agreement between the dealer and the financier is that the

---

[33.] See Chap. 2, above.

---

former can exchange the original goods with substituted goods of similar specification and value and that title in the replacement and renewals will vest in the financier. Such an arrangement is essential otherwise the dealer on every occasion would be required to seek specific approval for a replacement from the financier.

Legal problems

Introduction. Legal problems arise out of the receivables financing mechanism, typically where the finance house acts as a factor of book debts by undertaking to purchase either all or a proportion of the book debts of its client (the dealer) at the end of an agreed period. Factoring is almost invariably carried out by way of outright sale of receivables which, as we have seen, avoids the need to register an assignment of receivables as a charge on book debts under section 395 of the Companies Act 1985. Factoring may be without recourse or with recourse to the client if its customer defaults. The agreement may be facultative in the sense that only batches of receivables are sold, and under the master agreement the client is normally under no obligation to offer to sell any particular batch to the factor, although typically the client will be under an obligation not to factor his receivables elsewhere without consent.

Modern commercial law views the right to money due under a contract as a property right.[34] This represents the developed law because, as Cozens-Hardy L.J. pointed out in *Fitzroy v. Cave*[35]:

> "At common law, a debt was looked upon as a *strictly personal obligation*, and an assignment of it was regarded as a mere assignment of a right to bring an action at law against the debtor."

This was not the view of equity. Chancery imposed a duty on the assignor of allowing his name to be used by the assignee in an action for the enforcement of the chose in action in a court of common law. If the assignor would not voluntarily lend his name, the assignee would have to bring a suit in equity against the assignor, and equity would invoke the maxim that it acted *in personam* and would, thereby, compel the assignor to be a party to the action. This action was treated under the common law as the assignor's action, and the defences available to the debtor against the assignor could be employed and equity would not interfere where the equities were equal.[36] Where the action was purely equitable and was absolutely assigned, the assignee could sue in his own name in a court of equity. However, a non-absolute assignment of an equitable chose in action or any legal chose in action, required both the assignor and the assignee as necessary parties.

[34.] See *Camdex International Ltd v. Bank of Zambia* [1996] 3 All E.R. 431.
[35.] [1905] 2 K.B. 364 at 372 (emphasis added).
[36.] See *Wilson v. Gabriel* (1863) 4 B. & S. 243.

The Judicature Acts 1873 to 1875 introduced a statutory form of assignment which enabled an assignee to sue in his own name. These Acts have given statutory recognition to such assignments provided that the assignment is absolute and not by way of charge, that it is evidenced in writing, and written notice is given to the debtor. This approach was substantially replicated in section 136(1) of the Law of Property Act 1925 which states:

"Any absolute assignment by writing under the hand of the assignor (not purporting to be by way of charge only) of any debt or other legal thing in action, of which express notice in writing has been given to the debtor . . . is effectual in law (subject to equities having priority over the right of the assignee) to pass and transfer from the date of such notice—

(a) the legal right to such debt or thing in action;

(b) all legal and other remedies for the same; and

(c) the power to give a good discharge for the same without the concurrence of the assignor."

There are major problems which emerge from this formalistic approach.

Ad valorem duty. An assignment of a debt is a conveyance or transfer of property and any instrument evidencing such a conveyance or transfer is liable under section 1 of the Stamp Act 1891 to *ad valorem* duty. The rate of duty is one per cent, subject to an exemption which relates to any independent transaction whereof the consideration does not exceed £30,000. A sale of receivables is ordinarily liable to stamp duty if carried out through a *document* but not otherwise. It is a tax on instruments and not on transactions, so if the transaction can be carried out without an instrument then no duty is payable. Furthermore, whilst a *sale* of receivables attracts *ad valorem* duty, a mortgage does not.[37]

In the case of an equitable assignment which does not have to be evidenced in writing, the agreement will not attract *ad valorem* duty. From this it may follow that written notification *after* the creation of a valid equitable instrument is not liable, but the majority of the House of Lords held in *Oughtred v. Inland Revenue Commissioners*[38] that a subsequent conveyance of a prior oral contract of sale was liable to *ad valorem* duty: it did not matter that it constituted a formal act confirming that which, in equity, already belonged to the transferee. However, the better view here is that such reasoning does not apply in the assignment-of-receivables context for two main reasons: first, in the case of land, full title can only be transferred by instrument which is not true of receivables; secondly, written notification of a sale of receivables is *not* the instrument whereby receivables are sold as it constitutes merely evidence of the sale and this document is not thereby stampable.[39]

[37.] Finance Act 1971, ss. 63 and 69.
[38.] *Oughtred v. Inland Revenue Commissioners* [1960] A.C. 206.
[39.] *Inland Revenue Commissioners v. G. Angus and Co.* (1889) 23 Q.B.D. 579.

One further method of avoiding stamp duty, which is often regarded as distorting the economics of credit factoring, is through a device of keeping the schedules of receivables below £30,000. It is unlikely that this approach will succeed if it can be shown that, in reality, there is only one transaction. This is so, despite the logic of stamp duty which is a tax on instruments rather than transactions.[40] Furthermore, section 34(4) of the Finance Act 1958 provides that a certificate of value for the purposes of stamping is required to contain a statement certifying that the transaction effected by the instrument does not form part of a larger transaction, or a series of transactions, where the aggregate value of the consideration exceeds £30,000. In *Attorney-General v. Cohen*,[41] Greene L.J. held that the phrase "series of transaction" relates to the situation where the relationship between the transactions is not fortuitous but is an integral one. This must be the case with a factoring agreement on a facility or whole-turnover basis since these will be governed by a single master agreement.[42]

The question of notice. Section 136(1) of the Law of Property Act 1925 constitutes a procedural device which permits an assignor to pass legal title to the assignee so that the latter can sue the debtor in his own name. Even after the Judicature Acts 1873 to 1875, an assignee of a legal chose in action who could not bring himself within the statute is required to bring the assignor into the fray as either a co-plaintiff or co-defendant.[43] Non-joinder of the assignor is not a ground for dismissing the action, but the plaintiff will usually have to pay the costs involved in amending the pleadings so as to join the assignor.[44]

The formal requirements under section 136(1) are very strict: first the assignment has to be evidenced in a document; secondly, the assignment must be an absolute one, although this requirement does not preclude security assignments; thirdly, notice in writing must be given to the debtor. It is this last requirement which has posed the most difficulty. The courts have restrictively interpreted the express notice requirement as referring to the notice in the document itself rather than notice of assignment generally. Consequently, if the date of the assignment is wrongly stated on the notice it is ineffectual as notice under the section.[45] In *W.F. Harrison and Co. Ltd v. Burke*,[46] a gloss was introduced to the effect that if the wrong date was post the assignment this was

---

[40.] *Ingram v. Inland Revenue Commissioners* [1986] Ch. 585.

[41.] [1937] 1 K.B. 478.

[42.] *Cf. Lloyds and Scottish Finance Ltd v. Prentice* (1977) 121 S.J. 847; affd *sub nom. Lloyds and Scottish Finance Ltd v. Cyril Lord Carpets Sales Ltd* [1992] BCLC 609.

[43.] *Performing Rights Society Ltd v. London Theatre of Varieties Ltd* [1924] A.C. 1. *Cf.* liquidation where joinder is not necessary as in *Tolhurst v. Associated Portland Cement Manufacturers (1900) Ltd* [1903] A.C. 414.

[44.] R.S.C., Ord. 15, r. 6(1).

[45.] *Stanley v. English Fibres Industries Ltd* (1899) 68 L.J.Q.B. 839.

[46.] [1956] 1 W.L.R. 419.

valid on the basis that at least an assignment was in existence at this time. Such an approach is anomalous because the *purpose* of notice is to bring to the debtor's attention with reasonable certainty that the debt has been assigned.[47] Furthermore, as Widgery L.J. pointed out in *Van Lynn Developments Ltd v. Pelias Construction Co. Ltd*,[48] what is important is the date of notice to the *debtor* and not the date when the assignment took place, because the former is the relevant date pertaining to priority issues and also in ensuring that the debtor pays the factor directly.

As far as an equitable assignment is concerned, the question is whether the assignor has given plain and unambiguous notice to the debtor. Even here the courts have been restrictive in their construction of assignment clauses. Thus, in *James Talcott Ltd v. John Lewis and Co. Ltd*,[49] the words: "To facilitate our accountancy and banking arrangements it has been agreed that this invoice be transferred to . . . [James Talcott]" were not deemed to be sufficiently plain to give the creditor notice that the debt had been assigned to a third party.[50] One explanation for the approach adopted in this case is that the defendants did not expect a "notice" of this kind from its suppliers, a North American firm, in favour of James Talcott Ltd who were, at that time, the third largest factoring company in the United States of America. It is significant that following this case, factoring companies advise clients to inform their customers in writing that debts are now being assigned and, insofar as invoices are being stamped to this effect, the colour of the stamp is bright and the print is large so as to effectuate actual notice.

The assignee takes subject to "equities". One of the major policy dilemmas associated with receivables financing is the need to balance the use of receivables as the basis of security and, at the same time, protect the debtor by preserving his cross-claims and defences against the assignor. Of course, if the law were to permit a wide scope of cross-claims, this will punish the receivables financier who has no control over relations between the assignor and debtor. This explains why clauses are often inserted into factoring agreements whereby a client is required to provide an express warranty that he has performed what the invoice relates to, and he will fulfil his obligations to the customer. Sometimes, the client will even warrant that the customer will not reject the goods delivered! It is doubtful whether this later warranty can be enforced, and it is for this reason that the factoring company will reserve the right to convert an "approved" invoice to a "disproved" invoice.

The outer fringes of the rule that the assignee of receivables takes subject to equities having priority over his right are reasonably clear. First, the assignee takes no better right than the assignor had, so the assignment will be tainted by any defect in the underlying contract and

[47.] *Denney, Gaquet and Metcalfe v. Conklin* [1913] 3 K.B. 177.
[48.] [1969] 1 Q.B. 607.
[49.] [1940] 3 All E.R. 592.
[50.] *Cf.* Lord Goddard's strong dissenting judgment; *ibid.* at 603.

also any proper defences against the assignor available to the debtor at the date of notice of the assignment.[51] Interestingly, the debtor's right to rescind the contract is not barred by the assignee's intervention unlike the case of a bona fide purchaser for value of goods without notice. The exception to the *nemo dat* rule, whilst protecting transferees of the *goods* from the buyer, does not extend to transferees of the seller's right to receive payment. Secondly, the assignee takes subject to the state of the account between the debtor and the assignor at the date of notice of the assignment. Thus, a debtor who has a liquidated cross-claim against the assignor at the date he receives notice of the assignment can set it off against the assignee, even though the cross-claim has no connection with the debt assigned.[52] Of course, it is otherwise where the cross-claim arises *after* notice of the assignment.[53] A closely connected concept here is the debtor's right of abatement at common law for defective performance of sale of goods with a warranty,[54] so the assignee will take subject to this right. The doctrine of abatement[55] is confined to a strictly limited group of contracts of work and materials.[56]

Rights of set-off

Undoubtedly, the debtor's rights of set-off constitute the most important arm of his enforceable equities, not least because monetary cross-claims dominate the debtor's equities. In the case of an equitable set-off, the claim and cross-claim whilst not necessarily arising out of the same contract must, nevertheless, be closely connected so much so that it would be inequitable not to allow credit for it.[57] Thus, it is reasonably clear that unliquidated damages unconnected with the contract from which the debt arose cannot, in the absence of a contrary agreement, be set-off against the debt.[58] The classical exposition of this approach can be seen in the House of Lords decision in *Rawson v. Samuel*,[59] a case involving a single agreement which gave rise both to the plaintiff's claim and to the counterclaim which, it was argued, constituted a set-off. It was held by Lord Cottenham in this case that in order to be effective as a set-off, the counterclaim had to be of such a kind that it "impeached the title to the legal demand". On the other hand, where the contract between the assignor and debtor provides that the debtor may deduct from the debt sums due to him from the assignor, this will apply to post-

---

[51.] *Christie v. Taunton, Delmard, Lane and Co.* [1983] 2 Ch. 175.
[52.] *Roxburgh v. Cox* (1881) 17 Ch. D. 520; *Young v. Kitchin* (1878) 3 Ex. D. 127.
[53.] *N.W. Robbie and Co. Ltd v. Witney Warehouse Co. Ltd* [1963] 1 W.L.R. 1324.
[54.] Sale of Goods Act 1979, s. 53(1)(a).
[55.] See *Street v. Blay* (1831) 2 B. & Ad. 456; *Mondel v. Steel* (1841) 8 M. & W. 868.
[56.] *Gilbert-Ash (Northern) Ltd v. Modern Engineering (Bristol) Ltd* [1974] A.C. 689 at 717.
[57.] *Dole Dried Fruit and Nut Co. v. Trustin Kerwood Ltd* [1990] 2 Lloyd's Rep. 309.
[58.] *Axel Johnson Petroleum AB v. MG Mineral Group (AG)* [1992] 1 W.L.R. 270.
[59.] (1841) Cr. & Ph. 161.

notice cross-claims for the simple reason that the debt and the contract of set-off arise from the *same* transaction, and the assignee cannot take this debt independent of this obligation since this was included in the original contract to which the debt relates.

It has been suggested that in cases concerning an inseparable connection, the assignee may take subject not only to a right of equitable set-off available to the debtor as a defence to an action brought against him by the assignor, but also, in some cases, subject to an unliquidated demand that could only have been brought forward as a counterclaim in the assignor's action, that is, not susceptible of equitable set-off. Indeed the Privy Council in its judgment in *Government of Newfoundland v. Newfoundland Railway Co.*,[60] specifically referred to counterclaims, though it is by no means clear that the Privy Council was using the term in its technical sense because the nature of the cross-claim here was one of a true equitable set-off. As a matter of principle, it would be anomalous to allow the debtor to enforce a true counterclaim, especially where the latter has no set-off against the assignor, perhaps, because of the absence of a relevant connection. When it is said that an assignee takes subject to equities, the epithet "equities" is intended to connote rights in the nature of defences available to the debtor against the assignor. Before the Judicature Acts 1873 to 1875, a cross-claim possessed by the defendant in an action had to be prosecuted in a totally separate action at law against the plaintiff unless it could be employed in a set-off. It did not constitute a defence; nor did it give rise to an equity analogous to a defence available to the defendant in the plaintiff's action. The Judicature Acts 1873 to 1875, in introducing a right to counterclaim, only affected matters of procedure: it was not intended to alter the rights of the parties.[61] Consequently, it should still be the law that an assignee does not take subject to a cross-demand that could not have formed the basis of a set-off in an action brought by the assignor. The significance of this analysis is that if set-off is purely a procedural matter, then reliance on set-off to withhold payment essentially contributes to a breach of obligations which will likely trigger any acceleration clause or cross-default clauses in the main contract.

The effect of notice

The effect of notice is that it fixes the date for determining the debtor's equities subject to which the factor takes, although this does not deny post-notice equities so long as there is an inseparable connection with the underlying contract to which the assignment relates. Nevertheless, the general rule is that notice of assignment crystallises the debtor's equities enforceable against the assignee. Thus, where the cross-claim is a contingent liability, this must be due before the notice date and also

---

[60.] (1888) 13 App. Cas. 199.
[61.] *Stumore v. Campbell and Co.* [1892] 1 Q.B. 314.

payable before the assigned debt becomes payable. The justification for not recognising contingent cross-claims in this context is the unfairness of requiring the assignee, who may have given present value, to wait until the cross-claim has matured into an actual payable debt.[62] The legal position was summarised by Templeman J. in *Business Computers Ltd v. Anglo-African Leasing Ltd*[63]:

> "The result of the relevant authorities is that a debt which accrues due before notice of an assignment is received, whether or not it is payable before that date, or a debt which arises out of the same contract as that which gives rise to the assigned debt, or is closely connected with that contract, may be set off against the assignee. But a debt which is neither accrued nor connected may not be set off even though it arises from a contract made before the assignment."

Further interesting problems arise in respect of future choses in action where an assignee gives notice of his assignment before the debt arises, and the debtor subsequently raises cross-claims based on subsequent events but before the assigned debt arises. As a matter of principle, the cross-claim will be enforceable against the assignee because the debt generated by the executory contract was always subject to the debtor's cross-claim. This is particularly pertinent in the context of a "whole turnover" factoring agreement where what is involved is an assignment of expectant receivables.[64] An illustration of this phenomenon can be seen in the facts of *Canadian Admiral Corporation Ltd v. L.F. Dommerich and Co. Inc.*[65] Here there was an agreement to factor receivables, but the notice of assignment was stamped on each invoice sent. It was held that the customer of the client could not set-off a subsequent debt since, it was argued, only the *specific* assignment in respect of which invoices were sent to the debtor were operative for the purpose of the notice element, irrespective of the date of notice of the master factoring agreement.

The scope of the assignment

In equity it is possible to have an assignment of future receivables so long as they can be identified as falling within the scope of the agreement without the need for appropriation. No problems should arise in respect of identification, especially with regard to the assignment of a special category of receivables.[66] In the case of a whole turnover factoring arrangement, the debts will vest in the factor when they came into existence only so long as the factor is under an obligation to purchase

---

[62] See *Christie v. Taunton, Delmard, Lane and Co.* [1893] 2 Ch. 175.
[63] [1977] 1 W.L.R. 578 at 585.
[64] See *Rother Iron Works Ltd v. Canterbury Precision Engineers Ltd* [1974] Q.B. 1.
[65] (1964) 43 DLR (2d.) 1 (S.C. Can).
[66] *Tailby v. Official Receiver* (1888) 13 App. Cas. 523.

the receivables. In equity it is necessary for such a future interest to be supported by executed consideration,[67] and in this respect the agreement is construed as a whole so that credits by the factor to the client in respect of earlier receivables will constitute good consideration.

The position of the client

In accordance with conventional equitable principles, once assignment has taken place then the client is under a duty to account to the factor for any proceeds received. If these are paid into an overdrawn account, the issue will centre around the bank's notice of the factor's rights. Of course this does not absolve the liability of the client in conversion for the face value of the cheque paid into the account. Furthermore there will be personal liability on the director of the client company itself if he causes it to commit the act of conversion.[68]

Priority Questions

Introduction

The conceptual development of the rule in *Dearle v. Hall*[69] is still pertinent in the factoring context. The rule provides that priority is accorded not in terms of first in time by way of creation but rather first in time to give notice to the debtor. However, the rule only determines priority between competing *assignees*[70]; it is necessary in the case of a competition between the assignee and third parties to apply a different analysis which can be problematical especially in the context of a receivership or liquidation of the client company.

Factor assignee versus floating chargee

The general effect of a floating charge is that it allows the chargor to dispose of its receivables in the ordinary course of business which will therefore ensure priority to the assignee. In so far as there is an attempt to restrict assignment in the instrument creating the charge, the factor should still prevail as the assignment of debts would appear to be within the scope of the client company's apparent authority. It is otherwise if the factor has notice of the prohibition, but in this context registration of the prohibition with the floating charge does not constitute notice. The reason is that registration of a floating charge is notice only of the existence of the agreement and not of its contents.[71] Nonetheless it may

---

[67.] *Re Ellenborough* [1903] 1 Ch. 697.

[68.] *International Factors Ltd v. Rodriguez* [1979] Q.B. 351.

[69.] (1829) 3 Russ. 1.

[70.] See *Compaq Computer Ltd v. Abercorn Group Ltd* [1991] B.C.C. 484.

[71.] Under the Companies Act 1989 the Secretary of State has new powers of regulation of very wide scope to require the notification to the registrar for registration purposes of such further particulars, information or documents as may be prescribed by regulation. Until the terms of future regulations are known the priority protection obtained by a registered chargee cannot be stated.

be considered that prohibition of assignment clauses are so common place that this constitutes inferred knowledge in the sense that there is a duty to make reasonable inquiries. It is plausible, therefore, that restrictive covenants in prior floating charges could impeach the factor's proprietary rights to the debts.[72] Clearly the factor should exact a waiver from the chargee, before commencing a factoring operation, which should bind any subsequent assignee of the chargee on the basis of proprietary estoppel.[73] If the factoring arrangement precedes the floating charge, then so long as the debts automatically vest in the assignee the latter will have priority irrespective of notice of the prohibition in the floating charge, since the debt is always informed by the factoring company's equity.

Factor assignee versus fixed chargee

In this situation a subsequent assignee will take subject to the fixed charge, because a fixed charge over book debts, postulates in terms of its very nature such a restriction on assignment. If, however, the assignee had no notice of the fixed charge, then the rule in *Dearle v. Hall* will apply, typically when a floating charge has crystallised.

Factor assignee versus liquidator or administrator

Receivables arising within the scope of the factoring agreement will vest in the factor, even after liquidation, unless they came into existence as a result of the post-liquidation activity by the liquidator or the administrator.[74]

Factor assignee versus "Romalpa" type supplier of goods

It is anticipated here that the supplier of goods with a retention of title clause claims the proceeds of the goods either because the sale was unauthorised resulting in a constructive trust of the proceeds, or, if the dispositions were authorised, there was an agreement to account *in specie* for the proceeds of the goods. There is no doubt that factoring companies justifiably fear for their priority because the seller's equitable interest will be first in time, *qui prior est tempore potior est jure*. The question then arises whether the factor may, by giving value and without notice, gain priority by subsequently taking a statutory assignment even if by then he knows of the seller's interest, that is, *tabula in naufragio*. It could be maintained that because retention of title clauses are common, the factor will have imputed notice of the seller's equitable interest. Nevertheless, the courts have been reluctant to apply the doctrine of

---

[72.] *Cf. Tay Valley Joinery Ltd v. C.F. Financial Services Ltd* [1987] S.L.T. 207.
[73.] See *Eastern Distributors v. Goldring* [1957] 2 Q.B. 600.
[74.] *Cf. Re Lind* [1915] 2 Ch. 345; *Re Collins* [1925] Ch. 556.

notice to commercial transactions and indeed, in *E. Pfeiffer Weinkellerei-Weineinkauf GmbH & Co. v. Arbuthnot Factors Ltd*,[75] it was accepted that it could not be suggested that the defendant factoring company had constructive notice of the proceeds clause.

A serious difficulty for the factor is that section 136 of the Law of Property Act 1925 makes a statutory assignment of a legal chose in action effective in law "subject to equities having priority over the right of the assignee". Essentially, the matter is one of policy depending upon which of two schemes for regulating priority interests is adopted. The first, as already noted, consists of determining priority according to the *time* of creation of the interest and is the equitable equivalent of the common law *nemo dat* doctrine. As an alternative, the rule in *Dearle v. Hall*[76] calls for a determination of which of the two innocent parties had contributed most to his unfortunate position. In practice, it appears that the factoring company will give notice of its rights to the debtor, as was the case in *Pfeiffer Weinkellerei-Weineinkauf (E) GmbH & Co. v. Arbuthnot Factors Ltd*, thereby ensuring the factoring company's priority under the *Dearle v. Hall* rule. It is a matter of controversy whether the rule in *Dearle v. Hall* should be applied to the competition between a supplier's equitable interest in proceeds by virtue of a retention of title clause, and the interest of the factoring company under its factoring arrangement with the dealer. In the *Arbuthnot Factors Ltd* case the rule was uncritically applied by Phillips J., although technically the observations made by his Lordship are *obiter*. This was because of the finding that the retention of title clause was void as an unregistered charge and, as a matter of logic, the rule in *Dearle v. Hall* presupposes the existence of two *valid* claims. Even so, this approach was mirrored by Mummery J. in *Compaq Computer Ltd v. Abercorn Group Ltd*.[77]

It is unfortunate that the courts in *E. Pfeiffer Weinkellerei-Weineinkauf GmbH & Co. v. Arbuthnot Factors Ltd*[78] and *Compaq Computer Ltd v. Abercorn Group Ltd*[79] accepted the proposition that the rule in *Dearle v. Hall* must apply in all cases of equitable assignments. Such a conclusion leads to substantial injustice where a first assignee does not give notice to the debtor-obligor, perhaps because he is aware of a prohibition of assignment clause in the latter's contract with the assignor. If it is the case that the obligor can prevent the assignee from acquiring rights against him, the whole point of giving notice evaporates. The rationale here for such notice is, as Buckley J. pointed out in *Re Dallas*,[80] to enable the assignee to acquire a right *in rem* against the fund as distinct from "a right against the conscience of the assignor of the fund". Furthermore, if *Dearle v. Hall* is the nearest approach to taking possession, it should

---

[75.] [1988] 1 W.L.R. 150.
[76.] (1828) 3 Russ. 1.
[77.] [1991] B.C.C. 484.
[78.] [1988] 1 W.L.R. 150.
[79.] [1991] B.C.C. 484.
[80.] [1904] 2 Ch. 385 at 396.

have no relevance where the obligor can prevent this. At least by applying a first-in-time rule, provided the equities are equal, the courts could take into account the effect of a non-assignment clause.

Securitisation of Receivables

Introduction

In a sense the process involved in securitisation is the reverse side of credit factoring, in that the raising of finance on receivables is geared towards financial institutions rather than manufacturing industry. The essential framework of securitisation involves a sale of a stream of receivables, or a sale coupled with a sub-charge by the purchaser. Pools of receivables are "packaged" together and are then transferred to a special-purpose company. The purchase price is raised by this special-purpose company through the transfer of the original debt obligation into a new instrument that can be negotiated.

It is worth emphasising that the term "securitisation" refers to the transfer of financial assets from the original lender to the market and, as such, it does not denote security for payment. An alternative method of securitisation is through the issue of loan notes secured on the receivables. Under this arrangement, the transferor has the benefit of any profit margin constituting the difference between the interest rate paid to the shareholders and that paid on the original loans by the borrowers.

Economic advantages of securitisation for issuers

Cheaper source of funds. Securitisation lowers the cost of funding because it isolates risk, that is, investors can buy a specific package of receivables generated from a particular retail sector (or in the case of land, house mortgages) with a knowable level of risk, for example, receivables generated from the financing of a particular make and model of a car, caravan or boat.

Off-balance sheet financing. Off-balance sheet financing can be very important where the issuer is a bank, because securitisation takes assets off the balance sheet, thereby allowing banks to meet capital adequacy requirements laid down by the Bank of England. Furthermore, risky assets can be transferred off balance sheet which can help the issuer's overall credit standing. Securitisation assists in the issuer's risk management and this can be extremely beneficial to finance companies that are highly sensitive to interest-rate fluctuations. Moreover, it provides a means of overcoming any mismatch there may occur in the issuer's portfolio of assets, for example, between fixed interest rates and market rates.

Legal impediments to securitisation

Stamp duty. We have already considered stamp duty in the context of credit factoring, and the same considerations apply to the securitisation of receivables.

The impact of consumer protection laws. Consumer protection laws may have a significant impact on the ability of the seller and buyer to enforce an obligation against the borrower.[81]

The legal nature of the transfer of the original debt

The major difficulty is the English rule that obligations cannot be transferred.[82] Nevertheless, it is possible for financial assets to be transferred in one of three ways. The cleanest transfer of risk is achieved by *novation* which is essentially the process of substitution. A properly structured legal or equitable *assignment* can be an effective method of transferring the seller's rights and remedies. The third and probably most common technique is *sub-participation* which does not, strictly speaking, involve any transfer of rights, remedies, or obligations from seller to buyer, as it constitutes a separate non-recourse funding arrangement in that the buyer places funds with the seller in exchange for a beneficial interest only in the underlying loan.

Dealer Stock Unit Financing

Introduction

The simplest method of taking security in stock and receivables is by way of floating charge and indeed, as we have seen,[83] it may be possible to take a fixed charge over revolving assets, including receivables.[84] However, the conventional method in England of providing stocking facilities is through utilising the retention of title mechanism. Traditionally finance houses have preferred this method of financing because they will retain absolute legal title in the stock, and whilst the debtor will have interest in the stock (arising out of the stocking agreement) this will only apply so long as the stocking contract remains on foot and on termination the finance house will enjoy absolute title in the goods as owner.

The purpose of stocking finance is self-evident, namely, to fund dealers to acquire and maintain stock. However, since by definition the dealer will need to replenish the stock, then any accommodation made tends to be of a revolving character. It is for this reason that a fixed charge on stocking finance assets is not a practical option for finance houses since, by definition, it is anticipated that the dealer should have

---

[81.] See Chap. 3, above.
[82.] *Tolhurst v. Associated Portland Cement Manufacturers (1900) Ltd* [1902] 2 K.B. 660.
[83.] See Chap. 2, above.
[84.] *Siebe Gorman and Co. Ltd v. Barclays Bank Ltd* [1979] 2 Lloyd's Rep. 142.

the liberty of the stock in the ordinary course of business which is more consistent with a floating charge mechanism. A floating charge has the disadvantage of being somewhat of a rough and ready means of financing since the amount of units at any one time may vary greatly. One danger here is that the financier may be either over-collaterised or under-collaterised as the case may be. It is for this reason that finance houses prefer unit-stocking facilities, that is, where the finance is actually tailored to actual units in stock and which goes hand in hand with audit monitoring of these identified units.

In practical terms the finance house has several options in providing a unit stocking facility and, whichever option is adopted, this will often reflect the assumption of risk which the finance house is happy to bear in respect of the dealer. The common theme is the bailment mechanism whereby the dealer derives his interest from the finance house either through a pledge mechanism (field warehousing), a hirer under a hire-purchase agreement, or a consignee under a consignment or sub-consignment.

Field Warehousing

Field warehousing is not a developed concept in the United Kingdom as it is essentially an American invention which emerged during the depression of the 1930s. The essential mechanism is that the borrower/manufacturer creates a field warehouse by leasing a portion of his premises containing the materials to a warehouse company; the employees of the borrower, who normally control the stock-in-trade, are hired and bonded by the warehouse company pursuant to formal written agreements. Signs are posted throughout the leased area giving notice of the warehouse company's possession. Keys to the warehouse area are retained by the bonded employees, and warehouse receipts, usually non-negotiable in form, are issued for commodities deposited by the borrower. The crucial element for a valid field warehousing arrangement is that "dominion and control" is held by the supplier. There is nothing preventing an English supplier from adopting the same mechanism.

Field warehousing in the United States of America is usually undertaken by a professional warehousing company which is insured for loss or dissipation of the collateral, and thus the lender achieves excellent security. Furthermore, since the goods are under the pledgee's control, he can release them to the debtor in accordance with a pre-arranged collateral-to-loan ratio. Where there is, for example, creditor risk-aversion, or a limited need for direct access (as in stockpiles of out-of-season goods with relatively high unit values), the field warehouse is an excellent monitoring mechanism. Thus, when the manufacturer desires to process the materials, he can obtain temporary possession for that purpose and is policed by the warehouseman. Of course, if the goods or warehouse receipts are released there is always the danger of an unscrupulous borrower repledging them as security for another loan.[85] If

---

[85.] See *Lloyds Bank v. Bank of America* [1938] 2 K.B. 147.

147

the goods are released and sold on credit, the lender will often have an account receivable assigned to it as substitute security for the warehouse receipt covering the goods. Alternatively, the borrower/manufacturer could obtain a warehouse receipt from the lender on a trust receipt and, after processing, either the finished product could be turned over to the warehouse or it could be sold and the proceeds used to pay off the outstanding indebtedness.

Stocking or Floor Plan

The dealer receives possession, the finance house having acquired title direct from the manufacturer/supplier then proceeds to supply to the dealer on hire-purchase terms. Under such an arrangement the dealer will sell as principal, although he may possibly sell as agent for the finance company as owner. If an attempt was made in the hire-purchase agreement to prohibit the dealer as hirer from disposing of the goods, it is unlikely that such a clause will have effect since on conventional agency principles the dealer will have ostensible authority to dispose of them and that a bona fide purchaser from the dealer will acquire title under section 2(1) of the Factors Act 1889.[86]

Consignment and Sub-consignment Plans

The legal environment here is regulated by section 18, rule 4 of the Sale of Goods Act 1979 which provides as follows:

> "When goods are delivered to the buyer on approval or sale or return or other similar terms, the property in the goods passes to the buyer:
>
> (a) when he signifies his approval or acceptance to the seller or does any other act adopting the transaction;
>
> (b) if he does not signify his approval or acceptance to the seller but retains the goods without giving notice of rejection, then, if a time has been fixed for the return of the goods, on the expiration of that time, and, if no time has been fixed, on the expiration of a reasonable time."

It is interesting that this does not refer to goods as being "sold" but rather refers to delivery. It is clear that through this method Chalmers, the draftsman of the Act, accommodated both a "contract of sale" and an "agreement to sell". The latter analysis does not entirely fit conceptually the "sale or return" transaction, that is, here there is an agreement to sell subject to the buyer adopting the transaction. Moreover, in the case of "sales on approval" many of these are "sales" (in the sense of property passing) subject to a right of rescission. The crucial question then is

---

[86.] See *St Margaret's Trust Ltd v. Castle* (1964, C.A.; unreported; Bar Library, No. 247); R.M. Goode, *Hire Purchase Law and Practice* (2nd ed.) p. 616.

whether the buyer has engaged in an "act adopting the transaction". This was considered by the Court of Appeal in *Kirkham v. Attenborough*,[87] where the plaintiff, a jewellery manufacturer, entrusted the jewellery to a rogue on a sale or return basis. The rogue pledged the goods with the defendant, but the Court of Appeal refused the plaintiff in his claim for the return of the goods on the basis that the rogue, by pledging the goods, had adopted the transaction.[88] The other criterion of determining approval or acceptance, the lapse of a reasonable time, cannot be stated in the abstract and much depends upon the facts in each particular case. In *Poole v. Smith's Car Sales (Balham) Ltd*[89] this period was deemed to be three months where a car dealer had delivered a car to another dealer who had driven it for 1,600 miles, and it had been damaged as a result of an accident.

The question of what constitutes a true consignment sale is highly pertinent in that there is a natural judicial hostility to disguised security interests. A key consideration to the establishment of a true consignment as distinct from a security bill of sale, is that if a consignee is not obligated to pay the price of the goods until sale and can return unsold goods before sub-sale, this is a true agency relationship. The relevant factors are:

1. Reservation of title until sale.

2. The consignor's right to demand return of the goods at will.

3. The consignee's right to return unsold goods.

4. The consignee's authorisation to sell the goods at a fixed price or above a "floor".

5. The consignee's obligation to segregate the goods from his own.

6. The consignee's obligation to hold sales proceeds in trust and forward them to the consignor.

7. A requirement that the consignee retain separate books and records.

8. The consignor's right to inspect goods, books, records and premises.

9. All shipping papers being required to refer to the goods as consigned.

The determining feature of a "false" consignment is whether the consignee is absolutely liable for the price of the "consigned" goods with no right to return the goods unsold. Nevertheless, it has to be admitted

[87] [1897] 1 Q.B. 201.
[88] See also *Genn v. Winkel* (1912) 107 L.T. 434.
[89] [1962] 1 W.L.R. 744.

that the tests identified are not always easy to apply, because the consignment legal form seems so responsive to changing market factors that any test articulated is only going to be marginally useful.

The typical stock financing plan structure of new vehicles would appear as follows:

	CONSIGNMENT/ SUB CONSIGNMENT	INVOICE/CONSIGNMENT
Description	Title remains with the manufacturer until vehicle either adopted or registered by the dealer.	Title passes from manufacturer to finance company who then consigns to the dealer. Title remains with the finance company until vehicle either adopted or registered by the dealer.
Credit period	180 days	180 days
Invoicing	Manufacturer consigns vehicles to finance company. Finance company pays the wholesale price (excluding taxes and VAT) to the manufacturer either: (a) at the end of any free credit period; or (b) on consignment in which case the finance company charges interest to manufactuer during the free credit period.	Manufacturer invoices the finance company at wholesale price and pays taxes. Finance company pays whole amount to the manufacturer with payment options sale as for consignment/ sub-consignment.
Status of Vehicle	Title remains with manufacturer until payment received via the finance company. Manufacturer is liable to accept return of any unsold/unregistered new vehicles and repay to the finance company the wholesale price funded to them. Finance company registers a charge over the vehicles.	Title remains with the finance company until payment received. Manufacturer liable for return of vehicles as per consignment/sub-consignment. Charge over vehicles not necessary.
Payment Terms	On adoption dealer pays consignment price plus taxes to finance company who will pay over taxes to manufacturer. Alternatively the dealer may pay wholesale price to finance company and taxes direct to manufacturer. Dealer can pay a unit deposit or bulk deposit to offset interest charges after the initial interest free period.	On adoption dealer pays consignment price plus taxes (total amount funded from day 1) direct to the finance company. Dealer can pay a unit deposit or bulk deposit to offset interest charges after the interest free period.

It would appear from the above that manufacturers will typically consign batches of vehicles to the dealer on a sale or return basis collecting from the dealer the wholesale price excluding VAT. Appropriation will take place on resale and the dealer will have to account for the tax. The role of the finance house is as an intermediary in financing the wholesale price. This can be done in two ways: first, by way of loan secured by a floating charge on the stock and receivables and/or any other security; secondly, by way of sub-consignment whereby title passes through the finance house (the consignee) to the ultimate acquirer via the dealer (the sub-consignee). This mechanism is preferred by finance houses because the act of adopting the transaction is within their control and it also has the advantage of deferring VAT payment provided that the vehicle(s) is not held for more than a year.[90]

Retention of Title Clauses

The use of retention of title clauses has become widespread since the seminal Court of Appeal decision in *Aluminium Industrie Vaasen BV v. Romalpa Aluminium Ltd.*[91] Such an arrangement pre-supposes that the finance house will purchase the stock directly from the manufacturer/ supplier and supply them to the dealer on conditional sale terms, normally by way of retention of title to the goods until full payment of the price for the goods supplied under a particular contract or all contracts. The clause may also seek to extend to new goods manufactured or incorporated by the dealer/possessor and may also extend to proceeds on sub-sale.[92]

[90] Value Added Tax Act 1994, s. 6(2)(c).
[91] [1976] 1 W.L.R. 676.
[92] See Davies, *Effective Retention of Title* (1992); McCormack, *Reservation of Title* (1995, 2nd ed.).

Chapter 5

The Relationship Between the Lessee and the Dealer

Introduction

Where there is a contractual agreement entered into between the lessee/hirer and the dealer, the normal rules of contract as to consensus, consideration and certainty will apply. The most problematical feature here is the tripartite nature of especially the finance leasing transaction, as there would appear to be no contract directly created between the dealer and the lessee because the structure of the transaction is that of an intermediary financing lessor who concludes a lease contract with the lessee and another contract with the supplying dealer. If the equipment proves to be defective, questions arise as to whether the lessee has a remedy against the dealer especially if a false representation was made by the dealer to the lessee in the course of negotiations. Such an action may be important for the following reasons: first, the lessor may have successfully excluded liability for quality and fitness for purpose in the sense that the reasonableness test under the Unfair Contract Terms Act 1977 and the fairness test under the Unfair Terms in Consumer Contract Regulations have been satisfied; secondly, the issue of remoteness of damages for loss may be pertinent; thirdly, it will also be relevant in relation to the issue for the return of any deposit paid (including part-exchanged goods) where for some reason the anticipated lease agreement is not concluded.

The Dealer as the Finance Company's Agent

The Common Law Position

Agency generally

At common law a dealer is not normally deemed to be the agent of the financier/lessor in respect of representations made, even though the dealer may carry stocks of the lessor's forms.[1] In particular the following factors militate against the agency determination at common law: first,

---

[1] *Williams (J.D.) and Co. v. McCauley Parsons and Jones* [1994] C.C.L.R. 78, C.A.

the dealer is selling his goods to the lessor; secondly, it is the dealer who decides what is the cash basis for the finance agreement; and thirdly, when a dealer submits a proposal to the lessor, this is done very much in terms of a trader offering a business proposition to the lessor and not as his agent.

The developing case law

It is clear that the agency determination is a question of fact, so the emerging trend in the case law is inevitably inconsistent. The early Court of Appeal decision in *Campbell Discount Co. Ltd v. Gall*[2] would seem to have scotched any argument that the dealer was the finance company's agent. In this case the defendant had agreed with a dealer to buy a car on hire-purchase terms for £265. He paid a deposit of £65 to the dealer, understanding that the balance would be discharged by weekly instalments of £2, and signed in blank the finance company's form of hire-purchase agreement, leaving the dealer to fill in the details. The dealer, by mistake or fraud, inserted a total price of £825 and monthly instalments of £18. The finance company accepted the transaction on this footing, and sent a copy of the agreement to the defendant. The defendant then objected that this was not the agreement he had made; he refused to pay any instalments and did not use the car. The finance company retook possession of the car, and sued the defendant for £52, representing four instalments of hire unpaid. The defendant counterclaimed for the return of his deposit. The county court judge decided in favour of the plaintiffs on both the claim and the counterclaim, holding that the defendant had clothed the dealer with authority to complete the form of agreement, and that, although the dealer had exceeded his actual authority, the defendant was bound by the agreement the dealer had in fact made.

The Court of Appeal allowed the defendant's appeal and rejected the argument that the dealer was in reality the finance company's agent on the basis that the dealer determined the price and that merely accepting commission on the transaction did not *before the transaction was effective* make him an agent. Furthermore, acceptance by the dealer of the initial rent and also the dealer's provision of hire-purchase forms were rejected as evidence of agency, because at the time of the receipt of the initial rental there was no effective agreement and the finance house was not bound to accept the proposition. Furthermore, the provision of hire-purchase forms merely showed that the financing company hoped for business from the dealers and, as Holroyd Pearce L.J. put it, "that hope does not constitute an agency".[3]

The approach taken by the Court of Appeal in *Campell Discount* was not followed before a differently constituted Court of Appeal in *Financings Ltd v. Stimson*.[4] In this case the defendant wished to buy a car which

[2] [1961] 1 Q.B. 431.
[3] *Ibid.* at 441.
[4] [1962] 2 All E.R. 386.

he had seen on the premises of a dealer, and he had signed the plaintiff finance company's form of hire-purchase agreement, which the dealer had produced to him. That was on March 16, 1961. The agreement provided, *inter alia*, that it should only be binding on the finance company when they had accepted it by their signature, and that the goods should be at the risk of the hirer from the time of purchase by the owner. On the 18th the defendant paid the first instalment to the dealer, and was allowed to take the car away. He was, however, dissatisfied with it, and on the 20th he returned it to the dealer and offered to forfeit his deposit in order to settle the matter. By an oversight the company was not informed of this turn of events. On the night of the 24th the car was stolen from the dealer's premises and it was recovered badly damaged. On the 25th the company finally signed the agreement; they took the car back and sold it, and now claimed damages from the defendant. Their action failed in the county court, and their appeal was dismissed by the Court of Appeal.

It was held by the Court of Appeal that the signing of the form of agreement by the defendant constituted an offer to the finance company, which would only ripen into a contract upon acceptance by the company in the manner indicated in the agreement, namely by the company's signing it, and that this offer was conditional upon the car being in substantially the same state at the time when the offer was accepted as it was when the offer was made. The damage suffered on the night of the 24th meant that the condition was not satisfied, and the company's acceptance on the 23rd accordingly came too late. Furthermore Lord Denning M.R. and Donavan L.J. held that the dealer was the agent of the finance company for the purpose of receiving notice of the defendant's revocation of his offer, so that revocation of the offer on the 20th was *ipso facto* communicated to the finance company. Lord Denning expounded a wide view on agency:[5]

> "It seems to me that, in this transaction before us, as indeed in most of these hire-purchase transactions, the dealer is for many purposes the agent of the finance company. Counsel for the defendant in his argument pointed out a number of matters in which it cannot be denied that the dealer is the agent of the finance company. The dealer holds the necessary forms; he hands them over to the hirer to sign; he forwards them to the finance company; he receives the deposit as agent for the finance company; he receives from the finance company information that they are willing to accept the transaction; and he is authorised to pass on that communication to the hirer. He was in this very case the agent of the finance company to see that the insurance cover was all in proper order. He rejected the first cover which was offered and accepted the comprehensive cover which he said was satisfactory. Most important of all, he was the agent of the finance company to hand over the motor car to the hirer."

Lord Denning distinguished *Campbell Discount* as a case confined to its own facts, that is, whether the dealer had filled in the form of agreement

<hr>

5. *Ibid.* at 388.

as agent of the hirer or the finance company or neither. This, however, is to ignore the principle applied by the court in reaching its conclusion.

In *Northgran Finance Ltd v. Ashley*[6] the Court of Appeal concluded that the dealer was an agent without applying either *Campbell Discount* or *Financings Ltd v. Stimson*. The defendant had one car on hire purchase from finance company A, and he wished to trade this car in to the dealers in part exchange for another, and cheaper, one. He obtained A company's consent to his transferring the first car to the dealers, but only on condition that the dealers paid A company the amount of the outstanding hire-purchase instalments. The dealers agreed, and took the defendant's car, arranging for the hire-purchase by the defendant of the second car from the plaintiffs. Unfortunately for the defendant, the dealers failed to pay A company the amount owing to them, and being unable to support two hire-purchase agreements the defendant threw up the second one. The plaintiffs now brought an action for damages. The action succeeded, and the defendant appealed.

It was argued that the dealers were the finance company's agents to the extent that the agreement with the plaintiffs was subject to the condition precedent that the dealers would pay off finance company A. This argument was rejected. As Ormerod L.J. said[7]:

> "There can be no doubt that the dealers were agents for the company for some purposes, but there is nothing to show that such agency extended to entering into a transaction such as the present one on its behalf. We have been referred to a number of authorities, but this is not a matter in which decided cases can be of much assistance. The extent and nature of the authority must be decided on the facts of each case. In my judgment, there was no sufficient authority here."

On principle it is difficult to identify a meaningful agency relationship in this tripartite scenario. The dealer's agency of communicating acceptance of the finance company's proposal is very limited—he is merely an authorised channel of communication. In no sense can the dealer be regarded as having general authority to act on behalf of the finance company. Delivery up of the asset is done according to the instruction of the finance company—this is a ministerial agency—it has no authority to create an obligation binding on the company. As to the receipt of the deposit the agency point is still difficult to sustain. As Hughes has pointed out[8]:

> "There are two contracts, and two debts, involved in this situation. The hirer owes the finance company the amount of the deposit, and the company, in turn, owes the dealer the cash price of the car. If the company now discharges part of its debt to the dealer by directing its own debtor, the hirer, to pay what he owes the company straight to the dealer, then it is the hirer who is

[6] [1963] 1 Q.B. 476.
[7] *Ibid*. at 488.
[8] (1964) 27 M.L.R. 395 at 405.

the agent of the company in making the payment to the dealer, not the dealer who is the agent of the company in receiving the money."

Certainly where the finance agreement has not become binding, there is direct authority in *Cambell Discount* that the dealer is not an agent of the finance company to receive the deposit and cannot therefore be liable for the return of the deposit following the dealer's insolvency.

In *Branwhite v. Worcester Works Finance*,[9] the House of Lords reviewed the agency question in relation to the following facts. The customer signed a hire-purchase proposal form in blank leaving the dealer to insert later the agreed cash price of £430 and instalments of £5–£6 per month. However, the dealer inserted a price of £649 and instalments of over £18 per month. The finance company accepted the "offer" they had received. When the customer received a copy of the completed document he saw that the terms were not those he had agreed and he complained and refused to pay any instalments. The finance company re-possessed and sued for arrears. It was held that there was no contract following *Campbell Discount Co. Ltd v. Gall*.[10] The hirer then instituted proceedings claiming the return of his deposit (£130). This matter was considered by the House of Lords on two bases: first, that the finance company had received from him £130 he had paid to the dealer and that the consideration had wholly failed; secondly, that the dealer had received the £130 as agent for the finance company. The hirer succeeded in the House of Lords with all the members of the panel of judges supporting the first contention. There was however a considerable difference of opinion regarding the second matter. The majority cited with approval (Lords Morris, Guest and Upjohn) the dictum of Pearson L.J. in *Mercantile Credit Co. Ltd v. Hamblin*[11] when he said:

> "In a typical hire-purchase transaction the dealer is a party in his own right selling his car to the finance company, and he is acting primarily on his own behalf and not as a general agent for either of the other two parties . . ."

The authority of *Branwhite* established that only where there are exceptional facts will a relationship of principal and agent arise. The practical effect of this is that a finance company will not be fixed with any knowledge that the dealer, who is not its agent, may have of any defective title in the goods,[12] although the practical effect of this in relation to motor vehicles will be limited especially by virtue of section 27(6) of the Hire-Purchase Act 1964.[13]

The general position which emerges is that the lessor is not liable for any misstatements by the dealer. Moreover the dealer is not considered

[9.] [1969] A.C. 352.
[10.] [1961] 1 Q.B. 431.
[11.] [1965] 2 Q.B. 242.
[12.] See *Car and Universal Finance Co. Ltd v. Caldwell* [1964] 1 All E.R. 290.
[13.] See Chap. 6, below.

to have actual or ostensible authority to accept on behalf of the financier notice of termination of a lease agreement. Neither is the dealer the agent of the finance company in a hire-purchase transaction the agent of the finance company to receive a pre-contract down payment. Nonetheless, if the nature of the financing transaction is to acquire the equipment by lease, then the financier will be deemed to have received this down payment in a balance of account with the dealer and will be liable in money had and received if the agreement is subsequently avoided through, for example, rescission due to misrepresentation.

The modern position

In *Woodchester Equipment (Leasing) Ltd v. British Association of Canned and Preserved Foods Importers and Distributors Ltd*[14] the Court of Appeal confirmed the orthodox position regarding the relationship between the dealer and the finance company when Millett L.J. held[14a]:

> "There is no rule of law that in a hire purchase transaction the supplier is the agent of the finance company for the purpose of procuring the customer to offer to acquire goods on hire purchase. There is equally no rule of law that the supplier is not the agent of the finance company for that purpose. The question is a question of fact in each case . . . In my judgment the same applies to a leasing agreement."

In this case the employee of the supplier of a fax machine (Magnum Business Machines) misrepresented to the acquirer that a previous supply agreement entered into by him with another company was ineffective. This induced the acquirer to sign a new agreement in relation to the leasing of a new machine. Almost immediately after the leasing agreement was signed with the plaintiffs the machine was delivered and installed. A few days later the machine which had been the subject-matter of the previous agreement arrived. The defendants then rejected the Magnum machine and kept the other. After the machine had been returned to Magnum the company went into liquidation. The plaintiffs were unable to recover their payment to Magnum and therefore sued the defendants for their losses under the leasing agreement. The relevant issue was whether Magnum's employee was the agent for the plaintiffs in his negotiation of the deal with the defendants and that as a result of his fraudulent misrepresentation this induced the defendants to enter into the contract which the defendants were then entitled to rescind.

At first instance *Branwhite* was distinguished on the basis that the immediate facts at issue in *Woodchester* related to a lease as distinct from a hire-purchase contract. In the Court of Appeal reference was made to the authority of *J.D. Williams and Co. t/a Williams Leasing v. McCauley Parsons and Jones*[15] which dealt with the leasing point. The facts

---

[14.] [1995] C.C.L.R. 51.
[14a.] *Ibid.* at p. 60.
[15.] [1994] C.C.L.R. 78.

involved a company called Channel 9 Limited which conceived the idea of making available video and projection television equipment to clubs, and also making arrangements with advertisers for the provision of commercial advertising cassettes to the clubs. Channel 9 achieved this by selling the equipment to a leasing company who in turn would then lease the equipment to the club. The leasing agreement between the club and the leasing company would be made after the salesman from Channel 9 got the club to complete the draft lease agreement on a form provided to Channel 9 by the leasing company, Channel 9 at the same time taking from the club an initial deposit. Channel 9 would make a separate agreement with the club for the provision of advertising cassettes to the club and they used the fees payable to the club (for showing these cassettes) to be used to pay rentals under the leasing agreement. All of that was how things were done in the present case where the club fell into arrears with payments under the lease agreement and the leasing company terminated the agreement and commenced proceedings against the defendant club for the outstanding payments due under the lease agreement. The defendant club denied liability under the lease agreement on the grounds that the club had been prepared to deal only with Channel 9 and had been the victim of a fraudulent misrepresentation by Channel 9's salesman, the misrepresentation being that the plaintiff leasing company was part of Channel 9. In the High Court, judgment was given for the plaintiff leasing company. The club appealed on the grounds, *inter alia*, that Channel 9 was agent of the plaintiff leasing company and therefore the latter was bound by the misrepresentation of Channel 9's salesman. It was held by Bingham L.J.[16]:

> "In the present case there is, in my judgment, very little if anything to suggest that these plaintiffs did authorise Channel 9 to act as their agents. It is true that they cooperated, and it is quite plain that the plaintiffs indicated willingness if Channel 9 should chose to direct proposals to them, to consider them and, if they thought fit, to accept them. No doubt this was a profitable line of business for the plaintiffs. But in my judgment there is nothing whatever to suggest that the plaintiffs had authorised Channel 9 to act as their agents; still less to act as their agents to make the sorts of representations which are in issue here."[16a]

The courts have in other recent cases adopted a robust view of when the negotiator is in fact the agent of the owner. Thus in *Woodchester Leasing Equipment v. Clayton*,[17] representations made as to the merits of leasing, as opposed to buying, by the supplier's representative was treated as if the latter was agent of the owner. The facts involved a regulated consumer hire agreement for the defendants to hire from the

[16.] *Ibid.* at 83.
[16a.] It would appear from this case that there must be exceptional factual circumstances to justify the finding of an agency relationship arising out of the conduct of the finance company.
[17.] [1994] C.C.L.R. 89.

finance company a fax machine for the defendants' business. The defendants had signed the agreement at their own premises during the second of two visits there by the supplier's salesman. At the first visit, the defendants had been initially undecided whether to buy the machine outright for cash or to take it on some other terms. From the supplier's point of view, the latter would be much more profitable, since the cash price payable if the defendants bought the machine outright was £995 + VAT, whereas if the machine were taken by the defendants on lease from the finance company, the cash price payable by the finance company to the supplier would be £1,715 + VAT. It is not surprising therefore that at that first meeting, the representations made by the supplier's salesman to the defendants were directed at "selling" the idea of the lease via the finance company. The machine was delivered and the signed proposed agreement accepted by the finance company. Approximately 10 days later, the defendants wrote to the finance company cancelling the agreement. At the subsequent hearing the issue centred around whether the supplier had been the agent of the finance company. It was held that the supplier was the agent of the finance company on the basis that this was a leasing, not a hire-purchase case, and one where it was greatly to the supplier's advantage to persuade the customer to lease rather than to make an outright purchase, and where the thrust of the supplier's sales talk was to the virtues of leasing rather than the virtues of the product to be supplied. Nonetheless, in the light of the Court of Appeal decision in *J. D. Williams* the authority of this case must now be doubted.

A further example of an agency relationship being held to have been established involves eponymous subsidiaries, as seen in *Purnell Secretarial Services Ltd v. Lease Management Services Ltd*.[18] The facts involves a supplier, Canon (South West) Limited, from whom the customer had bought several photocopiers over previous years. During the visit of the supplier's sales representative, the customer made plain that it was essential that any new machine should be capable of making "paper plates" as indeed the demonstration model was. Subsequently the customer signed a leasing agreement to hire a new machine only to discover later that the machine was incapable of making "paper plates". It transpired that the customer had made the leasing agreement not, as the customer had thought, with the supplier, but with Lease Management Services Limited. This was a surprise to the customer since the agreement was headed "Canon (South West) Limited", the word "Canon" being printed in that company's distinctive logo. Much further down the page, in more tightly typed print, there appeared the words "Lessor/Owner: Lease Management Services Limited trading as Canon (South West) Finance". After some efforts to sort out the dispute, the unwanted machine was repossessed by Lease Management Services who brought proceedings, and obtained judgment, against the customer for

[18.] [1994] Tr.L.R. 337.

rentals under the agreement less a discount for accelerated payment and a deduction for the secondhand value of the repossessed machine. The customer, the lessee, appealed to the Court of Appeal and the appeal was allowed on the basis that Lease Management Services Limited was estopped from asserting that it was not part of the same group as Canon (South West) Limited and thus estopped from denying the authority of Canon (South West) Limited's staff to speak for Leasing Management Services Limited. This estoppel arose because Leasing Management Services Limited had chosen to identify itself, by the design of its form, with Canon (South West) and thereby had misled the customer into thinking the contract was with Canon (South West) Limited. In effect therefore the common practice of "customising" forms in the leasing industry to associate the finance company with the supplier can have the effect of creating an agency by estoppel.

In the absence of agreement or estoppel, the dealer will not normally be considered to be the agent of the lessor. However, in certain circumstances there has been statutory intervention, notably in the consumer credit field where there is a deemed agency concept to be found in section 56 of the Consumer Credit Act 1974.

Statutory Intervention and Deemed Agency

Legislative background

The deemed agency concept is set out in section 56 of the Consumer Credit Act 1974 and negotiations are deemed to be conducted by the negotiator in the "capacity of the agent of the creditor" so enabling the debtor in appropriate circumstances to rescind the credit agreement or to treat it as repudiated. An error in drafting section 56 has given rise to an anomalous position, that is, it does not bind the owner under a hire agreement to antecedent negotiations entered into by the negotiator, unless the negotiator was the owner's agent.[19] Whilst section 56(4) provides for the point of time at which antecedent negotiations are taken to begin, it is silent as to when these are concluded. As a matter of implication this must be at the time when the regulated agreement is concluded, although the fraud of the negotiator may actually prevent this occurring.[20] Section 56 provides as follows:

"(1) In this Act "antecedent negotiations" means any negotiations with the debtor or hirer—

(a) conducted by the creditor or owner in relation to the making of any regulated agreement, or

(b) conducted by a credit-broker in relation to goods sold or proposed to be sold by the credit-broker to the creditor before forming the subject-matter of a debtor-creditor-supplier agreement within section 12(a), or

[19.] *Lloyds Bowmaker Leasing Ltd v. MacDonald* [1993] C.C.L.R. 78.
[20.] *Branwhite v. Worcester Works Finance Ltd* [1969] 1 A.C. 592.

(c) conducted by the supplier in relation to a transaction financed or proposed to be financed by a debtor-creditor-supplier agreement within section 12(b) or (c),

and "negotiator" means the person by whom negotiations are so conducted with the debtor or hirer.

(2) Negotiations with the debtor in a case falling within subsection (1)(b) or (c) shall be deemed to be conducted by the negotiator in the capacity of agent of the creditor as well as in his actual capacity.

(3) An agreement is void if, and to the extent that, it purports in relation to an actual or prospective regulated agreement—

(a) to provide that a person acting as, or on behalf of, a negotiator is to be treated as the agent of the debtor or hirer, or

(b) to relieve a person from liability for acts or omissions of any person acting as, or on behalf of, a negotiator.

(4) For the purposes of this Act, antecedent negotiations shall be taken to begin when the negotiator and the debtor or hirer first enter into communication (including communication by advertisement), and to include any representation made by the negotiator to the debtor or hirer and any other dealings between them."

Scope

Section 56(1)(a) is concerned with negotiations conducted by the creditor or owner (either himself or by his employees or agents) in relation to the making of any regulated agreement.

Section 56(1)(b) on the other hand applies to negotiations conducted by a dealer in relation to goods sold or proposed to be sold to a creditor under a conventional sale. It is immaterial whether the dealer did or did not introduce the particular credit transaction, so long a he has the status of a credit broker. In *Powell v. Lloyds Bowmaker Ltd*,[21] the plaintiff part exchanged a motor vehicle which was still on hire purchase from a third-party finance company. The motor dealer undertook that the garage would repay the third-party finance company from the cash element, and arrange new finance for the purchase of a new car. The garage failed to settle the hire-purchase agreement. The plaintiff claimed in damages against the defendants, firstly by virtue of section 56(1)(b) and secondly that the garage acted as agents for the defendants. Both counts failed, the Edinburgh Sheriff Court held that the deemed agency created by section 56(1) and (2) was limited to statements, representations and undertakings made by the dealer (credit-broker) "in relation to goods sold or proposed to be sold" by the dealer and that the undertaking to settle existing finance was not a representation in relation to the goods. That being so, that undertaking was subject to the ordinary rule at common law that the dealer is not the agent of the finance company. Even so, it could be argued that for the customer the

---

[21.] (1996) unreported.

---

whole transaction is financially unworkable without including the elements of trading in the old car and paying off the debt relating to it, and that the statement made therefore relates to the acquisition of the new car because it is concerned with the price of the car.[22]

Section 56(1)(c) covers negotiations conducted by a supplier preparatory to an agreement for a loan by the finance house to the debtor for the purchase of goods or services from the supplier provided that the agreement is made by the finance house "under pre-existing arrangements" or in "contemplation of future arrangements" between the finance house and the supplier.

Section 56 of the CCA 1974 does not make the dealer the finance company's agent in the case of a regulated consumer hire agreement.[23] This is because paragraph (b) of section 56(1) of the CCA 1974 deals with negotiations conducted by a credit-broker in relation to goods sold or proposed to be sold by the credit-broker to the creditor before forming the subject-matter of a two party debtor-creditor-supplier agreement.[24] This paragraph typically covers a dealer selling goods to a finance company to be let on hire purchase or supplied on conditional sale to the debtor introduced by the dealer to the finance company.[25] This section arose because the draftsman had to "cover" the dealer, who is not normally considered to be the agent of the finance company, by bringing him within the definition of a negotiator.[26] This consequence has the unfortunate result that general negotiations conducted by a dealer, in the case of a leasing contract, will not fall under the applicability of paragraph (b),[27] and will not be treated as those of the owner.

An examination of the Crowther Committee Report on Consumer Credit leaves no doubt that protection in such an agreement was anticipated, for it states that "to a considerable extent the finance house and the dealer are engaged in a joint venture".[28] Also, when one examines the debates that took place surrounding the passing of the Consumer Credit Act, the Minister for State, Department of Prices and Consumer Protection,[29] confidently states that "we want the Bill to control credit as a whole, not one particular type of credit, such as hire-

---

22. *UDT v. Whitfield* [1987] C.C.L.R. 60. See now *Forthright Finance Ltd v. Ingate and Carlyle Finance Ltd* (1996) unreported.
23. See R. Goode *Consumer Credit Law* (1989) p. 496.
24. See *Lloyds Bowmaker Leasing Ltd v. MacDonald* [1993] C.C.L.R. 65. This was also confirmed in the case of *Moorgate Leasing v. Gell and Ugolini* [1988] C.C.L.R. 1. Leasing agreements are then seen to be consumer hire agreements under CCA 1974, s. 15.
25. See R. Goode *op. cit.* p. 432.
26. The effect of this is to make the dealer the deemed agent of the creditor under CCA 1974, s. 56(2).
27. This is because the paragraph is confined to a credit-broker selling goods to a *creditor* and *not* an *owner*.
28. Cmnd 4569, para. 6.6.22.
29. Mr Alan Williams M.P., Swansea West.

---

purchase, . . . we want identical protection as far as possible for *all* debtors".[30] However, not one single debate subsequently picked up the anomaly surrounding section 56(2). It can only be assumed that the fault lay in the drafting of the Act, for indeed in other jurisdictions the protection has been extended to such agreements.[31]

Exclusion of liability

Section 56(3) attempts to prevent exclusion by the contract of liability for the acts of the negotiator as such agent in relation to regulated agreements. This only applies to the assumption of the deemed agency and section 56(3)(b) does not prevent the contracting out of liability that arises out of the deemed agency insofar as the law provides for this, notably, a term exempting liability for misrepresentation is effective only if it is reasonable.[32]

Extent of deemed agency

Liability for antecedent negotiations is very wide and by virtue of section 56(4) extends to "any representations made by the negotiator to the debtor or hirer and any other dealings between them". A question that arises is whether the creditor's liability in tort is only for such acts of the negotiator as he would have been liable for if the negotiator had been his actual agent. A literal interpretation of section 56(2) of the words "shall be deemed to be conducted by the negotiator in the capacity of agent of the creditor as well as in his actual capacity" would be that any tort committed by the negotiator will be deemed to have been authorised by the creditor. As a result the creditor could be guilty of an offence under this deemed agency provision, for example, under the Trade Descriptions Act 1968 and the Consumer Protection Act 1987, subject to the relevant defences under that legislation, notably, under section 24 of the 1968 Act (offences due to the act or default of another person) and also sections 10(4), 24 and 39 of the 1987 Act.

There will be a right of contribution to the creditor for the liability incurred under section 75(2) of the CCA 1974. In any case a right to contribution would arise under the Civil Liability (Contribution) Act 1978 in respect of *civil* liability since both the creditor and the negotiator are liable in respect of the same damage.[33]

The following consequences arise out of credit brokerage under the CCA 1974:

    1. Deemed agent of the creditor for such purposes as:

[30.] See *Hansard*, H.C. Vol. 877 col. 46, (emphasis added).
[31.] See *A.L. Hamblin Equipment Pty Ltd v. Federal Commissioner of Taxation* (1974) 4 A.T.R. 208.
[32.] UCTA 1977, s. 8.
[33.] Civil Liability (Contribution) Act 1978, s. 1.

    (a) notice of withdrawal from a prospective agreement;
    (b) notice of cancellation in respect of a cancellable agreement;
    (c) notice rescinding the agreement;
These deemed agency provisions cannot be excluded under the CCA .[34]

2. By virtue of Regulations 1(2) and 2 of the Consumer Credit (Quotations) Regulations 1989,[35] a credit-broker is authorised to receive a request for a quotation and if he receives this request, is obliged to give or cause to be given to the person requesting such a document a quotation in accordance with the Regulation. Furthermore by virtue of section 10(3) Supply of Goods (Implied Terms) Act 1973 and sections 4(4)(b), 9(4)(b) of the Supply of Goods and Services Act 1982, if a customer makes known to a credit-broker the purposes for which he proposes acquiring the goods or hiring the goods, then there is an implied condition that the goods supplied must be fit unless it is possible to demonstrate non-reliance.[36]

Nature of credit brokerage

The material element of credit brokerage entails effecting introductions of individuals desiring to obtain credit or goods on hire to persons carrying on a consumer credit or a consumer hire business, or the introduction of individuals desiring to obtain credit or to obtain goods on hire to other credit-brokers.[37] Whilst the emphasis is upon a one-way introduction, individuals to creditors, it probably also extends to introductions of prospective creditors to debtors. Merely advertising credit facilities is not an introduction and neither is making the creditor's application forms available in display boxes or helping to complete these forms.[38] The issue of what constitutes an introduction is a question of fact. However, a person is engaged in credit brokerage even where the introduction is effected by his agent.[39] Furthermore, it is not a credit-brokerage business merely to advertise another's credit or to recommend a source of credit, where there is no commission or other arrangement between the party recommending the source of credit and the credit provider. This also applies to consumer hire. The activity of introducing only corporate customers to sources of credit or hire is also not credit brokerage.

    A consumer credit licence is required for the conduct of a credit-brokerage business and it is an offence to conduct business as a

---

[34.] CCA 1974, s. 173.
[35.] S.I. 1989 No. 1126.
[36.] See Chap. 3, above.
[37.] CCA 1974, s. 145(2).
[38.] See *Brookes v. Retail Credit Cards Ltd* (1985) 150 J.P. 131. [1986] Crim.L.R. 327.
[39.] See *Hicks v. Walker* (1984) 148 J.P. 636.

credit-broker without a licence, whilst agreements entered into with an unlicensed credit-broker are only enforceable on the order of the Director General of Fair Trading pursuant to an application made to him.[40]

Collateral Contract

Where a dealer makes to a prospective lessee a representation concerning the goods to be leased and such a statement is intended to have contractual force, an action for damages will lie at the suit of the lessee against the dealer if the representation is untrue and as a result the lessee has suffered damage. The consideration for such a collateral contract is that the intending lessee will enter into the finance lease agreement.[41] Thus is *Charnock v. Liverpool Corporation*,[42] the plaintiff's car was damaged and repaired under an insurance contract between his insurance company and a garage. It was held that there was a collateral contract by which the garage promised the plaintiff to do the repairs reasonably quickly, the consideration being that by leaving the car with the garage this gave the latter the opportunity of the repair contract with the insurance company.

The obvious analogy in the finance leasing context in establishing a collateral contract is *Andrews v. Hopkinson*.[43] In this case the plaintiff approached the dealer with a view to buying a second-hand car on hire-purchase terms. He obtained the following assurance from the dealer: "It's a good little bus. I would stake my life on it; you will have no trouble with it". The plaintiff then agreed to hire the car from a finance company, to whom the dealer sold it, and unfortunately the car turned out to be exceedingly troublesome. McNair J. held that the promise by the dealer constituted a collateral contract by which the dealer warranted the goods in consideration of the plaintiff signing a hire-purchase proposal for submission to the finance company. This was clearly a case where the statement was made with a contractual intention and was not a mere misrepresentation.[44]

It will be necessary to demonstrate that the statement made by the dealer had contractual force. One inevitable consequence of such an approach is that it would appear to undermine even further the parol

---

[40.] CCA 1974, s. 149.
[41.] See *Webster v. Higgin* [1948] 2 All E.R. 127.
[42.] [1968] 1 W.L.R. 1498.
[43.] [1957] 1 Q.B. 229.
[44.] See *Independent Broadcasting Authority v. EMI Electronics* (1980) 14 Build. L.R. 1.

evidence rule and also, perhaps more fundamentally, to attack the base common law position which is hostile to the recovery of damages for innocent misrepresentation. Unless there is a written contract there is the possibility that the parol evidence rule may prevent the successful incorporation of extrinsic evidence. Nevertheless, the rule is subject to so many exceptions that they have practically destroyed the rule. Thus, it does *not* apply: (1) where the evidence established the existence of a collateral contract; (2) where it can be shown that the document was not intended as a complete record of the contract terms; (3) where its existence or operation was dependent upon some prior unexpected stipulation; or (4) where it was procured by some illegality or misrepresentation. It is not surprising, therefore, that the Law Commission has recommended no reform of the parol evidence rule, declaring that the "rule" is not as extensive as traditionally expounded.[44a]

The question of whether a statement made during the course of negotiation remains a mere representation or becomes a contractual term, turns on the intention of the parties. Such a criterion is notoriously elusive, but in determining the precise legal status of a statement some reliance has been placed upon the *point* during the negotiations at which the statement was made.[44b] The further away from the making of the contract it was made the more likely it is to be considered as a misrepresentation. In *Routledge v. McKay*,[44c] the seller of a motorbicycle incorrectly told the buyer that it was a 1942 model, but the contract was not concluded until one week later and the Court of Appeal held that this statement was not, thereby, a term. In the same way, if after an oral representation the terms of the sale are reduced into writing which does not include the representation, this may indicate that it did not form part of the agreement. However, in this circumstance, the court will readily infer a collateral contract as illustrated by the case of *Couchman v. Hill*.[44d] Here, a statement at an auction by the auctioneer that a heifer was "unserved" was held to amount to a collateral warranty, for breach of which the auctioneer was liable even though the main contract excluded liability for fault, imperfections and errors of description. Most of the cases where collateral contracts have been upheld[44e] have been where the representation has induced the representee into a contract not with the representor himself but with a third party.

The significance of the collateral contract issue lies in the measure of damages available. Whilst most lease transactions are structured to minimise the privity of contract problems[45] posed in a finance leasing

---

[44a.] See *Law of Contract—The Parol Evidence Rule* (Law Com. No. 154 (1986)).

[44b.] See *Oscar Chess Ltd v. Williams* [1957] 1 W.L.R. 370; *Dick Bentley Productions Ltd v. Harold Smith (Motors) Ltd* [1965] 1 W.L.R. 623.

[44c.] [1954] 1 W.L.R. 615.

[44d.] [1947] K.B. 554.

[44e.] See *Brown v. Sheen and Richmond Car Sales* [1950] 1 All E.R. 1102; *Andrews v. Hopkinson* [1957] 1 Q.B. 229.

[45.] These have been discussed in Chap. 3.

context, typically through the lessor agreeing to assign to the lessee those warranties created in the supply agreement, nonetheless this will not give the lessee adequate protection in relation to those warranties given to the lessee in dealer-lessee negotiations. In any case, the lessee as the assignee of the warranties may be limited to damages suffered by the lessor due to the supplier's breach rather than recovering for its own damages. The difficulty here is that the interests of the lessor and the lessee are not the same, nor are the damages suffered by each. In the case of a delay in delivery when payment is conditional upon delivery, the loss or damage to the lessor may be minimal. On the other hand, the lessee may have suffered huge consequential losses. The question is not of transferring rights from the lessor to the lessee, but of giving the lessee an independent cause of action against the supplier. Significantly, in the absence of agreement, some United States courts have allowed a direct action against the supplier on the basis of the latter's strict liability, the lessor being regarded as merely performing a financing function.[46]

The quantification of damages can only be assessed in the light of the impact of the breach of the collateral contract on the main lease agreement.

Damages for a Non-Repudiatory Breach of Lease Agreement

Where the defect can be repaired then the damages recoverable will be the out of possession cost (hiring a substitute) together with the reasonable cost of repairs. As such these losses are easily quantifiable.

Damages for Rescission of Lease Contract

Where the equipment cannot be used and the lessee returns the goods to the lessor, if the lessee incurs a liability on termination as stipulated by the contract or alternatively is liable under a minimum payment clause, this liquidated sum may properly be regarded as constituting a loss flowing from the dealer's breach which would fall within the first limb of the test laid down for remoteness in *Hadley v. Baxendale*,[47] that is the loss is sufficiently connected to the breach. Under the second limb of the rule, the defendant is made liable for such losses as may reasonably be supposed to have been in the contemplation of the parties at the time of the contract as the probable result of its breach. In the context of equipment leasing, where the asset is of an income-producing kind, the lessee should be able to recover for the loss of profit that the dealer could reasonably have contemplated as flowing from the breach. This can be

---

[46.] See *Citicorp Leasing Inc v. Allied Inst'l Distribs Inc.* 454 F.Supp. 511 (1977); *Atlas Indus v. Nat'l Cash Register Co.* 216 Kan. 213 (1975).
[47.] (1854) 9 Exch. 341.

illustrated in the famous case of *Victoria Laundry (Windsor) Ltd v. Newman Industries Ltd*[48] where the defendants were late in supplying a boiler required by the plaintiffs for their laundry and dyeing business. It was held that the plaintiffs were liable for loss of normal profits resulting from the plaintiffs' loss of business, but not for additional losses relating to the special contracts entered into on particularly lucrative terms, as these could not have been foreseen by the seller. Of course, the transferee is under a duty to mitigate his loss where he can, for example, by hiring substitute goods pending delivery.

Remedies

Consequential Loss

Consequential loss claims may well arise upon the acceptance of goods which prove to be defective. The rules in *Hadley v. Baxendale* (1854) provide a sound and rational basis for paying due regard to the normal and foreseeable results which flow as a result of breach of contract. Nonetheless, there are difficulties with constructing a single formula which expresses the degree of foreseeability necessary. In *The Heron II*,[49] the House of Lords seems to have settled on "not unlikely" as expressing the degree of foreseeability. The problem here is that it may not be just always to impose liability for foreseeable consequences, especially as other factors may be relevant. Thus, in the case of sale of goods, the price of the goods will normally reflect the scarcity value of them.[50]

In the context of equipment leasing the lessee will be able to recover for consequential losses if they fall within the reasonable anticipation of the defendant in the light of the circumstances known to him. Thus, the lessee will have to prove that the supplier had knowledge of any special contract, such as a particularly valuable sub-contract, and that it was reasonably foreseeable that such a contract would be lost as a result of the breach. In practice, this will be a difficult burden to displace.

A dramatic illustration of the difficulties posed by the foreseeability test can be seen in *H. Parsons (Livestock) v. Uttley and Co. Ltd*.[51] In this case, the defendants supplied and installed a large hopper for holding animal foodstuffs for the plaintiff, a pig farmer. A ventilator at the top of the hopper, which could not be seen from the ground, was left closed with the result that some of the food became mouldy. The pigs became ill and subsequently a more serious condition was triggered off by the first illness with the result that many of the pigs died. The farmer recovered for all his lost and diseased pigs on the basis that this was foreseeable. The Court of Appeal rejected the view that the duty of fitness for purpose, which is implied under the Sale of Goods Act 1979,

---

[48.] [1949] 2 Q.B. 528.
[49.] [1969] 1 A.C. 350.
[50.] See *Victoria Laundries v. Newman Industries* (n. 50, above).
[51.] [1978] Q.B. 791.

excludes the operation of the normal rule in *Hadley v. Baxendale*, but nonetheless upheld the verdict in favour of the plaintiff. In this case Lord Denning M.R. held that there was no distinction between the "natural contemplation" test of remoteness in contract and the "reasonable foreseeability" test in tort, where the loss suffered resulted from physical injury to the property in question. The majority, however (Scarman and Orr L.JJ.) did not support this distinction, but it was held unnecessary for the plaintiffs to show that the defendants ought reasonably to have contemplated that pigs would die from being fed mouldy nuts: it was sufficient that there was an appreciation of the serious possibility of pigs suffering injury or death if fed with nuts stored in a hopper unfit for storage purposes. As Scarman L.J. put it[52]:

> "The assumption [to be made] is of the parties asking themselves not what is likely to happen if the nuts are mouldy but what is likely to happen to the pigs if the hopper is unfit for storing nuts suitable to be fed to them. While, on his finding, nobody at the time of contract could have expected *E. coli* to ensue from eating mouldy nuts, he is clearly—and as a matter of common sense, rightly—saying that people would contemplate, upon the second assumption, the serious possibility of injury and even death among pigs."

There does seem to be an air of unreality about the foreseeability test here, because it would seem that the only events which can be regarded as unforeseeable, following this case, are those in which the train of events has been interrupted by conscious human intervention. This sees to go too far, especially in the light of the finding of fact that, whilst it was usual for pigs to suffer illness through eating mouldy nuts, the event in question related to the toxicity in pig food. It would appear that the remoteness test laid down by Scarman L.J. destroys the distinction between the rules of remoteness in contract and those of tort.

If the lessee does not take the normal precautions with a view to discovering any patent or latent defect concerning goods delivered, this may be a *novus actus interveniens* preventing the supplier being liable for the consequences of his breach. Thus in *Lambert v. Lewis*,[53] a farmer who continued to use a coupling, which he knew or ought to have known was defective could not claim indemnity from the seller in respect to the farmer's liability to the plaintiff, who was injured when the coupling gave way. However, where the goods have been put to their contemplated use and the defect amounts to a breach of the contract of supply, it has been held that the buyer may recover for personal injury as well as injury to other property.[54]

Particular dilemmas have arisen where defective goods are of an income-producing kind. It is clear that the hirer cannot claim both the diminution in the warranted value at the contract delivery date and the

---

[52.] *Ibid*. at 812.
[53.] [1982] A.C. 225.
[54.] *Bostock and Co. Ltd v. Nicholson and Sons Ltd* [1904] 1 K.B. 725.

full loss of profit resulting from the nonconformity of the goods, as this would allow him to duplicate his compensation. The problem is that there are several ways of calculating loss of profit. In the troublesome case of *Cullinane v. British 'Rema' Manufacturing Co*,[55] the Court of Appeal held that the buyer, in that case, could not split his claim as between capital loss and income loss. This was an indefensible position and it is hoped that in future the decision will not be followed. Of course, this does not mean that the plaintiff should be free to split his claim in arbitrary fashion. Reference must surely be made to what a reasonable hirer would do to mitigate his loss, for example by hiring substitute goods in appropriate cases. The problem of double recovery can be seen in *George Mitchell (Chesterfield) Ltd v. Finney Lock Seeds Ltd*,[56] where a seed merchant sold defective seed to a farmer with the result that the latter's crop failed. It was said that the damages included "all the costs incurred by the [farmer] in the cultivation of the worthless crop as well as the profit [he] would have expected to make from a successful crop if proper seeds had been supplied".[57] In this regard the reference to "profit" must refer to the proceeds of a successful crop less the cost of cultivating this type of crop, and this cost, of course, might well be lower than the cost of attempting to cultivate an unsuccessful crop.

Contributory Negligence

Where the defendant has broken a contractual obligation which is expressed in terms of taking reasonable care, but which does not correspond to a common law duty of care, it is unclear whether the provisions of the Law Reform (Contributory Negligence) Act 1945 apply. However, where the defendant is sued for the breach of a strict contractual duty, then the 1945 Act is inapplicable and damages cannot be reduced on the ground of contributory negligence.[58] In this respect the plaintiff may be overcompensated as no reduction is made to reflect the plaintiff's contribution to the loss which has arisen.[59]

Mitigation of Loss

Where the supplier is in breach, the lessee will have a duty to mitigate loss, the policy being to encourage reasonable self-reliance. The term "duty" is somewhat of a misnomer since the plaintiff cannot himself be

[55.] [1954] 1 Q.B. 292.
[56.] [1983] A.C. 803.
[57.] *Ibid.* at 812.
[58.] *Forsikringsaktieselskapet Vesta v. Butcher* [1989] A.C. 852.
[59.] See Law Commission Report, *Contributory Negligence as a Defence in Contract* (No. 219) (1993).

sued for a failure to comply with this, rather the consequence of such a failure is that damages are reduced for the avoidable loss. There are two aspects to the mitigation principle, the first focusing on inaction whilst the second centres around unreasonable action.

Under a finance lease where there has been a breach of a collateral contract between the dealer and the lessee, it will be unreasonable for the plaintiff to turn down an offer of alternative performance from the dealer[60] or, perhaps, even to refuse an offer of late delivery.[61] Even so, the plaintiff need not take action which will put his commercial reputation or good public relations at risk.[62] The overriding issue concerning the duty to mitigate is whether or not the lessee's conduct is reasonable having regard to the character of the equipment and the sub-contract in question. Nevertheless, the plaintiff need not take steps which he financially cannot afford, that is impecuniosity. Thus in *Muhammud Issa El Sheikh Ahmed v. Ali*[63] and *Trans Trust SPRL v. Danubian Trading Co. Ltd*[64] loss flowing from impecuniosity, at least in a contract scenario, are recoverable so long as they satisfy the normal test for remoteness.[65] Even in the context of the tort of negligence, Beldham L.J. has recently said "... it is only in an exceptional case that it is possible or correct to isolate impecuniosity ... as a separate cause and as terminating the consequences of a defendant's wrong".[66]

One interesting problem that arises in the finance leasing context is the status of the main-lease contract and the lessee's action against the dealer under a collateral contract. It may be an unreasonable action if the lessee refuses to rescind the lease contract if his failure to do so results in greater loss. Whilst it is true that the duty to mitigate cannot be used by the guilty party to force rescission or termination of a contract,[67] nonetheless, the contract of rescission relates to one which is a totally separate contract, notably the finance lease. If, however, the lessor disputes the lessee's right to rescind, then it is an established principle that the plaintiff need not take steps which would involve him in complicated litigation.[68] It is otherwise if the continuance of the equipment lease is blatantly unreasonable where it is likely that the dealer would succeed under the so-called duty to mitigate loss.

---

[60]. *Payzu Ltd v. Saunders* [1919] 2 K.B. 581.
[61]. *Sotiros Shipping Inc. v. Sameiet Solholt; The Solholt* [1983] 1 Lloyd's Rep. 605.
[62]. *James Finlay and Co. Ltd v. Kwik Hoo Tong* [1929] 1 K.B. 400.
[63]. [1947] A.C. 414.
[64]. [1952] 2 Q.B. 297.
[65]. *Cf. Owners of Dredger Liesbosch v. Owners of Steamship Edison; The Liesbosch* [1933] A.C. 449.
[66]. *Mattocks v. Mann* [1993] R.T.R. 13.
[67]. *White and Carter (Councils) Ltd v. McGregor* [1962] A.C. 413.
[68]. *Pilkington v. Wood* [1953] Ch. 770.

The Position in Tort

Economic loss

The doctrine of privity of contract only means that a non-contracting party cannot bring an action on the contract, and it does not exclude a successful action being brought in tort.[69]

Misrepresentation

If the lessee suffers loss as a result of acting in reliance on a fraudulent statement from a dealer, then he can recover damages in an action for deceit. He can do this whether he rescinds the lease contract or not,[70] although he cannot pursue both remedies at once since this would be tantamount to double recovery for the same loss.[71]

The test for fraudulent misrepresentation is laid out in the famous case of *Derry v. Peek*[72] where the House of Lords held that a statement is fraudulent only if it is made (1) with knowledge of its falsity; (2) without belief in its truth; or (3) recklessly, not caring whether it is true or false. More recently the test has been expressed in terms of recklessness in making a false representation.[73] Such a test is, of course, a very heavy burden for the plaintiff to discharge and it is for this reason that an action under section 2(1) of the Misrepresentation Act 1967 will normally be the preferred course, because the burden of proof is shifted onto the representor to show that it was not negligent whilst the "fiction of fraud" device employed in the section would appear to require the court to apply the deceit rule, namely, the measure of damages is the loss directly flowing from the fraud and any consequential damage suffered.[74] There is growing judicial support for this view.[75] Even so, an action in deceit may be important where a contract is not concluded, notably, the equipment lease, so that a statutory action under section 2(1) of the Misrepresentation Act 1967 will fail as would an action based on a collateral contract, because the consideration for the dealer's warranty (the prospective lessee's entry into the equipment lease agreement) will not have materialised.

Product liability

The liability of the dealer as a supplier of defective goods which results in personal injury or damage to property is discussed in Chapter 3, above.

[69.] See Chap. 3, above.
[70.] See *Smith New Court Securities Ltd v. Scrimgeous Asset Management Ltd* [1994] 4 All E.R. 225.
[71.] See *Archer v. Brown* [1985] Q.B. 401.
[72.] (1889) 14 App. Cas. 337.
[73.] See *Thomas Witter Ltd v. TBP Industries Ltd* [1996] 2 All E.R. 573.
[74.] *Doyle v. Olby (Ironmongers) Ltd* [1969] 2 Q.B. 158.
[75.] *Royscot Trust Ltd v. Rogerson* [1991] 2 Q.B. 297.

Recovery of Pre-Payments

The common law position

In the case of a deposit paid by the prospective lessee to the dealer in connection with an equipment lease to be entered into with a finance lessor which does not materialise, the lessee will normally be entitled to recover the deposit from the dealer. The payer will recover his pre-payment either because there is deemed to be a total failure of consideration or because it is an implied term in the contract of sale between the dealer and the prospective lessor that the lessee should be restored to his original position in the event of non-completion of the sale.

The orthodox common law position is that any part payment made will depend upon whether it is a genuine advance instalment of the purchase price, or whether it is a deposit intended to operate as security for the due performance of the buyer's obligations. In the case of the former, if the supply contract is not concluded part payment may be recovered on the basis of total failure of consideration. Under the common law the deposit in this circumstance is forfeited. Nevertheless, in the case of prospective regulated consumer credit agreements, section 59 of the CCA 1974 provides that the intended deposit becomes recoverable on the ground of total failure of consideration.

In *Dies v. British and International Mining etc. Corp.*,[76] the buyers paid 37 per cent of the price of the goods in advance and then defaulted in the payment of the balance, so the sellers refused to deliver the goods. The buyers admitted their liability for damages but recovered the advance payment on the basis of total failure of consideration. The distinction between a part payment which is recoverable and a forfeitable deposit which is not, is a matter of construction of the contract. In this respect, the *Dies* case may be construed as the buyer's obligation to pay the whole price being replaced by their liability to pay damages. Significant problems arise where a buyer is required by the contract to pay a deposit in advance which has not been paid and where this would have been forfeited on breach. In principle, the time of payment should not be relevant. This is confirmed in *Damon Cia Naviera v. Hapag-Lloyd; The Blankenstein*[77] where a buyer contracted to buy a ship for $2.36 million and to pay a deposit of 10 per cent of the price. The contract expressly provided that, if the buyer failed to complete, the deposit would be irrecoverable. It was held that this deposit was forfeitable even though the seller had resold the ship at a small loss which was far less than the amount of the deposit. The plaintiff, as seller who was suing for the recovery of the deposit, succeeded in upholding what was, in essence, a penal claim. As such, the case demonstrates the court's

[76.] [1939] 1 K.B. 724.
[77.] [1985] 1 W.L.R. 435.

disinclination to extend equitable relief to forfeiture in commercial contracts.[78]

The House of Lords in *Johnson v. Agnew* (1980) drew a distinction between rescission of the contract *ab initio* which has retrospective effect, and a mere subsequent termination of the contract. This has repercussions if a buyer is under an obligation to pay in advance but does not do so, and the contract is subsequently terminated. Thus in *Hyundai Heavy Industries Co. Ltd v. Papadopoulos*,[79] a shipbuilding case in which the price was payable by instalments as the work proceeded, the House of Lords held that the buyer could be sued for an instalment which fell due on July 15 despite the fact that the seller exercised a cancellation right on September 6. This approach is over-formalistic and overlooks that the buyer's duty to pay is surely conditional on subsequent performance by the other party. Even if the contract involves an element of manufacture and sale, it cannot be appropriate that the seller can sue for the recovery of an advance substantial payment where he has incurred only minimal advance expenditure prior to cancellation.

Equitable relief against forfeiture

Equity's jurisdiction to relieve against forfeiture extends to commercial transactions, where a transaction or where a transfer of proprietary or possessory rights has taken place. In exercising its discretion whether or not to grant relief the test is whether the retention of the money would be unconscionable in the light of the conduct of the parties, the nature and gravity of the breach and the amount of money which might be forfeited.[80]

Part-Exchange Goods

There has been very little discussion in the case law concerning the nature of the part-exchange transaction, whereby a lessee gives in an old vehicle or equipment and trades it in by way of part-exchange for new goods on lease or hire provided by a lessor. The status of the part-exchange goods needs now to be considered.

Liability prior to delivery of the part-exchange goods

In the case of a part-exchange transaction there is no difficulty in categorising the supply of new goods as a sale simply because the supplier will be receiving a composite consideration. Thus in *Aldridge v. Johnson*[81] there was an agreement to transfer 32 bullocks valued at £192

[78.] See *Goker v. NWS Bank, The Times*, May 23, 1990. See Chap. 3 above.
[79.] [1980] 1 W.L.R. 1129.
[80.] See Chap. 3, above.
[81.] (1857) 7 B. & B. 855.

in return for 100 quarters of barley valued at £125, the set-off of £23 to be paid in cash, this was construed as a reciprocal sale.[82] Surprisingly, there appears to be only one English decision which deals with the trading-in of motor vehicles in part-exchange, even though it is such a common place everyday experience. The facts in this case, *G.J. Dawson (Clapham) Ltd v. H. and G. Dutfield*,[83] are worth elaboration. The plaintiffs were dealers in secondhand lorries and agreed to transfer to the defendants two lorries for £475 and take in exchange two other lorries valued at £225, provided that they were delivered within one month. The defendants paid in cash the balance of £250 but did not deliver the lorries. It was held that this was a contract for sale and the plaintiffs were therefore able to sue for the price. The decision would have been otherwise if no value had been assigned, as in the Irish Court decision in *Flynn v. Mackin*.[84]

Whether the transaction is a sale or exchange is a question of contractual intention. Normally the position would appear to be that by agreeing to take in the part-exchange goods, this is an option for the prospective lessee to sell the goods to the dealer which will form part of a deposit for the purposes of the finance lease transaction. The grant of this option is part of the consideration for the lessee entering into the finance lease transaction. In the ordinary course this option must be exercised at the time the lease is concluded, which coincides with delivery of the part-exchange goods, or if no time is stipulated then presumably within a reasonable time.

After delivery of the part-exchange goods

Problems may arise if the dealer has agreed with the lessee to discharge any outstanding finance on the equipment perhaps by way of hire-purchase. Clearly this will be a condition precedent before property can pass, although the dealer may have a power to pass a good title in the goods.[85]

Contractual matters

Introduction. The normal rule is that property and risk will pass in the part-exchange goods on delivery. If, however, as a result of searching with HPI plc an outstanding finance interest is recorded and this fact is known, property will only be "fed" to the dealer on discharge of the outstanding sums. Certainly the implied title terms will apply as between the prospective lessee and the dealer with respect to the part-exchange goods.[86] The issue of satisfactory quality and fitness for

[82] See also *Forsyth v. Jervis* (1816) 1 Stark. 437; *Sheldon v. Cox* (1824) 3 B. & C. 420.
[83] [1936] 2 All E.R. 232.
[84] [1974] I.R. 101.
[85] See Chap. 6, below.
[86] See SGA 1979, s. 12.

purpose under the Sale of Goods Act 1979 will only apply if the sale is in the course of a business. Clearly the issue of reliance especially on the description will be pertinent since the presumption must be that the dealer will rely on his own skill and judgment.[87]

In so far as the dealer has a remedy for breach of the contract of sale with the prospective lessee, then the normal principles will apply following the delivery of the goods, namely rejection of the goods for breach and recovery of the price. This will depend upon whether the remedy is exercisable which is linked to the question of acceptance. The seller must afford the buyer a reasonable opportunity to examine the goods.[88] Acceptance is an interrelating rule to this right of examination under section 35(1)–(3) SGA 1979. From this it appears that the buyer will lose his right to reject in the following circumstances.

Express acceptance. As the buyer has a statutory right to examine the goods, in order to bar his right to reject, it must be shown that the buyer has elected to accept the goods delivered as conforming with the contract. This could amount to a complete waiver of all claims arising under the sale and supply contract.

Inconsistent Act. This has already been discussed.[89]

Lapse of time. If the dealer/buyer has not rejected the goods, section 35 provides that he is deemed to have accepted them if he retains them beyond a reasonable time. The issue is one of fact and the court must balance the interests of the parties. Clearly, if the market is a fluctuating one or is seasonal, protection of the seller's interest requires a speedier notification of rejection than when the market remains constant. The period of acceptance will depend upon the nature of the goods.

Remedies for misrepresentation

The dealer can rescind the part-exchange contract for misrepresentation and in the case of fraudulent or negligent misrepresentation, claim damages.[90] Where there is an innocent misrepresentation it is possible to recover under section 2(2) of the Misrepresentation Act 1967 for damages in lieu of rescission.[91]

Where the lease contract is not concluded

It is probable that the part-exchange transaction and the finance lease will be categorised as interdependent contracts, so that the part-

[87.] See *Harlingdon and Leinster Enterprises Ltd v. Christopher Hull Fine Art Ltd* [1991] 1 Q.B. 564.
[88.] Sale of Goods Act 1979, s. 34.
[89.] See Chap. 3, above.
[90.] See pp. 125–128.
[91.] *Ibid.*

exchange element may be construed as a sale subject to a condition subsequent, thereby, making it determinable if the financier does not accept the transaction. There is also a special provision under section 73(2) of the Consumer Credit Act 1974 for a part-exchange allowance in respect of a cancelled regulated agreement where property has been transferred.

Duties following cancellation of a regulated agreement under the Consumer Credit Act 1974

Where notice has been given, in the case of a hire-purchase or conditional sale transaction, section 72 generally places upon the debtor a legal duty to redeliver the goods subject to a lien for any part-exchange goods tendered by him.[92] Under section 73(2) the primary entitlement of the debtor or hirer is to recover the "part-exchange allowance". In the case of loan finance in a regulated debtor-creditor-supplier agreement, the creditor and the supplier are jointly and severally liable to him.[93] Within a period of 10 days from the date of cancellation, the duty to pay the part-exchange allowance will be discharged by the return of the part-exchanged goods where they are in substantially the same condition as originally delivered to the negotiator.[94] If both sides agree, any deterioration or delay regarding the return of the part-exchanged goods can be ignored.[95] As far as the debtor's obligations are concerned, he must retain possession of the goods and make them available for the creditor to collect, taking reasonable care of them in the meantime.[96] The duty to take reasonable care is confined to the period of 21 days after cancellation[97]; therefore he usually becomes an involuntary bailee with a duty to refrain from wilful damage.

Where money has been paid over to the debtor before the end of the "cooling-off" period, the CCA 1974 gives the debtor a choice: first, to take a month's free credit before repaying the credit already advanced[98]; or secondly, with regard to money already spent, he can repay the money with interest, as provided for in the credit agreement, so that the effect of the cancellation only relates to the linked supply transaction.[99] Cancellation of a credit agreement also entails the cancellation of linked transaction[1] as this has no effect until the principal agreement is made.[2] Here again the debtor must allow the goods to be collected and take

---

[92.] CCA 1974, s. 73(5).
[93.] CCA 1974, s. 70(3).
[94.] CCA 1974, s. 73(2).
[95.] CCA 1974, s. 173(2).
[96.] CCA 1974, s. 72(4).
[97.] CCA 1974, s. 72(8).
[98.] CCA 1974, s. 71(2)(a).
[99.] CCA 1974, s. 71(3).
[1.] CCA 1974, s. 69(1).
[2.] CCA 1974, s. 19(3).

reasonable care in the meantime, whilst sums paid out by him must be repaid. Cancellation of a directly financed transaction will leave the sale from dealer to financier still outstanding; this though should normally be covered through a contractual repurchase provision.

Wrongful Dealings in Leased Assets and Third Party Conflicts

Part 3

Wrongful Dealings in Leased Assets and Third Party Conflicts

Chapter 6

The Security of Property Principle

In this chapter we shall focus upon the general position involving a wrongful disposition by the hirer/lessee to a third party. The wrongful dealing may be by the hirer/lessee or it may be by the dealer through whom the hire-purchase/lease agreement was concluded. The disposition in question may be by way of outright sale or the creation of an encumbrance such as a lien[1] or by acting in a manner which destroys the owner's title such as affixing the goods to the land or destroying their identity through accession to or confusion with other chattels.[2]

The Property Principle

Introduction

There is a certain logic in the proposition that one cannot transfer what one does not have. Indeed this reflects the common law concept of *nemo dat quod (qui) non habet*, and the primacy of this principle is retained in the Sale of Goods Act 1979 (the SGA 1979) subject to the exceptions contained in sections 21 to 25 of that Act. There must, therefore, be compelling reasons for an owner to lose his interest in his goods. When considering the exceptions to this principle several policy factors emerge: estoppel; ostensible ownership and possession; protection of purchasers. Before considering these exceptions it is important to bear in mind that since title under English law is relative, even the exceptions to *nemo dat*, which must be treated as curing the seller's defective title, do not necessarily mean the granting of an absolute indefeasible title. This helps to explain why title can pass in property even under an illegal contract.

Title Claims and Illegal Transactions

It is sometimes asserted that title to property can pass under an illegal contract only where the plaintiff can establish the title without relying

[1.] See Chap. 7.
[2.] See Chaps 8, 9.

on the contract or on its illegality. [3] However, the case law in the hire-purchase and equipment lease context would tend to support the proposition that the law allows a party to rely on the illegal contract if it is for the purpose of showing title has passed as a matter of law. As the Privy Council held in *Singh v. Ali*[4]:

">. . . the transferee, having obtained the property, can assert his title to it against all the world, not because he has any merit of his own, but because there is no one who can assert a better title to it. The court does not confiscate the property because of the illegality—it has no power to do so."

Clearly, it is otherwise in non-title claims.

In *Belvoir Finance Co. Ltd v. Stapleton*,[5] the plaintiff finance company sued a third party for the conversion of goods which they had bought under an illegal contract. In order to succeed they had to show an immediate right to possession which could only be based upon their ownership of the goods. In order to do so they had to rely on the illegal contract of sale and their claim succeeded because, as Lord Denning held:

"Although the plaintiffs obtained the car under a contract which was illegal, nevertheless, inasmuch as the contract was executed and the property passed, the car belonged to the finance company (the plaintiffs) and they can claim it."[6]

This appears to be judicial confirmation of the finance company relying upon an illegal contract to establish title. Indeed as du Parcq L.J. held in *Bowmakers Ltd v. Barnet Instrument Ltd*[7]:

">. . . a man's *right to possess* his own chattels will as a general rule be enforced against one who, *without any claim of right*, is detaining them, or has converted them to his own use, even though it may appear from the pleadings, or in the course of the trial, that chattels in question came into the defendant's possession by reason of an illegal contract between himself and the plaintiff."

The General Effect of Unlawful Dispositions

The Equipment Lease

The security of property principle protects the lessor in the case of a wrongful disposition by the lessee in the absence of any exception to the

---

[3.] See Treitel, *The Law of Contract* (9th ed. 1995) pp. 438–447.
[4.] [1960] A.C. 167 at 176–177.
[5.] [1971] 1 Q.B. 210.
[6.] *Ibid.* at 218.
[7.] [1945] 1 K.B. 65 at 71.

principle applying. The lessor/owner will be able to sue and have the option of recovering the goods from the sub-buyer/lessee,[8] but if the lessor elects to affirm the sub-bailment then this may be categorised as a sub-bailment on terms.[9] If the lessor elects to determine the lease, an interesting problem that arises is whether in this context the lessee can invoke equity's jurisdiction to relieve against forfeiture.

Hire-Purchase and Conditional Sale

Different considerations apply to hire-purchase and conditional sale transactions. The purported sale is not wholly ineffective since the hirer can transfer his interest in the goods including, crucially, the option to purchase irrespective of whether the hire-purchase agreement contains a prohibition against assignment. This principle was established by the Court of Appeal in *Wickham Holdings Ltd v. Brooke House Motors Ltd*,[10] where it was held that even if the agreement prohibited the hirer from assigning the benefit of the agreement as well as from disposing of the goods, the finance company was entitled to recover only what it had lost from the hirer's unlawful act, namely, the outstanding balance of the hire-purchase price. Notwithstanding this important decision, the general approach of the English courts was to continue to pay lip service to the notion of two distinct elements to the hire-purchase agreement, namely the bailment and the option to purchase. The option to purchase was treated as a separate and severable part of the agreement,[11] whilst instalments were held to be rentals payable in consideration of the use and possession of the goods and not, as in a conditional sale agreement, as payments on account.[12] It took legislation, the Hire-Purchase Act 1964, the Supply of Goods (Implied Terms) Act 1973 and the Consumer Credit Act 1974 to generally formally assimilate hire-purchase to sale on credit.

As a result of legislative intervention, dispositions by a buyer holding under a conditional sale agreement are excluded from section 25(1) of the SGA 1979 and section 9 of the Factors Act 1889 (FA 1989). "A conditional sale agreement" means an agreement for the sale of goods which is a consumer credit agreement within the meaning of the Consumer Credit Act 1974. In this case it is provided that the buyer shall be deemed not to be a person who has bought or agreed to buy goods. However a conditional sale that does not pass the consumer credit test continues to carry the buyer's power to transmit title under section 25. Such an approach is hardly rational and gives the law an almost whimsical appearance, especially since motor vehicles where the

---

[8.] See Chap. 11, below.
[9.] See Chap. 2, above.
[10.] [1967] 1 All E.R. 117.
[11.] See *Whitelet Ltd v. Hill* [1918] 2 K.B. 808.
[12.] The issue of form versus function is still important. See *Forthright Finance Ltd v. Carlyle Finance Ltd*, January 28, 1997, C.A., unreported.

---

bulk of *nemo dat* problems arise is subject to its own special legislative regime.[13] A more rational reform would have been to have extended section 9 of the FA 1889 and section 25(1) of the SGA 1979 to apply to hire-purchase transactions but this did not occur.

Remedies of Innocent Purchaser

A person buying goods has the following remedies against a lessee or hirer who wrongfully disposes of the goods:

Rescission

Rescission is the restoration of the *status quo ante*, so that the price of the equipment can be recovered and also damages by way of an indemnity. However, in order to recover the loss of a bargain the remedy of rejection of the goods by way of the disposer's repudiation of contract for breach of the implied condition as to the right to sell under section 12(1) of the SGA 1979 would appear to be appropriate.

Rejection

Where there is a chain of sales, each buyer has a cause of action in contract for breach of condition.[14] A thorny dilemma is whether the seller can "cure" an initial defective title, for example, by paying out the lessor or financier under a hire-purchase or conditional sale contract.

A "right" to cure?

There appears to be nothing wrong in legal logic with the idea that a seller can cure a defective title. As the number of encumbered goods in the economy increases, it may be unfair to shift to the seller all of the credit and crime risks with regard to the title to chattels. One way of doing this is through adopting a limited notion of "cure". Just as the vendor selling goods to which he has no title is estopped from denying the validity of the transfer, so also, where the seller subsequently acquired a good title, the buyer is protected by the estoppel, that is, the estoppel is "fed". The basic problem here is determining at what stage the estoppel arises in the absence of waiver by the buyer. This is especially problematic in view of the fact that section 12(1) of the SGA 1979 envisages that a seller who does not have a right to sell at the time of the sale commits a breach of condition. This point arose and was considered in *Barber v. NWS Bank plc*[15] the facts of which are set out below.[16] It may be that a way of avoiding this dilemma is through

13. See below.
14. See *Bowmaker (Commercial) Ltd v. Day* [1965] 1 W.L.R. 1396; 2 All E.R. 856n.
15. [1996] 1 All E.R. 906.
16. See pp. 188–189, below.

section 11(4) which relegates a breach of condition to that of a warranty in a non-severable contract where the buyer has accepted the goods. The main difficulty here is that Atkin L.J.'s judgment in *Rowland v. Divall*[17] would seem to preclude this possibility:

> "The whole object of a sale is to transfer property from one person to another, and I think that in every contract of sale of goods there is an implied term to that effect that a breach of the condition that the seller has a right to sell the goods may be treated as a ground for rejecting the goods and repudiating the contract notwithstanding the acceptance within the meaning of the concluding words of [the sub-section] . . ."

In fact, there is no warrant for this view in the Act itself, and it is doubtful whether Atkin L.J. contemplated that his proposition would apply in cases where the seller had been able to remedy the breach before the repudiation by the buyer. It is noteworthy that in *Rowland v. Divall* the seller never acquired the right to sell the car, which was recovered from the buyer after four months' use, and it follows, therefore, that the buyer could not be regarded as having accepted the goods.

It does seem harsh that if the seller can and does cure his defective title before the buyer's repudiation, the latter can nevertheless repudiate the contract, despite prolonged use and perhaps depreciation of the asset. The Law Reform Committee's 12th Report, *Transfer of Title to Chattels*,[18] recommended that the buyer should not be able to recover the price in full in the situation where he had use of the goods. This approach has been echoed in subsequent Law Commission reports, but interestingly in the most recent Law Commission report,[19] the problems of quantifying the buyer's unjust enrichment have precluded any recommendation for reform in this area.[20] Although it may be the case, as the Law Commission Report on *Sale and Supply of Goods* points out,[21] that the valuation of the buyer's unjust enrichment on termination through his prolonged use of the goods will be uncertain, nonetheless if there has been a subsequent acquisition of title there can be no objection in principle to this feeding the title of the buyer if the latter had not, by that time, elected to treat the contract as repudiated. Indeed this is illustrated by *Butterworth v. Kingsway Motors Ltd*[22] where the hirer of a car under a hire-purchase agreement sold it but continued to pay the instalments as they fell due. After almost a year's use, the plaintiff was notified by the finance company that the car was on hire-purchase and he promptly terminated his contract with the defendant. Within a very

---

[17.] [1923] 2 K.B. 500 at 506–7.
[18.] Cmnd 2958 (1966) para. 36.
[19.] *Sale and Supply of Goods* (No. 160 (1987)).
[20.] *Ibid*. para. 6.4.
[21.] *Ibid*. para. 6.5.
[22.] [1954] 1 W.L.R. 1286.

short time, the hirer paid her final instalment, and it was held that this "fed" the titles of the intermediate buyers. Thus, although the plaintiff could recover the full price, all the intermediate buyers who had not terminated before their titles were "fed" could only recover damages for breach of contract.

A jurisprudential problem arises where the acquirer accepts delivery of the previously encumbered goods on hire-purchase or conditional sale. In this respect a distinction may be drawn between hire-purchase and conditional sale contracts in that in the case of the former the finance company warrants that it will be able to pass title in the goods at the time when the hirer exercises his option to purchase, whereas, in the case of a conditional sale the finance company at the time of the sale warrants that he has a right to sell at the time of entering into the agreement. This issue arose in *Barber v. NWS Bank plc*.[23] In this case the appellant, Barber, financed the acquisition of a car from Kestrel Garages (Eastbourne) Ltd by means of a conventional conditional sale agreement with NWS. In fact the car was subject to a prior hire-purchase interest and when Barber sought to sell the car to a motor trader in order to clear his debt with NWS, the sale was declined because of this prior interest which continued to be recorded on the outstanding finance register operated by HPI plc. Shortly afterwards Barber rescinded the agreement and it was held by the Court of Appeal, in proceedings brought under Order 14A of the Rules of the Supreme Court 1965 (as amended), that he was entitled to recover the whole amount paid under the conditional sale agreement, including the deposit paid by way of part-exchange since the Court of Appeal determined that the dealer received this in its capacity as NWS's agent. The Court reinforced the view that an express term as to title is a condition, so that Sir Roger Parker, who gave judgment on behalf of the Court of Appeal, held:

> "In my judgment there can be no doubt that the term was a condition. It was fundamental to the transaction that the bank had the property [in the car] at the time of the agreement and would retain it until paid in full the monies due under the agreement."[24]

At the time of the rescission NWS did not have the right to sell the vehicle, although by the time of the application to the Court, NWS had settled the outstanding amount with the previous finance company owner. It would seem from this that the crucial question is not whether the party to a contract has received any benefit at all, but whether he has received the benefit which he was entitled to expect under the contract. Similarly, in hire-purchase agreements, the question is whether the hirer has enjoyed both possession and a valid option to purchase. In *Karflex Ltd v. Poole*,[25] it was held that despite the fact that the hirer had

---

[23.] [1996] 1 All E.R. 906.
[24.] *Ibid.*
[25.] [1933] 2 K.B. 251.

defaulted on his instalments under a hire-purchase agreement, he was nevertheless entitled to repudiate the contract and recover his deposit because the finance company was not the owner of the car at the date of delivery.

Affirmation and damages

If the defect of title is cured by reason of a payment to the owner by the ultimate purchaser himself, this payment represents the measure of his loss and he is entitled to recover this from the vendor.[26]

Exceptions to the Security of Property Principle

Estoppel

Section 21(1) of SGA 1979 provides:

> "Subject to this Act, where goods are sold by a person who is not their owner and who does not sell them under the authority or with the consent of the owner, the buyer acquires no better title to the goods than the seller had, unless the owner of the goods is by his conduct precluded from denying the seller's authority to sell."

Although the SGA 1979 adopts the term "precluded" rather than "estopped", section 21(1) is usually classed as an example of the doctrine of estoppel, the rationale of which, according to Coke, is that "a man's own act or acceptance stoppeth or closeth up his mouth to allege or pleade the truth".[27] Inasmuch as it is true to say that a rule which prevents the owner from asserting his rights in effect takes them away from him, it cannot be the case that the estoppel of such a person can bind another (who is not privy to the estoppel) with a title paramount. Thus, Battersby and Preston have suggested[28] that the word "owner" in section 21(1) must mean "the owner of the title that is being transferred", since otherwise it would have an extremely limiting effect on the section because the doctrine of estoppel would not apply against a possessor with a defeasible title.

The Proprietary Effect of Estoppel

Introduction

The position of the third party successor to the vendor is pertinent. It has sometimes been maintained, drawing upon the approach taken by

---

[26]. *Cf. Warman v. Southern Countries Car Finance Corporation Ltd* [1949] 1 All E.R. 711.

[27]. Co. Litt. 352a.

[28]. (1972) 35 M.L.R. 268.

Devlin L.J. in the Court of Appeal in *Eastern Distributors Ltd v. Goldring*,[29] that the effect of section 21 of the SGA 1979 is to transfer to the buyer a real title and not a metaphorical title by estoppel. In this case a van owner signed hire-purchase proposal forms which made a dealer appear to be the owner. This was part of a scheme to enable the customer to obtain another vehicle on credit, without having to pay the deposit required by the then current credit regulations. The scheme failed but the dealer used the documents which the owner had given him; he was able to sell the van to a hire-purchase company although having no right to do so. The hire-purchase company acquired a good title because, although the dealer had no right to sell, the owner's conduct in completing false forms estopped him from asserting this. It was held:

"... that apparent authority to sell is an exception to the maxim *nemo dat quod non habet*; and it is plain from the wording that if the owner of the goods is precluded from denying authority, the buyer will in fact acquire a better title than the seller."[30]

Subsequent case law has experienced difficulty in determining the exact basis of the decision. In *Stoneleigh Finance Ltd v. Phillips*,[31] Davies L.J. referred to an "ostensible title to sell" in connection with *Eastern Distributors*, while in *Snook v. London and West Riding Investments Ltd*,[32] Russell L.J. stated that the plaintiff in that case was estopped by his own conduct.[33] Other decisions have referred to the *Eastern Distributors* case as being based on ostensible ownership and not ostensible agency. It appears that the position is very confused especially since, on the facts, the decision in *Eastern Distributors* could have been justified on more conventional agency principles, because the owner had consented to give the van to a mercantile agent for the purpose of sale as well as relevant documentation relating to the van.

There are real difficulties in reconciling the proprietary estoppel doctrine with statutory interpretation since section 17(1) of the SGA 1979 adopts the rule that property passes by agreement and not by conduct. Moreover, the proprietary estoppel approach fails to take into account the dynamic nature of the sale transaction, as it concentrates on the assumption that there are three parties: *viz.*, an owner, a rogue and a bona fide purchaser. In fact, the goods may have passed through several hands and the innocent purchaser may have been persuaded to enter into the sale transaction by a rogue who knew the extent of an agent's authority. If title is a rule of evidence or impressed with an equity and not of absolute conveyance, the rogue, as sub-purchaser, will not prevail

---

[29.] [1957] 2 Q.B. 600.
[30.] *Ibid. per* Devlin L.J. at 611.
[31.] [1965] 2 Q.B. 537.
[32.] [1967] 2 Q.B. 786.
[33.] *Ibid.* at 803–804.

against the owner. The essential issue is whether goods are freely negotiable: the development of the doctrine of estoppel in the context of chattels has stressed the need for a representation either by words or by conduct.

The limited extent of the doctrine of estoppel is illustrated by *Shaw v. Commissioner of Police of the Metropolis*,[34] where the owner of a Porsche motor car entrusted it to a rogue to find a buyer. Unfortunately, the owner signed a letter stating that he had sold the car to the rogue. Relying on that letter, a bona fide purchaser agreed to buy the car under a conditional contract which did not pass property until the rogue vendor was paid. The Court of Appeal held that the owner of goods was precluded by section 21 of the 1979 Act from denying an intermediate seller's authority to sell goods of which the seller was not the owner, only if the goods were "sold" by the intermediate seller. Statutory estoppel did not apply where there was merely an agreement to sell since, under section 2(5) of the SGA 1979, an agreement to sell does not involve a transfer of property.

Apparent ownership and apparent authority

Apparent ownership is where the agent appears to be the owner himself whereas apparent authority is where the agent appears to act within the scope of his agency with a principal (whether disclosed or undisclosed). Two broad categories of case are involved in the apparent authority context: first, a specific representation made by the owner which is a branch of estoppel; secondly, where the agent is put in a position which carries with it usual authority to sell the goods and, as such, is the rationale of the Factors Act 1889 (the FA 1889). The basis of the distinction goes to the limit of the agents apparent ability to sell. In this regard the issue of appearance of ownership or authority is decided objectively, that is, whether the third-party purchaser was acting under a reasonable belief in the light of the circumstances of the case. Of course mere possession of a thing does not confer either apparent authority or ownership, and it was this conclusion which was at the heart of the criticism surrounding the DTI Consultation Paper on Transfer of Title (1994).[35] Something more is necessary, for example, a holding out by means of documentation or, in the case of a mercantile agency, then his possession of it, at least in his capacity as a mercantile agent, will lead the third-party purchaser to suppose that he has the authority to sell the goods in the ordinary course of business.[36]

The issue of apparent authority was considered by the Court of Appeal in *Sovereign Finance plc (formerly Sovereign Leasing plc) v. Netcom Systems Ltd and Others*[37] and the facts are worthy of detailed consideration as they illuminate the principles involved. The case involved a

[34.] [1987] 1 W.L.R. 1332.
[35.] See Chap. 1, above.
[36.] Factors Act 1889, s. 2(1).
[37.] (1995) C.A. unreported.

purported sale and leaseback of a BMW car by N, who was a director of the defendant company, to the plaintiffs. The sale and leaseback was arranged by a third party intermediary, Abbey Vehicle Leasing, and the motivation for the arrangement was seen as tax benefits for N. In November 1989, N wrote to Abbey agreeing to sell the car to them on various terms including an inelegantly drafted retention of title clause which provided as follows:

> "Before the legal title to be passed to your company and for me to hand over the vehicle to be handed over to Netcom Systems [the defendant], the full amount must be paid to me (less deposit)."

A short time later, Abbey sent N a leasing application form of Sovereign Leasing and this was the first time that N had notice of the plaintiffs and he concluded that Abbey must have acted as agents or brokers for them. Having completed the form, in contractual terms, N offered to the plaintiffs to lease the car according to the conditions set out in the document which included the following term: "The . . . vehicle remains the property of [N] until the invoice is paid in full." This document was passed on by Abbey to Sovereign who accepted the document by signing it. A short while later Sovereign sent the invoice sum of nearly £14,000 to Abbey but this was not passed over to N. Some time later N refused to honour the leasing payments due on the basis of repudiation and he claimed back the car for his own personal use. There was no question of recapturing possession since the car remained throughout in N's personal possession.

One of the major issues before the court was whether Abbey had implied authority to sell the car and to pass good title to Sovereign. The main difficulty here was the express term in the contract retaining title in the car until payment. Furthermore, it was held that there had been no holding out by N which could amount to a representation. Insofar as N had signed the application form for leasing, this constituted an offer by *Netcom* to enter into a lease at some future date and did not amount to a representation that Abbey was owner. As Stuart-Smith L.J. held:

> ". . . it seems to me that Sovereign relied upon the implied representation and warranty by Abbey by virtue of section 12(1) of the Sale of Goods Act 1979, that it was the owner of the car and could sell and pass a good title to Sovereign. They did not rely upon anything said or done by [N]."

Estoppel: the need for an express representation

When the owner has enabled the representation to be made, the question of whether he owed a duty of care and, if so, whether he had broken that duty, must be material. The *locus classicus* here is *Henderson and Co. v. Williams*,[38] the facts of which are as follows. Bags of sugar

---

38. [1895] 1 Q.B. 521.

belonging to O (the original owner) were stored in Williams' warehouse. O was defrauded by a rogue into "selling" the goods to the rogue and in this respect, O instructed Williams to hold the goods on behalf of the rogue. This enabled the rogue to sell the goods to Henderson. Before buying, Henderson inquired from Williams who assured him that the rogue did have a right to the goods. The fraud was then discovered. The first contract, between O and the rogue, was held void for mistake. The warehouseman therefore refused to deliver up the goods to Henderson, the innocent buyer. It was held that both the warehousemen and O were estopped from denying the rogue's title because they had held him out as having a right to the goods. This case may be contrasted with *Farquharson Bros and Co. v. King and Co. Ltd*,[39] which involved a clerk employed by the plaintiffs, who had authority to send delivery orders to the dock company with whom timber belonging to the plaintiffs was lodged. The clerk fraudulently transferred the timber to himself through the dock company under a fictitious name, and using that name he purported to sell the timber to the defendants. The House of Lords held that the plaintiffs were not estopped from denying the title of the defendants, on the grounds that the plaintiffs had made no representation of any kind to them. Their Lordships were clearly of the opinion here that the plaintiffs owed no duty of care to the defendants in this situation.

It is necessary not only to establish a duty of care but also to demonstrate that there has been a breach of such a duty. This is a difficult burden to discharge, as is evident in the case law. Perhaps the most celebrated instance of a duty of care being established in recent times is *Mercantile Credit Co. Ltd v. Hamblin*.[40] In *Hamblin* the defendant signed hire-purchase forms in blank which she entrusted to an apparently respectable dealer to complete so that she could obtain a loan on the security of a car. She kept possession of her car throughout but by her actions she enabled the dealer to offer to sell the car as his own to the plaintiff finance company and offer the defendant to take the car on hire-purchase terms from the plaintiffs. The defendant, however, thought that she was signing some sort of mortgage instrument. The Court of Appeal held that there was a sufficient relationship of proximity between the finance company and the defendant to give rise to the duty of care, because had she read the document she would have seen that the finance company was a specified recipient of the form and would have relied upon the form for the purpose specified in the form. However, it was held that, although a duty of care was established, she had not failed to take care in that it was not unreasonable for her to have trusted the dealer, so that her negligence was not the proximate cause of the finance company being induced to buy the car.

The *Hamblin* case was applied by the Court of Appeal in *Beverley Acceptances Ltd v. Oakley*[41] where the pledgee of two Rolls Royce cars was

---

[39.] [1902] A.C. 325.
[40.] [1965] 2 Q.B. 242.
[41.] [1982] R.T.R. 417.

held to owe a duty of care to the plaintiff financiers where the pledgor had been given temporary possession of the two cars and the registration books. The pledgee gave up the keys of the compound (where the cars were kept) for a specific purpose, namely, because the pledgor had represented to him that temporary possession was necessary for assessment of insurance. It was held that although a duty of care was owed to the persons who accompanied the pledgor, since this was the purpose of giving up possession, there had nevertheless been no breach of this duty. As Donaldson L.J. put it[42]:

> "These were elderly and valuable cars, and [the pledgee] would no doubt have been wise to have insured his own interest in them. But, whether he did so or not [the pledgor] had a very clear insurable interest in the motor cars, because he would remain liable to [the pledgee] to repay the loan even if the cars were stolen or destroyed. As the cars were both elderly and valuable, it was not an improbable story which [the pledgor] told, namely, that he had representatives of the insurers with him and they wanted to inspect the cars. Such representatives might well want to verify the age . . . they might want to see the registration documents."

The scope of the estoppel doctrine is extremely limited and it is well to recall the approach of Lord Wright in *Mercantile Bank of India Ltd v. Central Bank of India Ltd*[43]: "There are very few cases of actions for conversion in which a plea of estoppel by representation has succeeded". The emphasis on wilful conduct means that the common law doctrine does not go very far in entrustment cases, since it is settled that mere possession of property does not convey a title to dispose of it.[44] At the same time it should not be forgotten that possession is at the root of title (*beati possidentes*). It is still the case that the purchaser in good faith can acquire ownership through adverse possession in England by being in possession for six years. The Limitation Act 1980 purports to bar the owner's right to bring suit to recover his property or its value after the prescribed period.[45]

Estoppel and implied representations

Where the owner gives possession of the asset to the agent to dispose of the goods in the agent's name, he thereby, makes an express representation that the agent is the owner and can dispose of the goods in the ordinary course of business which will bind the owner even if the agent exceeds his mandate. Of course, this is the position only in so far as the sale was within the scope of the agent's apparent authority, that is, if the agent was selling in the ordinary course of business. Even so, the

---

[42.] *Ibid.* at 424–425.
[43.] [1938] A.C. 287 at 302.
[44.] *Central Newbury Car Auctions Ltd v. Unity Finance Ltd* [1957] 1 Q.B. 371.
[45.] Limitation Act 1980, ss. 2, 3.

entrustment must be to the agent as part of his capacity to dispose of the vehicle as distinct from any other capacity such as repair.[46] If the agent is not a dealer but a private individual then, since there is no ordinary course of business test which would apply, the position is that the agent's power to sell to the third-party is limited to his *actual authority*.[47]

It is often the case in the finance lease context that at the end of the primary period the finance lessor appoints the lessee to dispose of the goods. In *Lloyds and Scottish Finance Ltd v. Williamson*[48] the agent sold a car to the defendant at a price above the minimum authorised by the owners (the plaintiffs). The defendant without the authority of the plaintiffs, agreed that the price instead of being paid to the agent should be paid to the agent's creditor. The defendant then sold the car and paid the money to his creditor. The plaintiffs claim against the defendant for conversion failed on the ground that since the plaintiffs had authorised the agent to sell and they knew that there was a real possibility that he would sell in his own name so that he would appear as an owner, the plaintiffs could not later deny that he was only acting as agent and that he had exceeded his authority. Herein lies the difference with apparent authority because had the defendant known that the agent was disposing of the motor vehicle in his capacity as an agent, then the defendant would not have had good title as paying the agent's creditor could not on any analysis be considered to fall within the ostensible authority of the agent. Thus, in the case of a dealer stocking plan, if the nature of the underlying contract is *hire-purchase* and the finance company knows that this stock is going to be sold, then apparent ownership principles will apply to pass good title in the vehicle to a bona fide purchaser in the ordinary course of business, despite a prohibition of sale clause in the agreement which is vulnerable under the doctrine of sham.[49] It is otherwise in the case of a leasing contract since the very function of such a transaction militates against sale in the absence of an express agency arrangement.

Estoppel by negligence

The principal is not bound merely because he has let the agent have goods and/or the documents of title; rather, he must have done something more, for example, given the agent an acknowledgement that the agent had bought and paid for the goods or entrusted the goods to a person who in the normal course of a business sells the goods as his own.[50] In this respect, an issue which has exercised the courts is whether

---

[46.] See *Fry v. Smellie* [1912] 3 K.B. 282.

[47.] See *Central Newbury Car Auctions Ltd v. Unity Finance Ltd* [1957] 1 Q.B. 371.

[48.] [1965] 1 All E.R. 641.

[49.] See *St Margaret's Trust Ltd v. Castle* (1964), C.A. unreported; Bar Library, No. 247.

[50.] See *Motor Credits (Hire Finance) Ltd v. Pacific Motor Auctions Pty Ltd* (1963) 109 C.L.R. 87, rvsd. on other grounds [1965] A.C. 867.

there are any legal effects of a failure by a finance company to register a hire-purchase or related agreement such as a lease or contract hire arrangement with a motor file information register operated by either HPI plc of more recently CCN Systems.

The failure by a finance company "owner" of a car to register with HPI was fully considered by the House of Lords in *Moorgate Mercantile Co. Ltd v. Twitchings*.[51] In that case, the plaintiff finance company brought an action in conversion against a dealer, which turned on the issue of estoppel as a source for protecting the defendant motor dealer/ purchaser of the vehicle. The minority approach in the House of Lords and the Court of Appeal judgments referred to the possibility of finance companies registering with HPI as a mechanism for protecting property, and failure here formed the basis of a duty of care, that is, common membership by the major financiers of motor vehicles of the HPI scheme created a relationship of propinquity between them. By contrast, the majority were reluctant to substitute a desirable practice into a requirement. It is clear from the majority judgments that the mere fact that the true owner could reasonably foresee that his carelessness would lead the buyer to believe that the seller was the owner of the goods or that the true owner had no interest in the goods, did not give rise to a duty. The decision would appear to be squarely in line with current case law which restricts liability in negligence to economic loss.[52] Of course the position would be otherwise if there was a contractual duty to register with either HPI and/or CCN.

The extent of the duty of care in negligence also arose in *Debs v. Sibec*,[53] illustrating a failure by a private individual to report the theft of a car to the police, a report which could ultimately have resulted in registration of this information with HPI. In August 1987, the plaintiff bought for £57,000 a Mercedes Benz car equipped with many extras. He was robbed of this car and, during the robbery, his life was threatened unless he signed a document containing his name and address, together with an acknowledgement that he had received a sum of money in full and final settlement for it. The robbers, in taking the ignition key and registration document, maintained the threat (through subsequent phone calls) against going to the police and reporting the incident, by promising to kill his children on the occurrence of this eventuality. A month passed by before the plaintiff was persuaded to go to the police. In the meantime, the car was sold to a dealer merely on the production of the "receipt" and the top half of the registration document. The dealer checked with HPI that the car was not stolen or on hire-purchase and agreed to buy it for £46,950. This was done without either checking the address of the immediate seller or through making contact with the plaintiff. The car was then sold to a second dealer and then, at the defendant's request, to Forward Trust Ltd for £51,000 who also had

[51.] [1977] A.C. 890.
[52.] See *Caparo Industries plc v Dickman* [1990] 2 A.C. 605.
[53.] [1990] R.T.R. 91.

checked with HPI. Soon afterwards, the police traced the car to the defendants. The plaintiff succeeded in his claim for damages for conversion against the defendant. One argument put forward was that there had been an estoppel by representation by virtue of the written receipt. This was rejected quite properly on the basis that the representation was not a voluntary one in that it had been induced by force. The case neatly illustrates the narrowness of the estoppel by negligence doctrine. In this respect, Simon Brown J. adopted a suppositive argument: even if the plaintiff had been negligent in failing to report on the theft, supposing he had reported it, this would not have been included on the HPI register when the first dealer checked the records. It followed that if the defendant was to succeed, the scope of the duty of care would have to extend to each purchaser in a chain of purchasers with the result that protection would or would not be gained, according to when an inquiry of HPI would reveal the theft. This was rejected by the court on the basis of *Twitchings*. From this it would appear that in the absence of a legislative initiative, the common law environment which champions security of property is unaffected by the failure to register credit or other information.

A Wrongful Disposition by the Dealer

Principle of apparent ownership

The Factors legislation incorporates the principle of apparent ownership. The key to the FA 1889 is section 2(1) which provides:

> "Where a mercantile agent is, with the consent of the owner in possession of goods or of the documents of title to goods, any sale, pledge or other disposition of the goods, made by him when acting in the ordinary course of business of a mercantile agent, shall, subject to the provisions of this Act, be as valid as if he were expressly authorised by the owner of the goods to make the same; provided that the person taking under the disposition acts in good faith, and has not at the time of the disposition noticed that the person making the disposition has no authority to make the same."

Who is a mercantile agent?

In a sense the FA 1889 is curiously named since it deals with classes of agent other than the factor. The broad definition of mercantile agent makes it no longer necessary to distinguish between factors and brokers so, according to section 1(1) of the 1889 Act, "mercantile agent" means:

> " . . . a mercantile agent having in the customary course of his business as such agent authority either to sell the goods, or to consign goods for the purpose of sale, or to buy goods, or to raise money on the security of goods."

The essential issue is that a "mercantile agent" is one who, by way of business, is customarily entrusted with goods as agent. In this respect, a person who induces another to let him have goods on the representation that he can sell them to another is not, without more, a mercantile agent. Quite often the presence of a commission will help to assert his status. Thus in *Budberg v. Jerwood and Ward*[54] it was held that the Act did not apply to defeat the title of an owner who entrusted her jewellery to a friend for the purposes of a business relationship. There is an apparent conflict between section 1(1) which refers to "customary course" and section 2(1) which alludes to "the ordinary course of business of a mercantile agent". In *Oppenheimer v. Attenborough*,[55] the question arose whether the agent for sale is authorised to pledge. The court expressed the opinion that the 1889 Act made no difference to the pre-existing law. With respect, this approach cannot be sustained especially in view of the inclusion of "ordinary course of business". Moreover, the definition of mercantile agent stipulates four kinds of activity and it is obvious that the ordinary kind of business of each will be different. Indeed, it appears from *Hansard* that the clause as originally drafted contained the words "such a mercantile agent" which shows what the intention of the draftsman was.[56]

The essential question is whether a dealer when disposing of goods is doing so in his capacity as a mercantile agent. Normally there should be no difficulty in establishing this, although if a dealer disposes of goods subject to a contract of hire or lease then no title can pass to a purchaser under this provision. The reason for this is that the basis of the dealer's possession is *not* as a mercantile agent but rather as a bailee. In order for the purchaser to succeed in this scenario some other independent basis would have to be demonstrated, for example an actual or apparent authority to sell.[57]

Disposition in the ordinary course of business

The entrusting concept found in previous nineteenth century factors legislation is incorporated in the 1889 Act through the provision in section 2 that the sale or pledge must be "in the ordinary course of business of a mercantile agent". A degree of illogicality has entered into English law because although the courts recognise, for example, that a car log book and registration certificates are not documents of title, nevertheless they have given them some special status in relation to "ordinary course of business of a mercantile agent". Thus in *Pearson v. Rose and Young Ltd*,[58] the Court of Appeal unanimously held that a disposition of a car with its log book was not in the ordinary course of business because the mercantile agent was in the possession of the log book without the consent of the owner. The fact of physical possession was ignored for the purpose of the disposition.

[54] (1935) 51 T.L.R. 99.
[55] [1908] 1 K.B. 221.
[56] See *Hansard* (3rd ser.), col. 339, p. 230.
[57] See pp. 191–192, above.
[58] [1951] 1 K.B. 275.

This was taken a stage further in *Stadium Finance Co. Ltd v. Robbins.*[59] In this case a dealer had been given possession of the owner's Jaguar car in order that he should find a buyer. The owner kept the ignition key, clearly intending to control the sale himself. Inadvertently he left the registration book in the locked glove compartment. It was held by the Court of Appeal that as the dealer had not been given possession of the registration book and ignition key, a subsequent sale could not be in the ordinary course of business, even though he obtained a duplicate key and was able to hand a key and the registration book to the hirer. However, it is difficult to accept such reasoning and perhaps the best approach is to draw a distinction between the possession of the car itself, which must require the subjective consent of the owner, and the subsequent disposition which objectively requires a log book or registration document for the sale to be within the ordinary course of business. Significantly in *Astley Industrial Trust Ltd v. Miller,*[60] Chapman J. considered that the Court of Appeal decisions were wrong on this latter point. He did distinguish the two cases on the ground that with brand new cars the registration book is by no means so important regarding title, and that the sale of a new car without the book or registration document can apparently be in the ordinary course of business.

Consent of the owner

The English courts have adopted a wide approach with regard to the question of the consent of the owner. Thus in cases involving jewellers, the courts would point to evidence of a contrary intention which overrode section 18, rule 4 of the SGA 1979.[61] While there must be actual consent to the agent's possession by the owner, it is irrelevant that this consent was obtained by a trick. In *Folkes v. King,*[62] a motor agent was given possession of the owner's car and authorised to sell it for him for not less than £575, but in fact he sold it for £340. The buyer knew nothing of the cash restriction which the owner had placed upon the agent's actual authority and bought it in good faith. The agent was a mercantile agent and the buyer, therefore, obtained a good title. Moreover, so long as possession was originally given by the owner, withdrawal of that consent is immaterial[63] unless the buyer knew that it had been withdrawn, in which event he might no longer take in good faith in any case. The burden of proof is upon the buyer that he took in good faith and without notice that the sale was made without the owner's authority.[64] In the case of multiple sales by a dealer to finance houses, this section does not in practice prove to be problematical since

[59.] [1962] 2 Q.B. 664.
[60.] [1968] 2 All E.R. 36.
[61.] *Weiner v. Gill* [1906] 2 K.B. 574. See Chap. 4, above.
[62.] [1923] 1 K.B. 282.
[63.] Factors Act 1889, s. 2(2).
[64.] *Heap v. Motorists Advisory Agency Ltd* [1923] 1 K.B. 377.

the matter will normally be governed by section 8 of the FA 1889 (section 24 of the SGA 1979).

In so far as the dealer accepts goods from the lessee or hirer for disposal at the end of the term, the dealer will not pass a good title in the absence of an authority to receive the equipment from the finance owner. It is otherwise if the transaction in question is governed by Part III of the Hire-Purchase Act 1964 (as amended) which is discussed later.[65]

Sale by a Seller in Possession

Legislation generally

Section 8 of the FA 1889 deals with the case of a seller under a sale or agreement to sell, in possession of goods or of the documents of title to the goods. This was virtually duplicated in section 25(1) of the SGA 1893 (now section 24 of the SGA 1979) which provides as follows:

> "Where a person having sold goods continues or is in possession of the goods, or of the documents of title to the goods, the delivery or transfer by that person, or by a mercantile agent acting for him, of the goods or documents of title under any sale, pledge or other disposition thereof, [or under any agreement for sale, pledge or other disposition thereof], to any person receiving the same in good faith and without notice of the previous sale, has the same effect as if the person making the delivery or transfer was expressly authorised by the owner of the goods to make the same."

The words in brackets are additional words included in the FA 1889.

A literal construction of section 24 of SGA 1979 would suggest that, although the owner is deemed to authorise the delivery of the goods or the transfer of the documents of title, he is not deemed to have given his authority to the sale, pledge or other disposition. This contrasts with the "notional mercantile agency" device adopted in section 9 of the FA 1889 where the buyer in possession is treated as if he were such a mercantile agent. The significance of this is that section 2(1) of the FA 1889, the main mercantile agency provision, allows the mercantile agent, within certain constraints, to pass title by delivery of goods unaccompanied by documents. As a result of this notional mercantile agency, the effect of section 9 is wider than section 8. The differences between the two sections were noted by Pearson L.J. in *Newtons of Wembley Ltd v. Williams*[66]:

> "Under section 8, the effect of the disposition by the seller is that it shall have 'the same effect as if the person making the delivery or transfer were expressly authorised by the owner of the goods to make the same'. On the other hand,

---

[65.] See pp. 211–223, below.
[66.] [1965] 1 Q.B. 560 at 577–578.

in section 9, there is a different provision as to the effect of the transaction, because it is to have 'the same effect as if the person making the delivery or transfer were a mercantile agent in possession of the goods, or documents of title with the consent of the owner'. It is also to be observed that almost identical provisions were inserted in section 25 of the Sale of Goods Act 1893. Section 25(1) of the Act of 1893 is almost exactly the same as section 8 of the Act of 1889; section 25(2) of the Act of 1893 is almost identical to section 9 of the Act of 1889; and the same difference in the effect of the transaction is preserved in those two subsections. Thus there cannot be any suggestion that the difference in language is merely *per incuriam*."

The good faith notice requirement

The question of the notice requirement for bona fide purchase is particularly pertinent under a literal interpretation of section 24 of the SGA 1979. This section provides that goods may be delivered "under any sale, to any person". Thus, delivery need not be to the first purchaser from the seller but to a sub-purchaser direct from the original seller. The problem revolves around the question concerning the obligation to act in "good faith and without notice of the previous sale" which is required in section 24. The material words read as follows: ". . . the delivery . . . of the goods . . . under any sale . . . to any persons receiving the same in good faith and without notice of the previous sale . . .". This suggests that only the sub-purchaser needs to be in good faith, and even if the latter is in bad faith, he will acquire title by virtue of the buyer's good faith. The approach taken under section 25(1) of the 1893 Act, which substantially reproduced section 8 of FA 1889, differed from its forerunner, section 3 of FA 1877. This provided that title passed to "any other person who . . . purchases such goods" so that title is linked to any person who purchased the goods without notice of the previous sale. The present rule, however, requires not only sale but also a delivery. So long as the delivery is to a person (not necessarily a purchaser) who is acting in good faith, the buyer in bad faith may acquire title by virtue of a delivery to a person who takes delivery in good faith. In contrast, under the doctrine of estoppel or the provision in section 2 of the FA 1889, the second buyer is protected as from the moment of sale which does not necessarily coincide with delivery.

The capacity of the seller

The capacity in which the seller retains possession has engaged the attention of the courts. Some of the cases have suggested that if the seller retains possession but acts in relation to the goods as a hirer, the sub-purchaser will not be protected.[67] The modern position is that the capacity in which the seller remains in continuous possession is

---

[67.] See *Staffs Motor Guarantee Ltd v. British Wagon Co. Ltd* [1934] 2 K.B. 305; *Eastern Distributors Ltd v. Goldring* [1957] 2 Q.B. 600.

---

immaterial. Thus in *Pacific Motor Auctions Ltd v. Motor Credits Ltd*,[68] a dealer unsuccessfully attempted to achieve a stocking plan by way of a sale and rehiring, and the Privy Council held that the words "continues . . . in possession" referred to the continuity of physical possession, notwithstanding any private transaction between the seller and the first buyer which might have altered the legal capacity under which the possession was held. Of course, where physical possession has been given up, as in *Mitchell v. Jones*,[69] the second buyer is not protected because of the break in the continuity of possession.

Sub-sale and other dispositions

Section 24 of the SGA 1979 does not only apply to resale but extends to any "sale, pledge or other disposition". The words "other disposition" have been held to cover any transaction which, like sale or pledge, transfers some proprietary interest in the goods. This can be illustrated by the facts in *Worcester Works Finance Ltd v. Cooden Engineering Co. Ltd*,[70] where X bought a car from the defendants but paid with a cheque which was dishonoured. He then sold the car to the plaintiffs, although he retained possession for the time being. Meanwhile the defendants, the original owner, sought to rescind the contract because X's cheque had failed. X agreed to this and allowed the defendants to retake the vehicle. When the plaintiffs pointed out that the car now belonged to them and claimed the vehicle or its value from the defendants, the action failed. As against the plaintiffs, X was still a seller in possession, and when X accepted the defendants rescission of the original contract and returned the car, this was held to be a "disposition" within section 24 so that title had passed. The effect of this decision was that the plaintiffs had recourse only to X, if this was indeed a worthwhile remedy. In *Hanson (W.) Harrow v. Rapid Civil Engineering and Usborne Developments*,[71] it was held that the words "sale or disposition", included also in section 25(1) of the SGA 1979, did not cover the case where there was a term in the contract between the buyer in possession of timber supplied and a main contractor on a building site, whereby the latter could use the materials in construction. This did not defeat the seller where there was included in the contract of sale a simple retention of title clause relating to the timber, because in the absence of payment under the main building contract there was no sale or disposition to the builder.

Buyer in Possession

Introduction

Section 9 of the FA 1889 and section 25(1) of the SGA 1979 provide for property passing by virtue of the buyer's possession:

[68] [1965] A.C. 867.
[69] (1905) 24 N.Z.L.R. 932.
[70] [1972] 1 Q.B. 210.
[71] (1987) 38 Build. L.R. 106.

"Where a person having bought or agreed to buy goods, obtains, with the consent of the seller, possession of the goods or the documents of title to the goods, the delivery or transfer by that person or by a mercantile agent acting for him, of the goods or documents of title under any sale, pledge, or other disposition thereof [or under any agreement for sale, pledge, or other disposition thereof] to any person receiving the same in good faith and without notice of any lien or other right of the original seller in respect of the goods, shall have the same effect as if the person making the delivery or transfer were a mercantile agent in possession of the goods or documents of title with the consent of the owner."

The words in brackets are omitted in section 25(1) of SGA 1979.

If good title has passed to the buyer then section 25(1) will rarely apply. The section refers to a contract of sale where the buyer has "bought" the goods, which appear to be surprising for the simple reason that in any case the *nemo dat quod non habet* principle will apply. However, the subsection may be important in regard to where the buyer has obtained both property and possession of the goods but title has subsequently been avoided by the seller. Thus section 2(2) of the FA 1889 specifically states that the subsequent withdrawal of the consent by the seller does not prevent the application of the Act. It is clear from *Cahn v. Pockett's Bristol Channel Steam Packet Co. Ltd*[72] and *Newtons of Wembley Ltd v. Williams*,[73] that the issue of consent in section 9 of the FA 1889 and section 25(1) of the SGA 1979 is subject to section 2 of the FA 1889's treatment of the seller's consent.

The importance of legal form

The limitation imposed by the words "agreed to buy" should not be under-estimated. This is the distinction between hire-purchase[74] and conditional sale.[75] It is significant that in accordance with the general assimilation of conditional sale agreements to hire-purchase agreements, it is now provided that for the purposes of section 9 of the FA 1889 and section 25(1) of the SGA 1979, "the buyer under a conditional sale agreement is to be taken not to be a person who has bought or agreed to buy goods".[76] It would appear that such conditional sales are governed by the CCA 1974. However, with respect to other conditional sales not covered by the 1974 Act, for example, if the total credit provided is in excess of £15,000, or if the buyer is a body corporate,[77] section 25(1) of the SGA 1979 still applies. Of course, this is of great importance for the lessor under a finance leasing or a contract hire transaction. Moreover, consignment sales, including sale-or-return transactions, are not covered

[72] [1899] 1 Q.B. 643.
[73] [1965] 1 Q.B. 560.
[74] *Helby v. Matthews* [1895] A.C. 471.
[75] *Lee v. Butler* [1893] 2 Q.B. 269.
[76] Sale of Goods Act 1979, s. 25(2)(a).
[77] Consumer Credit Act 1974, s. 189.

by section 25(1) of the SGA 1979 because the possessor is not a person who has agreed to buy goods, even though, in a certain sense, he has made a conditional contract of sale. This emphasises the continued existence in English law of legal form as a phenomenon triumphing over economic substance. This is also important in relation to stocking plans especially of motor vehicles.[77a]

Good faith and notice

The third party under section 25(1) of the SGA 1979 must take the goods "in good faith and without notice of the goods". This provision is repeated in section 2(1) of the FA 1889 and sections 23 to 25 of the SGA 1979. At the outset it is important to draw a clear distinction between notice and knowledge. Notice is not necessarily knowledge since, essentially, the former is a mechanism by which the latter is attributed. Thus, the terms are not interchangeable since knowledge is a question of fact, whereas notice is a more expansive concept as it can anticipate knowledge being attributed to a person.

Although in its extreme form actual notice is co-extensive with knowledge in that the person with such notice has, as a matter of fact, conscious awareness, it should be recognised that notice is an aspect of a continuum and, on the other extreme, constructive notice is treated as being knowledge. Great difficulties have emerged in distinguishing actual notice from constructive notice. The modern approach is to eschew the evidence-orientated approach and concentrate rather on the question of whose actions are relevant. If the state of the mind of the party to be charged is relevant, then this is a question of actual notice. It is submitted that this is the case under section 25(1), because the issue of notice is qualified by the "good faith" requirement which would otherwise be redundant.

The question of "good faith" is defined in section 61(3) of the SGA 1979 as follows:

"A thing is deemed to be done in good faith within the meaning of the Act when it is in fact done honestly, whether it is done negligently or not."

It is clear that negligence, when surrounded by other circumstances, will go to the question of knowledge. For the sake of convenience, knowledge may be categorised as actual, "Nelsonian", that is, wilfully shutting one's eye to the obvious, and "naughty" knowledge where there has been an element of recklessness concerning circumstances which would indicate the facts to an honest and reasonable man.[78] Nonetheless, the doctrine of constructive notice does not normally apply to commercial transactions,[79] and there is no general duty on the buyer of goods in

---

[77a.] See Chap. 4 above.
[78.] See *Heap v. Motorists' Advisory Agency Ltd* 1 K.B. 577; *Pearson v. Rose and Young Ltd* [1951] 1 K.B. 275.
[79.] *Manchester Trust v. Furness* [1895] 2 Q.B. 539.

an ordinary commercial transaction to make inquiries as to the right of the seller to dispose of the goods. Certainly, it would be anomalous to punish knowledge by the sub-buyer of the buyer's non-payment, especially since it is a common business occurrence for a seller to be paid for goods before he himself can pay for them. It would be unreasonable in this respect for a sub-buyer to be put on notice merely because of his knowledge of a retention of title clause, not least because there are so many types of retention of title clauses including consignment sale, many of which include proceeds provisions. In the case where property has passed to the buyer, the sub-buyer's knowledge of non-payment cannot be described as bad faith because this can hardly be considered a right "in respect of the goods"; it is merely a personal right in respect of the contract of sale. The principles were expanded by Neil J. in *Fuer Leather Corp v. Frank Johnstone and Sons*[80]:

> ". . . (2) For this purpose the court is concerned with actual notice and not with constructive notice. (3) In deciding whether a person in the position of the defendants had actual notice: (a) the court will apply an objective test and look at all the circumstances; (b) if by an objective test clear notice was given liability cannot be avoided by proof merely of the absence of actual knowledge; (c) a person will be deemed to have had notice of any fact to which it can be shown that he deliberately turned a 'blind eye' . . . (d) on the other hand, the court will not expect the recipient of goods to scrutinise commercial documents such as delivery notes with great care; (e) there is no general duty on a buyer of goods in an ordinary commercial transaction to make inquiries as to the right of the seller to dispose of the goods; (f) the question becomes: looking objectively at the circumstances which are alleged to constitute notice, do those circumstances constitute notice? This must be a matter of fact and degree to be determined in the particular circumstances of the case. (4) The burden of proving a bone fide purchase for value without notice rests on the person who asserts it.

The construction of section 9 of the Factors Act 1889 and section 25(1) of the Sale of Goods Act 1979

The reference to mercantile agent. agent. In *Newtons of Wembley Ltd v. Williams*[81] the owners of a car sold it in return for a cheque, but it was expressly agreed that ownership should remain in the seller until the cheque was cleared. The rogue resold the car in Warren Street, London, a recognised market for second-hand cars. It was held that the sub-buyer prevailed since the rogue, as a buyer in possession, could transfer a good title by virtue of section 25(1) of the SGA 1979. The Court of Appeal took a literal approach to the requirement of acting in the capacity of being a mercantile agent. In this respect, the resale by the rogue had been in circumstances (that is at an established second-hand car market) such that the sub-buyer could reasonably assume that he was buying

---

[80.] [1981] Com. L.R. 251 at 253.
[81.] [1965] 1 Q.B. 560.

from a mercantile agent in the ordinary course of business. Thus Pearson L.J. pointed out[82]:

> "When the provisions of s. 2 are applied to the s. 9 position . . . this is the prima facie result: if the transaction is made by the person concerned when acting in the ordinary course of the business of a mercantile agent, the transaction is validated: on the other hand, if the transaction is made by him when not acting in the ordinary course of business of a mercantile agent, the transaction is not validated."

This *obiter* approach would, if unrestricted in its application, severely limit section 9 of the FA 1889 and section 25(1) of the SGA 1979. Moreover, it is difficult to understand the development of the hire-purchase mechanism as a device to avoid section 9 if this indeed was the strict position. Certainly, the conventional legal position before the *Newtons of Wembley* case was that section 9 and section 25(1) were considered to validate a sale as if the buyer in possession were a mercantile agent, but did not include that he should act in such a way. To clarify the position, the 1966 Law Reform Committee's 12th Report recommended that the law be amended to restore this position. Certainly, Clarke J. in *Forsythe International (UK) Ltd v. Silver Shipping Co. Ltd*[83] appeared to champion the pre-1964 position while at the same time conceding that he was bound by *Newtons of Wembley*, although he did cite contrary Commonwealth authority.[84]

The significance of possession as an indication of ownership

The dilemma posed by the conflict between security of property and the protection of purchasers can be conveniently illustrated in *Four Point Garages Ltd v. Carter*,[85] since it deals with the significance of possession as an indication of ownership.

The *Four Point Garage* case was brought before Simon Brown J. in the Queen's Bench Division and was tried on affidavit evidence. The plaintiff sought a declaration of ownership concerning a new Ford Escort XR3i sports car, relating to events less than four weeks before the case came to court. The considerable speed with which this case was expedited demonstrates the importance attached to "newness" in motor cars *vis-à-vis* their saleability and quality. The facts are fairly simple. The defendant desired to buy a new car, and after having made a number of inquiries primarily concerned with price from a number of garages, agreed on October 2, 1984 to purchase the car with accessories from Freeway (Cougar) Ltd for £6,889. Following the completion of independent financial arrangements, the defendant posted the necessary moneys

---

[82.] *Ibid.* at 578.
[83.] [1994] 1 All E.R. 851.
[84.] See *Gamer's Motor Centre (Newcastle) Pty Ltd v. Natwest Wholesale Australia Pty Ltd* (1987) 163 C.L.R. 236 at 259, *per* Dawson J.
[85.] [1985] 2 All E.R. 12.

to Freeway and arranged with the latter for delivery of the motor car on October 10, 1984. The car was not in stock with Freeway, but they made arrangements to purchase a car of the same specification from the plaintiffs who believed that Freeway were engaged in the leasing and hiring business. On October 9, 1984, the plaintiffs invoiced Freeway for the car to the sum of £6,746 and were persuaded before payment to deliver the car direct to the defendant. This they completed on October 10, 1984, assuming the defendant to be a customer of Freeway rather than a sub-purchaser. The defendant, on the other hand, thought that delivery had been made to him direct by Freeway. Three days after delivery, notification was given to the plaintiffs that Freeway was going into liquidation. In response, the plaintiffs sought to recover the car relying on their contract of supply with Freeway which contained the following retention of title clause: "The buyer is advised that title to the goods contained in this invoice remains with the seller until such goods are fully paid". By establishing ownership, the plaintiffs would simultaneously establish the better right to possess and could then, presumably, resell the car. Clearly, as unsecured creditors, neither the plaintiffs nor the defendant were likely to recover their loss from the insolvent Freeway.

The court held in favour of the defendant, and one of the main strands to Simon Brown J.'s judgment was based on section 25(1) of the SGA 1979. It was held that Freeway had constructive possession of the goods following *E. & S. Ruben Ltd v. Faire Bros & Co.*,[86] and could thereby pass good title to an innocent sub-purchaser. Nevertheless, it is difficult to see how the *Ruben* case applies here. This case was concerned with the buyer's right to reject, and quite different policy considerations are involved in section 35 of the SGA 1979 than those posed in section 25. Moreover, in *Ruben* it was said that the buyers had acted inconsistently with the seller's ownership by taking constructive delivery at the seller's premises; contrastingly, in *Four Point Garage* the seller had expressly reserved title and sub-delivered the goods believing its ownership in the vehicle to be still subsisting. A further problem concerns the difficulty inherent with basing a decision on constructive possession. This expression is used in many different senses so that, for example, Salmond treats constructive possession as covering those cases where the law grants possession to one who is not in actual physical control,[87] whereas Pollock and Wright, in their seminal essay on *Possession*, confine the expression to cases where there is a mere right to recover possession.[88] It is very difficult to determine a unitary concept of possession in English law, and Professor Stoljar has suggested that, because possession is a ductile and intuitive concept, it should be rejected as even a foundation for any meaningful theory of bailment.[89]

[86.] [1949] 1 K.B. 254.
[87.] *Jurisprudence* (ed. Fitzgerald, 1966) p. 286.
[88.] *Possession and the Common Law* (1888) pp. 25–27.
[89.] (1935) 7 Res Judicatae 160.

In *Sovereign Finance plc* (1995)[90] it was argued that by virtue of the leasing agreement, factual possession was with Netcom and that there had been constructive possession in Sovereign and Abbey. This argument was based upon *E. & S. Ruben Ltd v. Faire Brothers and Co. Ltd*[91] and also *Four Point Garages Ltd v. Carter*[92] where the following principle was said to emerge namely:

"Where A sells goods to B, and B sub-sells them to C, and it is agreed that A shall deliver them direct to C without passing through B's hands, B nonetheless obtains constructive possession of the goods at the time that they are delivered to C, sufficient to pass a good title to C under s. 25."

This argument was rejected quite simply because there had been no delivery to Netcom as the car had remained in the personal possession of N throughout. Indeed it was a condition of the contract in this case that the vehicle was not to be handed over until the full price had been paid. As Stuart-Smith L.J. held:

"It is one thing to say, following the *Ruben* and *Four Point Garage* cases, that, where an owner actually delivers the goods into the possession of the sub-purchaser at the request of the purchaser, delivery involves constructive possession by the purchaser, since it is clear that the delivery direct is simply a convenience to avoid the unnecessary step of delivery to the purchaser. It is quite another to extend that doctrine to a case where the owner [N] does not in fact deliver to the sub-purchaser (either Sovereign or Netcom) and is unwilling to do so, but by virtue of a legal fiction that, because there was a lease, Netcom was the only person entitled to legal possession and was therefore in actual possession. Furthermore . . . [this] begs the question that there was a valid lease."

The requirement of "delivery" or "transfer"

More recently doubt has arisen in respect of whether actual delivery is required for the purposes of section 25(1) of the SGA 1979 and section 9 of the FA 1979 despite the fact that this would seem to be implied in the criterion of "receiving" the goods in good faith. In the celebrated decision of *Gamer Motor Center (Newcastle) Pty Ltd v. Natwest Wholesale Australia Pty Ltd*,[93] the High Court of Australia held that constructive delivery was sufficient where the character of the buyer's possession was transferred into a bailment. In this case, car dealers immediately "sold" the vehicles to a finance company, but they retained possession of them for display purposes and they were authorised to sell the units on the finance company's behalf. Essentially, the approach of the court represents a policy decision of protecting the innocent third-party purchaser

[90] The facts are set out at pp. 191–192.
[91] [1949] 1 K.B. 254.
[92] [1985] 3 All E.R. 12.
[93] (1987) 163 C.L.R. 236.

arising out of the ostensible ownership of the seller or buyer in possession of the chattel in question, because following a sale the nature of the disposer's possession will necessarily change to that of being a bailee.[94] Even so, the general approach adopted in *Gamer* was applied by Clarke J. in *Forsythe International (U.K.) Ltd v. Silver Shipping Co. Ltd*.[95] In this case the plaintiffs contracted with charterers to supply oil bunkers for a vessel which was on a time-charter from the owners. The contract of supply contained a reservation of title clause. Before the charter expired the owners withdrew the vessel from the charterers for non-payment of hire. At this time the vessel was carrying bunkers for which the plaintiffs had not been paid. It was common ground that property in the bunkers had not passed to the charterers as they had not paid for them, but the owners of the vessel contended that they had acquired a good title to the bunkers by virtue of the buyer in possession exception to the *nemo dat* rule. The judge took the view that under section 25(1) there must be some voluntary transfer of possession, rather it had come about automatically as a result of the termination of the charterparty by the owners.

Voidable Title and Avoidance by Seller

Since English law fails to distinguish between contract and conveyance, no property can pass if the contract of sale is void. Section 23 of the SGA 1979 provides as follows:

> "When the seller of goods has a voidable title to them, but his title has not been avoided at the time of sale, the buyer acquires a good title to the goods, provided he buys them in good faith and without notice of the seller's defect of title."

The formalistic position adopted depends upon the intention of the parties; whether the owner intends to transfer possession only or whether he intends to transfer title to the wrongdoer. However, the fundamental flaw with the voidable title approach is, how can the owner's subjective intent supply the innocent purchaser with realistic criteria for judging the legitimacy of the transaction? In addition, the owner-intent cases can be seen as an example of inductive judicial reasoning.[96]

One of the most celebrated cases in this context is *Cundy v. Lindsay*.[97] A rogue persuaded Lindsay to "sell" linen to him on credit by pretending to be Blenkiron and Co., a known and reputable customer. The rogue then resold to Cundy whilst Lindsay, unpaid by the rogue,

---

[94.] *Cf. Nicholson v. Harper* [1895] 2 Ch. 415.
[95.] [1994] 1 All E.R. 851.
[96.] See *e.g. Ingram v. Little* [1961] 1 Q.B. 31; *Lewis v. Averay* [1972] 1 Q.B. 198.
[97.] (1879) 23 App. Cas. 459.

sued Cundy for conversion. In this case, a risk analysis based on fault may have stressed that in the supply of cotton there was a rapid turnover, unlike the slower legal mechanism for the transfer of realty which often involves noting a property interest on a register, and that the owners having been tricked acted quickly and tried to reduce the risk to third parties. On the other hand, it is possible to argue that the owners were negligent in not spotting the discrepancy on the letter heading, which they should have done, given the fact that the degree of commercial pressure was less than in an *inter praesentes* shopping situation. The House of Lords rejected any analysis based on fault, preferring a formalistic approach.[98]

It is interesting how the courts have ensured the primacy of the security of property principle by taking a wide approach to the question of rescission in the voidable title context. Thus, in *Car and Universal Finance Ltd v. Caldwell*,[99] the owner of a car sold it to a plausible rogue and allowed the rogue to take it away in return for a cheque. The cheque was dishonoured and the seller immediately informed the police requesting them to try to get his car back. After this, the rogue resold the car to X who took it in bad faith knowing of the fraud; X then re-sold it to the plaintiffs who bought it in good faith. It was held that since the rogue could not have been contacted, the original seller had rescinded the contract by informing the police and doing everything practicable to make public his intention to rescind, for example, by informing the AA. Subsequently in *Newtons of Wembley Ltd v. Williams*,[1] it was held that informing the police and a motorists' organisation like the AA or RAC was sufficient to rescind the contract when the rogue could not be found. Of course, this is of little comfort to the innocent buyer and it is for this reason that the Law Revision Committee[2] recommended that the rule as to avoidance laid down in *Caldwell's* case should be reversed and actual communication required. Nevertheless, the approach taken in *Caldwell* (1965) has been indorsed in *Thomas v. Heelas*[3] In this case the court held that, when an owner sought to recover goods in the possession of somebody who was not a party to the voidable transaction, the onus was on the possessor to show that he had good title. Clearly this is an onerous task especially where the chain of title is long. Indeed, over six months had elapsed between the owner's original rescission by informing the police and the eventual recovery of the car.

The Abolition of Market Overt

Under English law, recovery is based not on ownership in the sense of absolute title, but rather on the better right to possess, and the *jus tertii*

[98] *Cf. Phillips v. Brooks* [1919] 2 K.B. 243.
[99] [1965] 1 Q.B. 525.
[1] [1965] 1 Q.B. 560.
[2] Transfer of Title, 12th Report (Cmnd 2958, 1966) paras. 16, 40(4).
[3] November 27, 1986 (CAT No. 1065).

cannot be pleaded against a possessor. Consequently, there is no theoretical reason why a thief should not sue a second thief although, in practice, the first thief will probably not want to draw attention to himself. It was only in the case of market overt that an indefeasible absolute title to chattels was known to the common law. The Law Reform Committee[4] recommended that the rule should be extended to the sale of goods in all retail establishments. The effect of this recommendation would have been to shift the right of action available to the bona fide purchaser of goods under section 12 of the SGA 1979 to the owner. Significantly, the abolition of the market overt doctrine, by the 1994 Sale of Goods (Amendment) Act (c.32), represents a swing away from such an approach which would champion transactions as distinct from ownership.

Supplies of Motor Vehicles

Background to Part III of the Hire-Purchase Act 1964

The strict common law *nemo dat* would compromise purchases especially of second-hand vehicles. It was for this reason that the Molony Committee[5] recommended reform but did not indicate which solution it favoured. Given the primacy of the *nemo dat* principle, it is little wonder that the first legislative proposal for reform encapsulated in the Hire-Purchase (No. 2) Bill 1963 included an elaborate system of notification in an attempt to balance the financier's ownership interest and also protect prospective purchasers of motor vehicles. These proposals were criticised by the finance industry as being too burdensome, which may explain why the Finance Houses Association (which represented the major financiers of motor vehicles) agreed to support an Opposition amendment to the original Bill that title should in any event pass to a private bona fide purchaser without notice of a hire-purchase or conditional sale agreement. Even though this approach was tantamount to a reversal of the traditional common law *nemo dat* doctrine, legislation to this effect was forthcoming, which was incorporated into Part III of the Hire-Purchase Act 1964.[6]

Part III provided a special legislative regime in the context of dispositions involving motor vehicles. The general effect of this legislation is to champion security in transactions in non-motor trade dispositions.

The Object of the Legislation: Motor Vehicles

Introduction

The conventional definition of "motor vehicles" seen under road traffic legislation is adopted in Part III of the Hire-Purchase Act 1964, so

---

[4] See para. 11 (n.2, above).
[5] *Consumer Protection* (Cmnd. 1781 (1962)).
[6] This has since been substituted by the Consumer Credit Act 1974, s. 192(2), and Sched. 4, para. 22.

section 29(1) provides that: " 'Motor Vehicle' means a mechanically propelled vehicle intended or adapted for use on roads to which the public has access". The courts have consistently adopted an expansive approach to this conventional definition. Thus in *Newberry v. Simmonds*[7] it was held that a motor car which had its engine removed was still a mechanically-propelled vehicle, and this reasoning has been extended to a vehicle being towed because of a defective engine.[8] The question of the *scope* of the definition of "motor vehicle" for the purpose of Part III revolves around the "use on roads to which the public has access". Plant or equipment may be mechanically propelled but they are not treated as motor vehicles because they are not "intended or adapted for use on roads". Consequently, dump trucks used in building works have been excluded on this basis, as would be, presumably, fork lift trucks used extensively in factory premises. On the other hand, in *Childs v. Coghlan*[9] a "Euclid earth scraper" was held to be a motor vehicle; although its primary function was for use on building sites, because of its size it was not easily transportable and had to go on the roads under its own power to get from one site to another. The relevant test was laid down by Lord Parker C.J. in the *Childs* case as follows:[10]

> "The real question is: is some general use of the roads contemplated as one of the uses? In the present case, if a reasonable person looked at the vehicle with the knowledge that it had to go from site to site and had to use the roads in so doing, and was capable of speeds of up to 45 mph it seemed clear that such person would have said that one of the uses of the vehicles would be a road use."

Undoubtedly, the courts are rightly concerned to ensure that vehicles are covered by the safety requirements laid down by the Road Traffic Acts. However, while this approach is appropriate for promoting safety, there are different policy considerations applicable in legislation which is solely concerned with protecting consumers against asset financiers purely in a title dispute. In this context, it is conventional wisdom to distinguish between the type and kind of goods, that is, whether they are consumer goods, equipment or stock-in-trade. The point of substance here is that the unwieldy definition applied in Part III extends the protection accorded beyond the simple consumer context.

The parties affected: the debtor

Section 29(4) of the Hire-Purchase Act 1964 (as amended) states:

> "In this Part of the Act the 'debtor' in relation to a motor vehicle which has been bailed or hired under a hire-purchase agreement, means the person who

---

[7.] [1961] 2 Q.B. 345.
[8.] See *Cobb v. Whorton* [1971] R.T.R. 392.
[9.] (1986) 112 Sol. Jo. 175.
[10.] *Ibid.*

at the material time (whether the agreement has before that time been terminated or not) either -

    (a) is the person to whom the vehicle is bailed or hired under that agreement, or

    (b) is, in relation to the agreement, the buyer, including a person who at the time is, by virtue of section 130(4) of the Consumer Credit Act 1974 treated as a bailee or (in Scotland) a custodier of the vehicle."

The inclusion of the wording in brackets is obviously intended to cover *ipso facto* termination clauses so that nothing hinges upon the current contractual status of the debtor.

The main difficulty with the above approach is that it fails to distinguish between cases where the debtor is in possession of the vehicle from those situations where the finance company has repossessed the vehicle. As a matter of principle, repossession of the vehicle must terminate the ability to pass good title, and in any case, lack of possession should affect the *fides* of the disponee, given that the mischief of the legislation was to deal with the ostensible ownership problem of the hirer being in possession of the motor vehicle. It is suggested that in sections 8 and 9 of the FA 1889 the ability to pass good title is dependent upon the giving up of possession through delivery.

A further dilemma is posed by the capacity in which the debtor is holding the motor vehicle. If the relevant agreement is illegal, this should not prejudice the ability of the debtor to pass title under Part III because the general effect of illegality is not to render the contract totally void but merely to make it unenforceable. Where, however, the contract is voidable and has been avoided by the owner before the wrongful disposition takes place, for example, because of fraud or misrepresentation, this will not be covered by Part III, which refers to termination of an agreement rather than *avoidance* of it. Misrepresentation allows for rescission, which is a powerful remedy providing for the restoration of the *status quo ante*, that is an *ab initio* avoidance of the transaction. This is potentially an important limitation of the scope of the consumer protection element in Part III.

The parties affected: the private purchaser

The provisions of Part III bite upon the contradistinction between a "trade or finance purchaser" who does not acquire a good title, and a private purchaser who as a person in good faith and without notice can acquire a good title. The definition of "trade or finance purchaser" in section 29(2) of the Act encompasses a purchaser who at the time of the disposition is involved in a business consisting wholly or partly:

    "(a) of purchasing motor vehicles for the purpose of offering or exposing them for sale, or

    (b) of providing finance by purchasing motor vehicles for the purpose of bailing or (in Scotland) hiring them under hire purchase agreements or agreeing to sell them under conditional sale agreements . . ."

213

The emphasis upon business suggests a degree of regularity and also the element of holding out. Thus in *Stevenson v. Beverley Bentinck Ltd*,[11] a tool inspector, who had for less than two years bought and sold motor vehicles on a modest scale in his spare time, was held to have been partly (not wholly) involved in the business of purchasing motor vehicles for the purpose of offering them or exposing them for sale and was, thereby, covered by section 29(2) of the Act. The fact that the plaintiff in this case was buying the motor vehicle in his private capacity was irrelevant, since the Act draws the distinction between, as Browne L.J. pointed out, categories of persons, not between categories of transactions.[12]

Undoubtedly, the mischief of the Act is geared towards the protection of the public who are not engaged in the motor business or involved directly in the financing of motor vehicles through credit sales or hire-purchase. A private purchaser is defined in section 29(2) as "a purchaser who, at the time of the disposition made to him, does not carry on [motor trade or motor finance] business". Nevertheless the limitation of scope here has to be noted: contract hire and leasing contracts which as a matter of legal form are not *sale* contracts will therefore not be covered by section 29(2) of the Act.

The transaction affected: dispositions

The Act applies to dispositions made by a debtor subject to a hire-purchase or conditional sale arrangement. It would appear that Part III only applies in favour of a person who buys, agrees to buy, or takes the vehicle on hire-purchase and that the disposition must be made by the debtor himself and not by any other party such as a bailee of the debtor. There is, however, a presumption in section 28(2) that it is the debtor who disposes of the vehicle. Even so, agency principles will apply, so in *Ford Motor Credit Co. Ltd v. Harmack*[13] the Court of Appeal held that a person who was the managing director and controlling shareholder of a company had actual and ostensible authority of the hirer company (which had taken a vehicle on hire-purchase) to dispose of the car on behalf of the company and pass good title under section 27 of the Act.

It is clearly envisaged in the legislation that "disposition" refers to sale and analogous defined transactions, namely, hire-purchase and conditional sale. Consequently, "disposition" does not cover a special property interest like pledge or lien and neither does it cover a gift, mortgage or assignment by operation of law, set-off or contractual assignments, for example, initiated by so-called vehicle transfer agencies.[13a] These agencies operate by placing advertisements in the press targeted at members of the public who may be having difficulty maintaining finance

11. [1976] 1 W.L.R. 483.
12. *Ibid*. at 488.
13. [1972] C.L.Y. 1649.
13a. See *Bindi v. Cannon and Automodule (Automotive Financial Services)*, November 23, 1994; unreported.

repayments on their cars subject to hire-purchase, conditional sale or lease. In return for the vehicle, for which it claims to have a buyer, the vehicle transfer company will be settled. Research conducted by the Finance and Leasing Association has shown that in 90 per cent of the cases repayments were not maintained.[14] It would appear, therefore, that a buyer from a vehicle transfer agency would not get a statutory title under Part III, whilst disposal to such an agency would amount to repudiatory conduct on the part of the hirer/lessee.

It is often the case that hirers will "swap" vehicles, sometimes accompanied by a cash element. In this scenario the status of the transaction as being either as a matter of law categorised as a sale which is covered or, an exchange, which is not covered is crucial to the protection provision in Part III. A thorny problem is whether a forbearance to sue on a debt is a disposition or purported disposition covered by the Act. This issue was considered in *Royscott Trust v. Burno Daken Ltd and David Ball*[15] before Judge Astill sitting as a High Court Judge. In this case the plaintiff let out on hire-purchase terms a Range Rover car to Edwards, trading as Steel Services, who wrongfully passed it to the first defendant. The value of the car was stated to be £10,250 in an "Invoice" drawn by Steel Services to the first defendant. At the time Steel Services owed the first defendant £11,100.95 for goods supplied. Steel Services were unable to discharge that debt, and the Range Rover was taken by the first defendant in part satisfaction of it. Accordingly, the document entitled "Invoice" said "Invoice to be contra against steel supplied by Burns Dakin as agreed". At the same time the "Invoice" stated dishonestly that "No liabilities or encumbrances cover the vehicle". At all times the defendants were in good faith. Significantly, Judge Astill held concerning the definition of "disposition" in section 29 of the Act 1964 (as amended):

".... it appears to me that the consideration for this transaction was not money, albeit that a document called an "Invoice" was produced and the value of the vehicle agreed. Rather the consideration was a forbearance to sue for that part of the outstanding debt represented by the vehicle's value. It was not "an exchange of property for money" and not, therefore, a disposition as defined by section 29 sub-section 1 of the Hire-Purchase Act 1964."

Furthermore, neither was it a "purported disposition" in the sense that even though it was not a sale the parties, as a matter of contractual intention, meant it to be one. As Judge Astill held:

"I confess that I am not all sure what 'purported' means in this Act of Parliament. I do not think it can mean the intention of the parties as has been submitted. If 'purports' means what the transaction seems to represent, I find no difficulty in concluding that it seems to represent a foregoing of a part of the debt due, but not a money exchange and, therefore, not a disposition."

[14.] Finance Leasing Association Report 1995, p. 21.
[15.] July 9, 1993; unreported.

The transaction affected: hire-purchase or conditional sale

The current definition of hire-purchase can be found in section 189(1) of the Consumer Credit Act 1974 which states:

> "'hire purchase agreement' means an agreement, other than a conditional sale agreement, under which—
>
> (a) goods are bailed or (in Scotland) hired in return for periodical payments by the person to whom they are bailed or hired, and
> (b) the property in the goods will pass to that person if the terms of the agreement are complied with and one or more of the following occurs—
>
> > (i) the exercise of an option to purchase by that person;
> > (ii) the doing of any specified act by any party to the agreement;
> > (iii) the happening of any other specified event."

Section 189(4) further provides that the agreement may be constituted in more than one document, that is to say, a hire agreement with a separate option provision. The developed English position constitutes a statutory reversal of *R. v. R. W. Proffitt Ltd*,[16] where it had been held that the relevant definition of hire-purchase only applied where the bailee controlled the circumstances in which the property would or would not pass to him, and did not apply where the contingencies upon which the property was to pass were in the bailor's control.

A variation of the developed statutory position discussed above arose in the context of a conditional sale in *Dodds v. Yorkshire Bank Finance Ltd.*[17] The facts involved the disposition by a company director B of a Porsche car to the plaintiff, which was still subject to an outstanding hire-purchase agreement with the defendants. The relevant transaction was a conditional sale agreement by B to sell the vehicle to the plaintiff if he defaulted to pay back the plaintiff, money advanced as part of an elaborate financing arrangement for B's ailing business. When B failed to pay back the money advanced by the plaintiff, the condition precedent to the passing of property in the vehicle was satisfied. The fact that the condition for property passing was in the seller's control was irrelevant and, as such, is consistent with the position in hire-purchase. There is no doubt that the Court of Appeal adopted the legal *form* of the transaction, notwithstanding that as a matter of economic substance it is not possible to distinguish between an executory agreement to sell and a chattel mortgage.

Undoubtedly, Part III of the Hire-Purchase Act 1964 (as amended) constitutes an important exception to the *nemo dat* principle. Even so, ownership interests are not lightly overturned and the statutory exception here refers to the necessity of the purchaser being in good faith and without notice of the ownership interest.

[16.] [1954] 2 Q.B. 35.
[17.] [1992] C.C.L.R. 92.

The pre-requisite for protection: good faith and without notice

The purchaser must act in good faith and without notice at the time of the disposition. The issue of good faith is not defined in Part III, but section 29(3) of the Act defines "without notice" as meaning that the purchaser "has no actual notice that the vehicle is or was the subject of any hire-purchase agreement". From this it would seem to follow that actual notice of *any* hire-purchase agreement prevents the purchaser being without notice. However, the Court of Appeal in *Barker v. Bell*[18] held that there must be notice only of the *relevant* hire-purchase or conditional sale agreement that had been supposedly paid off. The main judgment was given by Lord Denning M.R. who explained his reasoning as follows[19]:

> "If a car was originally let on hire-purchase terms, the instalments have all been paid, or the settlement figure has been paid, that hire-purchase agreement is entirely irrelevant: and I see no reason why notice of it should affect the purchaser's title. So far as the words 'or was' are concerned, they should not be construed so as to apply to a past agreement which is entirely irrelevant. They can be given a sensible meaning (under which the owner now claims the car) which provides that, on an attempted sale or disposition of the car by the hirer, the agreement is automatically terminated. The words 'or was' do not apply to a past hire-purchase agreement which has been paid off. In short, a purchaser is only affected by notice if he has actual notice that the car is on hire-purchase. He is not affected merely by being told that it was previously on hire-purchase which has not been paid off."

There is no real symbiosis between good faith and notice. Thus for there to be bad faith, in terms of notice, mere carelessness is not sufficient—there must be conduct which evinces a deliberate design not to know more. The nineteenth century authorities suggest that mere suspicion is not notice unless suspicion is taken a stage further, that is, where the actor resolved to see nothing which was contrary to his interests.

The definition of good faith, which accords with the common law position at the end of the nineteenth century, is defined as we have discussed previously in section 61(3) of the SGA 1979, namely, as when a thing "is in fact done honestly, whether it is done negligently or not". It follows that notice and good faith include implied or constructive notice. This is the point which emerges from *Heap v. Motorists Advisory Agency Ltd*,[20] where Lush J. held that the sale of a car which the plaintiff wished to sell at £210 but was eventually sold for £110, was at such a low price that it should have put the defendants on their guard. The defendant had failed to do what any reasonable man would have done by failing to discover more about the car when he bought it—it was this failure which was held to constitute notice on the part of the defendant

[18]. [1971] 1 W.L.R. 983.
[19]. *Ibid.* at 986.
[20]. [1923] 1 K.B. 577.

of some want of authority on the part of the mercantile agent. Since the weight of authority is against constructive notice which, in any case, would render the good faith element unnecessary, it follows that the inclusion of this requirement ensures that the purchaser is protected where he is careless but not where he is wilful. Such an approach was confirmed in *Dodds v. Yorkshire Bank Finance Ltd* (1991) discussed above. Undoubtedly, the plaintiff purchaser was suspicious and was concerned about the possibility of the vehicle being on hire-purchase. In the Court of Appeal the question of good faith was treated as an aspect of honesty, and the purchaser satisfied this test when she insisted that the disposer signed a receipt to the effect that the vehicle was not subject to hire-purchase. The mere knowledge of the *possibility* of another's interest in the goods is not sufficient to constitute dishonesty.

The nature of protection: the title acquired

Introduction. The basis for understanding the passing of property pro-visions in sale of goods is that of relativity of title. In the context of Part III of the Hire-Purchase Act 1964 (as amended), what passes as a result of the disposition is the title of the financier to the hirer or the buyer under a conditional sale agreement. Herein, of course, lies a potential problem regarding the marketability of the motor vehicle, as there may be a shadow on the title thereby restricting the innocent purchaser's ability to dispose of the vehicle. The main difficulty is that section 12 of the SGA 1979, in setting out the seller's implied contractual obligation relating to the nature of the title that the seller must invest in the buyer, refers to an implied condition that the seller has the right to sell and pass good title, that is, not merely a *power* to sell which is invested upon him by virtue of, for example, Part III of the Hire-Purchase Act 1964 (as amended). As a matter of principle, a seller who by his action of selling the vehicle commits the tort of conversion cannot be said to have a "right" to sell the goods. Even so a private purchaser in good faith does enjoy a good title by virtue of this exception to the *nemo dat* rule, it follows that the breach of section 12(1) of the Sale of Goods Act 1979, which provides that the seller will have a right to sell the goods, is merely technical, because the buyer is given what he bargained for, namely, a good title.[21]

In the case of conditional sale account must be taken of the time factor for the right to sell under section 12(1) of the SGA 1979, which occurs "when the property is to pass". This would normally equate with the time when the buyer has completed his payment schedule. Where the buyer makes an accelerated payment, it could be argued, if the buyer is aware of the seller's difficulty in making title on early repayment, that the act of accelerated payment constitutes a waiver of this breach of condition. In a similar fashion, where there is a hire-purchase agree-ment, section 8 of SOGIT 1973 equates "right to sell" with when the

---

[21.] *Cf. Barber v. NWS Bank plc* [1996] 1 All E.R. 906.

general property is to pass, which coincides with when the hirer has completed his payments. The *purpose* of an executed sale transaction is to pass a perfect title, and this is not the case with an executory contract of sale or hire-purchase, at least until the time when property is to pass. Where there has been a technical breach of the right to sell, this will only sound in a right to reject the goods where there has been a breach of the quiet possession warranty in section 12(2) of the SGA 1979 and section 8(1)(b) of the SOGIT 1973. In this regard, the disturbance has to be substantial to justify repudiation, for example, the finance company owner repossessing the vehicle or the buyer/hirer having to engage a solicitor to handle his affairs in defending his claim.

It is sometimes the case that a potential trade purchaser or motor dealer, when running a search of hire-purchase interests with HPI plc, will discover the existence of the hire-purchase or conditional sale agreement and will refuse to take the vehicle in part-exchange. As a consequence, the marketability of the motor vehicle is severely impaired because the private purchaser who shelters under the title protection provisions of Part III of the Act is compromised. The possibilities for the private purchaser will now be considered.

The acquirer's dilemma: keep the vehicle indefinitely. The effect of keeping the vehicle indefinitely is to take the car outside the stream of commerce, and is not, therefore, a realistic option because one of the features of commercial law is that it recognises the need for marketability of commercial assets.

The acquirer's dilemma: repudiate the original contract of sale. In many instances repudiation of the original contract of sale is not a realistic option because the original fraudulent disposer will either be judgment-proof or beyond the reach of process. However, in the absence of this eventuality, for example, through the intervention of a financial intermediary in funding the disposition, there are considerable conceptual and practical problems associated with repudiation, especially the issue of "curing" a defective title.[22]

The acquirer's dilemma: sale to a private sub-buyer. In adopting the course of a sale to a private sub-buyers, the buyer runs the risk of liability for breach of the quiet possession warranty if the sub-buyer is disturbed at a later date, which is a question of assumption of risk. Herein lies the importance of the presumptions which operate to remove doubt as to the title of the bona fide purchaser.

The presumptions

Introduction. Section 28 of the Hire-Purchase Act 1964 (as substituted) lays out a system of rebuttable presumptions which operate in any

---

[22.] See pp. 186–189.

proceedings (civil or criminal) relating to a motor vehicle. It is provided for the purpose of section 28(1):

> "(a) that the vehicle was bailed or (in Scotland) hired under a hire-purchase agreement, or was agreed to be sold under a conditional sale agreement, and
> (b) that a person (whether a party to the proceedings or not) became a private purchaser of the vehicle in good faith without notice of the hire-purchase or conditional sale agreement (the 'relevant agreement')."

The presumptions do not apply where the circumstances of the disputed transactions are fully known. This point emerges clearly in the judgment of Orr L.J. delivering the judgment on behalf of the Court of Appeal in *Soneco Ltd v. Barcross Finance Ltd*[23] in the following terms:

> "It is entirely clear from a reading of the Act as a whole that section 27 is dealing with the case, which is the present case, where all the relevant dispositions of the vehicle are known, whereas section 28 is dealing with cases where all dispositions of the vehicle are not known, and its objective is to ensure that in such a situation a purchaser is not deprived of the relief granted by the Act, and for this reason section 28 provides that certain artificial assumptions are to be made in his favour ... It is only, in our judgment, necessary to go on to section 28 where, as does not arise in the present case, there is a missing link in the history of the car, in which event the purchaser is given the benefit of the statutory presumptions in section 28."

It is clear that the claimant is only protected in these circumstances where there has been a break in the chain of title which would otherwise make it very difficult for a claimant in any dispute with the owner, as financier, who had let the vehicle to the fraudulent hirer to prove that he came within the shelter accorded by Part III.

The first presumption[24] is that the disposition was made to the relevant purchaser who was a private purchaser from the debtor in good faith and without notice of the hire-purchase or conditional sale agreement. If this presumption fails, the second may operate,[25] namely, that the debtor disposed of the vehicle to a private purchaser who was a purchaser of the vehicle in good faith and without notice of the relevant agreement, and that the relevant purchaser is or was a person *claiming under the person to whom the debtor so disposed of the vehicle*. On that assumption that this presumption fails, the third will operate,[26] that is, the person who, after the disposition of the vehicle to the trade or finance purchaser in question, first became a private purchaser who took

---

[23.] [1978] R.T.R. 444 at 450–451.
[24.] Hire-Purchase Act 1964, s. 28(2) (as substituted).
[25.] *Ibid.* s. 28(3).
[26.] *Ibid.* s. 28(4).

in good faith and without notice and is or was a person claiming under the original trade or finance purchaser. Generally in order to invoke the presumptions in section 28, the claimant must show either that he himself had, or he derived, title from some other party in the chain of transaction. Thus, in *Worcester Works Finance Ltd v. Ocean Banking Corp Ltd*,[27] where a motor dealer could not establish that any intermediate private purchaser was in good faith, it was held that the dealer could not, by making a sale to a bona fide private purchaser, thereupon himself rely on the statutory presumption encapsulated in section 28 which could compromise the position of a subsequent private purchaser from the dealer.[28]

Even though the presumptions assist in establishing title, nonetheless the original buyer will still take the risk of quiet possession liability if the sub-buyer is disturbed by an earlier owner. Under section 12(2) of the SGA 1979, the seller has to warrant that neither he personally nor anyone claiming under him will disturb the buyer's possession, except in so far as this would be permitted under a disclosed or known encumbrance. It could be argued that any extension of the quiet possession warranty to include tortious acts of third parties would destroy the legal predictability of the warranty. However, the Court of Appeal in two cases has held the seller liable where the disturbance came from a third party and not from the vendor himself. In *Mason v. Burningham*[29] the buyer had to return a stolen typewriter to the owner, whereas, in *Microbeads AG v. Vinhurst Road Marking Ltd*[30] the seller was held to be in breach of the quiet possession guarantee when the holder of a patent claimed that the buyer was using a machine in breach of this intellectual property right. A careful distinction should be drawn here with interference which it totally unconnected with that of the seller, for example, the actions of a thief. The significance of this analysis is that by taking such a strict approach to section 12(2) it would appear that a buyer will have an action if his possession is disturbed by a previous owner (financier) seeking to assert title. The actions of the owner (financier) can hardly be considered to be illegitimate in the sense as that of a thief who is totally unconnected with the seller. Given the complexity of the title issue in this context, the behaviour of the owner (financier) may be perfectly reasonable in view of the fact that the chain of title can only become clear in the light of legal argument and emergent facts. In this circumstance in no sense can the financier's action be considered to be illegitimate, so there is no policy issue here of confining the scope of section 12(2) to only legitimate interference with the title.

The quiet possession guarantee is certainly problematical for the seller. This is further compounded by the fact that he cannot exclude

[27.] (1972) unreported.
[28.] But see the Hire-Purchase Act 1964, s. 28(5) with regard to admissions made.
[29.] [1949] 2 K.B. 545.
[30.] [1975] 1 W.L.R. 218.

liability here because exclusion of section 12 of the SGA 1979 implied terms are void under section 6(1)(a) of the UCTA 1977. However, section 12(3) of the SGA 1979 does contemplate the possibility of the sale of a limited title, and where this is the case section 12(5) provides for a warranty that neither the seller nor any third person whose title the seller is transferring by virtue of section 12(5)(c) nor "anyone claiming through or under the seller or that third person" will disturb the quiet possession of the buyer. The dilemma here is that this does not cover the case where a previous owner (financier) who loses out under the *nemo dat* exception in Part III wrongfully claims title, because in law the seller's claim is not a limited one.

The acquirer's dilemma: disposal of the vehicle to another trade purchaser. There is natural reluctance on the part of a trade purchaser to accept a vehicle with a shadow on its title. This is compounded by the fact that a dealer cannot himself rely upon the presumptions laid down in section 28 of the HPA 1964 (as substituted). This analysis was confirmed by the Court of Appeal in *Barber v. NWS Bank plc*[31] where reference was made to section 27(6) of the Act which restricts trade or finance purchasers from benefiting from the provisions of the Act, the mischief of which is to protect innocent *private* purchasers. Furthermore, the trade or finance purchaser does not derive title through the relevant bona fide private purchaser, because otherwise the strict common law position applies. Significantly, section 27(3) of the Hire-Purchase Act 1964 (as substituted) protects only the first purchaser from the trade or finance purchaser, so long as he is in good faith and has no notice of the hire-purchase agreement. Therefore, there will be shadow on the title if the conduit pipe in this regard, the first private purchaser, is not in good faith.

Part III of the Hire-Purchase Act 1964 (as substituted) recognises the economic equivalence of different legal forms of transaction, namely, sale, conditional sale and hire-purchase. Consequently, where a first purchaser is in good faith and without notice of the defect in title, so long as at the time of the *first* disposition to him he was without notice of the defect, good title will pass notwithstanding that when the hirer exercises his option to purchase by that time he had notice of the original hire-purchase transaction. In this respect, section 27(4) of the Act provides as follows:

"Where, in a case within subsection (3) above—

  (a) the disposition by which the first private purchaser becomes a purchaser of the motor vehicle in good faith without notice of the relevant agreement is itself a bailment or hiring under a hire purchase agreement, and

  (b) the person who is the creditor in relation to that agreement disposes of the vehicle to the first private purchaser, or a person claiming

[31.] [1996] 1 All E.R. 906.

under him, by transferring to him the property in the vehicle in pursuance of a provision in the agreement in that behalf,

the disposition referred to in paragraph (b) above (whether or not the person to whom it is made is a purchaser in good faith without notice of the relevant agreement) shall as well as the disposition referred to in paragraph (a) above, have effect as mentioned in subsection (3) above."

There is an anomaly here, given that section 27(2) protects any purchaser in good faith and without notice. Where a disposition is effected by a trade or finance purchaser, and the first private purchaser takes the vehicle on hire-purchase or conditional sale and the vehicle is repossessed and subsequently sold by the financier, the person to whom the vehicle is sold does not acquire a good title because he is not the first private purchaser. Furthermore, section 27(4) extends to hire purchase provided by a financier and does not apply where the vehicle is let to the private purchaser by the original debtor. Surely, this is a distinction without a difference given the access by both the dealer and the financier to the credit information reference agency HPI plc?

Miscellaneous Dealings in Goods

Execution and Seizure of Goods

The enforcement of debt by the seizure of goods is an effective, albeit a controversial, means of debt collection available in English law. Where there is a judgment or order given by the High Court, execution may be effected against the debtor's goods and chattels either by issuing a writ of *fieri facias* directed to the sheriff of the county of which the goods are situate[32] or by applying to the registrar of the appropriate county court for the issue of a warrant of execution.[33] When the judgment is that of a county court only, the latter method of execution is available. The sheriff or registrar enforces the writ or warrant by causing the goods to be seized and thus sold, which may be by auction or by private sale, on the application of the sheriff or the execution creditor or debtor or even, in the county court, by the district judge.[34] The sheriff can only seize goods of the debtor.

Section 15(1) of the Courts and Legal Services Act 1990 amends section 138 of the Supreme Court Act 1981 regarding seizable goods. These now comprise any of the debtor's goods, except:

"(a) Such tools, books, vehicles and other items of equipment as are necessary for use personally in employment, business or vocation.

---

[32] R.S.C., Ord. 45.
[33] *Ibid.* Ord. 26, r.1; C.C.R. 1981.
[34] See R.S.C., Ord. 47, r. 6; C.C.R., Ord. 26, r. 15.

(b) Such clothing, bedding, furniture, household equipment and provisions as are necessary for satisfying basic domestic needs of the
person and family."

Goods held jointly with third parties are not seizable.[35]

Once goods have been seized, the debtor must be provided with an
inventory and must be given advance notice of the auction. It is essential
for a lessor, who discovers that equipment leased by him has been seized
or threatened with seizure, to immediately give notice of his interest to
the sheriff or registrar entrusted with the execution. If the goods are sold
by the sheriff's officer or bailiff in ignorance of their true ownership, the
purchaser will acquire a valid title[36] and the officer executing the writ or
warrant is in such cases protected by statute from liability,[37] except
where he had notice or might by making reasonable inquiry have
ascertained that the goods were not the property of the judgment debtor.
In this circumstance, it is arguable that inquiry with HPI plc would
satisfy the reasonable inquiry provision, at least in relation to motor
vehicles. Where the goods are sold by a sheriff's officer or bailiff who has
no reason to believe that they are not the property of the judgment
debtor, the owner's only remedy is to sue the execution creditor for the
proceeds of sale.[38] He is entitled to recover these from the execution
creditor subject to a deduction in respect of the expenses of sale.[39]

If the sheriff or bailiff has doubt about the ownership of goods seized,
then the latter can gain protection by interpleading, for example where a
claim to those goods are made from a person other than a judgment
debtor.[40] In this situation the claimant may deposit certain sums or give
security and have his claim determined by the court. In default of this
the bailiff must sell the goods as though no such claim had been made.[41]

Distress

The entitlement of the landlord to distrain for goods is a well established common law right. There are also statutory remedies providing
for distress to recover rates and taxes and also for rights in relation to
land as well as for the enforcement of certain fines imposed by or by
order of magistrates' courts. These statutory remedies are more analogous to execution than to the common law right of a landlord to distrain
for rent. Furthermore the statutory rules governing the process of
levying distress for rent[42] are not applicable to distress for rates or for

[35] *Farrar v. Beswick* [1836] 1 M. & M. 682.
[36] County Courts Act 1984, s. 198.
[37] *Ibid*. s. 98(1).
[38] See *Ibid*. s. 98(2).
[39] See *Jones Bros (Holloway) Ltd v. Woodhouse* [1923] 2 K.B. 117.
[40] See R.S.C. Ord. 17, r. 2; C.C.R. Ord. 33, rr. 1–4.
[41] County Courts Act 1984, s. 100(3).
[42] Distress for Rent Rules 1988, S.I. 1988 No. 2050.

taxes or under the summary jurisdictions. These different forms of distress are considered in Chapter 10, below.

Liens

A lien is a right normally given by operation of law to one person over the goods of another person to secure payment of a sum of money owed by that other person to the lessee. There are well established rules as to the circumstances in which and the persons against whom a lien can be asserted. These rules are considered in detail in Chapter 7, below.

Forfeiture of Goods

Under section 36 of the Road Traffic Act 1991 there is a court power of forfeiture covering vehicles used in all imprisonable offences under the Road Traffic Act 1988, which are committed by driving, attempting to drive or being in charge of the vehicle. There may be a good public policy rationale for forfeiture, for example, it does reinforce a disqualification order in that it could make it more difficult for the offender to drive in defiance of the order, which is obviously significant in the case of a serious or persistent road traffic offender. In making any deprivation order which can only be made against personal property,[43] the court has to take into account the value of the property and also the likely financial and other effect on the offender. Thus, in *R. v. Richards*,[44] the facts involved an appeal of a deprivation order in respect of the appellant's rights in a motor car (in which he and others had driven to places where they had committed thefts) which was made on the basis that the car was worthless whereas, in fact, it was worth £3,000. The appeal against the order was upheld on the basis that the court had to have regard to the value of the property and to the likely financial and other effects on the offender in making the order, and the judge at first instance was not aware of the car's true value.

When a deprivation order or a confiscation order[44a] is made the property must be given up to the police for disposal. The disposal by the police is governed by the Police (Property) Act 1897, although this is excluded where property seized or detained as liable to forfeiture has come into police possession by virtue of section 139(3) and (4) of the Customs and Excise Management Act 1979. Under section 1(1) of the 1897 Act, there is a duty on the police to ascertain who is the owner. It could be maintained that a check with HPI plc is reasonable and simple, so a failure by the police could render the police liable in an action in

---

[43.] See *R. v. Khan* [1982] 2 All E.R. 969.

[44.] (1992) 13 Cr.App.Rep. 272.

[44a.] For a general discussion see Rees "Confiscating the Proceeds of Crime" (1966) 146 New L.J. 1270.

negligence for breach of a statutory duty by the financier/owner especially since the nature of the original court order can be made regardless of the rights of the true owner.

The powers of the authorities are extensive under the Customs and Excise Management Act 1979. In this repect, section 141 of the Act provides a process *in rem* against any vehicle or object used for the carriage of prohibited goods. It would appear, following *Customs and Excise Commissioners v. Air Canada*,[45] that liability for forfeiture is absolute and knowledge on the part of any person, whether as user or owner of the vehicle, was not a requirement of liability. This approach was upheld by the European Court of Human Rights in *Air Canada v. United Kingdom*,[46] where it was held that the seizure of Air Canada's aircraft by the Customs and Excise and its release subject to payment, did not amount to an unjustified interference with the peaceful enjoyment of possession as guaranteed in Article 1 of the First Protocol of the European Convention on Human Rights. Furthermore the Court concluded that the matters complained of did not involve the determination of a criminal charge and that the company's civil rights and obligations, as guaranteed by Article 6 of the Convention, had not been violated because no criminal charge had been brought and the English criminal courts had not been involved in the matter.

Sale under Common Law or Statutory Powers

The SGA 1979 preserves other exceptions to the general rule of security of property. By virtue of section 21(2)(b), nothing in the Act shall affect "the validity of any contract of sale under any special common law or statutory power of sale or under the order of a court of competent jurisdiction". Many of the statutory powers of sale developed from the common law, for example, the right of a pawnee under sections 120, 121 of the CCA 1974; those of a bailee of uncollected goods under sections 12 and 13 of the Torts (Interference with Goods) Act 1977; and innkeepers' powers to sell guests' goods to meet unpaid hotel fees under section 1 of the Innkeepers' Act 1878. Other important statutory powers relate to insolvency and bankruptcy and are consolidated under the Insolvency Act 1986.

The High Court has significant statutory power to order sale if the goods are perishing or depreciating rapidly in value while litigation over them is proceeding.[47] In addition, rules of court allow for the sale of goods seized in execution where a claimant alleges that he is entitled to the goods by way of a security for a debt.[48]

---

[45] [1991] 2 Q.B. 446.
[46] ECHR Case No. 9/1994/456/537.
[47] R.S.C., Ord. 29, r. 4; County Courts Act 1984, s. 38.
[48] R.S.C., Ord. 17, r. 6; County Courts Act 1984, s. 100.

Chapter 7

Liens and Wrongful Dealings in Equipment

Introduction

A lien is a right normally given by operation of law to one person over the goods of another person to secure payment of a sum of money owed by that other person to the lienee. A careful distinction should be drawn between possessory and non-possessory or equitable liens.

Possessory (Common Law) Liens

Introduction

A possessory lien confers no proprietary interest in the lienee and is not assignable: it is purely a personal right and cannot be taken in execution by the lienee's creditors. The possessory lien may be subclassified into general liens and particular liens.

General Liens

A general lien entitles the lienee to retain possession of *any* of his debtor's chattels to secure payment of all sums due on a general balance of account between them. Thus, a general lien is exercisable in respect of a debt or account which has no relation to the chattel subject to the lien. A general lien is usually created by usage and is confined to a small number of trades and professions. This is because they are not viewed with favour by the courts, since their comprehensive nature tend to prejudice other creditors in the event of the debtor's insolvency. On the other hand, where the parties deal with each other on a regular basis, the general lien is, in fact, mutually beneficial since it allows the lienee to release individual goods without immediate payment because he will have recourse to other goods as security for the debt if this proves necessary.

A trader seeking to establish a general lien bears a heavy burden of proof.[1] In practice, therefore, general liens are normally the creatures of

[1] See *Rushforth v. Hadfield* (1805) 6 East. 519, and (1806) 7 East. 224.

227

contract. Even so, long usage can establish general liens, and they are enjoyed by solicitors,[2] bankers,[3] factors,[4] and stockbrokers.[5] It should be noted that the transferee of an interest in goods held under a general lien takes it subject to the extent of the balance of account owing to the lienee when he receives notice of the transfer.

Particular Liens

Generally

A particular lien entitles the lienee to retain possession only of those of his debtor's chattels in respect of which the debt arose, that is, it entitles the lienee to hold the debtor's goods pending payment of charges incurred in relation to the goods detained, there being no right to retain the goods for the purpose of securing payment of some other debt due from the owner unconnected with the goods in question.

Particular liens are favoured by the courts because they are not seriously prejudicial to general creditors on the debtor's insolvency. Of course, the terms of the transaction may prevent the lien from coming into existence in the first place, as in the case of a credit period.[6]

Particular liens created by contract

Particlar liens created by contract may arise expressly or impliedly from a prior course of dealing between the parties. Custom is important here as many classes of traders have established usages in their favour.

Particular liens created by statute

The most important of the liens created by statute is the unpaid vendor's lien which arises under sections 39 to 43 of the Sale of Goods Act 1979.

Particular liens created by judicially recognised usage

Where the lienee is obliged by law to receive other person's goods, as in the case of innkeepers and common carriers, the courts have ameliorated this burden by the recognition of liens over guests' belongings and goods carried. The lien is enforceable against persons generally and not merely against the person for whom the charges are due.[7]

---

[2] *Ex p. Sterling* (1809) 16 Ves. Jr. 258.
[3] *National Westminster Bank Ltd v. Halesowen Presswork and Assemblies Ltd* [1972] A.C. 785.
[4] *Baring v. Corrie* (1818) 2 B. & Ald. 137.
[5] *Re London and Globe Finance Corp.* [1902] 2 Ch. 416.
[6] *Wilson v. Lombank Ltd* [1963] 1 W.L.R. 1294.
[7] *Marsh v. Commissioners of Police* [1944] 2 All E.R. 392.

Artificer's lien

An artificer's lien arises where the lienee has by his labour and/or skill improved another's chattel. The courts have taken a restrictive view of what constitutes an improvement, so that in *Re Southern Livestock Producers Ltd*,[8] it was held that a farmer housing, feeding and caring for pigs had no lien on them for sums spent, one of the reasons being that routine care was not improvement.[9] In contrast, there would be a common law lien on charges for veterinary attention and, in a similar way, professionals would have a lien on documents they work on, such as architects,[10] and accountants.[11] The lien only arises for work already *completed* or work done before the owner prevents completion.[12] In contrast in relation to a warehouseman's lien, this extends to goods in his possession to secure payment of warehouse charges for those goods. Moreover, a warehouseman may be able to establish a general lien by contract or usage and this is a normal provision in warehousing contracts. Such a lien will be effective even against strangers if they are aware of this contractual provision.[13]

The antithesis of the improver's lien is the salvor's lien for his services recognised in maritime law.[14] The essence of the salvor's lien is that he helps to prevent injury to another's goods which would, of course, not constitute an improvement for the purposes of the artificer's lien.

Non-Possessory Liens

Non-possessory liens are rights conferred by equity in various circumstances, which entitle creditors to have particular property in the possession of their debtors to be realised by legal process in order to satisfy their debts. Examples include the vendor's lien on land conveyed in respect of any unpaid portion of the price, and the purchaser's lien on land sold but not yet conveyed regarding any part of the price already paid.[15]

An unpaid seller of goods has only got a possessory lien.[16] Nevertheless, an equitable lien may arise in respect of personal property, other than "goods," which are the subject of a contract of sale, for example,

---

[8.] [1964] 1 W.L.R. 24.
[9.] See also *Hatton v. Car Maintenance Co. Ltd* [1915] 1 Ch. 621.
[10.] *Hughes v. Lenny* (1839) 5 M. & W. 183.
[11.] *Woodworth v. Conroy* [1976] Q.B. 884.
[12.] *Lilley v. Barnsley* (1844) 1 Car. & Kir. 344.
[13.] See *K. Chellaram and Sons (London) Ltd v. Butlers Warehousing and Distribution Ltd* [1977] 2 Lloyd's Rep. 292.
[14.] *The Goring* [1987] Q.B. 687.
[15.] *Cf. Re Wait* [1927] 1 Ch. 606.
[16.] Sale of Goods Act 1979, ss. 41–43.

patents and shares. Such liens bind all those acquiring interests in the property concerned, except bona fide purchasers of legal interests without notice of the lien, and are therefore unlikely to affect asset title financiers of equipment.

Possessory Liens and Equipment Lessors

Possession as the Base Concept

Possession generally

Possession is a highly fluid concept as it may be either factual or constructive. Moreover, constructive possession might take many forms, including attornment and symbolic delivery, for example, the handing over of keys to the store where the pledged goods are housed so as to ensure exclusivity of possession.[17] The indorsement and delivery of a bill of lading or some other document of title operates as delivery of the goods which it represents and may, therefore, be pledged. In *Official Assignee of Madras v. Mercantile Bank of India Ltd*,[18] Lord Wright summarised the position as follows:

> "In the common law a pledge could not be created except by a delivery of possession of the thing pledged, either actual or constructive. It involved a bailment. If the pledgor had the actual goods in his physical possession, he could effect the pledge by actual delivery; in other cases he could give possession by some symbolic act, such as handing over the key of the store in which they were. If, however, the goods were in the custody of a third person, who held for the bailor, the pledge could be effected by a change of the possession of the third party, that is by an order to him from the pledgor to hold for the pledgee, the change being perfected by the third party attorning to the pledgee, that is acknowledging that he thereupon held for him . . . But where goods were represented by documents the transfer of the documents did not change the possession of the goods, save for one exception, unless the custodier (carrier, warehouseman or such) was notified of the transfer and agreed to hold in future as bailee for the pledgee. The one exception was the case of bills of lading, the transfer of which by the law merchant operated as a transfer of the possession of, as well as the property in the goods . . . a pledge of the documents (always excepting a bill of lading) is merely a pledge of the *ipsa corpora* of them; the common law continued to regard them as merely tokens of an authority to receive possession."

The issue of exclusivity of possession is essential. In this respect, the lienee must have obtained actual or constructive possession *lawfully*, and must have the right to uninterrupted possession with no express or

---

[17.] *Hilton v. Tucker* (1888) 39 Ch. D. 669.
[18.] [1935] A.C. 53 at 58.

implied provision incompatible with this. Thus, in *Forth v. Simpson*,[19] it was held that a trainer had no lien over a racehorse because he had no right of *continuing* possession, since the owner could take the horse away for any race he chose and also select any jockey he chose. A related question concerns the legality of the creditor's possession which demonstrates the consensual basis of liens and pledges. Where true consent is not forthcoming the debtor will not be bound, for example, where there has been fraud or misrepresentation,[20] or where the goods have been obtained by force or any other tortious method.[21]

Where the creditor parts with the possession of the goods, this cannot normally be re-established by recaption.[22] It is otherwise in the case of sale of goods where the right of stoppage *in transitu* arises by operation of law under Part V of the Sale of Goods Act 1979 (as amended).

Effect of giving up possession

The natural presumption is that the effect of redelivery of the goods is that possession has been surrendered. There are some difficult authorities which uphold the creditor's rights where the capacity of the debtor's possession is that of a bailee. The typical context here is where the object is needed as a tool of trade for the debtor, for example, a chronometer where the debtor was the master of a ship[23]; or a taxi in the case where the debtor was a taxi-cab operator.[24] Clearly, ostensible ownership problems are presented here and it is little wonder that in jurisdictions which have sophisticated personal property security registers, such interests have to be registered in order to be perfected.[25]

The Assertion and Enforceability of a Lien Against the Owners of the Equipment

Introduction

There are established rules as to the circumstances in which, and the person against whom, a lien can be asserted.[26] In the equipment leasing context the issue revolves around the ability of the lessee to create a valid lien which binds the lessor, and this will arise typically where the equipment has been repaired and an artificer's lien is claimed.

The general rule

Where the lienee is under no legal obligation to accept the care and custody of goods, any charges which arise out of this which forms the

---

[19.] (1843) 13 Q.B. 680.
[20.] *Madden v. Kempster* (1807) 1 Camp. 12.
[21.] *Bernal v. Pim* (1835) 1 Gale. 17.
[22.] *Pennington v. Reliance Motor Works Ltd* [1923] 1 K.B. 127.
[23.] *Reeves v. Capper* (1838) 5 Bing. (N.C.) 136.
[24.] *Albermarle Supply Co. Ltd v. Hind and Co.* [1928] 1 K.B. 307.
[25.] See, *e.g.* in Canada, the Repair and Storage Liens Act 1989, s. 7.
[26.] See 28 *Halsbury's Laws of England* (4th ed.).

basis of a lien is not exercisable against the owner of the equipment, unless he either actually or ostensibly authorised the delivery of the goods to the lienee for the execution of the work giving rise to the lien.

Actual authority to repair. Actual authority may be express or implied, for example, a bailment for repair, or other work, on goods may expressly or impliedly authorise a bailee to sub-contract all or part of the work, as in the case of a trade custom.[27] It is established authority that a bailment which expressly requires the bailee to keep the goods in repair, impliedly authorises delivery to the repairer. In *Green v. All Motors Ltd*,[28] a hire-purchase contract relating to a motor car placed the repairing obligation on the hirer; the hirer took the car to a garage for repair, the garage proprietor being aware that the person who brought it in was a hirer. During the currency of the repair work, the owner demanded the return of the car from the defendants and they refused to deliver it up until their charges had been paid. The Court of Appeal held that the defendants had a valid lien as against the owner for the cost of repairs. The principle of law was expressed clearly[29]:

> "The law is clear. The hirer of a chattel is entitled to have it repaired so as to enable him to use it in the way in which such a chattel is ordinarily used. The hirer was therefore entitled, without any express authority from the owner, to have the motor car repaired so as to enable him to use it as a motor car is ordinarily used."

Implied authority to repair. Even where the agreement is silent as to an obligation to repair, it is settled that a bailee/hirer is entitled to deal with the goods in any manner reasonably incidental to their use.[30] The *locus classicus* here is *Tappenden v. Artus*[31] where the facts involved an informal contract of bailment, designed to accommodate the bailee until he could raise a sufficient deposit to acquire the vehicle on hire-purchase, the plaintiffs allowing the prospective hirer to use a certain motor-van on condition that he licensed it and insured it. The van broke down and the bailee ordered the defendants to tow it away and effect the necessary repairs. The defendants presumed him to be the owner. After the repairs were completed, the bailor located the van and demanded its return, but the defendants refused to surrender it until they were paid. The Court of Appeal rejected the argument of the plaintiffs that an authority to create a lien should be displaced when the bailor himself is in the business of carrying out repairs, on the basis that there may be occasions, for

---

[27.] See *Cassils and Co. and Sassoon and Co. v. Holden Wood Bleaching Co. Ltd* (1915) 84 L.J.K.B. 834.
[28.] [1917] 1 K.B. 625.
[29.] *Ibid.* at 633.
[30.] *Singer Manufacturing Co. Ltd v. London and South Western Rail Co.* [1894] 1 Q.B. 833.
[31.] [1964] 2 Q.B. 185.

example, when the vehicle broke down a long way from the bailor's premises. All that had to be shown was that the artificer's possession of the chattel was lawful at the time when the lien was alleged to have arisen, the criterion being whether the owner authorised (or is estopped as against the artificer from denying that he authorised) the bailee to give possession of the goods to the artificer. As Diplock L.J. held[32]:

> "He is entitled to make reasonable use of the goods, and if it is reasonably incident to such use for the bailee to give possession of them to a third person in circumstances which may result in such person acquiring the common law remedy of lien against the goods the bailee has the authority of the owner to give lawful possession of the goods to the third person ... The grant of authority to use goods is itself to be construed as authority to do in relation to the goods all things that are reasonably incidental to their reasonable use. If the bailor decides to exclude the right of the bailee to do in relation to the goods some particular thing which is reasonably incidental to their reasonable use, he can, of course, do so, but he must do so expressly."

Apparent authority to order repairs. A device which is sometimes employed is to expressly provide for the hirer to be responsible for effectuating repairs but at the same time to prohibit the creation of a lien for the cost of repairs. This was the issue in *Albermarle Supply Co. Ltd v. Hind and Co.*[33] In this case the hirer of taxi cabs, whilst not prohibited from delivering them up for repair, was nevertheless, as a matter of contract, not entitled to create a binding lien as against the owner/financier. It was held that by impliedly authorising delivery to a repairer, the owner holds out the hirer as authorised to order repairs, thereby creating a situation in which the repairer is led to assume, in the absence of notice to the contrary, that if he executes work on the goods he will have all the remedies which the law allows for recovery of his charges. The notable point about *Albermarle* is that there was in that case no prohibition of repair and as such this was reasonably incidental to the reasonable use of the goods. In this respect the dictum of Goddard C.J. in *Bowmaker Ltd v. Wycombe Motors Ltd*[34] is most instructive:

> "... an arrangement between the owner and the hirer that the hirer shall not be entitled to create a lien does not affect the repairer. A repairer has a lien although the owner has purported to limit the hirer's authority to create a lien upon that chattel, which he can exercise against the owner of the chattel if the owner of the chattel is the person who has placed the goods with him or has authorised another person to place the goods with him."

Prohibition of delivery up for repair

If the bailee has express or implied authority to deliver goods for repair, it is immaterial whether or not the repairer knows that the deliverer is a

---

[32]. *Ibid.* at 190.
[33]. [1928] 1 K.B. 307.
[34]. [1946] K.B. 505.

bailee and not the owner. However, if there is a prohibition of delivery up for repair then, in the absence of ostensible authority or ostensible ownership, receipt of the goods by the repairer is unlawful and it follows that prima facie the right of the lien against the owner is lost. Similarly, if the agreement is terminated before the repair work has started on the goods and also before the appearance of authority has been conveyed to the repairer, in the absence of ostensible authority, the repairer cannot at common law exercise a lien against the owner. The point is that the repairer must not have been misled by the appearance of authority, for example, work completed before termination of the hirer's actual authority. In this situation the repairer would be entitled to assume the continuation of this authority until notice of termination. Of course, it is otherwise if the repairers, when executing the previous repairs, were ignorant of the fact that the person ordering them was not the owner and, therefore, could not be said to have been misled by the appearance of authority.

It is important in discussing the creation of a valid enforceable lien to distinguish between actual or implied authority in the equipment leasing contract which will bind the equipment lessor, and ostensible authority which arises by some sort of holding out by the owner/ financier. In this respect the exceptions to the *nemo dat* or security of property principle are relevant.[35]

Ostensible authority

This is an aspect of estoppel and arises where the equipment lessor's conduct has induced the artificer into believing that the bailee had actual authority to perform the acts which caused the lien to attach. Mere delivery up of possession under an equipment lease is not sufficient and does not constitute an implied representation either of authority or ownership. Indeed, it was this proposal which provoked the hostile response from the asset title finance industry to the DTI Consultation Paper, Transfer of Title (1994).

In order to establish ostensible authority there must be a *positive* act by the lessor, although this can include acquiescence in a state of affairs. Thus in *Albermarle Supply* (1928),[36] the bailor, who had expressly prohibited the creation of lien, was held to be estopped from denying its validity after a lengthy period of acquiescence in the bailee's practice of garaging and servicing the taxi cabs with the defendant garage. This approach was mirrored more recently in Australia in the unreported case of *Associated Securities Ltd v. Cocks*.[37] In this case the plaintiffs leased a Lamborghini car under a three-year agreement. The lessee took it to the defendants for repairs on about 22 occasions during a period of 18

[35.] See Chap. 6, above.
[36.] [1928] 1 K.B. 307.
[37.] [1975] Australian Current Law DT 181 (N.S.W. S.C.). *Cf. Fisher v. Automobile Finance Co. of Australia Ltd* (1928) 41 C.L.R. 167.

months. The defendants, who were the sole distributors of Lamborghini cars in New South Wales, knew of the leasing agreement but were unaware of an express provision in the agreement which forbade the creation of a lien. Begg J. held that they were entitled to a lien for the cost of their unpaid repairs, because the lessee had been given ostensible authority to have the car repaired by them and the lien was therefore enforceable.

The strict common law position appears to disregard the issue as to whether the plaintiff's intervention has incontrovertibly benefited the defendant. However, it may be that a court could be persuaded to grant restitutionary relief, where a garage carries out *necessary* repairs, if it can be shown that the defendant himself would have entered into a similar contract, for example, to fulfil a statutory requirement with the garage like an MoT certificate. In this way any argument based on redistribution of contractual risks would be avoided.[38] It is sometimes asserted that the garage could, in any case, recover under section 6(4) of the Torts (Interference with Goods) Act 1977, but this provision is obscurely worded and the better view is that it has not amended the common law position.[39] If it had reversed the common law rule, then the Act would have the effect of cutting across contractual boundaries, unjustifiably redistributing to the owner the burden of risks, for example, the creditworthiness of a contracting party which the artificer assumed in his contract with the hirer. This was not the position in the difficult case of *Greenwood v. Bennett*[40] because the contract between the innocent improver and the rogue was one of *sale*. It follows from this that the innocent improver's restitutionary claim against the owner for the value of the repairs was independent of, and did not spring from, the contract of sale.

Powers of Sale

Lien

The common law lien, being a possessory lien, is enforced by retaining possession of the goods until the debt is paid. A lienee has no automatic right to sell the goods, and if he does so wrongfully then this would terminate the lien and amount to conversion. A power of sale may, however, be conferred by contract, trade usage or statute, for example, section 12 of the Torts (Interference with Goods) Act 1977. The sale must be conducted providently and the surplus proceeds must be disgorged to the lienor. Where there is a shortfall, the lienee can sue the lienor in debt for the balance due.

[38.] See Goff and Jones *The Law of Restitution* (4th ed. 1993) p. 56.
[39.] See *ibid.* p. 176.
[40.] [1973] 1 Q.B. 195. This is discussed in Chap. 8, below.

Termination of the interest

Where factual possession is lost, we have already seen that the interest of the lienee or pledgee will be prejudiced. In addition, the interest of the lienee or pledgee will be terminated in the following circumstances:

1. Tender of amount due.
2. Waiver, for example, the taking of some other security for the debt where it is clear that this is to *replace* the pledge or lien.[41]
3. Breach. It is difficult to establish a breach of the terms on which the pledgee holds the goods so as to terminate his interest short of intentionally destroying the goods or consuming them.[42] In the case of a lien, the lienee's interest will be divested for breach where the goods are used,[43] or where the lienee claims for an unjustifiable amount.[44]

[41.] *Bank of Africa v. Salisbury Gold Mining Co.* [1892] A.C. 281.
[42.] *Cooke v. Haddon* (1862) 3 F. & F. 229.
[43.] *Rust v. McNaught and Co. Ltd* (1918) 144 L.T. Jo. 440.
[44.] *Jones v. Tarleton* (1842) 9 M. & W. 675. *Cf. Scarfe v. Morgan* (1838) 4 M. & W. 270.

Chapter 8

Accession of Chattels

Introduction

In the equipment leasing context, a thorny problem relates to the legal position when the leased chattel is annexed to another chattel. This situation should be differentiated from confusion of goods where Roman lawyers distinguished between *confusio* (wet mixtures) and *commixtio* (dry mixtures). In the case of the former, because of the "absolute inter-penetration" of the substance, there was co-ownership in Roman law whereas in the case of dry mixtures the particles retained their integrity and so there could be no co-ownership unless there was an agreement to mix.[1] In fact, in the equipment leasing context, it is the accession problem which will focus the attention of financiers because the nature of the equipment leased will normally be specifically identifiable, for example as plant or equipment by serial number. A separate issue concerns the accession or otherwise to chattels of registration numbers issued under the authority of the Secretary of State for Transport.[2]

There has been little consideration in English law of the problem of accession. Indeed, what little authority there is has demonstrated the obscuration of English law in that it has attempted to resolve the issue from the vantage of tort as distinct from property. In this respect, two broad themes may be identified: first, the concept of accession and its proprietary consequences; secondly, the notion of improvement of goods and the remedies available for so-called innocent improvers.

The typical scenario is where equipment is leased and is subsequently improved by the addition of other parts, or alternatively the equipment is installed on a chassis, such as a refrigerated unit on a lorry or a cement mixer, or an air compressor as part of a bigger machine. It is standard practice to include in leasing and hire-purchase agreements a clause to the effect that any accessories or goods supplied with or for or attached to or repairs executed shall accede to the equipment leased or hired. Where the contract specifically provides for accession the fact that the degree of annexation is not such as would satisfy the common law tests for an accession is not relevant. Indeed in *Akron Tyre Co. Pty Ltd v. Kittson*,[3] tyres fitted to a vehicle were held to have acceded to it by virtue of such an express provision in the contract of hire-purchase. The question whether such an agreement constitutes a bill of sale does not

---

[1.] See Palmer and McKendrick ed, *Interests in Goods* (1993), Birks, Chap. 19.
[2.] See pp. 247–252 below.
[3.] (1951) 82 C.L.R. 477.

arise since the passing of property in the accessory takes place following the occurrence of an external act.[4]

The Concept of Accession and Proprietary Consequences

The Common Law Tests for Accession

Where there is no provision in the equipment leasing contract, then common law principles will apply. These principles centre upon the question of the degree of annexation necessary to cause an accession. Three tests have been identified.[5] The first test is that of injurious removal, that is where the annexation is so complete that removal will destroy the utility of the principal chattel. Such a test can be objected to on the basis that it is too harsh on the owner of the accessory as it involves another exception to the basic conveyancing rule in personalty, namely, *nemo dat quod non habet*. Significantly, in *Regina Chevrolet Sales Ltd v. Riddell*[6] the Court of Appeal in Saskatchewan held that tyres fitted to a truck became the property of the truck owner as they were an integral part of the truck and necessary for its proper working.

A second test is that of separate existence, that is whether the chattel which has been incorporated in another chattel has ceased to exist as a separate chattel. It is unlikely that this test will apply as it was disapproved by the leading Commonwealth authority on the law of accession in *Rendell v. Associated Finance Pty Ltd.*[7] In this case the test championed was whether the accessory is so affixed that it cannot be removed without material damage to the principal goods. The facts involved a financier who supplied a Chevrolet truck on hire-purchase to Pell subject to a provision for the ownership of any new accession. Pell obtained a second-hand engine for the truck from Rendell on hire-purchase. Following Pell's default under the main hire-purchase agreement, the defendants recovered the truck. The plaintiffs successfully sued in conversion for the engine and the court held that since there was no accession there was no conversion. The fact that the attached engine was obviously essential to the operation of the goods was considered irrelevant since the goods were identifiable and severable without much damage to the property. Thus, in a dispute between two security holders relating to the accession or otherwise of tyres to a motor vehicle, Laskin J. in the Supreme Court of Canada held in *Firestone Tyre and Rubber Co. v. Industrial Acceptance Corporation*[8]:

[4] See *Lunn v. Thornton* (1845) 1 C.B. 379.
[5] See Guest "Accession and Confusion in the Law of Hire-Purchase" (1964) 27 M.L.R. 505 at 502–504.
[6] [1942] 3 D.L.R. 159.
[7] [1957] V.R. 604.
[8] (1971) 17 D.L.R. (3d) 229.

"The present case is unembarrassed by any suggestion that the accessory chattels have lost their identity. Nor are we concerned with an accession to the title of the purchaser of a fabricated product, be it a ship or other chattel, by the maker thereof. Again, we are not concerned with the enhancement of a security holder's position against a conditional buyer or chattel mortgagor who improves the burdened chattel in some way. In my opinion, whatever be the rationale of the doctrine of accession in taking effect in the foregoing situations, it ought not to be applied to the present case where removable and identifiable accessory chattels are claimed by the holder of an original title thereto, retained as security for their value, against the prior security title holder of the principal chattel."

The modern position can be simply stated: in the case of components which can be easily detached or unbolted the doctrine of accession will rarely apply. Indeed the Supreme Court of New Zealand in *Thomas v. Robinson*[9] applied the following test:

"The accessories continue to belong to their original owner unless it is shown that as a matter of practicability they cannot be identified, or if identified, they have been incorporated to such an extent that they cannot be detached from the vehicle."

In some respects the claim of the original owner of the accessories which can be identified and detached from the principal chattel looks like a restitutionary claim but in effect it is a proprietary claim, that is, the claim is that the property in the chattels used to "improve" the principal chattel has not passed to the owner of this chattel.

The Proprietary Effects of Accession

Introduction

The mere fact that the property in an accession becomes vested in the owner of the principal goods does not mean that the owner can recover the goods in their improved state. The court has power to impose terms and section 3(6) of the Torts (Interference with Goods) Act 1977 stipulates that, an order for delivery of goods may contain such conditions as may be determined by the courts. This confirms the discretionary nature of an order for specific restitution. Furthermore, the court has power to impose terms including compensation for improvements. In addition section 6(1) provides that if in proceedings for wrongful interference against a person who has improved the goods it is shown that the improver acted in the mistaken but honest belief that he had a good title to them, an allowance for these improvements will be made. It is necessary therefore to consider further these third party rights.

[9.] [1977] 1 N.Z.L.R. 385 at 391.

The legislation

The Torts (Interference with Goods) Act 1977 is poorly drafted and in many respects may have been somewhat premature, for example, it would not apply to the facts set out in *Munro v. Wilmott*[10] where the improver *knew* that he did not have title to the goods but he wished to remove them from his land and could not find the owner of it. However, in setting out the allowance for innocent improvement to goods, the Act gives an example[11] of a person buying a stolen car in good faith from an improver and being sued by the owner. The defendant will be given the allowance but equally, if the purchaser of a stolen improved car sues an improver who acted in good faith for failure of consideration then an allowance will, where appropriate, be also made. The Act gives no direct guidance on valuation of the goods which is "attributable to the improvement". In principle this should be the difference in the improved value and unimproved value of the chattel. The assessment will be made at the time of the conversion or other tort and not at the time of judgment, so that any increases in value as a result of the improvement will normally be excluded. The main difficulty with this approach is that unless the improver commits a fresh act of conversion by selling the goods so improved, the improvement would normally be excluded from the award of damages. It should be noted that the allowance will only be made in "proceedings for wrongful interference" against the improver and it is doubtful, therefore, whether the improver under the statute will be entitled to an allowance if he accepts the goods. In this situation reliance will have to be made on the principle established in the infamous case of *Greenwood v. Bennett*.[12]

The main difficulty with the Act is its lack of precision: it does not define improvement and neither does it say who has the burden of proving that the goods have been improved and quantifying the value of these improvements. This is significant if the equipment lessor's claim is against a bona fide purchaser from the improver who is given an allowance similar to that of the improver.[13] If the reasonable value of the improver's services is less than the net increase in the value of the chattel attributable to the improvement, then in principle he should be awarded that lesser sum.

There is a provision in the Act which is meant to deal with the problem of double liability, that is, when an owner of goods has a multiple entitlement to sue in conversion. The broad principle is enshrined in section 7(4) which provides "where as the result of the enforcement of a double liability any claimant is enriched to any extent, he shall be liable to reimburse the wrongdoer to that extent". Even so, one problematical situation which is not obviously covered by the

---

[10.] [1949] 1 K.B. 295 .
[11.] Torts (Interference with Goods) Act 1977, s. 6(2).
[12.] [1973] 1 Q.B. 195. See below.
[13.] Torts (Interference with Goods) Act 1977, s. 6(2).

legislation is *Wilson v. Lombank*.[14] In this case the plaintiff obtained a car, by a purported sale, from a person who had no title and sent it to a garage with which he had a credit account, so that no issue of lien arose. Whilst the car was on the forecourt a representative of the defendants, who believed the car belonged to them, seized it. When the truth emerged, the defendants returned the car to the true owner. The plaintiff sued in trespass and recovered the full value of the car. In terms of the 1977 Act it is hardly likely that the true owners could have sued the defendants for more than nominal damages, it would, therefore be inappropriate to talk of double liability under section 7. In this situation it may be that section 8(1), allowing a defendant to show that a third party has a better title than the plaintiff, should be taken as providing a complete defence.

It is not the case that the 1977 Act applies to one of the most frequent causes of double liability, namely, suits by both bailor and bailee. A successful action by a bailee at common law bars an action by his bailor, whether or not the bailee accounts, because the bailor must look to the bailee for recompense and so no issue of double liability arises.[15] If the bailor sues first for harm to his reversionary interest, this does not prevent the bailee from suing for the value of his possessory interest in the goods, because such an action will not amount to double liability.[16]

Improvement of Chattels

Mistaken Improvements at Common Law

Introduction

Essentially mistaken improvements at common law involves a restitutionary claim based upon the principle of unjust enrichment.[17] The structure of such a restitutionary claim appears as follows: first, the plaintiff must show that the defendant has been enriched; secondly, the enrichment must have taken place "at the expense of" the plaintiff; thirdly, it is unjust to retain the benefit because of, for example, mistake of fact; fourthly, whether there are any defences to the claim. With these categories in mind it is appropriate to consider the case of the mistaken improver.

The *locus classicus* is *Greenwood v. Bennett*[18] when a person who had mistakenly improved another's chattel was allowed a restitutionary claim

---

[14.] [1963] 1 W.L.R. 1294.
[15.] See Bell, *Modern Law of Personal Property* (1989) pp. 83–84.
[16.] See McKendrick and Palmer, *Interests in Goods* (1993) Hudson, Chap. 21.
[17.] See *Lipkin Gorman (a firm) v. Karpnale Ltd* [1991] 2 A.C. 548.
[18.] [1973] 1 Q.B. 195.

against the owner. It is worth setting out the facts of this case as they illustrate the type of dilemma faced by an equipment lessor or owner. Mr Bennett who was the manager of a garage which was owned by X and, in the course of his employment, he purchased a Jaguar car which required some repair work before being put up for sale. He delivered the car to Y who had agreed to repair the car for £85. Instead of carrying out the repairs Y used the car for his own purposes. Unfortunately, he was involved in an accident and as a result the car suffered considerable damage. Y then sold the car to Z (a garage proprietor) who bought the car in all good faith for £75 and carried out repairs which, including labour and materials, cost £226. He then sold the car to a finance company who in turn let it on hire-purchase to A for £450. When Y failed to return the car, Bennett reported the matter to the police and they subsequently found the car in the possession of A and they assumed possession of it. Y was later tried and convicted of theft. The narrow issue was whether Bennett should be ordered to pay £226 to Z (the garage proprietor) in respect of the improvements which he had carried out to the car. The Court of Appeal held that Z had a direct action against Bennett for the value of the improvements he had done to the car. The principle of law was laid down by Lord Denning who said[19]:

> "The [owners] should not be allowed unjustly to enrich themselves at [Z] expense. The Court will order the [owners], if they recover the car, or its improved value, to recompense the innocent purchaser for the work he has done on it."

Unfortunately *Greenwood v. Bennett* was decided at a comparatively early stage in the articulation of restitutionary principles in English law, and some have argued that this lack of analysis detracts from its authority.[20] It is prudent therefore to consider the decision in the light of the restitutionary structure discussed above.

Enrichment

The essential question is why should an owner have to pay for so-called improvements which he has not requested and which he may not have desired or valued. This is the scenario in *Greenwood v. Bennett* as Mr Greenwood did not know that any work was being carried out by Z. Neither can it be said that the owner had an opportunity of rejecting the improvements made, not least because on conventional proprietary analysis these improvements would, by definition, have acceded to the car. Moreover, it cannot be said in the case of a mistaken improvement that the plaintiff had been saved a necessary or inevitable expense—the car may have been more aesthetically pleasing but this cannot be considered a "necessary" benefit.

[19.] *Ibid.* at 202.
[20.] See P. Birks *An Introduction to the Law of Restitution*, p. 125.

On the facts of *Greenwood v. Bennett*, the above issues were relevant given that Mr Bennett was a manager of a garage and he had delivered up the car to Y for the purpose of repairing it before putting it up for sale. The aesthetic element here, it could be argued, is a "necessary" expense as this would facilitate disposal of the vehicle in the motor trade. Moreover, this benefit had been realised by a subsequent sale. This is a relevant consideration which arises in the context of equipment leasing: in practice, the finance lessor is going to dispose of the equipment and in this sense will realise the benefit of the improvement. As Goff and Jones have put it[21]:

> "We are persuaded that it is normally just and reasonable to require the owner of a chattel, which is not unique, who has benefited from another's services rendered under mistake, to sell his chattel if that is the only way he can make restitution. In the past the common law has taken the position that an owner should never be required to pay for improvements which he did not want or request. But the merits of that defence must be balanced against the claim of the honest and mistaken improver."

At the expense

There was no doubt that on the facts of *Greenwood v. Bennett* it could be easily shown that the enrichment was at the expense of Z, who had expended time and money on the car.

Was it unjust for the owner to retain the benefit?

The position of the improver of a chattel who mistakenly thinks that he owns it is different from that of the improver who carries out repairs on the instructions of a person whom he mistakenly believes to be the owner. There is no reason why this restitutionary remedy should cut across contractual boundaries and redistribute risks which, for example, a garage proprietor may have assumed by entering into a repair contract with the thief of a car.[22] As a matter of principle, an innocent improver who knows or ought to know that the property does not belong to him, cannot claim for improvements made. This is demonstrated by reference to the case of *Grays Truck Centre Ltd v. Olaf Johnson Ltd*.[23] The plaintiff Ford dealer carried out repairs to the defendant's truck. For credit purposes, the plaintiff refused to contract with the defendant directly but required that the order be placed by another main Ford dealer, Reginald Tildesley Ltd. The plaintiff carried out the work but Reginald Tildesley went into receivership without paying the bill, so the plaintiff sought to recover the amount unpaid from the defendant, who refused to pay. The plaintiff's claim failed. In so far as the plaintiff relied upon

[21.] *The Law of Restitution* (4th ed.) p. 176.
[22.] See *ibid* p. 55.
[23.] Unreported, C.A., January 25, 1990.

Greenwood v. Bennett, the judge held that it was distinguishable because here there was no mistake as to the ownership of the car. Although it was clearly arguable that the defendant had been enriched because the repairs it had requested had been done without it having to pay anything towards the cost of these repairs, the plaintiff could not point to any recognised "unjust" factor. It had simply taken a risk and lost.

Defences

There were no defences, such as that of change of position, available to Bennett so long as Z could show that Bennett had been enriched. Moreover, as a matter or principle, had Bennett not recovered the car but had had to bring an action in conversion against Z, he could only recover the value of the goods at the time of the conversion, namely £75, so in this respect he would have had to give credit for the improvements made.

Annexation and Priority Conflicts

Annexation of Leased Equipment to Equipment Owned by the Lessee

In the situation of annexation of leased equipment to equipment owned by the lessee, the position of the lessee in annexing the goods to his own property depends upon whether he was acting wilfully or negligently or innocently in the sense that he had no reason to believe that he was acting wrongfully. This would be rare in the equipment leasing scenario. Where there is annexation, the English approach is Draconian in its extent, in that it would appear to give the property in the resultant product to the innocent party. In this respect, as early as 1615, Coke C.J.[24] stated the law to be:

> "... that if I.S. have a heap of corn and I.D. will intermingle his corn with the corn of I.S. he shall have all the corn, because this was so done by I.D. of his wrong . . . and if this should be otherwise, a man should be made a trespasser, *volens nolens,* by the taking of his goods again, and for the avoiding of this inconvenience, the Law in such a case is, that he shall now retain all."

Nevertheless there may be exceptions, most notably, if the amount of the goods wrongfully mixed is small in comparison with the wrongdoer's goods.[25] This must be correct in principle because there is no compelling reason why the supplier should enjoy a windfall which may be at the expense of the debtor's other creditors.

[24.] In *Warde v. Ayre* 2 Bulst. 323 at 323–324.
[25.] See *Sandeman and Sons v. Tyzack and Branfoot* [1913] A.C. 680.

The above approach is confirmed in *Indian Oil Corporation Ltd v. Greenstone Shipping Company SA*,[26] where it was known, with reasonable precision, how much was contributed by the innocent party. Here the owners of a vessel, on which the receivers' cargo of Soviet crude oil was shipped, had mixed that cargo with other oil belonging to the owners already on the vessel. It was possible to work out with considerable precision the amounts of oil belonging to the two parties. Any doubt about the quantity would have been resolved in favour of the innocent party. Indeed, Staughton J. approved a general statement of Lord Eldon in *Lupton v. White*[27] that in some cases, a decision has to be made "not upon the notions that strict justice was done, but upon this: that it was the only justice that could be done." The situation would appear to be, therefore, that where the equipment lessee acted innocently he would be liable only for the unimproved value of the accession.

Annexation of Goods Owned by Third Parties to the Goods under an Equipment Lease

Where there is an accession, the equipment lessor will become the owner of the goods as an aspect of property law. It will be necessary, however, to consider the application of restitutionary principles— the *Greenwood v. Bennett* case would not apply simply because the so-called improvement would be effected not by the owner of the accessory but rather by a third party, namely the lessee. If the article belonging to the third party does not constitute an accession in the sense that it falls within the injurious removal test, it will not be deemed to have vested in the equipment lessor merely because of the existence of a clause in the equipment lease to the effect that chattels added will vest in the lessor. The rationale for this approach is that on conventional property principles the lessee will have no title to pass on to the lessor.

Annexation of Equipment Lessors Goods to those of a Third Party

Because English law has approached this problem from the vantage of tort law, then much depends upon whether the third party or its servants or agents did the act of annexation wilfully. If so, the equipment lessor will recover the whole goods. On the other hand, if the annexation was effected not by the third party but by the lessee, then title will pass subject, of course, to the application of restitutionary principles. If the third party annexed the goods subject to the equipment lease in good faith, as where he purchased the article from the lessee, he will be entitled to retain his own goods including the accession, but will

[26.] [1988] Q.B. 345.
[27.] (1808) 15 Ves. 432.

be liable to the equipment lessor for the value of the accession or, in the case of a hire-purchase agreement, of the unpaid balance of the hire-purchase price, whichever is the less.

Accessions and Fixtures

Where the principal goods become fixtures, then the owner of the principal goods will lose these and the accession unless there is a right of removal, typically because they are trade fixtures.[28]

Specification and the Creation of a New Thing

There is very little English authority on the co-mingling of two or more products in such a way as to perpetuate a loss of separate identity. It seems probable that the maker of the new thing becomes its owner irrespective of whether he has contributed any of the materials used, the former proprietors being relegated to an action in conversion or wrongful interference. This approach was confirmed by Goff L.J. in the Court of Appeal in *Clough Mill Ltd v. Martin*[29] where Blackstone's *Commentaries* was cited as authority for the proposition that if A's material is lawfully used by B to create new goods, whether or not B incorporates other material of his own, the property in the new goods will generally vest in B, at least where the goods are not reducible to the original materials.[30] Certainly this appears to be the position in Scotland. A dramatic example is *International Banking Corporation v. Ferguson Shaw and Sons*[31] when A turned B's oil into lard; it was held that B was entitled only to compensation and not to the lard.

The Scottish Law Commission[32] has considered the problems regarding the ownership of a new product where another's materials have been used in the process of manufacture and there is neither a contract nor any question of bona fide purchase between the parties. Two alternatives are suggested. The first provides that where materials cannot be conveniently separated, *pro rata* common ownership shall be enjoyed. This alternative involves a tenancy in common and may lead to problems where the value and character of the different contributions vary considerably.[33] Section 188 of the Law of Property Act 1925 empowers the court to order a division of chattels according to a valuation or otherwise, but only on the application of a person or persons interested in a moiety or upwards. Section 10 of the Torts

---

[28.] See Chap. 9, below.
[29.] [1985] 1 W.L.R. 111.
[30.] *Ibid.* at 119.
[31.] 1970 S.C. 182.
[32.] *Corporeal Movables: Mixing Union and Creation* (Memorandum No. 28 (1976)).
[33.] See *Coleman v. Harvey* [1989] 1 N.Z.L.R. 723.

246

(Interference with Goods) Act 1977 provides that co-ownership is no defence to an action founded on conversion or trespass where there has been destruction of the goods or the giving up or the purported giving up of title in the goods. The second approach attributes specific ownership to the party who had economically contributed most to the new thing. However, it is questionable whether it is possible to measure relative economic worth of labour and materials, especially in a manufacturing environment requiring a large initial outlay in machinery and energy. Under both alternatives, it is envisaged that the court would be given a discretion where the producer is in bad faith. It is understandable that the improver should not receive any legal protection if he makes an improvement with full knowledge of the ownership rights of another. With such knowledge, the improver's conduct is little more that an effort to exact payment for work performed without the owner's consent.

Accession and Cherished Registration Numbers

Introduction

When a vehicle is first licensed, the Secretary of State for Transport must register the vehicle and assign to it a registration mark indicating the registered number of the vehicle in a prescribed manner.[34] Since 1976 it has been possible to effect transfers of registration marks upon request to the Secretary of State for Transport, as section 12 of the Finance Act of that year provides:

> "12—(1) Regulations under the Vehicles Excise Act 1971 may provide for a prescribed charge to be made in cases where, by request, a particular registration mark is assigned to a vehicle (whether on its first registration or later), having previously been assigned to another vehicle.
> (2) The regulations may (a) require the vehicle to which a mark is requested to be assigned, and also in prescribed cases the other vehicle, to be made available for inspection either at a place designated by or under the regulations or elsewhere."

A thriving trade has grown around this practice as number plates, which can be considered desirable (cherished registration numbers) in terms of combinations or numbers and letters of the alphabet, soon attracted considerable sums of money in their cherished number plate form. In the late 1980s the government recognised the potential for diverting to the Exchequer more proceeds from this trade, and under the Finance Act 1989 the Secretary of State for Transport was given more powers to

---

[34.] Vehicle Excise Act 1971, s. 19, consolidated in the Vehicle Excise and Registration Acts 1994: see ss. 21, 23, 27.

---

effectuate transfers of registration numbers. Thus, the Sale of Registration Marks Regulations 1989, which were made under a power conferred by section 12 of the Finance Act 1989, came into force on November 20, 1989 and provide a scheme whereby a person can acquire a right from the Secretary of State for Transport to have a particular registration mark assigned to a vehicle registered in his name on payment of such sum as is payable under an agreement as provided for. The current position is governed by the Sale of Registration Marks Regulations 1995[35] which applies to applications made on or after December 18, 1995. By virtue of regulation 2 a person may acquire a right from the Secretary of State to have a particular registration mark, to which section 12 of the Finance Act 1989 applies, assigned to a vehicle registered in that person's name or in the name of some other person nominated by him. The agreement for acquisition of the "relevant right" can, by virtue of regulation 4, be made by public auction, tender, or by private treaty. When payment is made under the agreement, the Secretary of State issues to the purchaser a certificate. This identifies the registration mark which is the subject-matter of the agreement as well as recording the name and address of the purchaser, the date of the agreement and the date by which the relevant right may be exercised. The normal period is one year, but the 1995 regulations provides that, upon payment of an appropriate fee, it is possible to extend this period upon application. There are certain conditions which pertain to assignment, notably, a mark as would give the vehicle the appearance of being newer than it is will not be permitted.[36] Furthermore, the relevant right is non-transferable save by operation of law, for example to a personal representative.[37]

Under section 11(1) of the Finance Act 1989 there is an enabling provision for the right of retention of a *registration mark pending transfer to another vehicle*. Regulations made under this power, the Retention of Registration Marks Regulations 1993,[38] provide for a person in whose name a vehicle is registered to be granted a right to have the registration mark which is assigned to the vehicle transferred to another vehicle which is registered in the name of that person or that person's nominee. The right of retention mirrors the regulations relating to the sale of registration marks, so that whilst the right of retention may be exercised within one year from the date on which the retention document was issued, there is provision, on the payment of the appropriate fee, for an extension on one or more occasions.

---

[35] S.I. 1995 No. 2880. These regulations replace the Sale of Registration Marks (Amendment) Regulations 1993 S.I. 1993 No. 986, which continue to apply to unexercised rights granted on or before December 17, 1995.

[36] *Ibid*. reg. 10(2)(a).

[37] *Ibid*. reg. 12.

[38] S.I. 1993 No. 987.

Can there be ownership in a Cherished Registration Number?

Introduction

There can be no question of ownership in an ascribed cherished number plate, which is good against the whole world. The reason for this is that under road vehicle licensing law in the United Kingdom a registration mark is assigned by the Secretary of State for Transport when it is first licensed. This mark remains with the vehicle until it is broken up, destroyed or taken out of Great Britain, except where the mark is assigned to another vehicle or another mark is assigned to the vehicle by the Secretary of State for Transport. Any rights of a person in relation to a given registration mark will therefore be temporal and will depend upon this person's ability to invoke them in relation to a vehicle at a given time. In this respect the exercise of the acquisition of a registration number and also the right to retention can only be made *inter alia* by surrender to the Secretary of State of the registration document (the V5), as it relates to the vehicle in which the name and address of the purchaser/grantee or, where appropriate, the nominated person, are stated to be the owner of the vehicle within the Registration and Licensing Regulations 1971.[39] In this context, regulation 3 of the 1971 Regulations defines the word "owner" in relation to a vehicle as "the person by whom a vehicle is kept. . ."[40] It is worth noting that under earlier corresponding regulations, a hirer for 12 months was held to be an owner.[41]

A careful distinction should be drawn between the ownership of the actual physical material which makes up the number plate which is then attached to the vehicle and the entitlement to use this registration mark as a specific identifier of the vehicle. In this respect as regards to the former issue the question of law is whether the registration number as a physical object accedes to the vehicle in such a way as to be part of it. As discussed above there is usually a provision in a hire/lease or hire-purchase document which deals with this so that the definition of "goods" in this context will be covered by the following typical provision:

> "Reference to the Goods include all accessories and all new replacement parts in or on the Goods and all additions to the Goods."

Has the lessor got an interest in the cherished registration number where the vehicle is described in the invoice of acquisition as including this?

The invoice from the motor dealer is the document evidencing the finance company's acquisition of the vehicle and will normally be

---

[39.] S.I. 1971 No. 450 as amended by S.I. 1976 No. 2089; S.I. 1977 No. 230; S.I. 1980 No. 1802.

[40.] As amended by S.I. 1995 No. 1470, reg. 2.

[41.] See *British Railway Traffic and Electric Lighting Co. v. C.R.C. Co. and LCC* [1922] 2 K.B. 260.

effected following a sale. This document will show the registration mark of the car as part of its identity. Whilst in law the finance company has title in the vehicle, it is not the "owner" of the registration mark assigned to the vehicle from the Secretary of State for Transport because as noted above, the Road Vehicles (Registration and Licensing) Regulations 1971, as subsequently amended,[42] defines "owner" for the purposes of licensing of vehicles under regulation 3(1) as "the person by whom the vehicle is kept". The logic here is that it is this person (the "keeper") who can effectuate the assignment to the vehicle of another registration mark in pursuance of a request to the Secretary of State for Transport.

Since the leasing company's customer may permit the transfer from the vehicle of a registration mark assigned to it for the time being, the difficulty then is whether the finance company is entitled to retain the proceeds (the value of the cherished registration number) for itself? It may be persuasively argued that because the cherished registration number goes to the identity of the vehicle, this conclusion must be correct in principle and, in any case, such an act (assignment) would amount to repudiation of the leasing agreement. The only case law which considers the ownership issue in a registration number is *Naylor v. Hutson and Others*[43] and as such is worthy of further consideration. The facts are somewhat complicated. A motor car which had a registration number plate, 1700 MG, was the subject of a sale and leaseback to a finance company, Holbeche Leasing Ltd. The lessee was a company called Naylor which was developing a prototype MG style motor vehicle. The company went into financial difficulties and an administrative receiver was appointed. In breach of the lease agreement the second defendant, who was purporting to acquire the business, transferred the registration mark, 1700 MG, to another car owned by the third defendant by representing to the authorities that he was the keeper of the first car. The second defendant was aware that this vehicle was subject to a lease. The transfer form signature was irregular because the registered keeper was Naylor plc which was in administrative receivership. From that time the registration mark was transferred to various cars belonging to the fourth and fifth defendants who made use of the mark for publicity purposes. The third, fourth and fifth defendants were owned or controlled by the first two defendants.

Sometime later Holbeche Leasing repossessed the car to which the registration number 1700 MG was originally assigned. By now this car had a different registration mark. The car was then sold to the plaintiff, Holbeche having at the same time assigned to the plaintiff all rights of action in respect of the car. The narrow issue related to the ownership of the registration mark, and it was held that this had been wrongfully transferred for the following reasons: first, the transfer form was

[42.] See S.I. 1976 No. 2089; S.I. 1977 No. 230; S.I. 1982 No. 1802; S.I. 1995 No. 1470.
[43.] [1994] F.S.R. 63.

irregular; secondly, it was in breach of the lease agreement. It was further held by Maddocks J. that in the absence of a stipulation to the contrary, a registration mark passed on sale with the vehicle. Accordingly, it was in the nature of the lease that the lessor would recover at the end of the term the vehicle including the cherished number, that is, the lessee had to return that which he had received under the lease. Insofar as the lessee purported to transfer the mark, he would be in breach of the lease without the consent of the lessor. Maddocks J. rejected the argument that the registration number was attached to the vehicle only for the benefit of the keeper for the time being. The number was held to be inseparable from the car and that the power of the keeper could only be exercised with due regard to the rights of the owner. As Maddocks J. pointed out[44]:

> "The mark, significantly, if not substantially affected the value, not because the car could not be driven on the road without it—but because the number was a feature of value to a car of this particular type a replica MG with a 1700cc engine."

On the basis of the facts in this case, Maddocks J. would have been prepared to hold that the defendants held the mark on a constructive trust, the subject-matter of the trust being the registered mark and the right to transfer it. In adopting the statement made by Millett J. in *Lanrho plc v. Fayed (No. 2)*,[45] Maddocks J. held[46]:

> "I certainly would be happy to adopt the statement of principle by Millett J. there, and I can see the application of the principle. . . In the first place the right of this registration mark was in Holbeche. When [the Second Defendant] purported to transfer and indeed did transfer it, he was acting wrongfully and committing an act of conversion, by passing it on to a company controlled by [the Second Defendant]. It is a right . . . that company . . . must be taken to be a constructive trustee of the benefit of the mark, so far as it is attached to some other car."

However it was not necessary to apply the constructive trust doctrine because the court in these circumstances had inherent jurisdiction under section 37 of the Supreme Court Act 1981 to make a mandatory order for re-transfer[47]:

> "The time has long since passed when this type of registration mark can be regarded as a mere formality for the benefit of the licensing authorities, not least because the licensing authorities themselves recognise the interest the public has, or some members of the public have, in obtaining particular registered marks. That being so, and certainly in the light of the history of

---

[44.] *Ibid.* at 76.
[45.] [1992] 1 W.L.R. 1 at 8, 10.
[46.] [1994] F.S.R. 63 at 78.
[47.] *Ibid.* at 78, *per* Maddocks J.

this case, justice would not, in my judgment, be done if I did not make a mandatary order for the mark to be re-transferred, and that I shall do."

At the same time damages were awarded for the use of the mark in the interim period which were assessed on the reasonable commercial value of the use.

A distinction should be drawn with the case where the lessee assigns to the vehicle another registration number which he subsequently seeks to dispose of. In the case of a leased asset the assignment to the vehicle of a cherished number plate by the keeper can hardly be considered to be an innocent improvement and thereby covered by the Torts (Interference with Goods) Act 1977, because the lessee knows that the vehicle does not belong to him and, furthermore, unlike conditional sale or hire-purchase, the lessee does not look forward to becoming owner in due course under the agreement. In this situation following repossession of the leased vehicle on default and the transfer of the keeper status to the lessor, the registration number can be said to accede to the vehicle and through this to the lessor. Of course this begs the question of equitable relief against forfeiture and also the prospect of penalty if the value of the cherished number plate is so great that it provides a windfall for the lessor.[48]

Where the lessee has a right of retention of a cherished number, as provided for under section 11 of the Finance Act 1989 and the 1995 Regulations, it may in fact, as a matter of practicality, be difficult for the lessor to repossess the leased vehicle to include the ascribed cherished number plate. It would appear that the exercise of the right of retention depends upon the lessee reserving a right of retention by having initially applied for a retention document and also by having in his possession the registration document of the vehicle (the V5) and also the vehicle licence.[49] Much depends, therefore, upon how swift the repossession is, and if it is tardily executed or not executed fully the lessee will easily dispose of and secure for himself the value of the cherished number in pursuance of a right of retention.

[48] See Chap. 3, above.
[49] See S.I. 1995 No. 2880, reg. 9(2)(a), (b).

Chapter 9

Equipment Leasing and Fixtures to Land

Introduction

This chapter will consider some of the problems which may arise with the leasing of plant or machinery which is of a structural nature and/or is attached to land. In this context the lessor is exposed to three possible consequences: first, the equipment may still be considered to be a chattel; secondly, the equipment may become so attached to the land that it is considered to be part of it; thirdly, the equipment may be considered in law to constitute a fixture.

The Crowther Committee Report on *Consumer Credit*,[1] recommended, in the context of fixtures and accessories that a party who has a security interest over goods which are annexed to land by the *hire-purchaser* who is also the tenant should be accorded priority in competition with the landowner. However, it was envisaged that the owner of the equipment should reimburse the landowner for physical damage caused by the severance or removal of the fixture.[2] In addition, the Crowther Committee recommended that because purchasers and mortgagees might be misled into believing that the hire-purchase fixture was *pars soli*, the hire-purchase owner's interest in these fixtures should be registrable in the land registry so as to cure any ostensible ownership problem that might otherwise have arisen. In the absence of this recommendation being implemented, it is necessary to consider the continuing common law position.

Permanent Annexation to Freehold

Introduction

A building is part of the freehold in the sense that it is irrevocably wed to it. It is not relevant that it may be physically possible to reduce the building to its constituent parts, since a building is part of a freehold in an absolute sense.[3] As such it is necessary to delineate clearly the extent to which items of a structural nature or equipment constitute fixtures.

[1.] Cmnd 4596, (1971).
[2.] *Ibid*. s. 7.78–7.79.
[3.] See *Whitehead v. Bennett* (1858) L.J. Ch. 474; *Pole-Carew v. Western Counties and General Manure Co. Ltd* [1920] 2 Ch. 97.

Fixtures: A Problem of Definition

Introduction

The maxim is *quiquid plantatur solo solo cedit* and the classical exposition can be found in Blackburn J.'s dictum in *Holland v. Hodgson* when he said[4]:

> "There is no doubt that the general maxim of the law is, that what is annexed to the land becomes part of the land; but it is very difficult, if not impossible, to say with precision what constitutes an annexation sufficient for the purpose. It is a question which must depend on the circumstances of each case, and mainly on two circumstances, as indicating the intention, *viz.*, the degree of annexation and the object of annexation. When the article in question is no further attached to the land than by its own weight, it is generally to be considered a mere chattel . . . But even in such a case, if the intention is apparent to make the articles part of the land, they do become part of the land . . . On the other hand, an article may be very firmly fixed to the land, and yet the circumstances may be such as to shew that it was never intended to be part of the land. . . Perhaps the true rule is that articles not otherwise attached to the land than by their own weight are not to be considered as part of the land, unless the circumstances are such as to shew that they were intended to be part of the land, the onus of shewing that they were so intended lying on those who assert that they have ceased to be chattels, and that, on the contrary, an article which is affixed to the land even slightly is to be considered as part of the land, unless the circumstances are such as to shew that it was intended all along to continue a chattel, the onus lying on those who contend that it is a chattel."

Where a chattel lies on the ground by its own weight, it is not a fixture, for example, a printing machine.[5] Much depends upon the intention or purpose of the physical attachment, but this is determined objectively. In this respect, it is well established that it is of no relevance that the chattel which is attached to the land has been let on hire-purchase or lease terms so that property has not passed to the tenant of the land.[6] This was confirmed by the House of Lords in *Melluish (Inspector of Taxes) v. BMI (No. 3) Ltd and related appeals*[7] when Lord Browne-Wilkinson held[8]:

> ". . . the intention of the parties as to the ownership of the chattel fixed to the land is only material so far as such intention can be presumed from the degree and object of the annexation. The terms expressly or implicitly agreed between the fixer of the chattel and the owner of the land cannot affect the

[4.] (1872) L.R. 7 C.P. 328 at 334–335.
[5.] See *Hulme v. Brigham* [1943] K.B. 152.
[6.] See *Hobson v. Gorringe* [1897] 1 Ch. 182; *Reynolds v. Ashby and Sons Ltd* [1903] 1 K.B. 87.
[7.] [1995] 4 All E.R. 453.
[8.] *Ibid.* at 461 (overruling *Simmons v. Midford* [1969] 2 Ch. 415).

determination of the question whether, in law, the chattel has become a fixture and therefore in law belongs to the owner of the soil. The terms of such agreement will regulate the contractual rights to sever the chattel from the land as between the parties to that contract and, where an equitable right is conferred by the contract, as against certain third parties. But such agreement cannot prevent the chattel, once fixed, becoming in law part of the land and as such owned by the owner of the land so long as it remains fixed. To the extent that *Simmons v. Midford* decides otherwise it was wrongly decided."

It may also be that chattels which are not fixtures in themselves can become accessories to fixtures, for example, components to machines.[9] The test appears to be whether the purpose of the fixture is for the more convenient use and enjoyment of the chattel as a chattel or rather to enhance the enjoyment of the realty as realty. Thus, in *Leigh v. Taylor*,[10] valuable tapestries were fixed to the walls of a mansion house. The House of Lords held that the tapestries never ceased to be chattels because affixing them to the walls of the mansion house was necessary for their enjoyment as items of personalty. As such, the base consideration in the case of realty is the purpose of annexation and if the purpose is to enhance and effectuate the use of the land or building then it is likely that this will be categorised as a fixture since the purpose of the machine is to enhance the business as a whole.[11] An illustration of this phenomenon can be seen in *University of Reading v. The Commissioners of Customs and Excise*,[12] where the facts revolved around the installation by the University of a new telephone system which was housed in a purpose built building for it. It was held to be:

"irrelevant that the telephone building could be stripped of its contents and converted to some other use. The question is what purpose the University has in installing the objects into the building when and where they are installed ... The apparatus has been installed and incorporated into the building permanently to enable the building to be used as a telephone exchange building."

Where the degree of annexation is insignificant, and where the purpose is not permanent annexation, then the status of the chattel in relation to the land will remain unchanged. As discussed above in determining the issue of purpose, the form of the contract between the supplier and the acquirer is irrelevant, as that purpose is determined from objective circumstances, that is, the mode and degree of annexation.[13]

[9.] See *Richards, ex p. Astbury, ex p. Lloyd's Banking Co.* (1869) L.R. 4 Ch. App. 630, where one of the issues related to components of weighing machines.
[10.] [1902] A.C. 157.
[11.] See *Reynolds v. Ashby and Sons Ltd* [1903] 1 K.B. 87.
[12.] Unreported, October 19, 1989 (London VAT Tri.).
[13.] See *Hobson v. Gorringe* [1897] 1 Ch. 182.

Tenant's fixtures

The origin of the tenant's right of removal was in order to encourage trade. As Lord Kenyon C.J. put it[14]: "What tenant will lay out his money in costly improvements of the land, if he must leave everything behind him which can be said to be annexed to it?" The modern law contemplates the removal by the tenant of any fixtures he may attach, unless they are clearly annexed with the intention that they should become a permanent part of the land. Even so, there are significant limitations: first, the tenant may not remove fixtures attached by way of replacement for fixtures which formed part of the demise[15]; secondly, the right to remove fixtures might be expressly negatived in the terms of the lease.[16] Even if these limitations are overcome, it is still necessary to ensure that the fixtures are removed before the termination of the lease. As Parker J has stated[17]:

> "A tenant who contracts for the surrender of his lease to his landlord is in the same position as if he had contracted to sell the lease, and cannot as against the surrenderee, any more than he could as against a purchaser, remove fixtures which were upon the freehold at the date of the contract, even though they might be of the nature of tenant's or trade fixtures. No contract for the surrender of the lease would, however, affect his sub-tenants or alter their rights without their consent, though, if a sub-lessee stepped in and rightfuly removed fixtures after such a contract to surrender might be unable to complete the surrender which he had contracted to make, or might be bound to make compensation for breach of his contract."

Of course, if the tenant remains in possession at the expiration of the term or if the land is re-let to the tenant, then there is a presumption of retention of removal rights. The conflicting authorities were considered by the Court of Appeal in *New Zealand Government Property Corp. v. H. M. and S. Ltd*[18] and Lord Denning in that case referred to the dictum of Alderson B. in *Weeton v. Woodcock*[19] when he said:

> "The rule to be collected from the several cases on this subject seems to be this, that the tenant's right to remove fixtures continues during his original term, and during such further period of possession by him, as he holds the premises under a right still to consider himself as tenant."

Even so the position is still unclear. Indeed in *Leschallas v. Woolf*[20] it was held that if a tenant surrenders his lease even though he has it in view to

14. *Penton v. Robert* (1801) 2 East. 88 at 90.
15. *Sunderland v. Newton* (1830) 3 Sim. 450.
16. *Lambourn v. McLellan* [1903] 2 Ch. 268.
17. *Leschallas v. Woolf* [1908] 1 Ch. 641 at 650.
18. *New Zealand Government Property Corp v. H. M. and S. Ltd* [1982] Q.B. 1145.
19. (1840) 7 M. & W. 14 at 19.
20. [1908] 1 Ch. 641.

obtain a new lease, if he has not reserved the right to remove tenant's fixtures, he will lose that right altogether despite remaining in possession as a tenant.[21]

Tenant's fixtures can be removed notwithstanding that by doing so this causes damage to the freehold, notably to the fabric of the building, since the landlord is protected by the doctrine of waste, that is, as Dillon L.J. pointed out[22]: "the premises must be made good to the extent of being left in a reasonable condition". Of course when removal will occasion great damage to the land then it may be presumed that the chattel was intended to be annexed to the land, that is, it is not a tenant's fixture.[23] Notwithstanding this, outside the landlord and tenant relationship the law has been far less inclined to alleviate the practical consequence of the conversion of the chattel to land attendant upon affixation.[24] Thus, agricultural tenants did not have a right at common law to remove tenant's fixtures. However, this deficiency was removed by legislation and the current position can be found in section 10 of the Agricultural Holdings Act 1986 which gives the tenant a right to remove at any time during the term or within two months of its determination. The exercise of this right is conditional upon written notice being given to the landlord, and is subject to the tenant having fully satisfied his obligations under the tenancy and also the making good of any damage done on removal.

Equipment Lessors and Fixtures

Introduction

Where the equipment becomes annexed to the land in the form of a fixture, then it ceases to exist as a chattel and becomes part of the land pending severance. It is appropriate therefore to include within the equipment lease contract a provision giving the equipment lessor an express right of entry onto the equipment lessee's land with additional rights of severance and removal in the event of default. This right constitutes an equitable interest in land which arises at the point of annexation, since until this time no interest of any kind in the land can arise in favour of the equipment lessor.[25] In no way can this right be considered to constitute a legal estate given its limited nature and also its uncertain duration.[26] Complex priority issues arise which will now be considered.

[21] See also *Slough Picture Hall Co. Ltd v. Wade* (1916) 32 T.L.R. 542.
[22] *Mancetter Developments Ltd v. Garmanson Ltd* [1986] 1 Q.B. 1212 at 1219.
[23] *Wake v. Hall* (1883) 8 App. Cas. 195.
[24] For a discussion, see Bennett (1994) 110 L.Q.R. 448 at 457.
[25] See Goode *HP Law and Practice* (1970) p. 738.
[26] *Shiloh Spinners Ltd v. Harding* [1973] A.C. 691.

Equipment Lessor versus Lessee's Disponee

Sale of land

The normal rule is that disposition of land will include all fixtures, even in the absence of an express term and notwithstanding the nature of the disposition as being by way of mortgage.[27] The vendor cannot remove these fixtures as soon as a binding contract of sale or mortgage is purportedly concluded[28] and it is irrelevant that they can be considered to be tenant's fixtures.[29]

In the case of unregistered land, where the mortgage is purportedly protected by the deposit of title deeds the position of the equipment lessor would be improved if it were possible to register the interest under the Land Charges Act 1972 since, by virtue of section 198 of the Law of Property Act 1925, this is "deemed to constitute actual notice . . . to all persons and for all purposes connected with the land affected". It is unlikely that such an interest can be categorised as a Class C (iii) general equitable charge, because as a matter of strict form it is not a security interest in the equipment and cannot therefore be a consensual charge. Neither is it a Class D (iii) equitable easement, which is defined in section 2(5)(iii) of the Land Charges Act 1972 as "an easement, right or privilege over or affecting land . . . being merely an equitable interest". The equipment lessor has no easement in the land and as far as the phrase "right or privilege" is concerned, Cross J. said *obiter* in *Poster v. Slough Estates*[30] that a right to remove fixtures at the end of a lease did not constitute a Class D (iii) land charge.[31] If registration of the equipment lessor's interest were possible such registration would ensure priority for the supplier as against any later purchaser or any mortgagee, legal or equitable.

Any priority conflict will be determined by common law rules and these would appear to be as follows:

1. Until completion, the equipment lessor should prevail because its equitable interest will be first in point of time unless the fixture occurred after the agreement to sell.[32] The effect of a contract for the sale of land is to render the purchaser the equitable owner of the estate in question.[33] The first express recognition of a supplier's equitable interest in goods, who

---

27. *Meux v. Jacobs* (1875) L.R. 7 H.L. 481.
28. *Clarke v. Ramez* [1891] 2 Q.B. 456; Re *Yates* (1888) 38 Ch. D. 112.
29. *Longbottom v. Berry* (1869) L.R. 5 Q.B. 123.
30. [1968] 1 W.L.R. 1515.
31. See also *Shiloh Spinners Ltd v. Harding* [1973] A.C. 691.
32. For a discussion of the position where a fixture has been annexed after exchange of contracts but before there is a valid contract, see Bennett (1994) 110 L.Q.R. 448.
33. *Lysaght v. Edwards* (1876) 2 Ch. D. 499.

supplied goods on retention of title terms, came in *Re Samuel Allen and Sons*[34] when Parker J. stated[35]:

> "Now I do not think I should be right if I were to hold that an agreement of this sort was of a purely personal nature. These agreements are very common and very useful, and, of course, it is open to a mortgagee, when he takes his mortgage, to make what inquiries he likes as to whether there are any agreements affecting the fixtures upon the property. If he does not do so, and it is a mere equitable mortgage, in my opinion he must be held to take subject to those agreements, and I think that these agreements . . . do create an equitable interest by which a subsequent mortgagee who has not got in the legal estate is bound."

In the later case of *Re Morrison, Jones and Taylor Ltd* [36] there was a hire-purchase agreement in respect of a fire sprinkler which was installed in premises which fell within the scope of a floating charge. The hire-purchase agreement provided that in the event of default the owner might enter upon the premises and remove the installation. It was held that the owner of the chattels took precedence over the debenture holders. Cozens-Hardy M.R. cited with approval the dicta of Parker J. in the earlier case *Re Samuel Allen & Sons Ltd*[37]:

> "I think that those agreements . . . do create an equitable interest by which a subsequent mortgagee who does not get the legal estate is bound, and that, applying the ordinary principles of priorities as between the interest of the hirer under the hiring agreement and the interest created by the equitable mortgage, the interest created by the hiring agreement takes precedence."

2. Equity's darling will apply, that is, the purchaser of a legal estate without notice will defeat the equipment lessor.

3. Where the land is mortgaged, the fixtures are part of the land and the mortgage covers the land. Thus, the equipment lessor will be defeated by an earlier mortgage because it is first in point of time or, alternatively, by a subsequent legal mortgagee where the mortgagee had no notice. This is the classical explanation of *Hobson v. Gorringe*.[38] In this case, the plaintiff let a gas engine to X which included a hire-purchase agreement. A clause in the agreement empowered the plaintiff to repossess and remove the engine upon default. The hirer affixed the engine to his land in such a way as to make it a trade fixture. He then mortgaged the land to the defendant and after X became bankrupt the defendant entered the land under the mortgage and took possession of

---

[34.] [1907] 1 Ch. 575.
[35.] *Ibid* at 581–582.
[36.] [1914] 1 Ch. 50.
[37.] [1907] 1 Ch. 575 at 582. *Cf. Gough v. Wood and Co.* [1894] 1 Q.B. 713.
[38.] [1897] 1 Ch. 182.

the engine. The plaintiff sued to recover the engine or the proceeds of sale but the claim was unsuccessful. As Smith L.J. put it[39]:

"It seems to me that the true view of the hiring and purchase agreement, coupled with the annexation of the engine to the soil which took place in this case, is that the engine became a fixture — i.e. part of the soil — when it was annexed to the soil by screws and bolts, subject as between Hobson and King to this, that Hobson had the right by contract to unfix it and take possession of it if King failed to pay him the stipulated monthly instalments . . . But this right was not an easement created by deed, nor was it conferred by a covenant running with the land. The right, therefore, to remove the fixture imposed no legal obligation on any grantee from King of the land. Neither could the right be enforced in equity against any purchaser of the land without notice of the right, and the defendant Gorringe is such a purchaser. The plaintiff's right to remove the chattel if not paid for cannot be enforced against the defendant, who is not bound either at law or in equity by King's contract. The plaintiff's remedy for the price or for damages for the loss of the chattel is by action against King, or, he being bankrupt, by proof against his estate."

Such priority rankings may be displaced as follows:

(a) If the mortgage was registrable but was not registered, then such a mortgage is void against anyone who "for valuable consideration, takes any interest in land"[40] and this will include the equipment lessor.

(b) In *Gough v. Wood*,[41] it was held by the Court of Appeal that by leaving the mortgagor in possession, the mortgagee impliedly authorises him to continue to use the premises in the ordinary course of business, so this will probably include the equipment leasing arrangement. The rationale for this, as Lindley L.J. pointed out,[42] that otherwise "persons dealing bona fide with mortgagors in possession will be exposed to very unreasonable risks; and honest business with them will be seriously impeded". The main problem with this approach from the point of view of the equipment lessor is the limitations on the doctrine which are:

   (i) The implied authority can be expressly negatived in the mortgage.[43]

   (ii) In any case the implied authority is revoked following repossession by the mortgagee.[44]

[39] *Ibid.* at 189.
[40] Land Charges Act 1972. s. 17(1).
[41] [1894] 1 Q.B. 713.
[42] *Ibid.* at 720.
[43] See *Ellis v. Glover and Hobson Ltd* [1908] 1 K.B. 388.
[44] See *Reynolds v. Ashby and Son* [1904] A.C. 466.

(iii) It has been suggested[45] that the implied authorisation doctrine only operates as against a legal mortgagee since the latter has a right of immediate possession. An equitable mortgagee has no such right, so the effect of this is that the continuing possession of the mortgagor is by right and cannot be invoked against the mortgagee.[46]

Where the title to the land is registered, the nature of the equipment lessor's interest is categorised as a minor interest.[47] It would appear that where the equipment lessee disposes of the land absolutely or by way of a legal estate for valuable consideration, the transferee will prevail unless the equipment lessor's interest is protected on the register by notice, caution or restriction.[48] The same rule pertains if the equipment lessee is also the registered proprietor of a leasehold interest in land.[49]

In *Poster v. Slough Estates Ltd*[50] Cross J. held that a right to re-possess chattels was not an overriding interest. Nevertheless, as Guest and Lever have pointed out,[51] even though it is not an overriding interest it is still protectable by restriction or caution. Typically a registration of a caution against further dealings will mean that no dealing with the land to which the caution relates will be registered until notice has been served on the cautioner. This is a form of temporary protection, but it has the advantage that there is no need for the registered proprietor to co-operate in the procedure, for example, by making his land certificate available. It could also be argued[52] that the right to repossess is in any case registrable in the form of a notice on registered land under section 49(1)(f) of the Land Registration Act 1925 which allows for the registration of creditors notices and "any other right, interest or claim which it may be deemed expedient to protect by notice instead of by caution, inhibition or restriction". Any disposition by a registered proprietor takes effect subject to all estates, rights and claims which are protected by way of notice on the register at the date of registration or entry of notice of the disposition.[53] The main difficulty with this approach is that such a notice may only be entered on the production of the land certificate.[54]

Where the equipment lessee mortgages his interest in registered land, if his mortgage is by a sub-lease or otherwise for a term of years absolute,

---

[45.] Goode, *Hire Purchase Law and Practice* (1970) p. 742.
[46.] See *Barclays Bank v. Bird* [1954] Ch. 274.
[47.] Land Registration Act 1925, ss. 2(i), 3(xv).
[48.] *Ibid*. s. 20(i).
[49.] *Ibid*. s. 23(i).
[50.] [1968] 1 W.L.R. 1515.
[51.] (1963) 27 Conv. (N.S.) 30 at 43.
[52.] See McCormack *Reservation of Title* (2nd ed., 1995) p. 200.
[53.] See Land Registration Act 1925, s. 52.
[54.] See *ibid*. s. 64(i)(c).

the mortgagee will take free of any unregistered minor interest[55] so long as the mortgage where necessary is perfected by registration. If the mortgage is by registered charge, then these charges will rank *inter se* by order of registration.[56]

Leasing of land by the equipment lessee

In the case of unregistered land, where the lessee acquires a legal estate for value and without notice of the equipment lessor's equitable interest then the third party (lessee) will have a right to undisturbed enjoyment of the fixture for the duration of the lease of land. If the third party's interest is equitable then if the equipment lessor's interest is first in point of time, this will prevail unless it could be argued that the equipment lessor impliedly or ostensibly authorised the equipment lessee to create an interest in land including the fixture. This will probably be the case if the equipment is used in the course of a business run from those premises.

In the case of registered land, occupation by the equipment acquirer's lessee will confer upon him an overriding interest under section 70(i)(g) of the Land Registration Act 1925, which will prevail against any prior unregistered or later interests.

Equipment Lessor versus Lessee's Landlord

As the lessee cannot bind his landlord's title, it would follow that the equipment lessor cannot rely on the lessee's interest in land. Nevertheless, assuming that the equipment supplied constitutes a fixture, the equipment lessor can require the lessee to exercise his tenant's right of removal[57] or even exercise that right himself.[58] If the equipment lessee surrenders the lease to his landlord, the equipment lessor's rights of severance are greater than those of his lessee by virtue of the doctrine laid down by Lord Coke C.J.,[59] namely:

"Having regard to the parties to the surrender the estate is absolutely drowned . . . But having regard to strangers who were not parties thereto (lest by a voluntary surrender they may receive prejudice touching any right of interest they had before the surrender) the estate surrendered hath in consideration of law a continuance."

The equipment lessor will have a reasonable time after notice of surrender in which to sever and remove the fixtures.[60] Where the

[55] *Ibid.* ss. 20(1), 23(1).
[56] *Ibid.* s. 29.
[57] *Crossley Bros Ltd v. Lee* [1908] 1 K.B. 86.
[58] *Becker v. Riebold* (1913) 30 T.L.R. 142.
[59] Co. Litt. 338b.
[60] *Cf. Saint v. Pilley* (1875) L.R. 10 Ex. 137; *Re Glasdir Copper Works Ltd* [1904] 1 Ch. 819.

equipment lessee's landlord himself disposes of the land, the disponee stands in no stronger position than the landlord himself.[61]

The Impact of the Consumer Credit Act 1974

Where the agreement is a "cancellable" agreement[62], the debtor is given a period of time in which he can hand the goods back and the *status quo ante* is then re-established. However, if incorporation of the goods has occurred in any land not comprised in the agreement[63], then the debtor becomes liable to pay the cash price of the goods. It is otherwise where the incorporation has taken place with the creditor's consent, and in this situation the debtor will acquire the goods for free unless the creditor can claim against him in unjust enrichment. It is unlikely that such a contention will succeed because this would be contrary to the consumer protection policy of the Act, namely, it would deprive the debtor of his cancellation rights.

The Equipment Lessor as the Holder of a Purchase Money Security Interest (PMSI)

Introduction

It is obviously problematical for an equipment lessor in assessing commercial risk when, on conventional principles, priority is lost in a fixture to a mortgagee who is first in point of time. Nonetheless, in the light of *Abbey National Building Society v. Cann*,[64] it may be persuasively argued that English law has successfully imported the concept of the PMSI and, as such, this should protect the position of the equipment lessor. The facts are worthy of further considerations. The appellant, an occupant of mortgaged property, claimed a prior interest as against the building society mortgagee. On completion, the appellant acquired an equitable interest in the property as a contributor to the purchase price. It was argued that this took priority as against the mortgagee because the mortgage had been created by the purchaser (the appellant's son) in whom was vested the legal title out of which was then carved the mortgagee's interest. It followed that there must have been a *scintilla temporis* when the purchaser held the legal title free from the mortgage. At this point the appellant's equitable interest attached, consequently arising within the *scintilla temporis* and before the building society's charge by way of legal mortgage. The House of Lords rejected this argument and their Lordships were not prepared to permit the interest

---

[61.] See *Saunders v. Davis* [1885] 15 Q.B.D. 218.
[62.] Consumer Credit Act 1974, ss. 67–73 .
[63.] *Ibid*. s. 69(2)(b).
[64.] [1991] 1 A.C. 56.

of the purchase money financier to be subordinated by an artificial construct, namely the *scintilla temporis* doctrine. As Lord Oliver of Aylmerton stated[65]:

> "The reality is that, in the vast majority of cases, the acquisition of the legal estate and the charge are not only precisely simultaneous but indissolubly bound together. The acquisition of the legal estate is entirely dependent on the provision of funds which will have been provided before the conveyance can take effect and which are provided only against an agreement that the estate will be charged to secure them . . . The reality is that the purchaser of land who relies on a building society or bank loan for the completion of his purchase never in fact acquires anything but an equity of redemption, for the land is, from the very inception, charged with the amount of the loan without which it could never have been transferred at all and it was never intended that it should be otherwise."

In adopting the above approach, the House of Lords approved three earlier decisions where the courts had upheld the interest of a PMSI holder.[66] By applying this reasoning to the scenario confronted by the equipment lessor, there is no doubt that as soon as the equipment has become a fixture the lessor has lost his legal title in the goods or at least they have been suspended. The point of principle is whether following *Cann* the supplier's equitable interest can be an effective PMSI? Certainly the equipment lessor has extended "credit" in relation to specific goods, and in so far as a PMSI can be established then this would be a "paramount" interest. The justification for championing the interest of the PMSI holder is the unfairness of allowing a prior chargee a windfall increase in his security brought about with new funds provided by the equipment lessor. In practice the effect of the PMSI is that it makes the issue of "creation" as against an alleged preceding interest, for example, that of a mortgagee, to be redundant. The whole approach in *Cann* is that priority should not be determined *scintilla temporis*, that is, artificial and fortuitous temporal minutiae. In maintaining a PMSI, the extent of the interest of the equipment lessor would only relate to that part of the land constituted by the fixture itself. The analogy therefore would be with the right to remove a tenant's fixtures.[67] In summary the argument is that *Cann* confers priority on the equipment lessor's interest even against a prior mortgagee by virtue of the PMSI.[68]

PMSI and registered land

The interest of the supplier is a minor interest as defined by section 3(xv) of the Land Registration Act 1925. Where the priority conflict is

[65] *Ibid.* at 92–93.
[66] See *Re Connolly Bros Ltd (No. 2)* [1912] 2 Ch. 25; *Coventry Permanent Economic Building Society v. Jones* [1951] 1 All E.R. 901; *Security Trust Co. v. Royal Bank of Canada* [1976] A.C. 503.
[67] See pp. 256–257, above.
[68] See Bennett and Davis "Fixtures, Purchase Money Interests and Disposition of Interests in Land" (1994) 110 L.Q.R. 448.

with other minor interests, then the PMSI will prevail on the basis of *Cann* since it will be regarded as applying first. This is also the case if there is a priority conflict with an overriding interest.

Problems arise where there is a contest between a minor interest and a subsequent purchaser of a legal estate. The equipment lessor's right will bind the purchaser only if it is protected by entry of a notice before the purchaser is registered as proprietor.[69] It is also the case that a registered chargee will not be bound by a pre-existing minor interest unless this was registered before the registration of the charge. The rationale here is that under section 29 of the Land Registration Act 1925 registered charges rank in order of registration, and it would be illogical if an earlier created unregistered charge (such as a minor interest) could have priority and then lose it on registration.[70]

PMSI and unregistered land

It may be arguable that the equipment lessor's interest is registrable as a Class C (iii) land charge. An analogy may be drawn with an unpaid vendor's lien over land sold, which is probably a general equitable charge for this purpose.[71]

After *Cann* the nature of the equipment lessor's interest, in the case where annexation occurs after the completion of the contract of sale or creation of a mortgage, is deemed to arise simultaneously with that of the purchaser or mortgagee and, as such, nothing in the Land Charges Act 1972 can defeat that priority because unregistered interests can only be defeated by subsequent purchasers of interests. In the case of completed purchase and a legal mortgage after annexation, if the equipment lessor's interest is not registrable it will be defeated by a bona fide purchaser for value of the legal estate. It is difficult to see what the supplier can do because the courts are reluctant to infer notice, for example, in *Hobson v Gorringe*,[72] the fixing of a plate to the machinery disclosing ownership details made no impact with the court.

The Dilemma of Fixtures and Capital Allowances

The leasing of "fixtures" gave rise to problems with which capital allowance legislation, prior to the amendments made by the Finance Act 1985, was not designed to deal with. A pre-requisite for the claiming of capital allowances is that the lessor must show that, in consequence of

---

[69.] Land Registration Act 1925, s. 20(1) (purchaser of freehold), s. 23(1) (purchaser of leasehold).
[70.] See *Williams and Glyn's Bank Ltd v. Boland* [1981] A.C. 487.
[71.] See (1994) 110 L.Q.R. 448 at 476.
[72.] [1897] 1 Ch. 182.

his incurring capital expenditure, the machinery or plant for the purposes of trade *belongs* or has *belonged* to him. In *Stokes v. Costain Property Investments Ltd*,[73] Fox L.J. traced the legislative history of the concept of "belonging" and confirmed that it connotes rights or an interest akin to "beneficial ownership" by holding[74]:

> "I agree that "belong" and "belonging" are not terms of art. They are ordinary English words. It seems to me that, in ordinary usage, they would not be satisfied by limited interests. For example, I do not think one would say that a chattel "belongs to X" if he merely had the right to use it for five years. Nor do I think it is an apt use of language to say that landlord's fixtures "belong" to the leaseholder. He cannot remove them from the building. He cannot dispose of them except as part of the hereditament and subject to the provisions of the lease and to the term of the lease."

The facts in this case involved a taxpayer who held a long leasehold interest and incurred substantial capital expenditure on fixed equipment in the course of constructing a building. It was held that he was not eligible to claim first year capital allowances because the equipment, as a "landlord's fixture", did not, as a matter of law, "belong" to the taxpayer lessee but instead "belonged" to the freeholder. This approach was upheld by the House of Lords in *Melluish (Inspector of Taxes) v. B.M.I. (No 3) Ltd*.[75]

The Capital Allowances Act 1990 attempts to provide a legislative framework[76] which enables items of fixed plant and machinery to be leased on terms such that the lessor can normally be assured of obtaining the desired capital allowances. The effects of this legislation is broadly to deem that machinery or plant affixed to the land belongs to the person who has incurred the capital expenditure on that machinery or plant. This is a successive provision to that seen under section 59 and Schedule 17 of the Finance Act 1985. The House of Lords in *Melluish* (1995) confirmed that these provisions provided a comprehensive and exclusive code regulating the entitlement to capital allowances in relation to expenditure on fixtures incurred after July 11, 1984. The case concerned a large number of leasing transactions under a master lease entered into with the local authority lessees. The equipment leased ranged from cremators at a crematorium on land owned and occupied by the lessee to central heating systems installed in council housing owned in fee simple by the local authority lessees, but where the houses and flats were leased to tenants who had a legal estate in the land in question. The lessor had anticipated difficulties with the "belonging" criterion and to that end included in the lease an express retention of title clause to the effect that "the equipment hereby leased shall remain

[73] (1984) 57 T.C. 688.
[74] *Ibid.* at 705.
[75] [1995] 4 All E.R. 453.
[76] Capital Allowances Act 1990, ss. 51–59.

personal or moveable property and shall continue in the ownership of the lessor notwithstanding that the same may have been affixed to any land or building . . .". In addition there was a severance provision to the effect that the lessee was required to remove and deliver up possession of the equipment to the lessor on the expiry of the lease term or an earlier termination of the lease in the event of the lessees' default.

The Inland Revenue's case was that: first, the equipment became part of the lessees' land when it was installed and the issue of what constitutes a fixture is a matter of law and not contract; secondly, the equipment being a fixture could not therefore "belong" to the lessor. The first proposition was accepted by Vinelott J at first instance when he stated[77]:

> "It is plain and cannot be doubted that judged by objective criteria the equipment became part of the local authority's land. BMI and a local authority could not by agreeing that the equipment should 'remain personal or moveable property', contradict the plain and obvious legal consequence of the incorporation of this equipment as part of the local authority's land."

Even so the learned judge went on to hold that despite the plant becoming part of the lessees' land it could in certain circumstances still "belong" to the lessor. In doing so Vinelott J. referred to Fox L.J.'s dictum in *Stokes* to the effect that "belong" and "belonging" are not terms of art when he said[78]:

> "In my judgment in the ordinary sense of the word the equipment installed on the local authority's land is aptly described as 'belonging' to BMI. BMI paid for the equipment and the cost of installation: they had the right to remove it on the expiry or earlier termination of the term; while it remained in the possession of the local authority they were entitled to rent; and their right to payment of rent and to require the equipment to be severed and restored on the expiry or termination of the lease were assignable. It makes no difference in my judgment that it might not be possible to remove the equipment as part of a functioning system or that it might not be in the commercial interests of BMI to require it to be dismantled and restored. BMI was entitled if they wish to have the equipment severed and restored on the expiry or termination of the lease even if in doing so equipment were to be so damaged that it could not be re-used and had no scrap value. The local authority was liable under the terms of the master equipment lease to make good any damage to the land. The decisive feature, in my view, is that the local authority had no right to retain the equipment except during the term and on payment of rent . . . the local authority had no rights beyond those it would have had if the equipment had retained its character as a chattel. The only effect of the affixing of the equipment to the local authority's land was that it would pass as a part of the land to any person who might acquire a legal interest in the land without notice of the BMI's rights."

This approach was sufficient to enable the lessor to claim allowances in the case of plant installed on land owned and occupied by the local authority lessees.

[77.] [1944] S.T.C. 315 at 352.
[78.] *Ibid.* at 353–354.

In the case of the central heating systems, the legal estate which the council tenant had in each case would, as a matter of law, prevail over any contractual right of BMI as lessor to repossess the equipment on termination of the lease. If the local authority, as landlord of the council house tenancy, had a right to enter and remove the plant, the tenant would have held his legal estate subject to these repossession rights. This was not the case, and it was held that the plant installed in the council houses did not "belong" to the lessor. This was upheld by the House of Lords and it would appear that the right of the lessor to maintain that the equipment "belonged" to it will be defeated by the existence of the rights of certain third parties without notice of the specific arrangements between the lessor and the lessee. Lord Browne-Wilkinson accepted that the rights which the master leases gave the taxpayer companies over the installed equipment were not "purely contractual (and as such only enforceable between the parties)", but amounted to "an equitable right in the equipment enforceable against any subsequent taker of the land to which it is affixed other than a bona fide purchaser for value without notice".[79] Furthermore, on conventional property principles, those rights would be defeated in any case where at the time when the lease was put in place there was already a third party with a legal estate in land. Nevertheless, in the House of Lords it was held that BMI was entitled to capital allowances under paragraph 3 of Schedule 17 of the Finance Act 1985 because if the local authorities had incurred the expenditure on the provision of the equipment, the equipment would "for material purposes" be treated as belonging to them and it would, therefore, be deemed by paragraph 3(1) to be treated for material purposes as belonging to BMI. In adopting this approach the House of Lords reflected the policy rationale underlying the provision of capital allowances which is, as Lord Browne-Wilkinson pointed out[80]:

". . . to stimulate capital investment by individual taxpayers and also to stimulate economic activity generally . . . I can find no good reason why the legislature should seek to produce differing results dependent upon whether or not the equipment purchased is fixed to the land."

[79.] [1995] 4 All E.R. 453 at 463. As such there is nothing in *Melluish* to suggest that neither an immediate right of possession which is bound to crystallise can constitute a form of property where both possession and general or residual ownership reside elsewhere. *Cf. Re Swan, Witham v. Swan* [1915] 1 Ch. 829. As to the immediate right of possession of a head-lessor, see Chap. 2, pp. 32–39, above.

[80.] *Ibid.* at 469–470.

Chapter 10

Distress

Introduction

The following definition of distress is given in Bradby[1]:

> "A distress is the taking of a personal chattel, without legal process, from the possession of a wrongdoer, into the hands of the person grieved; as a pledge, for the redress of an injury, the performance of a duty, or the satisfaction of a demand."

As such this is a self-help remedy and the principle may be simply put, namely, if a landowner finds property belonging to another on his land causing damage he can seize it and withhold it from the owner until adequate compensation is forthcoming in respect of the damage done (distress damage feasant).[1a]

There are statutory remedies providing for distress to recover rates and taxes and also for rights in relation to land as well as for the enforcement of certain fines imposed by or orders of magistrates courts. However, such statutory remedies are more analogous to execution than to the common law right of a landlord to distrain for rent. Moreover, the statutory rules governing the process of levying distress for rent[2] are not applicable to distress for rates or for taxes or under the summary jurisdiction. Accordingly, it is proposed in this chapter to focus mainly upon distress for rent.

Distraint for Rent

Background

The entitlement of the landlord to distrain for rent is a well-established right dating back beyond the Distress for Rent Act 1689 which is still in force. An important mitigation on the force of this legislation was the doctrine of reputed ownership and in the nineteenth century the Lodgers' Goods Protection Act 1871 protected lodgers' goods from the

---

[1.] *Law of Distresses* (2nd ed) p. 1.
[1a.] See *Arthur and another v. Anker and another* [1996] 3 All E.R. 783.
[2.] Distress for Rent Rules 1988, S.I. 1988 No. 2050.

scope of distraint. The provisions in this legislation were repeated and replaced by the Law of Distress (Amendment) Act 1908. Sections 1 and 2 of that Act provide that if a landlord levies distress on the goods of any person, other than a sub-tenant of, or a lodger in, the premises, that person may serve a declaration on the landlord that the goods in question are his property; and that, if after receipt of such declaration, the landlord proceeds with a distress on the goods, such distress will be illegal, and that person may take proceedings for the recovery of his goods. Similar protection is extended to the goods of sub-tenants and lodgers, subject to their undertaking to pay any rent due to the tenant. The sense of this provision can be seen in the statement at the beginning of the Lodgers Goods Protection Act 1871 which mentioned that lodgers are "subject to great loss and injustice by the exercise of the power possessed by the superior landlord to levy distress". By providing a lodger with a means of avoiding a sale through a declaration this alleviated the injustice even though a lodger was likely to learn of the distress and could then take all the necessary steps.

A remarkable feature of this branch of law is that the other persons' property may be distrained and sold without their knowledge and thus without their having an opportunity to serve the section 1 declaration. Even if they do find out about the distraint in time, the notice must be served at the very latest before the sale, and once the goods have been sold they have no remedy. A major difficulty is that the owner of the goods let on hire may not learn of the distress until it is too late. As a matter of principle, therefore, given the haphazard nature of the remedy involved, it has to be questioned whether the remedy of distress is appropriate within a coherent legislative regime especially involving insolvency which may explain why the Law Commission[3] recommended the abolition of the procedure of distress for rent in order to bring the law of landlord and tenant into line with the modern law of bankruptcy. In the absence of the implementation of this recommendation, it is necessary to examine closely the scope of the existing legislation in order to consider its impact upon lessors of equipment.

The Scope of Distraint

Essential elements

The essential elements of this technical remedy are: first, a demise in land notably a tenancy agreement or a specifically enforceable agreement of tenancy; secondly, the rent must arise out of the land; thirdly, the rent must be ascertainable and certain; fourthly, the rent must be owed in the sense that it is in arrears of the agreed stipulated date (which may require payment in advance); fifthly, the person distraining for rent

[3.] Law Commission Report, *Landlord and Tenant, Distress for Rent*, No. 138, (1991).

must have some sort of reversionary interest in the sense that there is a landlord and tenant relationship as distinct from a mere mortgagee and mortgagor relationship.

Under the common law a landlord could distrain for arrears in rent from all goods found at the premises out of which the rent arose irrespective of ownership. As Dallas C.J. put it in *Gilman v. Elton*[4]:

> "The rule grows out of the relation of landlord and tenant and out of the nature of the thing itself."

However, there are so many exceptions grafted by statute that the general rule is in fact severely compromised. The most notable exceptions for our purposes are:

1. goods which have been seized by virtue of an execution, that is, goods in custody of the law;

2. goods sent to a trader who is to carry out work in relation to them, for example, a diesel generator sent to be incorporated into a machine. The goods are absolutely privileged so long as they are in the possession of the general trader;

3. goods actually in use are not distrainable;

4. tools and implements of trade are not distrainable, although there is a limit of protection here of £50.[5] Significantly a cab used by a driver is an implement of trade[6] and whilst the rule is that at least £50 worth of tools must be left, if only one article is available for distress and its value exceeds £50, the protection of the statute is extended to that article.[7] In any case the tools used in trade are distrainable only if there are no other goods on the premises sufficient to deal with the arrears of rent. In *Lavell v. Richings*[8] it was held that the van of a van driver came within this exception;

5. agricultural or other machinery on an agricultural holding are subject to special statutory privilege provided they are the property of a person other than the tenant;

6. machines used in the manufacture of woollen, linen, cotton, flax, mohair or silk materials cannot be distrained;

7. railway rolling stock is not liable to be distrained for rent unless the rolling stock is the tenant's actual property, but the rolling stock must be sufficiently identified by a metal plate or other distinguishing mark which is conspicuously affixed[9];

[4.] (1821) 3 Brod. and Bing. 75 at 79.
[5.] Law of Distress (Amendment) Act 1908, s. 4; County Courts Act 1984, s. 89.
[6.] See *Lavell v. Richings* [1906] 1 K.B. 480.
[7.] *Ibid.*
[8.] *Ibid.*
[9.] Railway Rolling Stock Protection Act 1872, s. 3.

8. gas, water and electricity fittings so long as they are sufficiently identified are privileged.

In summary the general common law approach can now be said to hardly exist as a meaningful legal proposition. In addition to the above exceptions the landlord's behaviour may amount to estoppel or waiver in relation to the goods themselves. One sure way therefore of avoiding distraint is to seek the landlord's agreement not to seize or sell the goods by way of distress. Such an agreement, unless it is done by deed,[10] has to be supported by consideration moving from the equipment lessor and should also include as part of the agreement an undertaking not to claim the leased goods as fixtures. If it is provided that the consideration for the agreement is the equipment lessor letting the goods to the tenant lessee, the consent of the landlord should be obtained before the equipment lease is executed otherwise the agreement to distrain could be vulnerable on the basis of past consideration.

Exclusion: hire-purchase and lease agreements

The legislation. The Law of Distress (Amendment) Act does not protect goods as laid out in sections 4 and 4A which state as follows:

"4 Exclusion of certain goods

This Act shall not apply—
   (1)   to goods belonging to the husband or wife of the tenant whose rent is in arrear, nor to goods comprised in any . . . settlement made by such tenant nor to goods in the possession, order, or disposition of such tenant by the consent and permission of the true owner under such circumstances that such tenant is the reputed owner thereof, nor to any [agisted livestock within the meaning of section 18 of the Agricultural Holdings Act 1986 to which that section] applies;
   (2)   (a) to goods of a partner of the immediate tenant; (b) to goods (not being goods of a lodger) upon premises where any trade or business is carried on in which both the immediate tenant and the under tenant have an interest; (c) to goods (not being the goods of a lodger) on premises used as offices or warehouses where the owner of the goods neglects for one calendar month after notice (which shall be given in like manner as a notice to quit) to remove the goods and vacate the premises; (d) to goods belonging to and in the offices of any company or corporation on premises the immediate tenant whereof is a director or officer, or in the employment of such company or corporation:
   Provided that it shall be competent for a stipendiary magistrate, or where there is no stipendiary magistrate for two justices, upon application by the superior landlord or any under tenant or other such person as aforesaid, upon hearing the parties to determine whether any goods are in fact goods covered by subsection (2) of this section.

---

[10] Law of Property (Miscellaneous Provisions) Act 1989, s. 1(2), (3).

4A Hire purchase etc. agreements

(1) Goods—

(a) bailed under a hire-purchase agreement or a consumer hire agreement, or

(b) agreed to be sold under a conditional sale agreement,

are, where the relevant agreement has not been terminated, excluded from the application of this Act except during the period between the service of a default notice under the Consumer Credit Act 1974 in respect of the goods and the date on which the notice expires or is earlier complied with.

(2) Goods comprised in a bill of sale are excluded from the application of this Act except during the period between service of a default notice under the Consumer Credit Act 1974 in respect of goods subject to a regulated agreement under which a bill of sale is given by way of security and the date on which the notice expires or is earlier complied with.

(3) In this section—

'conditional sale agreement' means an agreement for the sale of goods under which the purchase price or part of it is payable by instalments, and the property in the goods is to remain in the seller (notwithstanding that the buyer is to be in possession of the goods) until such conditions as to the payment of instalments or otherwise as may be specified in the agreement are fulfilled;

'consumer hire agreement' has the meaning given by section 15 of the Consumer Credit Act 1974;

'hire-purchase agreement' means an agreement, other than a conditional sale agreement, under which—

(a) goods are bailed in return for periodical payments by the person to whom they are bailed, and

(b) the property in the goods will pass to that person if the terms of the agreement are complied with and one or more of the following occurs—

(i) the exercise of an option to purchase by that person,

(ii) the doing of any other specified act by any party to the agreement,

(iii) the happening of any other specified event; and

'regulated hire agreement' has the meaning given by section 189(1) of the Consumer Credit Act 1974."

Regulated agreements. In the case of a regulated agreement under the Consumer Credit Act 1974, the exclusion from protection does not apply to the period of the service of a default notice under that Act.[11] Even if there is a provision for automatic termination of the regulated agreement, if there is a threat of distress there are statutory restrictions on termination.[12] However, so long as the goods are still comprised in a hire-purchase, consumer hire or conditional sale agreement the general

[11.] Consumer Credit Act 1974, ss. 87–89.
[12.] Consumer Credit Act 1974, ss. 16, 98.

position is that protection is removed. It is vitally important to determine, therefore, whether the goods are still comprised in the agreement at the time of the distress.

Non-regulated agreements. Even in the case of a non-regulated agreement it has been held that if any contractual right or agreement subsists after a purported termination the remaining goods are still part of a hire-purchase agreement.[13] Typically when there is an *ipso facto* termination clause on the occurrence of an event, but which also provides on that eventuality a right upon the owner to enter the premises of the equipment lessee, the courts have analysed this as a continuing right under the agreement so that for this purpose the goods are still comprised in the agreement. In this respect the Court of Appeal held in *Jay's Furnishing Co. v. Brand and Co.*[14]:

> "Even if so much of the agreement as consisted of a demise had been brought to an end by the exercise of the plaintiff's right to determine it, the agreement was still subsisting and bound the chattels in the sense that it gave the plaintiffs certain rights against the chattels."

One way of avoiding this problem is to include a *Smart v. Holt* clause,[15] the relevant part of which states:

> "In case of any breach of any term hereof the owners may:
>
> (a) Without prejudice to their claim for arrears of instalments or damages for breach of this agreement forthwith without notice terminate the hiring and repossess themselves of and remove the goods:
>
> (b) Alternatively, by written notice sent (by post or otherwise) to or left at the hirer's last known address forthwith and for all purposes absolutely determine and end this agreement and the hiring thereby constituted and thereupon the hirer shall no longer be in possession of the goods with the owner's consent nor shall either party thereafter have any rights hereunder but such determination shall not discharge any pre-existing liability of the hirer to the owners."

Reputed ownership

Section 4(1) of the 1908 Act denies protection "to goods in the possession, order or disposition of such tenant by the consent and permission of the true owner under such circumstances that such tenant is the reputed owner thereof". These words are wider than the original reputed ownership provision in section 38(c) of the Bankruptcy Act 1914, when the goods were required to be in the possession, order or disposition of the bankrupt *in his trade or business*. In order to avoid this

---

[13.] See *Times Furnishing Co. Ltd v. Hutchings* [1938] 1 K.B. 775.
[14.] [1915] 1 K.B. 458 at 465.
[15.] [1929] 2 K.B. 303.

provision it is not only necessary for the agreement to automatically terminate but also for the equipment lessor to take some positive steps to recover the goods. As Humphreys J. pointed out in *Times Furnishing Co Ltd v. Hutchings*[16]:

"The true owner must show that he has taken some steps to indicate his intention, and probably that he has taken some steps to recover the goods, so that no person can say that the tenant has continued to be the reputed owner of the goods, as he has been up to that time."

Typically a written notice to the lessee should suffice. However, time is not neutral in the context of distraint especially since there is no duty on the distrainor to inform the owner of the goods that they are to be seized or sold.

There are two principal ways for the equipment lessor to avoid distraint: first, if he has negotiated previously with the landlord an agreement that the goods be exempt; secondly, by seeking a declaration under the 1908 Act preventing the landlord from proceeding further with the distress. Under section 1 the declaration must be in strict form but it need not be statutory—it must state that the tenant has no right of property or beneficial interest in the goods distrained or threatened to be distrained and that they are the property or in the lawful possession of the owner, and that they are not goods or livestock to which the Act expressly does not apply. To this declaration must be annexed a correct inventory of the items which are subject to the section 1 declaration under the 1908 Act. The declarations must be subsequent to the seizure or threat of seizure. The Law of Distress (Amendment) Act 1908 does not specify any time within which the declaration must be served. However, if after being served with the declaration distress on the goods is proceeded, then the person who levies the distress is deemed guilty of an illegal distress and by virtue of the 1908 Act[17] any person so protected may apply to a justice of the peace for an order for the restoration of the goods.

The issue of distress for non-payment of rent and the position of an owner of equipment let under a contract hire agreement was considered by the Court of Appeal in *Salford Van Hire (Contracts) Ltd v. Bocholt Developments Ltd.*[18] In this case the plaintiffs, who were large scale contract hirers of commercial vehicles, claimed the value (£6,100) of a Mercedes 7.5 ton van which they had hired in 1991 to a company trading as Surestyle which was in receivership. The defendants were the owners of the factory premises out of which Surestyle manufactured double glazing units and by 1992 Surestyle were in financial difficulties and owed their landlords £169,750 in arrears of rent. In early May 1992 the defendants took close possession of the premises and later that

---

[16.] [1938] 1 K.B. 775 at 784.
[17.] Law of Distress (Amendment) Act 1908, s. 2
[18.] *The Times* April 22, 1995.

month a receiver was appointed. It was not until June 1, that the plaintiffs first learned of the distress and they served a notice on the defendants, that is, serving a declaration and inventory on the landlord. A technical argument put forward by the defendants that the plaintiffs declaration was out of time, on the basis that the time limit for a declaration expired when the right of sale first arose (five days after the levy) unless extended at the tenant's request (to fifteen days under section 6 of the Law of Distress Amendment Act 1888), was dismissed and it was held that a declaration is validly served at any time prior to the moment of actual sale.

The issues in focus before the Court of Appeal were as follows: first, whether Surestyle were the reputed owners of the van in all the circumstances? If this question was answered in the affirmative, then, secondly, whether there was a well-established trade custom of hiring motor vehicles which would rebut or exclude the doctrine of reputed ownership? At first instance, it was held that the van was in reputed ownership for the following reasons: (1) the van was on the premises at the time of the levy; (2) the van was a plain white van with no markings on it whatsoever to indicate who the true owner was; (3) the van was a little over three years old; (4) the van had undergone an unusual conversion for a vehicle of its size with the installation of a sleeper cabin and tail lift. The test laid down by the Court of Appeal in determining reputed ownership was the "must" test, that is, it was for the landlord to establish:

> "(a) that the hypothetical reasonable person with knowledge of the general course of business, and having made all reasonable enquiries about the material facts, would infer that the goods must (not may or may not) be owned by the tenant, and
> (b) that the true owner consented not only to possession but also to the tenant's reputed ownership in that he must have realised that a reasonable person would draw such an inference."

From this it would appear that the key issue in the equipment leasing context is the extent of the doctrine and in determining this issue it is necessary to briefly consider the historical background.

The reputed ownership concept was first embodied in the Bankruptcy Act 1623 and successive legislation although it was omitted from the Insolvency Act 1986. The principle was elaborated upon in Re Watson[19] where the Court of Appeal stated in judgment[20]:

> "In our opinion it is essential before a Court can hold that one man's goods are to be taken to pay another man's debts, because of the reputation of ownership of the bankrupt, that the goods should be held and dealt with by the bankrupt in such manner and under such circumstances that the

---

[19.] [1904] 2 K.B. 753.
[20.] Ibid. per Vaughan-Williams, Romer and Cozens-Hardy L.JJ. at 756–757.

reputation of ownership must arise. We think that the cases of *Load v. Green*[21] and *Smith v. Hudson*[22] fully establish this proposition. Blackburn J. in his judgment in *Smith v. Hudson*[23] said '*Load v. Green* decides that the true owner as such must consent that the other side should be reputed owner, not being true owner.' The doctrine of reputed ownership was first embodied in the Bankruptcy Act, 21 Jac. 1. It has been couched in various words in the successive bankruptcy statutes, but this principle has run through them all, and the statement of Lord Redesdale in *Joy v. Campbell*[24] (a case which has been approved and acted on again and again . . .[25]), that the true owner must have unconscientiously permitted the goods to remain in the order or disposition of the bankrupt, justifies this statement. This does not mean, as we understand it, that he must have intended that false credit should be obtained by the bankrupt's apparent possession of the goods, but it does at least mean that the true owner of the goods must have consented to a state of things from which he must have known, if he had considered the matter, that the inference of ownership by the bankrupt must (observe, not might or might not) arise."[26]

The extent of the reputed ownership doctrine was considered at length in *Re Fox*.[27] In that case a trustee in bankruptcy of a bankrupt builder claimed under the doctrine of reputed ownership and the principle adopted was articulated by Jenkins J. as follows:[28]

"Mere proof of possession in given circumstances (with the requisite consent or permission) may indeed raise a *prima facie* case of reputed ownership only to be rebutted by proof—or judicial notice—or a custom negativing that view. But the primary question must always be whether, in the circumstances, the possession of the goods by the bankrupt involved the inference that he was the reputed owner. If the answer to that question is 'No', then *cadit quaestio*. It is only if the answer is 'Yes' that the question of custom enters into the matter at all."

Counsel for the plaintiff in *Salford Van Hire* (1995) pointed out that only 8 per cent of licensed vehicles in the United Kingdom in the 3.5–7.5 tonnes category were on contract hire and that, therefore, the "must" test had failed. However, the Court of Appeal was unhappy about extending the reputed ownership, particularly in the light of judicial criticism of the doctrine and also its castigation in several official reports. Thus the Cork Committee Report noted[29]:

[21.] 5 M. & W. 216.

[22.] (1865) 34 L.J. (Q.B.) 145.

[23.] *Ibid*. at 151.

[24.] 1 Sch. & Lef. 328, 336; 9 R.R.

[25.] Citing *Belcher v. Bellamy* 2 Ex. 303; *Hamilton v. Bell* (1854) 10 Ex. 545.

[26.] Citing *Hamilton v. Bell* (1854) 10 Ex. 545; *Gibson v. Bray* (1817) 8 Taunt. 76; 19 R.R.; *Ex p. Bright* 10 Ch.D. 566.

[27.] [1948] Ch. 407.

[28.] *Ibid*. at 413.

[29.] *Insolvency Law and Practice* (Cmnd. 8558 (1982)) para. 1088.

"The Blagden Committee expressed the view that the custom, already then increasingly prevalent, of obtaining on hire-purchase practically every article employed in trades and businesses, extending even to livestock in the possession of a farmer, had made it virtually impossible to establish a right in the trustee in bankruptcy to goods belonging to other parties. This view has been supported by evidence which we ourselves have received."

This was followed by the White Paper, "A Revised Framework for Insolvency Law," [30] and also the Law Commission in their Report [31] who commented:

"A particular handful of third parties are wholly disqualified from claiming the privilege for their goods. Some may consider it appropriate that the property of the tenant's spouse, and of persons connected with him in business, should not be distinguished from his own property even though that distinction is most firmly drawn in other contexts such as execution and bankruptcy. In the context of rent distress, such persons may be regarded as deriving some benefit from the tenant's lease, sharing occupation personally, or at least through their goods being on the premises; further, the property of such persons and of the tenant is likely to be mixed or shared, increasing the incidence and complexity of ownership disputes, while property arrangements or devices to avoid distress might be encouraged. Nevertheless, in no other context are such arguments regarded as justification for taking the goods of one to satisfy the liability of another. The same arguments cannot, in any event, be applied to the goods of those underlessees who fail to qualify for privilege, or to goods held on various consumer credit terms. There, the relationship between the owner and the tenant is likely to be a commercial one, wholly at arm's length. Also the concept of reputed ownership may have yielded practical results when a man's possession of goods would normally have justified an inference of ownership, but hire-purchase agreements (and retention of title clauses) are now so prevalent, that the inference should rarely be drawn."

The Court of Appeal in *Salford Van Hire* (1995) held that in evaluating the "must" test of reputed ownership it was appropriate to take into account the number of vehicles which were hired and that the obvious inference of the ambiguity in the tenant's possession of them as owner could then be drawn. It followed that this was an appropriate case for inquiries to be made and that a simple phone call to the DVLA or HPI plc would have revealed that the tenant was neither the registered keeper nor the owner of the vehicle. As Hirst L.J., who gave the principal judgement for the Court of Appeal, held:

". . . the court cannot, in any judgment, properly fail to take judicial notice of the huge expansions of hiring and hire-purchase since the second world war, especially of motor vehicles, so that is has become a major feature in our economic and social life, far more so that 60 or 100 years ago."

[30] (Cmnd. 9175) paras. 115, 116.
[31] *Op. cit.* (see n. 30, above) para. 2.4.5.

Remedies for Wrongful Distress

Introduction

An illegal distress renders rescue of the goods by the owner justifiable. For example, where privileged goods are seized or after a declaration or when distress takes place in breach of an agreement. However, the law jealously protects the distrainor and if his right to distraint has been improperly interfered with under section 3 of the Distress for Rent Act 1689 he is entitled to recover treble damages not only against the wrongdoer but also against the owner of the goods distrained so long as the goods end up back in his possession. The fact that the distress was irregular or excessive does not provide a defence here. Furthermore, if distress has taken place and the goods have been impounded they are in the custody of the law.[32] If the owner of the goods breaks into the pound and takes the goods away then he is guilty of poundbreach. This can never be justified even if the distress is illegal.[33] Moreover, poundbreach was an indictable misdemeanour at common law.[34] There must be actual possession. Accordingly, it was held in *Abingdon R.D.C. v. O'Gorman*[35] that where goods are constructively possessed under a walking possession agreement and the owner in good faith seizes them from the hirer in ignorance of the walking possession agreement, he is not guilty of poundbreach.

The essential elements of illegal distress

1. Where the distrainor has seized the goods or effectuated their seizure in a manner not authorised by law, for example at an unlawful hour (between sunset or sunrise) or by breaking door(s) or window(s) or by effectuating the distress off the premises.

2. Where there is no rent due or after the landlord has parted with the reversion.

3. In breach of an agreement not to distrain.

4. When the goods are privileged.

5. After a declaration and therefore in breach of the provision of the Law of Distress Amendment Act 1908.

Remedies for illegal distress

Recaption. Recovery of the goods distrained. This is available even against a *bona fide* purchaser for value.[36]

[32.] Distress for Rent Act 1737, s. 10.
[33.] *Parrett Navigation Co. v. Stower* (1840) 6 M. & W. 564.
[34.] *R. v. Butterfield* (1893) 17 Cox 598.
[35.] [1968] 2 Q.B. 811.
[36.] *Capel v. Buszard* (1829) 6 Bing. 150.

Replevin. The person divested of the goods can obtain redelivery upon finding sufficient security for the rent and probable costs of the action. Replevin is seldom used except where immediate recovery of the goods is essential. It should be noted that a judgment for the replevisor normally precludes any further action for damages for taking the same goods.[37]

Damages. An illegal distress is void *ab initio* and the distrainor and any persons who have wrongfully interfered with them will be liable for their full value in an action of trespass or conversion.

The equipment lessor's bases of action are as follows: first, an immediate right to possession (by virtue of the termination clause); or secondly, the permanent injury to the reversionary interest in the goods, for example, by virtue of the fact that they have been damaged. The owner under a hire-purchase agreement, as distinct from a lessor, cannot recover more than the value of his interest in the goods, namely the amount remaining under the hire-purchase agreement.[38] The hirer/lessee, on the other hand, is entitled to the full value of the goods, although he would have to account to the owner for such part of the damages recovered in relation to the value of the goods as exceeds the amount of the hirer's interest. If the hirer's right to immediate possession has been terminated as a result of illegal distress, he will have an independent cause of action against the distrainor for procuring by unlawful means the termination of the hire-purchase or hire contract so long as the distrainor knew of the relevant agreement at the time of the distress.

In one particular case the equipment lessor will have an action for double the value of the goods as a punitive action where the goods are sold following distraint where no arrears in the rent were outstanding.

Irregular and excessive distress

If the goods distrained are sold without the prescribed notice being served on the tenant or below price, then the tenant can recover special damages for the loss he has suffered.[39] This action is a personal action against the distrainor and thereby a purchaser from the distrainor is not vulnerable to an action for wrongful interference with goods.

Sale of goods distrained

By virtue of section 1 of the Distress for Rent Act 1689, goods and chattels distrained upon for rent which have not been replevied within five days after seizure and notice thereof may be sold for the best price

[37.] See *Gibb v. Cruikshank* (1873) L.R. 8 C.P. 454 at 460.
[38.] *Bloxham v. Hubbard* (1804) 5 East. 407.
[39.] Distress for Rent Act 1737, s. 19.

obtainable towards satisfaction of the arrears of rent accrued due. Where distress is illegal no purchaser acquires a good title as against the owner of the goods.

Distress in Magistrates Court

Distress is available where default is made in payment of a sum adjudged to be paid following summary conviction or an order. These sums are civil debts, damages, compensation and fines, which includes those from the Crown Court, Court of Appeal or House of Lords.[40] Seizure can only take place in relation to the money or goods of the named person.

Distress for Taxes

Under the Income and Corporation Taxes Act 1988 distress can be used where tax has been demanded and there has been a refusal or neglect to pay. The Collector can distrain on goods which belong wholly and personally to the defaulter,[41] that is, goods and chattels belonging to a lessor are not liable for distraint.

Distress for Rates

Prior to the introduction of the community charge and its replacement by the council tax, under the Local Government Act 1992, the payment of rates was primarily enforceable by distress. The modern position is that payment due for council tax is enforceable by various methods, one of which is distress.[42]

[40.] See the Magistrates Court Act 1980, ss. 75–78; Magistrates Court Rules 1981, r. 54 .

[41.] *Earl of Shaftesbury v. Russell* [1823] 1 B. & C. 666.

[42.] See Local Government Finance Act 1992, Sched. 4; Council Tax (Administration and Enforcement) Regulations 1992, S.I. 1992 No. 613, Part 6.

Chapter 11

Liability in Tort

Wrongful Interference with Goods

Introduction

Despite the passage of the Torts (Interference with Goods) Act 1977 which simplified, for procedural purposes, the law concerning protection of interests in property, the position continues to be complicated due to the interplay between several principles, namely, property, contract and tort. In large measure an opportunity was lost to systematise liability for interference with chattels under the 1977 Act. Although section 1 created the concept of "wrongful interference with goods" this was mainly defined within the context of the existing torts and, apart from statutory conversion under section 2(2), no new tort was created. Whilst the 1977 Act abolished *detinue*,[1] trespass to goods remains and the Act extended conversion to cover the case where a bailee in breach of duty to his bailor allows goods to be lost or destroyed—this was the only case of detinue not also constituting conversion. The Law Reform Committee[2] had, however, recommended the abolition of detinue, conversion and trespass to be replaced by a single new tort of "wrongful interference", that is, intentional acts interfering with chattels without lawful justification. Nevertheless, pressures of parliamentary time only allowed for a common treatment as regard to remedies in relation to *separate* torts, and in this respect, section 1 created merely a new name, "wrongful interference with goods", which covers:

1. conversion;

2. trespass;

3. negligence resulting in damage to goods (presumably extending to destruction) or to an interest in goods;

4. "any other tort so far as it results in damage to goods or to an interest in goods" — that is to any reversionary interest.

As a result certain consequences follow: first, the sub-divisions in section 1 are not mutually exclusive so that the alleged wrong may fall

---

[1] Torts (Interference with Goods) Act 1977, s. 2(1).
[2] 18th Report on "Conversion and Detinue" (Cmnd. 4774 (1971)) paras. 25, 27, 29.

within different headings; secondly, the common law basis of the torts still remains as do the differences with regard to the burden of proof ranging from foreseeability in negligence to strict liability in conversion; thirdly, it is only in relation to remedies that there has been a conceptual change, notably, conversion and trespass have been transformed from being purely personal actions as they now have a quasi-proprietary quality. The form of relief provided by section 3 of the Act gives the plaintiff a choice where the defendant is in possession or control of the goods or orders for specific restitution or for redelivery of the goods or payment of damages representing their value as alternatives to the traditional claim for damages only.

Conversion

The constituent elements of conversion

Introduction. Conversion is a deliberate act in relation to a chattel which denies or is inconsistent with another's right most notably to use and possess it. In addition there is the statutory conversion provided by section 2(2) which applies to a bailee who, in breach of duty to his bailor, allows the goods bailed to become lost or destroyed. There is a wide definition of "goods" for the purposes of the 1977 Act so section 14(1) provides that this includes "all chattels personal other than things in action and money". An obvious analogy can be drawn here with section 61(1) of the Sale of Goods Act 1979.

It is possible to identify various categories of conversion, which are discussed below.

Asportation or taking. A distinction is sometimes drawn here with trespass as there is an intention element in conversion, so that a mere taking without any intention to exercise even temporary control is not conversion. As Atkin L.J. put it:[3]

"An act of conversion differs from mere trespass inasmuch as the former must amount to a deprivation of possession to such an extent as to be inconsistent with the right of the owner and evidence of an intention to deprive him of that right, whereas the latter includes every direct forcible injury or act disturbing the possession of the owner, however slight the act may be."

In practice, this is a distinction without a difference because any asportation of a chattel for use amounts to conversion notwithstanding that the defendant did not intend to permanently deprive the owner. This also applies in a warehousing situation where goods are transferred to the disposal of another or where there has been an indorsement of a document of title.[4]

[3] *Sanderson v. Marsden and Jones* (1922) 10 L.I. Rep. 467 at 472.
[4] *Union Credit Bank v. Mersey Docks and Harbour Board* [1899] 2 Q.B. 205.

The characteristic of conversion is the transfer of, or facilitation in the transfer of, the chattels in question. There is sometimes a fine line— mere communication in the course of a regular business as a broker is probably not conversion by the broker where there is lack of lawful authority in his principal. However, it is almost inconceivable that an auctioneer would not be liable in conversion where it goes beyond this to actually facilitating the conversion, for example, through the passage of documents, notably a vehicle registration document.[5] In effect any assistance in the unlawful transfer is conversion[6] and there is no defence of contributory negligence.[7] However, a careful distinction needs to be drawn with the case where there is an involuntary bailment. Such a bailee is impliedly authorised to take reasonable steps to return the property, and so long as he acts with reasonable care there is no conversion where he mistakenly hands the goods over to a person who falsely pretends to be the true owner.[8] Under the Unsolicited Goods and Services Act 1971, the involuntary recipient may be entitled to keep unsolicited goods as his own after six months from receipt or 30 days after notice to the sender.

The creation of some right over the equipment, such as a pledge or lien, will constitute an act of conversion unless it can be implied in the case of a lease or hire-purchase transaction that the bailee is authorised to deliver the chattel to another for the purpose of repair.[9]

Wrongful selling of goods. It can be persuasively argued that even though the unlawful disposition is not governed by one of the exceptions to the *nemo dat* principle,[10] nonetheless the disposal will constitute conversion in that it causes the owner to lose the goods in the sense that his chances of recovery will decrease as the chain of transactions increases. Indeed this phenomenon lay behind the argument in *Barrow Lane and Ballard v. Phillip Phillips*[11] where it was held that goods which are stolen were effectively "perished" for the purposes of sections 6 and 7 of the Sale of Goods Act 1979. As a matter of policy it could be contended that any relaxation of the strict rule as to perishability (*res extincta*) could be seen to encourage dishonesty.

Unlawful detention of the chattel. Unlawful detention of the chattel depends upon the defendant's power to return the equipment. Thus, if the goods are seized by a third party or under a legal process whilst still in the defendant's possession, he cannot be liable in conversion because it is beyond his power to return the chattel and deliver it on demand.

---

5. *Willis (R.H.) and Son v. British Car Auctions* [1978] 1 W.L.R. 438.
6. *Hort v. Bott* L.R. 9 Ex. 86.
7. Torts (Interference with Goods) Act 1977, s. 11(1) .
8. *Elvin and Powell Ltd v. Plummer Roddis Ltd* (1933) 50 T.L.R. 158.
9. See Chap. 7, above.
10. See Chap. 6, above.
11. [1929] 1 K.B. 574.

Where the goods are in the "hands of a warehouseman" or an agent, they are entitled to a reasonable time to consult and ascertain the position and their authority to give up the goods.[12]

Use inconsistent with the terms of the bailment. Use inconsistent with the terms of the bailment depends upon the terms of the lease or hire contract. The misuse of the chattel must be in a manner calculated to produce an appreciable interference with the owner's interest. An owner out of possession without an immediate right to possession cannot during the continuance of the bailment term bring an action. However, the act of conversion itself may have brought the hire to an end according to the terms of the bailment, for example, an unauthorised loan or an act which results in the loss or destruction of the chattel in question. Thus in *Moorgate Mercantile Co. Ltd v. Finch*,[13] a hire car was used to smuggle contraband which led to the seizure of the goods and the car by custom authorities, where it was held that the hirer had abused his possession and that this amounted to conversion. As Danckwerts L.J. held[14]:

> "It seems to me that whether the second defendant intended that consequence to follow or not [seizure by the custom authorities] . . . he must be taken to intend the consequences which were likely to happen from the conduct of which he was guilty, and which did in fact result in the loss of the car to the plaintiffs."

The crux of the issue is whether there has been an impairment of the owner's immediate right to possession and here the terms of the lease contract will be relevant, for example, whether delegation of the lessee's duties to another can be envisaged. At the same time the consequences of the strict liability nature of the tort should not be forgotten, because conversion is available even though the owner enjoys an effective remedy against a third person, for example, following a sale, and that the owner's chances of recovery could even be strengthened as a result of the sale, that is, to a third party of economic substance where the original lessee's position was financially precarious which threatened his ability to maintain payment of rentals. The essence of the matter is that the act of sale by the lessee contradicts or weakens the owner's claim to the goods in that it increases the risk of the goods turning out to be untraceable.

A bailee who wrongfully and without authority sub-bails the goods to an independent third party commits an act of conversion because at least potentially this act impairs the bailor's ability to recover the goods. Again the *de minimis* principle will be relevant if the sub-bailment came about because of an emergency. The sub-bailee's innocence *may* be

[12.] *Alexander v. Southey* (1841) 5 B. & A. 247.
[13.] [1962] 1 Q.B. 701.
[14.] *Ibid.* at 709.

relevant unless of course he asserts a lien in respect of work he has done in relation to the goods.

Conversion by denial of right. Section 11(3) of the 1977 Act provides that even an absolute denial of title does not, by itself, amount to conversion—there must be a further element, namely an act of dealing with the goods which has the effect of barring the plaintiff's access to the goods and in this way repudiating the plaintiff's right to them. However, it should be noted that a mere denial of title, whilst not actionable as a tort, is still nevertheless actionable in the sense that the plaintiff can seek a declaration to the effect that he and not the defendant has the right to the goods.[15]

The basis of suing in conversion

It is necessary to show not absolute ownership but rather that the person had at the time of the conversion either actual possession or an immediate right to possess. Thus in *North West Securities Ltd v. Alexander Breckon Ltd*[16] a finance company acquired title to goods from a dealer before the execution of a hire-purchase agreement and this enabled the company to sue for conversion occurring before the hire-purchase became effective. The problem in the lease context is that by definition the undisputed owner is not (in the absence of default) in actual possession of the chattel. In this context, since the lessee has a possessory right he can bring an action in conversion notwithstanding that he has actual factual custody or not. Whilst the lessor may have an action for reversionary injury, the bailee is the only person who can bring an action in conversion against, for example, a lienee, unless of course the lease contract is determined.[17]

Merely determining the bailment does not necessarily give the bailor a right to sue in conversion. Typically, the act of conversion itself (for example, wrongful disposal) will be inconsistent with the term of the bailment but the terms of the bailment may not preclude the transference of the bailee's special property interest. Thus, a hirer's option to purchase may be a saleable interest but normally this benefit is made unassignable by an express term, which is now a standard feature of hire-purchase contracts. The issue of an immediate right to possession must be seen within the general legislative context, notably where a hire-purchase purports to give the owner an immediate right to possess upon default by the hirer but the Consumer Credit Act 1974 renders this illegal.[18]

An employee who has custody of the goods or equipment in focus does not have possession in the sense that he can maintain an action in

---

[15.] See *Loudon v. Ryder (No. 2)* [1953] Ch. 423.
[16.] [1981] R.T.R. 518.
[17.] *Lord v. Price* (1874) L.R. 9 Ex. 54.
[18.] Consumer Credit Act 1974, s. 87.

conversion, because the employer has not only the right to possession but he may also be deemed by the law to be constructively in possession.[19] However, the circumstance of the employee's factual custody will be significant here, for example, where an employee is given considerable discretion in relation to a company car (for example to use it for his own private purposes) he may be able to sue in conversion. In this respect, section 8 of the 1977 Act deals with the *jus tertii* where the convertor can insist upon joining the employer in order to avoid the potential problem of dual liability.

Conversion and police powers

Section 1 of the Police (Property) Act 1897, as amended by section 58 of the Criminal Justice Act 1972, provides that where the police have come into possession of property in connection with their investigation of a suspected offence, a magistrate may order its disposition as he thinks fit subject to proceedings being brought within six months by anyone entitled to the property. After such an order is made, the burden of proof is on a claimant to prove title independently of his prior possession and in the absence of such proof the defendant has a better right to possess.[20] However, this summary method of disposing of property is not for use when any serious question of title arises. As was pointed out by Lord Widgery C.J. in *Lyons and Co. v. Metropolitan Police Comr.*[21]:

> "I would actively discourage them [the Justices] from attempting to use the procedure of the Act of 1897 [s.1(1) Police (Property) Act 1897] in cases which involve a real issue of law or any real difficulty in determining whether a particular person is or is not the owner."

Goods impounded and distress

Although the goods are physically in the possession of the landlord or agent, they are considered as being in the custody of the law, so where the goods are converted the only action available to the landlord or agent is that of poundbreach and this is not an action for "wrongful interference" under the 1977 Act.[22] This does not stop the tenant, or whoever is entitled to possession of them, to demand the goods back from those removing them, and the refusal to return them will be evidence of conversion. Indeed since the custody of the law is brought to an end by the taking, the tenant can also sue for the taking of the goods as the right of possession has thereby been restored.[23]

[19.] See Pollock and Wright, *Possession in the Common Law* (1988) p. 39.
[20.] *Irving v. National Provincial Bank Ltd* [1962] 2 Q.B. 73.
[21.] [1975] 1 Q.B. 321 at 326.
[22.] See Chap. 8, above.
[23.] See *Turner v. Ford* (1846) 15 M. & W. 212.

Co-ownership and conversion

Co-ownership is now governed by section 10(1) of the 1977 Act. The key issue is that of "destruction or something equivalent", so short of this there is no tort, for example, where a co-owner creates a lien or when he changes the chattel by a process of manufacture in the ordinary and legitimate use of the chattel.[24] The statutory approach reflects the dictum of Parke B. in *Morgan v. Marquis*[25]:

> "It is well established that one tenant in common cannot maintain an action against his companion unless there has been a destruction of the particular chattel or something equivalent to it."

Innocent handling as a defence in conversion

Liability for damages in conversion is prima facie strict so that the tortfeasor is liable irrespective of the fact that he knew he was infringing or interfering with the rights of the owner. Given the strict liability nature of the tort, innocent handling is an important defence to this tort. This is particularly the case since there is now a statutory rule in section 11(1) of the 1977 Act to the effect that "contributory negligence is no defence to an action for conversion or intentional trespass to goods". The analogy here is with the law of negligence where English law has consistently denied that an owner owes a duty of care to safeguard his own property in respect of third party acquirers.[26] The main problem concerns the scope of the innocent handling. A distinction is drawn between ministerial handling of goods, perhaps at the request of an apparent owner in control of the goods, and where the act in question merely changes the location of the goods as distinct from any assumption of dominion over them.[27] The line between a purely ministerial act and an assertive one is very difficult to draw but, as a matter of principle, it is difficult to see how the law should distinguish between innocent handlers and innocent acquirers especially since the former will often be in the custody business, where conversion is an occupational hazard which could be insured against.

In the case of acting on the instructions of another as principal, it would appear that if the auctioneer is involved with the actual transference of title, for example, by handing over the proceeds of sale to his principal without notice of any defect of title, the true owner has recourse against the auctioneer. This approach is confirmed by the Court of Appeal in *R.H. Willis and Son v. British Car Auctions Ltd*[28] where Lord Denning held:

[24.] *Jacobs v. Seward* (1872) L.R. 5 H.L. 464.
[25.] (1854) 9 Ex. 145 at 148.
[26.] See Chap. 6, above.
[27.] *Cf. National Mercantile Bank Ltd v. Rymill* (1881) 44 L.T. 767.
[28.] [1978] 1 W.L.R. 438.

"It is now, I think well established that if an auctioneer sells goods by knocking down with his hammer at an auction and thereafter delivers them to the purchaser—then although he is only an agent—then if the vendor has no title to the goods, both the auctioneer and the purchaser are liable in conversion to the true owner, no matter how innocent the auctioneer may have been in handling the goods or the purchaser in acquiring them".[29]

This approach was extended by the Court of Appeal to the provisional bids procedure which involves the auctioneer, where the highest price fails to reach the reserve price, engaging in a brokerage, that is, obtaining the highest bidder's confirmation of his bid and the seller's (a hirer under a hire-purchase agreement who wrongfully disposed of the car) acceptance of that price subject to a reduction in commission. This procedure was not considered by the Court of Appeal to be a purely ministerial act within the dictum of Blackburn J. in *Hollins v. Fowler*[30]:

"[An agent] should be excused for what he does if the act is of such a nature as would be excused if done by the authority of the person in possession, if he was a finder of the goods, or intrusted with their custody."

There is some authority that an auctioneer who has not effected a sale is not liable in conversion.[31] However, there is a fine distinction because the intervention of the auctioneer in each case was the effective cause of the sale and indeed for which the auctioneer was paid a commission.

Some statutory protection is given. In this respect section 234(3) of the Insolvency Act 1986 provides that the receiver or liquidator of a company is not liable for any loss or damage resulting from dealings with property seized from the company, unless he had reason to believe that he was not entitled to act as he did. The reference to loss or damage means that a restitutionary claim for proceeds received is still available.[32] Similarly, section 307(4) of the Insolvency Act 1986 protects persons dealing with the bankrupt's property in good faith, for value and without notice of the bankruptcy, or any banker who enters into a transaction in good faith and without notice of the bankruptcy.[33]

The *jus tertii*

At common law the defendant wrongdoer could impeach the title of the plaintiff by showing that someone else had a better right. However, at the same time there were significant exceptions at common law which were designed to prevent the *jus tertii* defence being used to delay

---

[29.] *Ibid.* at 442. See also *Union Transport Finances Ltd v. British Car Auctions Ltd* [1978] 2 All E.R. 385.
[30.] (1874–75) L.R. 7 H.L. 757 at 767.
[31.] See *Cochrane v. Rymill* (1879) 40 L.T. (N.S.) 744; *National Mercantile Bank v. Rymill* (1881) 44 L.T. (N.S.) 767.
[32.] See *Welsh Development Agency v. Export Finance* [1992] B.C.L.C. 148.
[33.] See Insolvency Act 1986, s. 307(4)(b).

litigation. The Reform Committee[34] considered the *jus tertii* problem in great detail, particularly the issue of multiplicity of actions, and its recommendations were generally enacted in the 1977 Act. The modern position is that the defendant, even in an action brought by his bailor, can apply to have all known competing claims determined simultaneously thereby reducing the risk of double liability.[35] It would appear that section 8 materially alters the common law, in particular in the following ways:

1. The principle of right to possession only applies as against the defendant where the plaintiff can show that he has the *only known* possessory title. This arises out of the fact that a defendant who wishes to avoid the threat of double liability[36] may apply for directions to the court as to whether that person (identified as having a better right) should be joined in the action. The sanction against such a named person who fails to appear at the hearing or to comply with any directions given is that an order, either unconditionally or conditionally, may be made depriving him of any right of action against the defendant for the wrong.[37]

2. A bailee being sued by the bailor is no longer estopped from denying that his bailor had a good title at the beginning of the bailment, because the defendant in any action for wrongful interference may apply to join a named third party (*tertius*). This is significant in complex lease structures which are multi-layered. In this regard section 8 of the 1977 Act and the Rules of the Supreme Court, Order 15, rule 10A provide the machinery for joinder. However, when such joinder is impracticable, for example, where the bailor cannot be traced, the common law position will still persist, that is, the bailee may recover the full value but is then liable to account to his bailor,[38] although this will expose the bailor to the solvency risk of the bailee.

3. Unless the bailor authorises the bailee to sue on his behalf in writing, a plaintiff bailee must give particulars of his title and identify his bailor so that the wrongdoer may then apply for directions to join the bailor. In this way damages may be apportioned between them[39] according to their respective interests. Otherwise, irrespective of whether the bailor authorises the bailee to sue on his own behalf, the bailee may nevertheless recover the full amount of the loss or damage and would then be

---

[34.] *i.e.* 18th Report, (see n.2, above).
[35.] See Torts (Interference with Goods Act) 1977, s. 8(1).
[36.] *Ibid*. s. 7.
[37.] *Ibid*. s. 8(2)(d) and R.S.C. Ord. 15, r. 10A(4); C.C.R. Ord. 15, r. 4(3).
[38.] See *The Winkfield* [1902] p. 42.
[39.] Torts (Interference with Goods) Act 1977, s. 7(2).

accountable to disgorge the excess to the *tertius*.[40] Moreover, where, as the result of enforcement of a double liability, any claimant is unjustly enriched, he is liable to reimburse the wrongdoer to that extent.[41]

Forms of Relief for Conversion

Introduction

Following the abolition of detinue and its complete submergence into conversion, the new forms of actions are in reality actions *in rem*. Consequently, in claims for wrongful interference, section 3(1) and (2) of the 1977 Act provide for the following claims.

Order for specific delivery

Section 3(2)(a) provides for specific delivery where the goods are in the possession or control of the defendant. There is no alternative for damages to be paid. The court has a discretion here to order up delivery[42] and will only do so normally in the case of extraordinary items where damages would not provide adequate compensation. If following an order for specific delivery this is not complied with, the court may revoke this order, or relevant part of it, and instead award damages by reference to the value of the goods.[43] It should be noted that where the defendant is entitled to an allowance for improvement of the goods after any act of wrongful interference,[44] the court may assess the allowance and make its payment a condition of an order for specific delivery.[45] Following an order for specific delivery, the defendant must make the goods available most notably by informing the plaintiff where they are and that they are at his disposal. A co-owner cannot obtain an order for specific delivery or even an order for its assessed value unless he has the written authority of every other co-owner to sue on their behalf.[46]

The court has power to make interlocutory orders for delivery.[47] Such an order may require delivery either to the claimant or to a person appointed by the court for the purpose according to the terms and conditions laid down by the court.[48]

Judgment for delivery or damages

Under section 3(2)(b) of the 1977 Act the court may, at the plaintiff's election, make an order for the delivery up of goods but give the

[40] *Ibid.* s. 7(3).
[41] *Ibid.* s. 7(4).
[42] *Ibid.* s. 3(3)(b).
[43] *Ibid.* s. 3(4).
[44] *Ibid.* s. 6(1), (2).
[45] *Ibid.* s. 3(7).
[46] R.S.C. Ord. 42, r. 1A.
[47] *Ibid.* s. 4(2).
[48] *Ibid.* s. 4(3).

defendant the alternative of paying damages by reference to the value of the goods together, in either alternative, with payment of any consequential damages. This order may be enforced either by a writ of delivery to recover the goods or their assessed value or, by order of the court on application by summons, by a writ of specific delivery.[49] Where the orders are in the alternative, the value of the goods should be clearly shown to be separately assessed from consequential losses claimed.

Damages

Introduction. The normal rule is that the plaintiff is entitled to the market value of the goods together with any special losses as the natural and direct result of the wrong. As discussed above, the 1977 Act alleviates the problem of double liability by requiring the plaintiff to identify any other claimant with an interest in the goods and introduces apportionment,[50] in the cases of successive claims, by requiring any claimant who recovers more than he would have been awarded had the claim been simultaneous, to account for such excess to a superior claimant who, to the extent that he is unjustly enriched, is liable then to reimburse the wrongdoer.[51] In addition there is the wrongdoer's allowance.[52]

The abolition of detinue and its submergence into conversion inevitably affects the computation of damages. In detinue damages for detention were included along with their value as part of the normal computation of damages, whereas in conversion this was consequential loss. We shall now consider the general approach to the award of damages in conversion.

Damages: the general rule in conversion. The general approach to damages in the tort of conversion is different to other torts, such as trespass or negligence, because the claimant recovers not only his loss but also the value of the thing converted. The general rule in contract is that damages are compensatory, that is the plaintiff recovers only his loss subject to the rules of mitigation. In conversion there is no general requirement of mitigation and neither is it necessary for the plaintiff to be able to demonstrate a causal connection between the specific act of conversion and any loss suffered by him. Contributory negligence is also disregarded for this purpose.[53] However, this does not mean that an estoppel defence is unavailable to a non-owner in trying to assert title. The justification for this approach is that the effect of estoppel, notably under section 21(1) of the Sale of Goods Act 1979, is to pass a good title to the acquirer which therefore provides a complete defence to liability

---

[49.] R.S.C. Ord. 45 r. 4, C.C.R. Ord. 26 r. 16.
[50.] Torts (Interference with Goods) Act 1977, s. 7(2).
[51.] *Ibid.* s. 7(3), (4).
[52.] *Ibid.* s. 6. See Chap. 8, above.
[53.] Torts (Interference with Goods) Act 1977, s. 11(1).

for conversion against the owner/representor,[54] whereas section 11(1) of the 1977 Act only goes to the issue of reduction of damages as a result of conversion as distinct from ousting liability.

Damages for conversion are at large in the sense that the plaintiff need not prove financial loss in order to recover them. Thus it has been held that an owner can recover for the full value of the goods even where risk has passed to a third party and he has paid for them. The rationale for this approach is evident in Hobhouse J.'s judgment in *The Sanix Ace*[55] when he held:

"It has long been settled law that the owner of goods is entitled to sue and recover damages in respect of loss or damage to those goods. The only qualification is that, if he is suing in tort, his claim may be defeated if his title was a bare proprietary one and did not include any right to possession of the goods. In English law it is the claimants' property in the goods which gives the right to recover substantial damages. In tort the title to sue and recovery of substantial damages are concurrent. There is no such thing in the relevant context as a right to sue in tort for merely nominal damages . . . As soon as the goods are damaged the owner of the goods suffers loss. Formerly he was the owner of goods of full value and subsequently he is the owner of goods with only a reduced value. He has suffered a loss. Whether or not he may be able to recoup his loss from others is a separate question . . . Full damages assessed by reference to the sound arrived value of the goods are not affected by the fact that the owner of the goods has sold them on at a higher or lower price."

Moreover, there is authority that recovery will not be subject to the value of any lien in favour of a third party or even the defendant himself.[56] The reason for this is that a lien is a personal obligation and the *nemo dat* principle will prevail irrespective of whether there are any statutory powers of sale.[57] A careful distinction should be drawn with the case where there are obligations owed by the plaintiff to the defendant wrongdoer, for example, if the plaintiff has bought a car from the defendant which is wrongfully sold to X then the plaintiff's recovery is predicated upon him first paying for the goods.[58]

Damages in conversion: the hire-purchase anomaly. A conceptually difficult case to rationalise, although perhaps pragmatically the position may be understood, is the rule that a finance company as owner under a *hire-purchase* arrangement can only recover its loss, that is, the sums outstanding under the agreement. The authority for this approach is *Wickham Holdings Ltd v. Brooke House Motors Ltd*[59] and, as such, deserves

---

[54.] See Chap. 6, above.
[55.] *The Sanix Ace (Obestain) Inc. v. National Mineral Development Corporation* [1987] 1 Lloyd's Rep. 465 at 468.
[56.] *Mulliner v. Florence* (1878) 3 Q.B.D. 484.
[57.] See Chap. 6, above.
[58.] *Chinery v. Viall* (1860) 5 H & N. 288.
[59.] [1967] 1 W.L.R. 295.

further consideration. In this case the plaintiff finance company entered into in October 1964 a hire-purchase agreement with Patterson in respect of a Rover car. The agreement included the following normal terms and conditions—that the hirer's rights were not assignable and that "any assignment or disposition or attempted assignment or disposition . . . shall be void and shall render nugatory and absolutely determine the hirer's rights under this agreement". The total hire-purchase price was £889—the hirer paid £234 and was to pay the balance by 12 instalments of £54.10s. a month and the option fee of £1. After paying seven instalments (with the totals equivalent to £615.10s.) Patterson traded-in the car and the defendant dealers telephoned the plaintiffs and were informed of the settlement figure which was £274.10s. They were told that they would accept £270 so long as it was paid within seven days. By an oversight they failed to pay this sum but they did repairs on the vehicle worth £50. Over two months later the defendants offered £20 more than the settlement figure but the plaintiffs refused and sued in conversion. At first instance, Fenton Atkinson J. held that the plaintiffs were entitled to the trade value of the Rover as at the date of judgment, namely, £365 after deducting the £50 spent by the dealers on repairs and also adding £75 damages for detention making a total of £440.

On appeal this judgment was overturned at the same time overruling *UDT (Commercial) Ltd v. Parkway Motors Ltd*[60] where the full value of a van on hire purchase was recovered.[61] It was held by Lord Denning M.R.[62]:

> "The finance company is only entitled to what it has lost by the wrongful act of the defendants. I am well aware, of course, that prima facie in conversion the measure of damages is the value of the goods at the date of conversion. But that does not apply where the plaintiff, immediately prior to the conversion, has only a limited interest in the goods . . . In a hire-purchase transaction there are two proprietary interests: the finance company's interest and the hirer's interest. If the hirer wrongfully sells the goods or the benefit of the agreement, in breach of the agreement, then the finance company are entitled to recover what they have lost by reason of his wrongful act. That is normally the balance outstanding on the hire-purchase price. But they are not entitled to more than they have lost."

The rationale for this approach is that the converting hirer was deemed to have a proprietary interest in the vehicle. However, it could equally be argued that the wrongful sale by the hirer destroys any interest that he had in the goods. This would certainly be the case in a finance lease arrangement and there is no reason in principle why the full value of the goods should not be recoverable by the finance lessor in this situation. A clear distinction can be drawn between a chattel mortgage where it is

---

[60.] [1955] 1 W.L.R. 719.
[61.] *Cf. Belsize Motor Supply Co. v. Cox* [1914] 1 K.B. 244.
[62.] [1967] 1 W.L.R. 295 at 299–301.

well established that a mortgagor can only sue to the value of his equity of redemption, because beyond that he is not the owner.[63]

Special damages and conversion. Of course special damages are recoverable where the wrongdoer must have been aware that the chattel was required by the plaintiff for a special purpose and that this purpose had now failed, for example, a failure to sell stock.[64] Recovery twice over for the same loss is not admissible, for example, profitable use of a chattel because this function goes to the value of the chattel. However, the courts have adopted an artificial mechanism for reckoning consequential losses by allowing the recovery of hire charges by a plaintiff who would not in fact have hired out the goods concerned, so long as the chattel detained is one which is normally let out on hire by the plaintiff, or, where this is not the case, there is nevertheless a figure that might be considered a reasonable hire charge or something analogous to it.[65] Neither is there a rule that hire charges must not exceed the capital cost of the chattel itself.[66] However, if the chattel is disposed of by the wrongdoer, the hiring charge will cease at the time of disposal and the owner will get damages assessed as the value of the chattel at the time of conversion.[67] The advantage of this approach is that the bailor is not restricted to a sum which represents the "proceeds" of a wrongdoing. Thus in *Strand Electric* the defendants detained and used some portable switchboards belonging to the plaintiffs. The plaintiffs leased out such equipment as part of their normal business operations and the Court of Appeal held that where the goods detained are of a kind which the defendant normally leases for reward and the defendant has enjoyed the beneficial use of them during the relevant period, the plaintiffs can recover the normal market hire rate of the goods on the basis that to award a lesser sum would be to allow the defendants to profit from their own wrong. Significantly Denning L.J. (as he then was) enunciated a general restitutionary approach, namely any wrongdoer who makes use of a chattel which is not his own must pay a reasonable hire for it irrespective of whether the owner has suffered a loss. It may be that Lord Denning's principle is itself restrictive, because there are situations where the deliberate misuse of goods may not amount to a "wrongdoing", for example a sub-bailee who has misused the goods with the permission of an original bailee: even in this case the misuse is likely to be a repudiation of the original contract of lease and therefore amount to conversion.

Exemplary damages and conversion. Exemplary damages in the sense that they are punitive are only payable following Lord Devlin's principle in *Rookes v. Barnard*[68]:

[63] *Brierly v. Kendall* (1852) 19 Q.B. 937.
[64] *Brandeis Goldschmidt Ltd v. Western Transport Ltd* [1981] Q.B. 564.
[65] See *The Mediana* [1900] A.C. 113.
[66] *Hillesden Securities Ltd v. Ryjack Ltd* [1983] 1 W.L.R. 959.
[67] *Strand Electric & Engineering Co. v. Brisford Entertainments* [1952] 2 Q.B. 246.
[68] [1964] A.C. 1127 at 1129.

". . . where a defendant with a cynical disregard for a plaintiff's rights has calculated that the money to be made out of his wrongdoing will probably exceed the damages at risk, it is necessary for the law to show that it cannot be broken with impunity."

Thus in *Tufuga v. Haddon*[69] such exemplary damages were awarded in respect of a sham hire-purchase agreement whereby the creditor with full knowledge unlawfully seized the debtor's car.

The time of assessment of damages. The time of assessment of damages is important to determine, because the computation of damages refers to the market price at the time of conversion, irrespective of the fact in hire-purchase contracts that this is less than the amount outstanding on the finance agreement.[70] If there is no market price or if the plaintiff is a dealer in the object converted and has plenty of stock, the measure of damages is the cost of replacement.[71] However in *J. Sargent (Garages) Ltd v. Motor Auctions (West Bromwich) Ltd*,[72] the Court of Appeal held that the plaintiff motor dealers were entitled to the retail price at which they were expected to sell a car with unusual features for which there was no general market.

The time at which the value is taken can be problematical. The normal rule is that the relevant time is the time of judgment, subject to the following exceptions:

1. Where it can be shown that the owner would have disposed of the chattel between the time he demanded it and the time of judgment, then its value at that time will be taken. This principle emerges from the celebrated Court of Appeal decision in *I.B.L. Ltd v. Coussens*.[73] In this case the defendant was the chairman and at one time chief executive of the plaintiff company. Following a takeover of the company, disputes arose particularly in relation to the valuation of the company which eventually led to the dismissal of the defendant. Upon dismissal in February 1988, the plaintiff demanded the return of two cars belonging to the company, an Aston Martin and a Rolls Royce—in the alternative, he was given the option of purchasing the two cars for £62,000. When he failed to deliver up the cars and proceedings were commenced, the dilemma was to determine at what time the value of the goods were to be assessed—at the time of judgment or on the date on which the defendant converted the goods by refusing to return them (February 1988—the date of valuation). The problem in this case was that the Aston

---

[69.] [1984] N.Z. Recent Law 285.
[70.] See *Chubb Cash Ltd v. John Crilley and Son* [1983] 1 W.L.R. 599.
[71.] *J. and E. Hall Ltd v. Barclay* [1937] 3 All E.R. 620.
[72.] [1977] R.T.R. 121.
[73.] [1991] 3 All E.R. 133.

Martin, in particular, was worth considerably more that it was in February 1988. As noted above, the general rule in conversion, particularly following the abolition of detinue, is that damages are not compensatory in terms of loss but rather the measure of damages is the value of the goods at the time of conversion.[74] The Court of Appeal determined the issue of valuation pragmatically in the light of circumstances and it is worth setting these out in full[75]:

> "In my judgment when the damages are assessed it will be necessary for the court to proceed as follows: (1) to decide whether if the cars had not been converted IBL would have kept and used the cars or have disposed of them elsewhere; (2) to decide whether if the cars would have been kept and used IBL could and should have obtained replacement cars and, if so, when; (3) if (a) the cars would have been kept and used and (b) it is decided either that IBL were under no obligation to obtain replacements or that they would have been unable to do so, the Court will assess the damages in the light of those findings. It seems to me that the damages on this basis are likely to be assessed by reference to the value of the cars at the date of judgment . . . (4) if the court decides that the cars would not have been kept and used or replacements could and should have been obtained it seems clear that an earlier date should be used for the calculation of the damages; (5) to calculate any damages suffered by reason of the loss of use of the cars between the date of conversion and the date ascertained in accordance with (3) and (4)."

2. If the owner merely claims damages, then the value is determined at the time of refusal to give up the goods. The justification of this approach is that by claiming damages the owner is giving up his *in specie* claim to the chattel in question and therefore, presumably, any subsequent appreciation in the value of the chattel up to the time of judgment.

Damages and successive conversions. Where damages for wrongful interference are assessed on the footing that the claimant is being compensated for the whole of his interest in the goods, payment of the damages extinguishes the claimant's title.[76] Recovery of less than the full value means the claimant will have a right of action against subsequent parties but will not be able to recover twice over, so that any damages received in one action will have to be taken into consideration in any other. Indeed section 9 of the 1977 Act is couched in such wide terms as to permit two or more actions for wrongful interference with the same goods against successive wrongdoers to be heard together in the same court provided they are concurrent. The limitation period of six years is

---

[74.] See *BBMB Finance (Hong Kong) Ltd v. Eda Holdings and others Ltd* [1990] 1 W.L.R. 409.
[75.] *Ibid.* at 139–140, per Neill L.J.
[76.] Torts (Interference with Goods Act) 1977, s. 5(1), (2).

obviously relevant.[77] If the defendant has deliberately concealed from the plaintiff any fact relevant to his right of action, the period does not begin to run, except as against a subsequent purchaser for value who was neither party to nor actually or constructively aware of the concealment, until the plaintiff had or should have discovered the concealment.[78]

Damages and set-off. Payments received on account of damages by the owner can be set-off not only against one converter but against all others. Significantly this also applies if the property converted or the proceeds are used to discharge the plaintiff's obligations to a third party.[79] This rule is a strict one and there must be a connection between the converted property or proceeds and the reduction of an obligation. In this respect a bank can reduce conversion damages related to a cheque by showing that it collected the cheque on behalf of a creditor of the plaintiff whose debt was thereby discharged.[80] The strictness of the rule was illustrated in the Australian decision of *Hunter BNZ Finance v. ANZ Bank.*[81] This was a purported lease of chattels by the plaintiffs to a fraudster who had engineered an elaborate financing arrangement to the effect that the plaintiffs would supply him with finance to acquire equipment from X which would then be leased to the fraudster by the plaintiffs. In fact the fraudster misapplied the financing cheque by paying it into an account controlled by him. However he did pay a few lease instalments on the non-existent goods in order to maintain the charade and then disappeared. The plaintiffs successfully sued the fraudster's bank in conversion. In the damages computation the court disregarded the few instalments made, because their source was not clear and they were not made by the converter out of the proceeds of the conversion.

The effect of return of the chattel. When the chattel is returned, there is still a cause of action and indeed section 3(2)(c) of the 1977 Act provides that a judgment for damages cannot be satisfied by redelivery after judgment. Redelivery does not compromise an action for consequential damage or deterioration in value, although if there is none then the plaintiff may have to pay costs even though he recovers nominal damages.[82] The position is the same if the plaintiff repossesses the chattel.

Trespass

Section 1(b) of the 1977 Act provides that the second form of "wrongful interference with goods" is "trespass to goods". Whilst the essential

[77] Limitation Act 1980, s. 3(1).
[78] *Ibid.* s. 3(2).
[79] *A.L. Underwood v. Barclays Bank* [1924] 1 K.B. 775.
[80] See *Bannatyne v. McIver* [1906] 1 K.B. 103.
[81] [1990] V.R. 41.
[82] *Hiort v. London and North Western Ry* (1879) 4 Ex. D. 188.

characteristics of the different torts are not diminished by the Act, the procedural consequences that pertain to the remedies available under section 3 and issues of avoidance of double liability will apply equally.

Conversion is a wider more flexible remedy than trespass particularly in actions involving equipment lessors and lessees for the following reasons:

1. In trespass the computation of damages relates to loss as distinct from the value of the goods.

2. The conceptual basis for trespass is to protect *possession* and not to protect against damage to the chattels themselves. As such there must be harm or damage in the sense of deliberate interference.

3. There must be actual possession, that is there is generally no claim based upon the *right* to possession. It is otherwise where the bailment is determinable at will, because the characterisation of this relationship is that the bailee merely holds the goods as agent for the bailor so that in this sense the bailor retains sufficient possession to entitle him to sue third parties.[83] The general rule, however, is that trespass is founded upon possession because as Lord Kenyon C.J. put it in *Ward v. Macanley*[84]:

   "The distinction between the action of trespass and trover is well settled: the former is founded on possession: the latter on property."

4. The intention of the trespasser (blameworthiness) is also relevant, or at least that he was negligent in producing an injury.[85] As such this puts the bailor under a procedural disadvantage in having to prove negligence.

Reversionary Damage to Chattels

Introduction

A person who is not in possession and does not have an immediate right to possession, notably a bailor for a fixed term, cannot sue in conversion or trespass. However, if he is deprived of the benefit of his reversionary interest typically because the goods are damaged or sold and title passes under one of the exceptions to the *nemo dat* rule,[86] then the plaintiff can recover damages for his loss.[87] This is anticipated in section 1(d) of the 1977 Act, that is, wrongful interference with goods which extends to

---

[83.] *Manders v. Williams* (1849) 4 Ex. 339; *White v. Morris* (1852) 11 C.B. 1015.
[84.] (1971) 4 T.R. 489 at 490.
[85.] *Wilson v. Lombank Ltd* [1963] 1 W.L.R. 1294.
[86.] See Chap. 6, above.
[87.] See R.S.C. Ord. 42 r. 1A; C.C.R. Ord. 22, r. 4.

include "any other tort so far as it results in damage to goods or to an *interest* in goods".

The reversionary interest of the bailor consists in the return of his goods, on the expiration of the term, basically in the same condition as when they were bailed taking into account fair wear and tear. The loss an owner sustains due to any damage or destruction of the goods must be commensurate with the full cost of repair or the value of the chattel immediately prior to destruction. In *Tancred v. Allgood*,[88] Pollock C.B. held that mere "temporary" injury would not do, for example, deprivation of use during the time when the owner's right to possession is suspended. It is otherwise where there is "permanent" damage, so that in *Mears v. London and South Western Railway*,[89] an owner who had let out his barge on hire recovered for the damage done to it by the defendants when they were negligently lifting a boiler on orders from the bailee.[90]

What interest must the plaintiff show?

The plaintiff must demonstrate a proprietary right. It is well known that a mere contractual right cannot provide a basis for an action in conversion[91] and by analogy this would extend to the complaint of damage to the reversion. In the context of finance leasing or contracts of hire, plaintiffs who are actual owners have no difficulty in establishing a proprietary interest. In addition, there is also no reason in principle why a claimant with an undisputed but limited interest in goods, such as a pledgor or a mortgagee or a lienor, should not also have a claim against damage to a reversionary interest.

A thorny issue concerns the right of a defendant to plead the *jus tertii* in a claim for damages to a reversionary interest. Typically this may involve a lessee, where a third party has wrongful possession of the goods, in an action for damage to the lessee's reversionary interest being met by the lessor's title in answer. Section 8 of the 1977 Act only applies where the defendant has evidence as to who the true owner is and so, in this context, the common law position is vital. Essentially the *jus tertii* rule is an aspect of relativity of title, that is, who has the better inter-party claim? Of course the fact that a reversionary plaintiff's title is imperfect goes to the issue of actual loss and damages but nonetheless

---

[88.] (1859) 4 H. & N. 438.
[89.] (1862) 11 C.B. (N.S.) 850.
[90.] See also *Lancashire Waggon Co. v. Fitzhugh* (1861) 6 H. & N. 502.
[91.] *The Aliakman* [1986] A.C. 785.

what matters is whether the nature of claimed possessory or other right is better than that which the defendant can show.[92]

In the case of section 8 where the plaintiff is suing for "wrongful interference" the defendant can plead that a named third party has a better title than the plaintiff. The definition of "wrongful interference" in section 1 is: (a) Conversion and trespass to goods; (b) Negligence where it results in damage to goods or to an interest in goods[93]; (c) "Any other tort so far as it results in damage to goods or to an interest in goods".[94] Clearly "physical damage" cases to the reversionary interest are covered but more difficulty is posed by wrongful dispositions—how can they be considered to damage an interest in goods in a lease scenario since property cannot pass? It would appear to be the case that a *jus tertii* cannot be pleaded involving a wrongful disposition *per se* where no actual damage to the goods is involved. Even so this should not bar injunctive relief since whilst ultimately no loss will be caused in the case of a wrongful disposition, nevertheless it is possible to infer that this could cause significant inconvenience to the reversionary owner.

Damages

The measure of damages for trespass is the loss suffered by the plaintiff, whereas in conversion and negligence it is possible that a claimant may recover more than he has lost, that is, the value of the goods. In *The Charlotte*,[95] an owner recovered the full value of the goods even though they were at the risk of a third party.[96] In the case of negligence, so long as the plaintiff can show a proprietary interest he can recover the cost of repairs irrespective of whether he has to pay for them. Thus, in the Australian case of *Dee Trading v. Baldwin*,[97] a finance company was able to recover for damage to a car on hire-purchase even though the hirer himself was contractually bound to repair the car. In the case of wrongful disposition, however, the measure for damages will be related to the plaintiff's actual loss which is tied into the question as to what chance the plaintiff has to get his goods back. As a matter of principle

---

[92.] See, *e.g. Buckley v. Gross* (1863) 3 B. & S. 566. Commonwealth authorities include *Bird v. Fort Frances* [1949] 2 D.L.R. 791; *Russel v. Wilson* (1923–24) 33 C.L.R. 538. These cases support the general position that apart from pleading a *jus tertii*, prior possession confers a possessory title which is good against later possessors who cannot prove a superior title. In the case of a bailment, the bailor has possession of the chattel when he transfers it to the bailee irrespective of whether ultimately he is the owner. If he is the owner then he is not put to proof of that title in suing the bailee because he can rely upon previous possession before the transfer. See *Baker* (1990) 16 University of Queensland L.J. 46.

[93.] Torts (Interference with Goods) Act 1977, s. 1(c).

[94.] *Ibid.* s. 1(d).

[95.] [1908] p. 206.

[96.] See more recently, *The Sanix Ace* [1987] 1 Lloyd's Rep. 465.

[97.] [1938] V.L.R. 173.

the court will take into account whether the goods were readily available in the hands of a given person who is not the defendant and the appropriateness therefore of suing the defendant. It should also be noted that contributory negligence under the Law Reform (Contributory Negligence) Act 1945 will impact here as it is unlikely that the section 11 bar in the Torts (Interference with Goods) Act 1977 can apply to an action for reversionary damage.

Chapter 12

Criminal Liability

Introduction

It is necessary to consider the interaction between criminal and civil law in respect of delinquent hirers or lessees of equipment. In many respects the intervention of criminal law arises out of an initial bad credit decision despite the fact that there are elaborate mechanisms adopted by the credit instalment industry to avoid such decisions arising in the first place. Of course, at the same time there may be potential criminal activity which goes undetected, for example, where goods are disposed of unlawfully but the instalments continue to be paid by the delinquent hirer or lessee.

It is not the purpose of this section to consider criminal liability imposed upon credit providers by consumer protection law for the purposes of the efficient administration of the consumer credit business. In this respect any person who by way of business provides credit under regulated agreements must have a licence.[1] Indeed unlicensed trading activities are prima facie unenforceable and both criminal and civil sanctions may apply.[2] An elaborate machinery is provided for the making by the Director General of Fair Trading of an enforcement order following unlicensed activity.[3] In addition, Part 3 of the Fair Trading Act 1973 (the FTA 1973) gives the Director General powers to seek the cessation of business activities detrimental to consumers.[4] In identifying such conduct, reliance is placed on information forthcoming from local authority consumer protection departments. Moreover, a central registry of convictions is kept to enable the Office of Fair Trading to identify businesses for possible action. A recent example of the Director General threatening to use his licensing powers can be seen when he did so in relation to finance houses using eponymous names in the context of the supply of photocopiers, unless a clear signal has been given by the finance company that it is not part of the same group as the manufacturer or supplier.[5]

When the Director is satisfied that a trader is indulging in conduct detrimental to consumers, the FTA 1973 provides for a three-fold

[1] Consumer Credit Act 1974, s. 21.
[2] *Ibid.* ss. 39–40 .
[3] *Ibid.* s. 40.
[4] Fair Trading Act 1973, s. 34(1).
[5] *Cf. Lease Management Services Ltd v. Purnell Secretarial Services* (1994) Tr. L.R. 337, C.A.

procedure. First, section 34(1) instructs the Director to seek a written assurance from the trader or his "accessory" (for example, where a new company has been formed) that he will refrain from continuing that course of conduct. Secondly, where he is unable to obtain satisfactory written assurances, the Director may bring proceedings before the Restrictive Practices Court.[6] In respect of "small traders" there is an alternative power to bring proceedings in the county courts.[7] The appropriate court may order the respondent to refrain from such conduct or, alternatively, accept an undertaking from the respondent in this respect. Lastly, breach of such an undertaking or court order will amount to a contempt of court. It should be noted that there are wide powers to prevent avoidance of the process by transferring business between companies in a group.[8] A list of assurances, court orders and contempt orders given each year can be found in the Office of Fair Trading Annual Report.

The general criminal law of the offences against property and the abuse of credit facilities will be considered in detail in this chapter. Typically the scenarios will involve the action of a hirer who, subsequent to a letter of termination, wrongfully disposes of the goods or destroys them or conceals them from the lessor/owner. In addition the behaviour of the dealer will be considered, such as where money is raised on fictitious invoices or where there is a misrepresentation as to the value of the goods which form the subject of the contract of hire. Finally we shall consider the position of the over-enthusiastic creditor who repossesses the equipment.

Offences by Lessee/Hirer Out of Possession

Conspiracy to Defraud

If the lessee/hirer and any other person conspire together to commit a fraudulent act the criminal law will infer a conspiracy to defraud. The issue is whether a conspiracy to defraud can act as a purpose stop-gap offence independent of a particular substantive offence committed. This was rejected by the House of Lords in *R. v. Ayres*,[9] where their Lordships interpreted section 3 of the Criminal Law Act 1977 to mean that, if by virtue of their arrangement, the parties had agreed to commit a substantive offence then the proper course was to convict for that

[6.] Fair Trading Act 1973, s. 35.
[7.] *Ibid*. s. 41.
[8.] *Ibid*. s. 40.
[9.] [1984] A.C. 447.

offence as a conspiracy to commit it. This approach was adopted despite
the fact that the Law Commission Report, which underlay the Act,
specifically recognised the need to preserve the general offence of
conspiracy to defraud.

In order to obviate the difficulties in the *Ayres* case, the Report of the
Criminal Law Revision Committee,[10] recommended that conspiracy to
defraud be reinstated and this has taken place in section 12 of the
Criminal Justice Act 1987 which provides as follows:

"(1) If—

(a) a person agrees with any other person or persons that a course of
conduct shall be pursued; and

(b) that course of conduct will necessarily amount to or involve the
commission of any offence or offences by one or more of the parties
to the agreement if the agreement is carried out in accordance with their
intentions,

the fact that it will do so shall not preclude a charge of conspiracy to defraud
being brought against them in respect of the agreement."

The significance of this offence is that it goes some way to circumvent
some of the inadequate penalties provided by parliament for the
substantive offence, since the penalty for the offence for conspiracy to
defraud under section 12(3) of the Act is 10 years' imprisonment and/or
an unlimited fine.

The modern position would appear to be that conspiracy to defraud
continues to exist alongside conspiracy to commit statutory offences. In
effect an indictment must include the various substantive offences
committed as well as a conspiracy to defraud. The significance of this
would appear to be that if the substantive offences fail on the basis of
insufficient evidence, then the trial judge may rule that the charge of
conspiracy be left to the jury. In the finance lease context, typically, this
would involve some kind of accommodation between the lessee and the
dealer where the former, at the request and for the accommodation of
the dealer, signs a lease or hire agreement for the goods which he knows
he intended neither to take nor pay for, the real purpose being to enable
the dealer to obtain an immediate advance from the finance house. It is
not necessary to prove an intention to deceive. Thus in *Scott v.
Metropolitan Police Comr*,[11] the appellants were copyright pirates who
bribed employees at cinemas to permit them to take films for the
purposes of copying them and subsequently returning them. It was held
that it was sufficient that the intention was to inflict economic loss on
the owners of the copyright and also the film distributors. Another
instance would be where the price of the goods were deliberately
overvalued,[12] and in this situation the dealer/hirer will certainly also run

---

[10.] *Conspiracy to Defraud* (Cmnd. 9873 (1986)).

[11.] *Scott v. Metropolitan Police Comr.* [1975] A.C. 819.

[12.] *Cf. Royscot Trust Ltd v. Rogerson* [1991] 2 Q.B. 297.

the risk of civil liability and will be estopped from denying the value of the goods as well as exposure to an action in the tort of deceit.

A major practical difficulty for the prosecution with the offence of conspiracy to defraud is that it cannot be charged summarily before magistrates as it is not an offence triable either way.

Theft

Undoubtedly theft will be the most common offence. The offence is very broadly defined in that section 1(1) of the Theft Act 1968 provides as follows:

"A person is guilty of theft if he dishonestly appropriates property belonging to another with the intention of permanently depriving the other of it."

It would appear that where there is no intention of paying for goods in possession then this constitutes theft. Moreover in *Lawrence v. Metropolitan Police Comr*[13] it was tentatively stated by the House of Lords that a person might be guilty of theft even if ownership had passed. In this sense the offence of theft would appear also to encompass obtaining by deception. Significantly in *Lawrence* the House of Lords clearly stated that the offence of theft could be committed even though the act of appropriation was expressly or impliedly authorised by the owner. The facts in *Lawrence* involved a taxi driver who took more than the permitted fare from a foreign student with his apparent consent. Viscount Dilhourne for the House of Lords said[14]:

". . . that there was an appropriation in this case is clear . . . Belief or the absence of belief that the owner had with . . . knowledge consented to the appropriation is relevant to the issue of dishonesty, not to the question whether or not there had been an appropriation. That may occur even though the owner has permitted or consented to the property being taken."

The above approach was confirmed in *R. v. Gomez.*[15] The facts in this case involved collaboration between an assistant manager and another whereby that other intended to "pay" for electrical goods with stolen building society cheques. The assistant manager sought the manager's approval to the transactions on the basis that the cheques were "as good as cash". They were dishonoured. Whilst this was a plain case of deception, the respondent was charged with and convicted of theft. It would appear, therefore, that the omission of the words "without the consent of the owner" from section 1(1) of the Theft Act 1968 is a deliberate expression of policy. The logic of *Lawrence* and *Gomez* is that all cases of deception are also theft.

13. [1972] A.C. 626.
14. *Ibid.* at 632.
15. [1993] A.C. 442.

The advantages for the prosecution in bringing a charge of theft, rather than a charge of obtaining property by deception under section 15 of the Theft Act 1968, is that it is not necessary to show "deception", that is someone being deceived and that the deception led to obtaining the property. One effect of *Lawrence* and *Gomez* is that they create an offence of theft where the *actus reus* is nothing more than a dishonest act.

Obtaining Property by Deception

Under section 15(1) of the Theft Act 1968, a person who by deception dishonestly obtains property belonging to another with the intention of permanently depriving the other of it, is liable on conviction on indictment to imprisonment to a term not exceeding 10 years. It is enough that he acquires possession or even control rather than complete ownership.[16] He must be shown to have had an intention to permanently deprive at the time the transaction took place.[17]

The typical scenario which applies in this context is where a lessee/hirer obtains the equipment by deception and then sells them or absconds with them leaving no trace of his whereabouts. However, it could be argued that the deception was employed in order to obtain the contract and that any property obtained in consequence is too remote to be the subject of an obtaining by false pretences charge. It may be that the difficulty of proving dishonesty from inception[18] makes it more attractive from a prosecution point of view to charge with theft because, following the House of Lords decision in *Gomez*, this offence is committed as soon as the deceiver takes possession. In most hire-purchase agreements, and certainly all lease agreements, there is a provision that the debtor should not re-sell without the prior written permission of the creditor. It would appear, therefore, that if the debtor does this without permission, such dishonesty will be treated as theft following *Gomez*. Nonetheless, if when he sold he intended to use the purchase price to pay off the outstanding balance of the debt, it is unlikely that such conduct will constitute dishonesty even though technically there is a breach of contract.

A jury may be reluctant to find for dishonesty where a lessee has been extravagant about his earning power or the extent of his financial commitments. Even so there is a sound basis for such an allegation where it can be shown that, but for that deception, the finance house would not have acted.[19] Nonetheless there is bifurcation in the offence

---

[16.] Theft Act 1968, s. 15(2). A significant amendment suggested by the Theft (Amendment) Bill in the new s. 15A of the 1968 Act. This is intended to deal with the effect of the House of Lords judgment in *R. v. Preddy* [1996] 3 All E.R. 481 and if implemented will create a new offence of dishonesty of obtaining a money transfer.

[17.] *Ibid.*, s. 6.

[18.] See below.

[19.] See *R. v. Allsop* (1976) 64 Cr.App.R. 29.

---

between deception and dishonesty—not every deception will be viewed as dishonesty. The issue of dishonesty is a matter for the jury and the test was laid down by the Court of Appeal in *R. v. Ghosh*[20]:

> "In determining whether the prosecution has proved that the defendant was acting dishonestly, a jury must first of all decide whether according to the ordinary standards of reasonable and honest people what was done was dishonest. If it was not dishonest by those standards, that is the end of the matter and the prosecution fails.
>
> If it was dishonest by those standards, then the jury must consider whether the defendant himself must have realised that what he was doing was by those standards dishonest. In most cases, where the actions are obviously dishonest by ordinary standards, there will be no doubt about it. It will be obvious that the defendant himself knew that he was acting dishonestly. It is dishonest for a defendant to act in a way which he knows ordinary people consider to be dishonest, even if he asserts or genuinely believes that he is morally justified in acting as he did."

In summary, the issue of dishonesty is a matter for the jury to determine in accordance with the standards of ordinary people, with all the uncertainties and incongruities that this may entail.

Obtaining Services by Deception

The main difficulties associated with the old offence of obtaining certain pecuniary advantages by deception under section 16(2)(a) of the Theft Act 1968 have been dealt with by section 1 of the Theft Act 1978, which provides as follows:

> "(1) A person who by deception dishonestly obtains services from another shall be guilty of an offence.
>
> (2) It is an obtaining of services where the other is induced to confer a benefit by doing some act, or causing or permitting some act to be done, on the understanding that the benefit has been or will be paid for. The Theft (Amendment) Bill will if implemented amend section 1 of the Theft Act 1978 in an attempt to clear up the problems in bringing appropriate charges in cases involving fraudulent mortgage applications. A new sub-section (3) will make it clear that there will be an obtaining of services within the meaning of section 1 where a party is induced to make a loan, or to cause or permit a loan to be made, on the understanding that any payment will be or has been made in respect of the loan."

In *R. v. Widdowson*[21] the appellant had completed a proposal form for the hire-purchase of a van in another's name. The appellant used a neighbour's name because he himself was a credit risk. The appellant's dishonesty was discovered because inadvertently he had signed the

[20] [1982] Q.B. 1053 at 1064.
[21] (1986) 82 Cr.App.R. 314.

document in his own name and he was charged with and convicted of attempting to obtain services by deception. The services here were "credit facilities to assist in the purchase of a van". Whilst technically the indictment was wrongly drafted in that a hire-purchase agreement cannot be described as credit facilities since on the making of an agreement the finance company does not give any "credit" to the hirer, nonetheless, such an arrangement does fall within the definition of services for the purpose of the legislation. The finance company does confer a benefit by delivering-up possession of the vehicle on the understanding that the hirer has or will pay an initial payment as well as subsequent instalments.

It is an offence to obtain goods on hire by deception, even though the defendant intends to return them, that is where there is no intention to permanently deprive. Typically this may occur when a hirer of a car presents the wrong driving licence, even though he intends to pay for the hire charge. This only applies in a commercial context where some payment is due, albeit a payment in kind, and does not apply to purely gratuitous social transactions.

Obtaining Exemption from Abatement of Liability

An offence is committed under section 2(1)(c) of the Theft Act 1978 in respect of a person who:

"by any deception—

. . .

(c) dishonestly obtains any exemption from or abatement of liability to make a payment."

This offence applies where the debtor is fraudulent at the inception of the debt transaction. The essence of the offence is where a retailer/financier provides a service more cheaply than otherwise he would by a misrepresentation as to status, for example membership of an organisation. This offence is committed even if the offender gets the service gratuitously or free of charge, and is therefore unlike section 1 of the Theft Act 1978 discussed above.

False Accounting

The Theft Act 1968 provides for the case where particulars on a form required to be completed are falsified. In this respect, section 17 states:

"(1) Where a person dishonestly, with a view to gain for himself or another or with intent to cause loss to another,

(a) destroys, defaces, conceals or falsifies any account or any record or document made or required for any accounting purpose; or

311

(b) in furnishing information for any purpose produces or makes use of any account, or any such record or document as aforesaid, which to his knowledge is or may be misleading, false or deceptive in a material particular;

he shall, on conviction on indictment, be liable to imprisonment for a term not exceeding seven years.

(2) For purposes of this section a person who makes or concurs in making in an account or other document an entry which is or may be misleading, false or deceptive in a material particular, or who omits or concurs in omitting a material particular from an account or other document, is to be treated as falsifying the account of document."

It has been held that a proposal form for finance, which is by way of inquiry and was strictly speaking preliminary to an accounting purpose, was covered by the Act. Thus in *A.-G.'s Reference (No. 1 of 1980)*[22] the defendant retailer was acquitted of the offence, having advised purchasers of his domestic appliances to give false personal particulars on loan proposal forms addressed to a finance company. The question referred for the opinion of the court was whether or not the proposal was "made or required for an accounting purpose" even before it had been accepted by the finance company, as the trial judge had ruled that at the time when it was completed it did not satisfy this requirement. In the Court of Appeal it was held that the words "made or required for an accounting purpose" included a proposal form, since it was "required for" an accounting purpose and that was in the contemplation of the parties when the document was made.

It would appear that the prosecution must show that the hirer/lessee intended that the proposal form should be forwarded to the finance company and that the latter would use it for an accounting purpose, that is in assessing credit worthiness. This would deal with the *mens rea* issue of dishonesty with a "view to gain" or "intent to cause loss". Furthermore it is not necessary that the false information has a direct bearing on the accounting purposes for which the document was required, so long as the statement was misleading in relation to "an important matter", for example the length of time in employment.[23] In this regard the issue is whether the statement is such that it could have affected the outcome of the proceedings had it not been made. It should be noted that even though the defendant may be aware that a statement is false, if he has not understood the significance of making the statement the requisite "intent to cause loss to another" or a "view to gain for himself or another" would appear to be missing and so also the requirement of dishonesty. If a dealer encourages false accounting by colluding with the customer, in order to avoid minimum deposit requirement set down by individual finance houses, then he may be charged with aiding and abetting the debtor's false accounting offences.[24] If other documentation

[22.] [1981] 1 W.L.R. 34.
[23.] *R. v. Mallett* [1978] 1 W.L.R. 820.
[24.] The statutory requirement for minimum deposits in hire-purchase transactions was abolished under the Control of Hiring and Hire-Purchase and Credit Sale Agreements (Revocation) Order 1982, S.I. 1982 No. 1034.

has been forged relating, for example, to the description of the vehicle, it is likely that both the dealer and the customer would be guilty of a conspiracy to defraud.

Forgery

The modern position would appear to be that almost any document that purports to contain a statement of fact which is untrue is in fact a forgery, for example the valuation of non-existent equipment[25] or a bogus applicant for credit facilities. Falsifying credit worthiness in an application for credit, for example mis-stating income, probably amounts to a forgery. This offence does not require dishonesty and it would appear that the offence is committed even though the document does not tell a lie about itself (automendacity) but rather contains false information.[26]

The relevant legislative provisions can be found in the Forgery and Counterfeiting Act 1981 and section 1 of that Act sets out the substantive offence as follows:

"A person is guilty of forgery if he makes a false instrument, with the intention that he or another shall use it to induce somebody to accept it as genuine, and by reason of so accepting it to do or not to do some act to his own or any other person's prejudice."

This a serious offence as it carries 10 years' imprisonment. The key issue centres around what is a false instrument. This is defined in section 9(1) of the Act as follows:

"An instrument is false for the purposes of this part of this Act—

    (a) if it purports to have been made in the form in which it is made by a person who did not in fact make it in that form; or

    (b) if it purports to have been made in the form in which it is made on the authority of a person who did not in fact authorise its making in that form; or

    (c) if it purports to have been made in the terms in which it is made by a person who did not in fact make it in those terms; or

    (d) if it purports to have been made in the terms in which it is made on the authority of a person who did not in fact authorise its making in those terms; or

    (e) if it purports to have been altered in any respect by a person who did not in fact alter it in that respect; or

    (f) if it purports to have been altered in any respect on the authority of a person who did not in fact authorise the alteration in that respect; or

---

[25] See *R. v. Donnelly* [1984] 1 W.L.R. 1017.
[26] *Ibid.*

(g) if it purports to have been made or altered on a date on which, or at a place at which, or otherwise in circumstances in which, it was not in fact made or altered; or

(h) if it purports to have been made or altered by an existing person but he does not in fact exist."

Obtaining Credit by an Undischarged Bankrupt

Section 360(1) of the Insolvency Act 1986, states as follows:

"The bankrupt is guilty of an offence if—

(a) either alone or jointly with any other person, he obtains credit to the extent of the prescribed amount or more without giving the person from whom he obtains it the relevant information about his status."

The offence is triable either way and when it is tried on indictment it carries two years' imprisonment. Under the old law a vexed issue was that of the concept of credit but the Insolvency Act 1986 has obviated some of the problems here in that section 360(2)(a) now provides that the bankrupt obtains credit "where goods are bailed to him under a hire-purchase agreement, or agreed to be sold to him under a conditional sale agreement". This should also be the case with leased equipment. It is established law that if rent is payable in arrears then credit will be "obtained".[27] Even if the rent is payable in advance, the court, in the context of a lease, will categorise this as obtaining credit especially where the lessee binds himself to a period of time in relation to the equipment.[28]

The offence is of a strict kind because it requires no proof of intent to defraud. Nonetheless where the bankrupt is not at fault, for example where he instructs an agent to obtain credit and to make full disclosure but the latter fails to do so,[29] the bankrupt can hardly be said to have "obtained" credit and should therefore be acquitted of the offence.

Offences by Lessee/Hirer in Possession

Theft

Theft is defined in section 1(1) of the Theft Act 1968 as follows:

[27.] See *R. v. Smith* (1915) 11 Cr.App.R. 81.

[28.] See *R. v. Hartley* [1972] 2 Q.B. 1 where, in the context of a lease of land, the court did not investigate whether the rent was payable in advance or in arrears.

[29.] *R. v. Duke of Leinster* [1924] 1 K.B. 311; *R. v. Salter* [1968] 2 Q.B. 793.

"A person is guilty of theft if he dishonestly appropriates property belonging to another with the intention of permanently depriving the other of it . . ."

The key concepts are appropriation and dishonesty. Appropriation is as much an offence against ownership as it is against interference with possession. A possessor who dishonestly treats property as though he were the owner of it is guilty of theft if he acts with the intention of permanently depriving the true owner of it, for example by dissipating it. However, not every use by a possessor amounts to an appropriation. At the same time it is important to note that a mere failure to re-deliver equipment at the end of a lease contract may be due to carelessness or negligence rather than dishonesty.

Section 3 of the 1968 Act states:

"Any assumption by a person of the rights of an owner amounts to an appropriation, and this includes, where he has come by the property (innocently or not) without stealing it, any later assumption of a right to it by keeping or dealing with it as owner."

For the purposes of criminal law, retention of title by the creditor is significant because, by virtue of section 5(1) of the Theft Act 1968, the property continues to belong to the creditor/seller because he has a "proprietary right or interest" in it, so a dishonest intention to defeat that interest might therefore amount to theft. Clearly, if the lessee sells the goods or gives them away this will constitute an act of appropriation. In offering the goods up for sale, this is an assumption of the owner's right to dispose of the entire interest in the property and therefore constitutes an act of appropriation.[30] Even so, dishonesty must be shown as well as an intention to permanently deprive. Nonetheless there are conceptual problems attendant with this concept of a "right" not to sell the goods by a third party because this party cannot pass good title without his authority. The exercise of such a power is simply an unsuccessful effort to usurp one of the powers of an owner. In the case of a hire-purchase agreement or conditional sale agreement, if the hirer/buyer honestly reveals his lack of ownership but states his intention to remit the proceeds of the sale and pay the balance of the purchase price to the finance company, there has been no dishonesty. On the other hand, if the seller does not reveal his lack of ownership in terms of a right to sell, the purported sale will not only constitute theft against the finance company but also criminal deception in relation to the purchase price.[31]

Where the hirer misstates his creditworthiness, the difficulty with the intention to permanently deprive requirement under section 15 of the Theft Act 1968 in the context of hiring, where the hirer may intend to return the goods at the end of the bailment, was covered by section 1 of

[30.] *R. v. Pitham and Hehl* (1976) 65 Cr.App.R. 45.
[31.] *R. v. Staton* [1983] Crim. L.R. 190.

the Theft Act 1978, that is obtaining services by deception. It is no defence that the hirer intends to give full consideration, as the basis of the offence is the deception. Where the lessee is dishonest from the inception of the lease agreement in that he never intended to pay for the goods, he is guilty of obtaining goods by deception and also theft. The act of appropriation occurs at that time and any subsequent appropriations are not in point since the thief will be deemed to be already enjoying the fruits of his theft.[32]

A thorny problem relates to the situation where a lessee/hirer wrongfully refuses to surrender the goods following termination of the contract by the financier/owner. Such refusal will amount to an act of appropriation and also, therefore, theft where the requisite dishonest intention can be shown. A balanced approach must be adopted here. In the case of a hirer of a television set who refuses to give it up to the rental company, there is hardly an act of appropriation if the hirer continues to view the set. The reason for this is that these actions are those of a recalcitrant hirer rather than those of an owner, that is, he does not deal with the property as though he were owner within the meaning of section 3(1) of the Theft Act 1968. There is, however, a fine line because, depending on the extent of the recalcitrance, the hirer by acting in this way has exercised dominion over the television to the exclusion of the person to whom the property belongs: the courts could treat this as appropriation for the purposes of section 3(1). Furthermore, if the hirer does some other act such as moving house without giving a forwarding address then this would amount to an act of appropriation. There are two related issues: first, if the finance company had no right to the goods because they are protected goods for the purposes of sections 90 and 91 of the Consumer Credit Act 1974, the hirer's refusal to return them under a regulated hire-purchase or conditional sale agreement is doing no more than the civil law allows him to do in any case. It would appear in these circumstances that such refusal will not amount to an act of appropriation. Similarly if the hirer is holding on to the goods as "security" in relation to some outstanding claim or dispute against the finance lessor, this act cannot amount to appropriation because he is not acting in relation to the goods *as owner* but rather as security for his claim.[33]

Significantly, section 90 of the Consumer Credit Act 1974 does not govern consumer hire agreements, so a lessor has greater freedom to repossess such goods than a financier/owner under a hire-purchase or conditional sale agreement. If the hirer/lessee's possession is outside the protection of the Act, a dishonest refusal to return them will amount to theft. Thus, if the hirer refuses to disclose the whereabouts of the goods, then evidence that the defendant has moved the thing from the place where it should be housed is evidence from which an assumption of the rights of an owner might be inferred. If this is accompanied by the *mens*

[32.] See *R. v. Atakpu* [1994] Q.B. 69.
[33.] *Cf. R. v. Wakeman* (1912) 8 Cr.App.R. 18.

---

rea of theft, this would constitute an assumption of the rights of an owner within the first part of section 3(1) of the Theft Act 1968. Moreover, the hirer will be guilty of an offence if he fails to disclose the whereabouts of goods upon request if there is a controlled agreement and under section 80(2) of the Consumer Credit Act 1974 if the default continues for a period of 14 days after the expiry of the time given under the Act (seven days under section 80(1)) a further offence is committed. Even if appropriation has taken place, it must be demonstrated that there is dishonesty. This is a matter of fact and section 2(1) of the Theft Act 1968 states that there is no dishonesty if the possessor acts "in belief that he has in law the right to deprive the other" of the property.

Appropriation and a Lessee/Hirer

As stated above, a person may be guilty of stealing even though his initial acquisition of the property was lawful and honest, for example, the possession by an equipment lessee under a lease contract. In determining whether appropriation has taken place much will depend upon the terms of the lease contract as this will generally govern the capacity in which the lessee holds the equipment. Thus if the lessee fails to return the goods on termination, in such a case it may be theft to dishonestly fail to return the property. The key issue is whether the acts succeeding the decision to steal indicate an act of assumption of ownership in relation to the property. In this respect it does not matter that the possessor's use of the equipment is consonant with that originally anticipated by the bailment contract. Thus in *R. v. Morgan*,[34] the appellant was held to have been properly convicted of stealing a leased car by an English court when he had taken the car to Ireland and sold it. The evidence showed that the defendant had abandoned his business in England and went to Ireland with no intention of returning to the United Kingdom.

All that is necessary to demonstrate is an act of appropriation. This may be the case where a bailment terminated on a particular date, and there was an obligation to return it by then, which the possessor failed to do. At the same time there are important policy issues, as it is unlikely that a charge of theft could be sustained merely as a result of inertia on the part of the hirer. There must be a prior demand for the return of the property otherwise any prosecution would appear to be vexatious.

Theft and Sub-Bailment

If the lessee parts with possession to a person who is honest at the time of receipt, it is unlikely that any subsequent act of appropriation will be

---

[34.] [1991] R.T.R. 365.

treated as theft from the bailee although it will probably constitute theft from the owner. Since the original bailee at the time of the appropriation is not in factual possession or control of the thing, it is difficult to see that there has been an appropriation against a proprietary interest of the bailee for the purposes of section 5(1) of the Theft Act 1968.

Unlawful Pledge

Where a hirer or lessee pledges the equipment which is the object of the agreement, if there is an intention to redeem the pledge the hirer/lessee will lack the intention to permanently deprive for the purpose of the offence of theft. Section 6(2) of the Theft Act 1968 provides as follows:

"Without prejudice to the generality of subsection (1) above, where a person, having possession or control (lawfully or not) of property belonging to another, parts with the property under a condition as to its return which he may not be able to perform, this (if done for purposes of his own and without the other's authority) amounts to treating the property as his own to dispose of regardless of the other's rights."

It would appear from this that the prosecution will have to show that the defendant must have realised that he could not redeem the pledge in order for the offence to be substantiated. There would appear to be a defence if the defendant believed that he could redeem, because in this circumstance the requisite degree of dishonesty will not be present.

Criminal Damage

The hirer/lessee must take care not to damage the equipment in his possession, otherwise there may be liability for criminal damage. Section 1(1) of the Criminal Damage Act 1971 provides that:

"A person who without lawful excuse destroys or damages any property belonging to another intending to destroy or damage any such property or being reckless as to whether any such property would be destroyed or damaged shall be guilty of an offence."

An objective approach has been adopted so that in *Metropolitan Police Comr v. Caldwell*[35] the House of Lords held that a person is guilty of an offence if the risk of his conduct in damaging the goods would have been obvious to others under the same circumstances, that is an ordinary prudent individual.[36] In the context of leasing it is unlikely that the lessee could have a defence of acting with lawful excuse under section 5(2)(a) of the 1971 Act, since the lessee is obliged to return the goods to

---

[35.] [1982] A.C. 341.
[36.] See *Elliott v. C. (A Minor)* [1983] 1 W.L.R. 939.

the lessor at the end of the lease period. It should be noted that fair wear and tear is by definition outside the terms of the statute because this can hardly constitute damage for this purpose.

Defrauding Creditors

The Theft Act 1978 replaces the unsatisfactory offence of obtaining pecuniary advantage contrary to section 16(2)(a) of the Theft Act 1968. The basis of the new offences is not to deal with failure to pay debts and criminalise such behaviour, rather the offences seek to outlaw debtor behaviour which impedes the creditor in the exercise of his legal remedies. The offences are as follows:

1. Securing the remission of a liability. By virtue of section 2(1)(a) of the Theft Act 1978 a person commits an offence if he:

   "by any deception—

   (a) dishonestly secures the remission of the whole or part of any existing liability to make a payment, whether his own liability or another's."

   A pre-requisite for this offence is that the liability must be legally enforceable. It is irrelevant that the remission is voidable for fraud, as the offence will be committed even though the fraudster does not obtain the benefit intended.

2. Inducing the creditor to wait for or to forgo payment. A person commits an offence under section 2(1)(b) of the 1978 Act if he:

   "by any deception—

   (b) with intent to make permanent default in whole or in part on any existing liability to make a payment, or with intent to let another do so, dishonestly induces the creditor or any person claiming payment on behalf of the creditor to wait for payment (whether or not the due date for payment is deferred) or to forgo payment."

   An offence is committed if it can be shown that the debtor intends to make permanent default, for example by disappearing or making it very difficult for the creditor to trace him. Payment by a worthless cheque is also treated for the purposes of section 3(3) of the Theft Act 1978 as an inducement to wait for payment.

3. Obtaining exemption from or abatement of liability by deception. This offence is provided by virtue of section 2(1)(c) of the Theft Act 1978 and has been discussed above.[37]

Offences by the Dealer

Implied Deception

A dealer who sells non-existent goods or goods that are not his or goods which he merely hopes to acquire may be guilty of obtaining property by

[37.] See p. 311, above.

deception. By offering the goods for sale the dealer must be taken to imply that they are in existence and that he has the right to sell them.

Theft

If the dealer is appointed to receive any deposit on behalf of the finance company and uses the money received for his own purposes and becomes bankrupt, section 5(3) of the Theft Act 1968 provides:

> "Where a person receives property from or on account of another, and is under an obligation to the other to retain and deal with that property or its proceeds in a particular way, the property or proceeds shall be regarded (as against him) as belonging to the other."

The key consideration is whether the dealer is under an obligation, as a matter of the contract between the parties, to deal with the money in a particular way, that is, as principal and agent as distinct from a debtor/creditor relationship.[38]

False Statements as to Goods

The legislation

The Trade Descriptions Act 1968 (the TDA 1968) and the Consumer Protection Act 1987 (the CPA 1987) go a long way to protect the position of consumers in relation to false trade descriptions, misleading pricing and also false statements about services to be supplied. The TDA 1968 creates two main strict liability criminal offences under section 1(1), namely, that of applying a false trade description to goods (section 1(1)(a)), and supplying goods to which a false trade description has been applied (section 1(1)(b)). These offences are confined to the course of a trade or business[39] so that private transactions are excluded. It appears that this includes a club having private membership.[40] The key issue is the question of supply of goods and there is separate provision, under section 14 of TDA 1968, for services. It should be noted that in no way does the TDA 1968 enhance the consumer's contractual rights,[41] its aim simply being to ensure, by criminal sanctions, that the consumer is not misled.

Applying a false trade description to goods

Proof of dishonesty is unnecessary for the offence of applying a false trade description to goods. Section 4 provides:

[38.] See *R. v. Brewster* (1979) 69 Cr.App.R. 375.
[39.] See Chap. 6, above.
[40.] See *John v. Matthews* [1970] 2 Q.B. 443.
[41.] Trade Descriptions Act 1968, s. 35.

"(1) A person applies a trade description to goods if he—

(a) affixes or annexes it to or in any manner marks it on or incorporates it with—

    (i) the goods themselves, or
    (ii) anything in, on or with which the goods are supplied; or

(b) places the goods in, on or with anything which the trade description has been affixed or annexed to, marked on or incorporated with, or places any such thing with the goods; or

(c) uses the trade description in any manner likely to be taken as referring to the goods.

(2) An oral statement may amount to the use of a trade description.

(3) Where the goods are supplied in pursuance of a request in which a trade description is used and the circumstances are such as to make it reasonable to infer that the goods are supplied as goods corresponding to that trade description, the person supplying the goods shall be deemed to have applied that trade description to the goods."

The offence extends to oral misdescription and is not necessarily confined to a contractual relationship with the customer.[42]

The definition of "false trade description" is contained in sections 2 and 3. Section 3 provides that a false trade description is one of material degree and this includes statements which, although literally true, are nevertheless misleading.[43] The term "trade description" is defined comprehensively in section 2(1) as follows:

"A trade description is an indication, direct or indirect, and by whatever means given, of any of the following matters with regard to any goods or part of goods, that is to say:

(a) quantity, size of gauge;

(b) method of manufacture, production, processing or reconditioning;

(c) composition;

(d) fitness of purpose, strength, performance, behaviour or accuracy;

(e) any physical characteristics not included in the preceding paragraphs;

(f) testing by any person and results thereof;

(g) approval by any person or conformity with a type aproved by any person;

(h) place or date of manufacture, production, processing or reconditioning;

(i) person to whom manufactured, produced, processed or reconditioned;

(j) other history, including previous ownership or use."

[42.] *Fletcher v. Sledmore* [1973] R.T.R. 371.
[43.] Trade Descriptions Act 1968, s. 3(2).

In *Cadbury Ltd v. Halliday*,[44] it was decided that the words "Extra value" written on the wrapper of a bar of chocolate did not relate to any of the items listed in section 2 so that no offence was committed. All the items listed in section 2 are matters of which the truth or falsity can be established as a matter of fact. That could not be said of "value" in this case which is essentially a matter of opinion. It was otherwise in *Fletcher v. Budgen*.[45] In this case a private seller wished to sell his car to a car dealer. The dealer said that there was no possibility of repairing the car and that it had only scrap value. As a result the car was sold to him for £2. The dealer spent £56 repairing it and then advertised it at a price of £135. It was held to be an offence under section 2(1)(a), the description falling within section 2(1)(c). The Act applied even though the description was applied by a prospective trade *buyer*, which is of course the reverse of the normal situation.

Section 1 of the TDA 1968 is a powerful deterrent and can apply to an honest trader who misdescribes his goods or, as we have seen, goods that he acquires. In *R. v. Ford Motor Company*,[46] the Court of Appeal had to determine whether the trade description "new" was a false one where a car, damaged in the care of forwarding agents, was repaired and supplied by the dealer as a "new car". The court held that a new car which is damaged and then repaired so as to be "as good as new" can still be regarded as "new". Much depends upon the type of damage and the quality of the repairs so that, for example, where an engine is damaged, a car may be restored to newness through a new engine being installed. It should be noted that the criterion "new" applies not just to the condition of the car but also with regard to whether the car has been registered. Thus in *R v. Anderson*,[47] the defendant had sold, as new, a Nissan car which, though in mint condition, had been registered in the retailer's name. The Court of Appeal upheld the defendant's conviction on the basis that a purchaser would understand the description "new" to indicate that the vehicle had had no previous registered keeper.

A mileometer reading on a motor vehicle is a trade description within the Act. A person who sells a vehicle in the course of his trade or business is supplying the vehicle with the description attached.[48] If, however, the motor trader defendant is not responsible for turning back the mileometer and covers up the reading,[49] the motor trader should be

[44.] [1975] 1 W.L.R. 649.
[45.] [1974] 1 W.L.R. 1056.
[46.] [1974] 1 W.L.R. 1200.
[47.] *The Times*, December 31, 1987.
[48.] *Holloway v. Cross* (1980) 125 S.J. 46; [1981] 1 All E.R. 1012; [1981] R.T.R. 146 D.C.
[49.] The doctrine of disclaimer has no application where the defendant himself is the culprit, that is, the one who has applied the description. Thus in *Newman v. Hackney L.B.C.* [1982] R.T.R. 296, a motor dealer turned back a mileometer from 46328 to 21000 and then stuck a disclaim over it. It was held that this later action did not prevent the commission of an offence under s. 1(1)(a). See also *R. v. Southwood* [1987] 1 W.L.R. 1361.

able to escape from liability on the basis that no false description was in fact applied to the goods.[50] Any notice of disclaimer, provided that it is "bold, precise and compelling",[51] should establish the defence. In the case where the disclaimer itself is misleading, this will amount to a false trade description.[52] Significantly, the TDA 1968 applies in auction situations strict liability to a false trade description which cannot be excluded by a disclaimer, even though, as a matter of civil law, such an exclusion clause could satisfy the reasonableness test under UCTA 1977.[53]

Supplying or offering to supply goods

The expression "offering to supply" was given a wide meaning by section 6 in order to avoid the difficulty found in *Fisher v. Bell*.[54] In this case flick knives displayed in a window were categorised by the court as an "invitation to treat" rather than an offer for sale. Section 6 avoids this problem by extending to "exposing goods for supply". The main issue here is "possession for supply" and it is sufficient if the goods are in a stock room so that, in effect, they do not have to be exposed for supply at the business premises of the supplier.[55] The word "supply" is a wide one and covers free gifts offered in the course of a business as well as extending to hire and hire-purchase transactions.

Where the false trade description has not been applied by the retailer, the special defence of "reasonable diligence" in section 24(3) of the TDA 1968 may be relied upon. This is different from the general defence of "due diligence" which looks for proof of mistaken belief. Under the special defence, the issue is whether the defendant did not know and could not with reasonable diligence have discovered, the false trade description. However, if the retailer knows of the trade description even though he is not aware of its falsity, the offence is committed.[56]

Trade Descriptions used in Advertisements

The TDA 1968 makes special provision for advertisements. "Advertisement" is widely defined under section 39(1) to include a catalogue, a

---

[50.] Trade Descriptions Act 1968, s. 1(1)(b). The practice of zeroing a mileometer amounts to "applying a false trade description". See *R. v. Southwood* [1987] 3 All E.R. 556. If a disclaimer is also included it could be argued that this does not mislead anyone. See *Lill Holdings v. White* [1979] R.T.R. 120. In *Waltham Forest London Borough Council v. T.G. Wheatley (General Garage) Ltd (No. 2)* [1978] R.T.R. 333 at 339, Lord Widgery held: "The purpose of the disclaimer is for it to sit beside, as it were, the false trade description and cancel the other out as soon as its first impression can be made on the purchaser".

[51.] See *Zawadski v. Sleigh* [1975] R.T.R. 113.

[52.] *Corfield v. Starr* [1981] R.T.R. 380.

[53.] See *Derbyshire County Council v. Vincent, The Times*, June 19, 1990.

[54.] [1961] 1 Q.B. 394.

[55.] *Stainthorpe v. Bailey* [1980] R.T.R. 7.

[56.] *Tarleton Engineering Co. v. Nattrass* [1973] 1 W.L.R. 1261.

circular and a price list. The trade description must be made in the course of a trade or business and be part of the advertisement, so that genuine news items are excluded. Section 5(2) states that the trade description shall be taken as referring to all goods of the class, whether or not in existence at the time the advertisement is published. In determining whether goods are of a class to which an advertised trade description relates, section 5(3) provides that regard shall be had not only to the form and content of the advertisement but also to the time, place, manner and frequency of its publication and all other matters making it likely or unlikely that a person to whom the goods are supplied would think of the goods as belonging to the class in question.

Misleading Price Indications

Misleading price indications is now regulated by Part 3 of the CPA 1987. A new general offence of giving a misleading price indication is provided in section 20. The question of what is misleading is determined under section 21 on the basis of an objective test and extends to both the price itself and any method of determining the price. It should be noted that the offence only applies where a misleading price indication is given to a consumer by a person in the course of his business. The new provisions apply not only to goods but also to services, accommodation or facilities. Section 20(6) defines "consumer" as follows:

"(a) in relation to any goods, it means any person who might wish to be supplied with the goods for his own private use or consumption;

(b) in relation to any services or facilities, it means any person who might wish to be provided with the services or facilities otherwise than for the purposes of any business of his; and

(c) in relation to any accommodation, it means any person who might wish to occupy the accommodation otherwise than for the purposes of any business of his."

In laying down the offences, section 20 distinguishes according to whether or not the price indication was misleading when it was given. If this is the case, two defences are available to the defendant. First, the due diligence defence in sections 24 and 39; secondly, that he was a prior party in the chain of distribution recommending a price which, under section 24(4), he reasonably believed was being followed. Where an advertisement becomes subsequently misleading, an offence is committed under section 20(2) if, in the course of a business, the supplier reasonably expected reliance on the advertisement and he has not taken steps which are reasonable to prevent reliance on this indication. It is not necessary in a section 20 prosecution for indicating misleading prices to produce an individual customer to whom the misleading price was indicated.[57]

[57.] *MFI Furniture Centres Ltd v. Hibbert, The Times,* July 21, 1995.

There is no doubt that in determining compliance with sections 20 to 21 of the CPA 1987, the initiatives of the Office of Fair Trading in encouraging business self-regulation through codes of practice will be highly relevant. This is anticipated under section 25(1) which gives the Secretary of State, after consulting the Director General of Fair Trading, the power to issue such codes of practice containing detailed guidance as to illegitimate price comparisons and price-related matters. Compliance by the defendant with the code may be relied upon by him for the purpose of showing that the commission of an offence under sections 20 and 21 has not been established. By containing such provision in a code, the Secretary of State has power to alter it or withdraw approval. Such an approach ensures flexibility in an ever-changing market situation.

Persons contravening section 20 are liable on conviction on indictment to a fine not exceeding the statutory maximum under section 20(4). Prosecutions under section 20, in common with other consumer protection legislation (for example section 19(1) of the TDA 1968), must be brought either by the end of the period of three years from the day that the offence was committed, or within one year of its discovery by the prosecutor, whichever is the earlier.[58]

Bribery and Corruption

The dealer and customer may set out to defraud a finance house, and this will often involve an inducement to the retailer/supplier. The substantive law can be found in section 1(1) of the Prevention of Corruption Act 1906, which provides:

> "If any agent corruptly accepts or obtains, or agrees to accept or attempts to obtain, from any person, for himself or for any other person, any gift or consideration as an inducement or reward for doing or forbearing to do, or for having after the passing of this Act done or forborne to do, any act in relation to his principal's affairs or business, or for showing or forbearing to show favour or disfavour to any person in relation to his principal's affairs or business; or
> If any person corruptly gives or agrees to give or offers any gift or consideration to any agent as an inducement or reward for doing or forbearing to do, or for having after the passing of this Act done or forborne to do, any act in relation to his principal's affairs or business, or for showing or forbearing to show favour or disfavour to any person in relation to his principal's affairs or business; or
> If any person knowingly gives to any agent, or if any agent knowingly uses with intent to deceive his principal, any receipt, account, or other document in respect of which the principal is interested, and which contains any statement which is false or erroneous or defective in any material particular, and which to his knowledge is intended to mislead the principal; he shall be guilty of [an offence]."

[58.] Consumer Protection Act 1987, s. 20(5).

In addition, if the dealer acts in collusion with the buyer/acquirer in an attempt to deceive the finance house he can be convicted as an aider and abettor of the customer's offences.

Fraudulent Trading

It is an offence to trade whilst knowing that there was no chance of meeting the commitment made. In this respect section 458 of the Companies Act 1985 provides:

> "If any business of a company is carried on with intent to defraud creditors of the company or creditors of any other person, or for any fraudulent purpose, every person who was knowingly a party to the carrying on of the business in that manner is liable to imprisonment or a fine, or both.
> This applies whether or not the company has been, or is in the course of being, wound up."

This offence is punishable with seven years imprisonment.[59]

Dishonesty must be proven and this is a matter for the jury according to the standard of "reasonable and honest people".[60] The main difficulty with this offence is that it will not apply against an unincorporated individual businessman. However, following *R. v. Gomez*,[61] if the business man knows that he is unable to provide or may not be able to provide the goods or services for which he is still taking orders and cash deposits he may be convicted of theft. It is only necessary to show the assumption of any rights of the owner for there to be appropriation.[62]

Offences by Creditors

Introduction

Self-help is one of the oldest remedies available for the creditor. The possibility of repossession of the equipment by the lessor is predicated upon the idea that the equipment is worth more than the costs involved with repossession. In this respect, it may be possible for the financier/owner to insure against depreciation in the residual value of the equipment at the end of the lease term. Often the equipment will be unique and not easily marketable so that, for example, a lessor may have difficulty in recovering the cost of his investment in a film by seizing it if the film suffers at the box office. It would follow that, as a matter of

[59.] Companies Act 1985, Sched. 24.
[60.] *R. v. Lockwood* [1986] Crim. L.R. 244.
[61.] [1993] 1 All E.R. 1.
[62.] See pp. 314–317, above.

prudence, the lessor should institute a thorough credit-check on every prospective lessee, and to assist in this regard, sophisticated computer programs have been devised which assess such factors as the financial soundness of the lessee, the type of equipment to be leased, and the conditions of the leasing contract. Additionally, the lessor should monitor the lessee's creditworthiness throughout the term of the lease so that problems can be identified and acted upon as soon as possible.

Repossession and the Consumer Credit Act 1974

Repossession, as the most dramatic illustration of self-help exercised by the creditor, is rigorously controlled by the Consumer Credit Act 1974 (the CCA 1974) with regard to regulated hire or hire-purchase or conditional sale agreements.[62a]

Repossession without the issue of a statutorily required default notice may give rise to an action for wrongful interference with goods under the Torts (Interference with Goods) Act 1977. Such an action will not normally constitute theft by the creditor, as section 170(1) of the Consumer Credit Act 1974 makes it plain that no criminal liability is incurred merely as a result of a breach of the terms of the Act.

Repossession outside of the Consumer Credit Act 1974

Introduction

In exercising recovery of goods outside of the Consumer Credit Act context, the creditor must exercise the greatest care to ensure that he does not commit the numerous offences to which he is potentially exposed.

Theft

The Theft Act 1968 qualifies possession under section 5(1) of the Act by providing that property belongs to:

"any person having possession or control of it, or having in it any proprietary right or interest (not being an equitable interest arising only from an agreement to transfer or grant an interest)."

It has been held that a person may be guilty of theft from his bailee at will for example, a repairer of a vehicle.[63] Such an approach is difficult to reconcile with principle, because surely the creditor in that circumstance (lawful termination) will have a better right to immediate possession so it can hardly be said that repossession in those circumstances will amount to

[62a.] See above pp. 120–121.
[63.] *R. v. Turner (No. 2)* [1971] 1 W.L.R. 901.

an appropriation. Furthermore, where the creditor acts genuinely in the belief of a right to possession there would appear to be an overwhelming difficulty of proving the requisite dishonesty of intention.[64]

Blackmail

This is defined in section 21 of the Theft Act 1968 as follows:

"(1)   A person is guilty of blackmail if, with a view to gain for himself or another or with intent to cause loss to another, he makes any unwarranted demand with menaces; and for this purpose a demand with menaces is unwarranted unless the person making it does so in the belief—

(a)   that he has reasonable grounds for making the demand; and

(b)   that the use of the menaces is a proper means of reinforcing the demand.

(2)   The nature of the act or omission demanded is immaterial, and it is also immaterial whether the menaces relate to action to be taken by the person making the demand."

The issue is whether the creditor has or believes that he has a reasonable ground for making the demand. It is likely that the defaulting debtor will have committed one of the documentary offences, or other offences, and that in this circumstance the action of the creditor in threatening to call the police would appear to be a proper means of reinforcing the demand.

Unlawful entry

Where a creditor acts in the belief that he has a right to property, then by definition he cannot commit burglary because he does not intend to commit theft. Nonetheless, if violence is used for the purpose of entry to repossess the goods, it is likely that an offence will be committed under section 6(1) of the Criminal law Act 1977, which provides as follows:

"Subject to the following provisions of this section, any person who without lawful authority, uses or threatens violence for the purpose of securing entry into any premises for himself or any other person is guilty of an offence, provided that—

(a)   there is someone present on those premises at the time who is opposed to the entry which the violence is intended to secure; and

(b)   the person using or threatening the violence knows that that is the case."

The offence is punishable summarily so the creditor will expose himself to the potential penalty of six months imprisonment.

[64.] *R. v. Gomez* [1993] 1 All E.R. 1.

There is also the criminal offence of unlawful harassment of debtors encapsulated in section 40(1) of the Administration of Justice Act 1970, which provides:

"(1) A person commits an offence if, with the object of coercing another person to pay money claimed from the other a debt due under a contract, he—

  (a) harasses the other with demands for payment such, in respect of their frequency or the manner or occasion of making any such demand, or of any threat or publicity by which any demand is accompanied, are calculated to subject him or members of his family or household to alarm, distress or humiliation."

The Act is notoriously imprecise in scope. It provides a defence for anything done by a person which is reasonable for the following purposes under section 40(3)(a): "of securing the discharge of an obligation due, or believed by him to be due, to himself or to persons for whom he acts, or protecting himself or them from future loss"; or, under section 40(3)(b) "of the enforcement of any liability by legal process". The difficulty here is the precise determination of reasonableness within the meaning of section 40(3).

A closely related concept is that of criminal damage to the goods in the process of recovery. If the lessor has the right to repossess the goods, then the fact that the lessee has custody of the goods should not take priority over the superior right of the owner/ lessor. In this respect in *R. v. Judge*[65] the seller of a car on a conditional sale agreement was held to be not guilty of criminal damage when he smashed its windows but was unsuccessful in removing it from the buyer's garage, who had not paid the instalments due under the agreement.

[65.] (1974) 138 J.P. 649.

Part 4

Insolvency and International Leasing

Chapter 13

The Impact of Insolvency

Introduction

A distinction should be drawn between the fact of insolvency and the *status* of bankruptcy (in the case of an individual) or winding up (in the case of a company). It is possible for insolvency proceedings to take place in response to a cash-flow crisis, that is where assets are not sufficiently liquid to satisfy present liabilities or, alternatively, insolvency proceedings may be initiated in the case of absolute or balance sheet insolvency where the total debts, present, future, contingent, exceed the assets even if they were realised at their most favourable rate. Bankruptcy is a status conferred by law, namely, a creditor to whom full and timely payment has not been made can initiate insolvency proceedings on the basis that the debtor's insolvency can be inferred from all the circumstances.

Insolvency proceedings form an important exception to the general hostility of English law to class actions, so section 130(4) of the Insolvency Act 1986 provides that an order for winding-up operates in favour of all creditors and contributories of the company, as if made on a joint petition of a creditor and of a contributory. This chapter will focus mainly upon the equipment lease in the various stages leading up to the bankruptcy or winding-up of the lessee/hirer.

Enforcement of Equipment Leases and Insolvency

The Equipment Lessor and Liquidator or Trustee in Bankruptcy

The essence of the legal mechanism of an equipment lease is ownership and, as such, this may be exercised to recover possession of the goods by the financier/lessor.[1] It is otherwise in relation to leased rentals due, where the liquidator only assumes personal liability in respect of these if he has used the goods for the purposes of assisting the winding-up. In the case of bankruptcy, the trustee in bankruptcy will be personally liable for rentals during the bankruptcy, but will be able to recover this

---

[1] See *General Share and Trust Co. v. Wetley Brick and Pottery Co.* (1882) 20 Ch. D. 260; *Ezekiel v. Orakpo* [1977] Q.B. 260 (bankruptcy proceedings).

sum from the estate as an expense of the bankruptcy, and this constitutes a super-preferential right.

The Equipment Lessor and Administrative Receiver

Administrative receivership is not a true collective insolvency proceeding because, in substance, it is a method by which the debenture holder can enforce his security. There is no personal liability against the administrative receiver in relation to current or outstanding rentals. An automatic termination clause in the equipment lease contract will visit personal liability upon the administrative receiver, as his possession and continued use will be under a new contract with him. In this regard he will have a right of indemnity out of the assets of the company.[2] Of course the equipment lessor will be able to recover possession of the asset as owner on termination of the lease or otherwise as a result of repudiation by virtue of non-payment of rentals.

The Equipment Lessor and the Administrator

Introduction

Although insolvency proceedings promote the collective will, it is doubtful whether the repossession of collateral by the secured creditor should interfere with this insolvency goal since, if the secured party's collateral is worth more to the firm than the third party, the collateral should end up back in the hands of the firm, notwithstanding its repossession by the secured creditor in the interim. In practice though, there is no doubt that such repossession would hinder efforts to preserve the firm as a "going concern", and there may be substantial costs involved in repossession and subsequent repurchase. One way of balancing the tensions here is to substitute for a secured party's actual substantive *rights* a requirement that the secured creditor accept the equivalent *value* of those rights.[3] There is nothing anomalous in this approach, because if the firm is worth more as a going concern than if it is broken up, giving the secured creditor the benefit of his bargain should not prevent a firm from staying together. Indeed, a failure to recognise the secured creditor's rights in full would prejudice the bankruptcy goal of ensuring the assets are used to advance the interests of everyone.

An overall strategy advocated by the Cork Committee,[4] was for the provision of effective alternatives to the winding up of an insolvent, or near-insolvent company, where there exist reasonable prospects of

---

[2.] Insolvency Act 1986, s. 44(1).
[3.] See generally the Insolvency Act 1986, s. 43(1).
[4.] See Cork Committee Report, *Insolvency Law and Practice* (Cmnd. 8558 (1982)).

reviving the company. The administration order was one of the main planks to this objective. This procedure envisages the appointment of an administrator whose task is one of creative rehabilitation of the company with a view to leaving it in a better economic condition than when he found it while, at the same time, safeguarding the interests of the secured creditors. In a sense, the administrator is the official corporate "rescuer" who attempts to salvage the company before it becomes too damaged by the problems of insolvency. In this respect, he enjoys wide-ranging powers to deal with situations which may hinder the realisation of this aim.

The effect of administration

The corollary to the transfer of all managerial power to the administrator is that the powers of the directors are, in practice, suspended for the duration of the administration order.[5] Furthermore, the administrator has power to remove any director in order to achieve the purposes for which he was appointed.[6]

The presentation of a petition for an administration order marks the beginning of a statutory moratorium over the company's affairs. During this period, no security can be enforced,[7] and neither can goods held under retention of title agreements be repossessed without the leave of the court. No resolution for winding up can be made.[8] This does not preclude the presentation of a *petition* for the winding up of the company, but the petition will not be disposed of until the administration order is dismissed. Finally, no other proceedings, and no execution or other legal process may be commenced or continued, and no distress may be levied against the company or its property without the leave of the court.[9] It is worth noting that the general effect of these provisions is that they do not constitute a freeze on the enforcement of other proprietary rights. Of course, there is a problem of legal form here because, presumably, a purchaser of book debts would not be covered, whilst a mortgagee or chargee of such debts who, without consent, collects payment from the account debtor would fall within the scope of the prohibition.

When the administration order has been made, the moratorium on enforcement is similar to that which applies on presentation of the petition, but with the additional option of enforcement taking place with the consent of the administrator.[10] However, no administrative receiver may be appointed and, except with the consent of the administrator or the leave of the court, no winding-up petition may be presented.[11] The

---

[5.] Insolvency Act 1986, s. 14(2).
[6.] See *Re P. & C. and R. & T. (Stockport) Ltd* [1991] B.C.L.C. 366.
[7.] Insolvency Act 1986, s. 10(1)(b).
[8.] Insolvency Act 1986, s. 10(1)(a).
[9.] Insolvency Act 1986, s. 10(1)(c).
[10.] Insolvency Act 1986, s. 11(3)(c).
[11.] Insolvency Act 1986, s. 11(3)(d).

question of the enforcement of security and the rights of creditors, as well as the particular issue of obtaining the leave of the courts under section 11(3)(c), arose in *Re Atlantic Computers Systems plc*.[12] It is worth setting out the facts as they illustrate starkly the issues involved in this context.

An administrative order was made in relation to *Atlantic Computers plc* in April 1990. The problem was that, in many cases, the computers being leased were not actually owned by the company but by "funders" who included the Norwich Union and the Allied Irish Bank plc. The computers were let to the company under hire-purchase agreements or leases and then sub-let to end users. The administrators requested the end users to continue paying their rental to the company, which amounted to over £1.7 million in the period April to June. However, no payments had been made to the funders under the head-leases and hire-purchase agreements. Section 11(3)(c) of the Insolvency Act 1986 provides that during the period of an administration order, no steps may be taken to enforce security over the company's property or to repossess goods in the company's possession except with the administrator's consent, which had been refused, or the leave of the court.

The funders applied to the court so as to determine whether they could receive their contractual payments during the administration; whether the goods were in the company's possession for the purposes of seeking leave under section 11(3)(c) when technically they were in the hands of the end users; and whether that leave would be granted. They finally resorted to the last-ditch protection provision in section 27 of the Insolvency Act 1986, which allows a creditor to apply for relief of unfairly prejudicial conduct in the management of the company by the administrator (which is similarly worded to the provision in section 459 of the Companies Act 1985). At first instance,[13] Ferris J. held[14] that where property belonging to another was used in the company's business whilst the administration order was in force, the contractual payments were "an expense of the administration" and had to be paid to the owner. The question of leave was not relevant because Ferris J. held that the equipment was in the physical possession of the end users and was not in the company's possession within section 11(3)(c).

The Court of Appeal did not agree with any of these points and in particular stated that, although it was clear that there was a concept of liquidation expenses and that the court had an overriding discretion under section 130(2) of the Insolvency Act 1986 to direct the liquidator to make payments as an expense of the liquidation in a situation such as this, there was no such entitlement in respect of administrative receivership. The essence of an administration was flexibility, and the hard and fast rules of the liquidation were not relevant. Therefore, such expenses would not automatically rank as administration expenses. Thus it would

---

[12] [1992] Ch. 505. For a discussion of the commercial context see pp. 16–17 above.

[13] [1990] B.C.C. 439.

[14] *Ibid*, at 454.

appear that contractual payments were unlikely to gain any priority and the real issue, therefore, was the question of leave actually to enforce the security.

On the question of leave, the Court of Appeal first held that section 11(3)(c) did apply because the goods were within the company's possession and so could not be repossessed, except with the administrator's consent or the leave of the court; secondly, the court referred to the principles governing the exercise of this leave which will be an important question for many creditors in this situation. Not surprisingly, the Court of Appeal held that leave would not automatically be granted and referred to the decision of Peter Gibson J. in *Re Meesan Investments Ltd*,[15] where it had been held that the court had a general discretion, and had to have regard to all the relevant circumstances. It would appear to be very much a balancing exercise between the likely outcome of the administration and the effect on the applicants if leave is refused. The Court of Appeal granted leave (which had been refused in *Re Meesan Investments Ltd*) after looking at the terms of the hire-purchase and lease agreements, the company's financial position, the administrator's proposals, the effect on the administration if it was refused. Other factors were the prospect of a successful outcome to the administration if leave was refused, and the conduct of the parties.

Certainly, there must be some sympathy with the position of the funders because large sums of contractual payments which were due to them were being used to keep the company in business, but the deciding factors seem to have been the realisation that the position was hopeless, in any event, since the administration was only a prelude to liquidation. The Court of Appeal stressed that section 11(3)(c) was not intended to strengthen the administrator's negotiating position when he sought to modify the funders' proprietary rights under an administration proposal. The balance, therefore rested with the funders.

This decision is important in laying down some guidelines which assist in assessing when the court will grant leave for a creditor to enforce his security or repossess his property. Nevertheless, it should not be viewed as any relaxation of the moratorium rule. In order for the balance to be weighed in favour of the creditor, it may be that he would have to be seeking repossession of his own property in circumstances where the administration cannot succeed in rescuing the company. Any counterbalancing points will more likely than not result in leave being refused. It was stressed in *Re Meesan Investments Ltd* that the onus of establishing that leave should be granted is firmly on the creditor and that the bank, in that case, was likely to be repaid in full within a reasonable time, even though the administration had continued for 10 months. Accordingly, the secured creditor, when seeking leave under section 11(3) to enforce his security, must show that it was a proper case for leave to be given. In this respect, the discretion exercised by the court

[15.] (1988) 4 B.C.C. 788.

will take into account all the circumstances, and it is not essential to demonstrate some criticism of the administrator's conduct.[16] In the Practice Guidelines (Insolvency Administration) issued by the Court of Appeal following its decision in *Re Atlantic Computers*, the following factors were highlighted as being relevant for the granting of leave under section 11(3):

1. Where the existence, validity or nature of the security sought to be enforced was in dispute, the court only needed to be satisfied that the applicant had a seriously arguable case.

2. Each case called for the exercise of judgment, in which the court sought to give effect to the purpose of the statutory provision having regard to the parties' interests and all the circumstances of the case.

3. In carrying out the balancing exercise, great weight was to be given to proprietary interests.

4. It would normally be sufficient ground for the grant of leave if significant loss would be caused to the applicant, but this has to be balanced with loss caused to others by the grant of leave. In assessing these respective losses, the court would have regard to such matters as the company's financial position, the administrator's proposals, the period during which the administration order had been in force and was expected to remain in force, the effect on the administration if leave were given, the effect on the applicant if leave were refused, the end result sought to be achieved by the administration and the prospects of it being achieved.[17]

5. It was necessary to balance the probability of suggested consequences of leave being granted or refused.

6. The conduct of the parties might be relevant to the issue of granting or refusing leave, to a decision to impose terms if leave was granted, or conditional upon the administrator's particular conduct of the administration.[18]

In *Re David Meek Plant Hire Ltd*[19] it was held that goods let on hire-purchase and physically in the possession of the company were subject to the moratorium provisions in administration. The court referred to the need of completing a balancing exercise, and it was held that the loss to individual finance companies in not being allowed to repossess the goods was outweighed by the following factors: first, if these finance

---

[16.] See *Royal Trust Bank v. Buchler* [1989] B.C.L.C. 130.
[17.] See *Bristol Airport plc v. Powdrill* [1992] Ch. 744.
[18.] See Insolvency Act 1986, ss. 14(3), 17.
[19.] [1994] 1 B.C.L.C. 680.

companies succeeded it would he hard to resist like claims from other finance companies thereby aborting any possible proposals to the creditors' meeting from the administrators; secondly, the abrupt termination of trading would have endangered the collection of outstanding book debts given the nature of the business, that is equipment used by the construction industry held by the hirer under hire-purchase but then hired out by them to end-users.

Powers of the administrator

The general powers conferred upon an administrator are wide-ranging and he is expressly empowered to do "all such things as may be necessary for the management of the affairs, business and property of the company".[20] A principle aspect of the legal status of the administrator is that, in exercising his powers, he is deemed to be acting as agent of the company.[21] The effect of this is that the company is bound by and is liable in respect of all acts validly performed by the administrator. Moreover, third parties are protected in their dealings with the administrator, because so long as they are dealing in good faith and for value, they need not inquire whether the administrator is acting within his powers.[22]

Once in office, the administrator has considerable power to deal with charged property under section 15 of the Insolvency Act 1986. Under section 15(1), where there is property of the company subject to a security which, as created, was a floating charge, the administrator may dispose of or otherwise exercise his powers in relation to that property as though it was not subject to the security. Sub-section (4) supplies the necessary protection for the holder of the security in question by providing that where property is disposed of in this manner, the charge-holder shall have the same priority, in respect of any property directly or indirectly representing the property disposed of, as he would have had in respect of the property subject to the security in its original form. The administrator can dispose of goods in the company's possession which are subject to a retention of title clause, including hire-purchase, conditional sale and chattel leases, as if they were unencumbered. This is achieved following an application by the administrator to the court under section 15(2). However, the court must be satisfied that the disposal would be likely to promote the purpose or one or more of the purposes specified in the administration order.[23] In this respect, section 15(5) and (6) provide:

"(5) It shall be a condition of an order under subsection (2) that—

(a) the net proceeds of the disposal, and

[20.] Insolvency Act 1986, s. 14(1), Sched. 1.
[21.] Insolvency Act 1986, s. 14(5).
[22.] Insolvency Act 1986, s. 14(6).
[23.] Insolvency Act 1986, s. 8.

(b) where those proceeds are less than such amount as may be determined by the court to be the net amount which would be realised on a sale of the property or goods in the open market by a willing vendor, such sums as may be required to make good the deficiency,

shall be applied towards discharging the sums secured by the security or payable under the hire-purchase agreement.

(6) Where a condition imposed in pursuance of subsection (5) relates to two or more securities, that condition requires the net proceeds of the disposal and, where paragraph (b) of that subsection applies, the sums mentioned in that paragraph to be applied towards discharging the sums secured by those securities in the order of their priorities."

This would appear to allow the administrator to transfer the full rights of ownership, even in a complex lease structure binding upon a head-lessor. Furthermore, whilst consent is conditional upon the net proceeds of disposal being applied in accordance with section 15(5), this is especially problematical in the equipment leasing context. The reason for this is that the outstanding sums payable under the agreement may be far less than the full value of the lessor's interest in the goods, but it would appear that only the outstanding sums must be accounted for. However, it is probable that the court in giving its consent under section 15(2) will require that the lessor's full interest is protected. In addition the court is under an obligation to account to the owner for the net proceeds of sale or open-market value, whichever is higher. In this respect the court is under no obligation to view the invoice value at the time of supply as being equivalent to the market value on disposal.[24] An estimate must be made of the price which would be realised in an open market, on a particular date, where there existed reasonable competitive conditions.[25]

The effect of automatic termination clauses

A pre-condition to the application of administration is that the goods are in the possession of the company at the time of the administration. It could be argued that a provision in an equipment lease providing for termination before administration would mean that the company's continued possession at the time of administration was unlawful. This argument was rejected in *Re David Meek Access Ltd*, where it was held that the phrase "goods in the company's possession under any hire-purchase agreement" in sections 10(1)(b), 11(3)(c) and 15(2)(b) of the Insolvency Act 1986 covered goods which were still in the company's physical possession, irrespective of any automatic termination clause which terminated the agreements before presentation of a petition for an administration order. A distinction was drawn, however, in respect of the situation where finance companies had actually sought to recover

[24.] See *Re ARV Aviation Ltd* [1989] B.C.L.C. 664.
[25.] See *Duke of Buccleuch v. Inland Revenue Commissioners* [1967] 1 A.C. 506.

their equipment before the petition for the administration order was presented, but had been prevented from doing so.

Sub-Letting of the Goods on Insolvency or Assignment of Sub-Rentals

Clearly, the finance lessor will be interested in continuing the sub-lease on the insolvency of the lessee. The alternative of repossession will be costly, and full recovery of damages under a minimum payment clause or otherwise may be impossible where there are insufficient funds. The lessor will often re-lease the goods on different terms to those in the original lease in order to satisfy the needs of the new lessee. Determining the fair market value of the lease in order to award market price damages will be extremely difficult when the only evidence of the secondary market is the re-lease itself. Some leases set forth the anticipated value of the goods following the termination of the lease, providing that upon breach the lessee is liable for all future rentals plus the termination value minus the proceeds of any release. As an alternative, it is possible to set forth the depreciated value of the goods at given periods during the lease and provide that the lessee should have a credit against future rentals for the depreciation saved by early cancellation. If the figures in these schedules represent bona fide approximations of the actual values, such clauses should be upheld.

The assignment of the benefit of the lease, for example the rights of the lessee under the sub-lease including the right to terminate or to accept termination by the sub-lessee, will only bind the lessee's liquidator if it was made before the commencement of the compulsory winding up of the company.[26] Such an assignment to the finance lessor of the sub-rentals due could be categorised as a charge of the lessee's book debts which will be void as against the liquidator unless registered.[27]

Disclaimer of Leases in Liquidation and Bankruptcy

Introduction

The power to disclaim is available to liquidators and trustees to enable the assets of the company or the bankrupt's estate to be effectively wound up. Where the lessee is in administrative receivership or administration the objective is not generally to wind-up affairs and there is therefore no power for an administrative receiver or administrator to disclaim. A liquidator (whether in voluntary or compulsory liquidation) or trustee in bankruptcy may disclaim the lease under the powers given by sections 178 to 182 of the Insolvency Act 1986 (for liquidation) and

---

[26.] *Cf. Re Atlantic Computers Systems plc* [1992] Ch. 505.
[27.] Companies Act 1985, s. (1)(e). See pp. 114, above.

sections 315 to 320 of the 1986 Act (for bankruptcy), which consolidate and modify the law as formerly stated in the Bankruptcy Act 1914 and the Companies Acts.

The liquidator or trustee can disclaim "onerous property", which means any unprofitable contract which is unsaleable or not readily saleable or is such that it may give rise to a liability to pay money or perform any other onerous act.[28] An equipment lease will normally be onerous property as it will give rise to a liability to pay money and contain other onerous covenants.

The effect of disclaimer

In general disclaimer ends the relationship between the equipment lessor and lessee. It also absolves a trustee in bankruptcy from personal liability. One of the technical oddities of disclaimer was the principle laid down in *Stacey v. Hill*,[29] to the effect that where the lease had not been assigned and it was the original equipment lessee in possession who was insolvent, the effect of the disclaimer was that it ended the liability even of a guarantor. The rationale of this rule was expressed in terms of the principle of co-extensiveness in the law of guarantees, under which the liability of a surety is dependent upon the continuing existence of the liability of the principal debtor.[30] Whilst this proposition is true it fails to take into account the effect of section 178(4)(b) of the Insolvency Act 1986 to the effect that whereas disclaimer operates to determine the insolvent's liabilities under the lease, it does not affect the rights or liabilities of other persons, including a surety. In this respect the House of Lords in *Hindcastle Ltd v. Attenborough Associates Ltd and others*[31] expressly overruled *Stacey v. Hill*. The policy position was eloquently expressed by Lord Nicholls[32]:

"... it is essential to have in mind that the fundamental purpose of an ordinary guarantee of another's debt is that the risk of the principal debtor's insolvency shall fall on the guarantor and not the creditor. If the debtor is unable to pay his debt when it becomes due, his bankruptcy does not release the guarantor ... The guarantor has a right of proof for whatever that may be worth as a creditor of the debtor's estate ... The guarantor remains liable to the landlord. The guarantor loses his right to an indemnity from the insolvent tenant, but in place the statute gives him a right to prove as a creditor of the insolvent tenant's estate. Thus there is no question of the guarantor's right to an indemnity being confiscated. After disclaimer the guarantor's position is no different from the position of any unsecured guarantor of a debtor who becomes insolvent. Had there been no disclaimer the guarantor's right of indemnity would have led only to a right to prove

[28] Insolvency Act 1986, ss. 178, 315(2).
[29] [1901] 1 K.B. 660.
[30] See *Murphy v Sawyer-Hoare and Another* [1994] 2 B.C.L.C. 39.
[31] [1996] 1 All E.R. 737.
[32] *Ibid.* at 753.

against the insolvent's estate. The disclaimer provisions do not change this. The Act leaves the loss consequent upon the tenant's bankruptcy where the parties to the guarantee intended. In addition, the guarantor can take steps to obtain some return from the property by applying to the court for a vesting order, if necessary seeking an extension of time for this purpose."

In the context of landlord and tenant law, it should also be noted that the guarantor may now be entitled to an overriding lease under section 19 of the Landlord and Tenant (Covenants) Act 1995. An important effect of this legislation, which abolishes the doctrine of privity of contract in relation to assignments by landlords and tenants, is that a tenant who assigns premises demised to him is released from his obligations under the tenant covenants, and under the new legislation this will also release the guarantor. However, in the case of a lease granted before January 1, 1996 (the date of the coming into force of the Act), the effect of a disclaimer under section 178 of the Insolvency Act 1986 is that the termination of an insolvent company tenant's liabilities does not affect the obligations to the landlord of a guarantor of the company, whether the company is the original tenant or an assignee.[33]

Automatic Termination Clauses and Insolvency

Where a clause providing for automatic termination on insolvency is included in the leasing agreement, the lessor is seeking to recover the physical possession of the equipment only. Such a provision is a standard term in hire-purchase agreements. In that context, where an option to purchase is provided, it would seem to be contrary to the principle of the equality of creditors, but it has nevertheless been upheld in some cases mainly as a result of a concession made on the part of the liquidator.[34] Significantly, in *Re Piggin Dicker v. Lombank Ltd*,[35] such an automatic termination clause was struck down as it was held to contravene the *pari passu* rule on insolvency distribution. It was further held that even if the clause was not void, equity would grant relief against forfeiture if the trustee in bankruptcy undertook to pay all sums due under the agreement.[36]

As we have already discussed in *Re David Meek Plant Hire Ltd*,[37] it was held that goods let on hire-purchase and physically in the possession of the company were subject to the restrictions imposed by the Insolvency Act 1986, notably the moratorium provisions in administration.

[33.] See *Hindcastle Ltd v. Attenborough Associates Ltd and others* [1996] 1 All E.R. 737.

[34.] See *Re Apex Supply Co. Ltd* [1942] Ch. 108.

[35.] [1962] 112 L.J. 424.

[36.] See Chap. 3, above.

[37.] See pp. 338–339, above.

Recovery of Minimum Payments and Insolvency

In *Robophone Facilities Ltd v. Blank*,[38] it was held that a clause providing for the pre-estimate of damages involving the repudiation of an operating lease was a genuine estimate of loss. The clause required payment as liquidated damages of 50 per cent of the gross rents which would have been payable, and this was accepted by the court as a *via media* of the actual loss of the plaintiff which was estimated to lie within a range of 47–58 per cent of the gross rents for the unexpired term of the contract. Where the minimum payment clause exceeds the true owner's loss, this clause would be open to challenge on the basis that it contradicts, in terms of effect, the *pari passu* principle for distribution.[39]

Insolvency and the Recovery of Insurance Proceeds

In the equipment leasing context, it is necessary to distinguish between loss or damage caused to the equipment which is insured and the situation where the lessee has insured against its liability for loss or damage. In the case of the former situation, the general rule is that the insurance proceeds will not form part of the lessee's estate and will be recoverable by the lessor, since the lessee has a contractual obligation to insure the equipment.[40] As a matter of prudence, the interest of the lessor should nevertheless be noted on the policy. In the case of vehicles on hire purchase, conditional sale or lease, insurance companies will search with HPI plc in order to determine whether there are any outstanding financial interests in motor vehicles which have been the object of a total loss claim.

Where the lessee has liability insurance in respect of loss or damage to the equipment, the common law position is that the proceeds of such insurance are not held on trust for the lessor.[41] However, under the Third Party (Rights Against Insurers) Act 1930, where a debtor, insured in respect of a liability to a creditor, becomes subject to specified insolvency procedures, the debtor's rights are transferred to and become vested in the creditor. The key consideration is the effectuation of an insolvency procedure and if this has not occurred then the Act will not apply. Significantly, applications for an injunction to restrain insurance settlement until initiation of the insolvency procedure on the grounds

---

[38.] [1966] 1 W.L.R. 1428.

[39.] See *British Eagle International Airlines Ltd v. Campagnie National Air France* [1975] 2 All E.R. 390.

[40.] In *Re E. Dibben and Sons Ltd* [1990] B.C.L.C. 577, the issue revolved around the nature of the contractual relationship between the bailor and bailee, especially as to whether this was supplemented by a fiduciary obligation to account for insurance proceeds. See *Interests in Goods* (eds. Palmer, McKendrick, 1993) Chap. 26, Furey, *Goods, Leasing and Insolvency*.

[41.] *Re Harrington Motor Co. Ltd* [1928] Ch. 105.

that it would deprive the plaintiff of its rights under the Act, failed in *Normid Housing Association Ltd v. Ralphs*.[42] Lastly, it should be noted that the provisions of the 1930 Act do not apply where a company is wound up voluntarily merely for the purposes of reconstruction or amalgamation with another company.[43]

[42] [1989] 1 Lloyd's Rep. 265.
[43] Third Party (Rights against Insurers) Act 1930, s. 1(6)(a).

Chapter 14

Facilitation of Leasing in International Trade: The Role of UNIDROIT

Introduction

With the expansion of international trade in leased assets it is clear that conflicts of laws problems are bound to occur. Indeed this phenomenon has inspired ambitious attempts by UNIDROIT towards even the international regulation of security interests in mobile equipment, that is, the development of internationally accepted rules for the regulation of security interests that have international implications. In addition there is the UNIDROIT Convention on International Financial Leasing which was adopted at the conclusion of a diplomatic conference in Ottawa in 1988. By 1996, it appears that 13 states have become signatories whilst France, Italy and Nigeria have gone on to become parties to the Convention. Before considering these two significant initiatives it is important to briefly consider the English position with respect to the recognition of foreign security interests in movables.[1]

The Law Applicable to Rights *in Rem*

The law governing proprietary rights in movables is the *lex situs*, that is the validity of a right *in rem* is determined according to the place where the equipment was situated at the time of the relevant disposition. The position has been summarised by Zaphirou as follows[2]:

> "The law of country Y [the country of importation] cannot apply retrospectively to facts which have taken place while the chattel was situated in country X [the country of export]; on the other hand the facts which will take place in country Y will be governed by the law of country Y and the law of country X can have no say in the matter. Thus, if the domestic law of country Y provides that A, the real owner of the chattel, is estopped from denying B's apparent ownership a contrary provision of the law of country X would be immaterial."

[1.] For a detailed discussion see North and Fawcett, *Cheshire and North's Private International Law* (12th ed., 1992).
[2.] See Zaphirou, *The Transfer of Chattels in Private International Law* (1956) p. 187.

The application of the *lex situs* has been justified on the principle of certainty, in that it is the best way to protect the rights accrued and enforce them against the whole world. Of course, for such a system to work effectively, these rights must be known generally by, for example, a system of public registration established at the place where the objects are situated.

The apparent simplicity of the *lex situs* rule disappears when the movables subject to a perfected ownership or security interest in State A are moved to State B and thereby acquire a new *situs*. The English position is that the foreign security interest is treated as valid in the new *situs* unless and until it is displaced by a new title acquired in accordance with the law of the new *situs*. In contrast, the approach of some European jurisdictions is that the continued existence of rights in the form of a security interest created under the original *situs* depends upon whether or not the foreign interest can be accommodated in the municipal law of the new *situs*. As Schilling has stated[3]:

> "The question asked by common lawyers is rather the question of which law governs the transfer of encumbered movables or their seizure on behalf of creditors. The latter question implies that the mere change of *situs* does not change the law governing the *jura in rem* in chattels but only the law applicable to a possible transfer or seizure of the chattel . . . In contrast, it is the near-unanimous continental view that a change of *situs* is sufficient to bring about immediately a change of the law applicable to the *jura in rem* themselves."

Even if the law of the second *situs* recognises that the security interest created under the first *situs* is valid, there is still the problem of translating that to the law of the second *situs*. This may involve conformity with public notice disclosure obligations in the law of the second *situs*.

In many respects it could be argued that where equipment is movable, it "is only a matter of chance that the security interest created under the original *situs* will be given sufficient recognition in the new *situs* to ensure the economic efficacy of the security agreement between the debtor and the secured party".[4] It is for this reason that UNIDROIT is working towards a proposal that will deal with the regulation of security interests in international mobile equipment as well as the priority conflicts between holders of different security interests, and also ownership disputes with bona fide purchasers of equipment.

---

[3] See Schilling, "Some European Decisions on Non-possessory Security Rights in Private International Law." (1985) 34 I.C.L.Q. 87 at 93.

[4] See Cuming, *International Regulation of Aspects of Security Interests in Mobile Equipment* (1989) p. 26.

The Role of UNIDROIT

Introduction

UNIDROIT is one of a limited number of organisations which has as a principal focus the improvement of international private law.[5] Drafting a law which it is aimed will be adopted by many states is not a simple matter. The process UNIDROIT follows is initially to first investigate existing law as to the subject about to be considered to see whether there is a common thread, or whether the lack of relevant law, or the lack of agreement between countries as to the relevant law, discourages international trade. At the same time, a questionnaire is sent to a considerable number of business entities and people who are potentially interested in the problem; the results are then studied by a group of experts in the field to ascertain the desirability of establishing a uniform law. If there seems to be a need for the contemplated law, the UNIDROIT Governing Council decides whether of not a project is feasible and if so, to what extent. If the decision is to proceed with the project, a small study group is constituted consisting of both academics and professionals in the area, who after careful study determine what is the better rule. A set of simple rules is then drawn up. The document containing the proposed rules is then sent to interested groups in different countries and to their governments for their comments and reactions. At this point, the effort to forge a political consensus begins and when this is achieved a Diplomatic Conference is arranged. In the context of leasing UNIDROIT has already as we have already noted completed a Convention on International Financial Leasing.

The UNIDROIT Convention on International Financial Leasing 1988

UNIDROIT's work on this subject commenced in 1974 and in its Convention the *sui generis* characteristic of the finance leasing transaction is recognised. The scope of the Convention is broad and the characteristics of a finance lease are identified to include in Article 1(2) the following:

1. The lessee specifies and selects the equipment and supplier without relying primarily on the skill and judgment of the lessor.

2. The supplier knows of the connection between the lessor and lessee.

[5.] See Matteucci, "UNIDROIT: The First Fifty Years" [1976] Uniform Law Review 15.

349

3. The rentals payable are calculated so as to take into account in particular the amortisation of the whole or a substantial part of the cost of the equipment. This is one of the main ways in which a finance lease differs from an operating lease, and the committee of governmental experts took the view that this distinguishing feature should be brought out clearly. The Rules eschew many of the troublesome questions of distinguishing between a "true" lease and one intended as a security. Thus an option to purchase is not important as far as the scope of the Convention is concerned as is made clear in Article 1(3).

The Rules are only concerned with the civil law aspect of international finance leasing, that is, when the lessor and the lessee have their place of business in different states. The choice of the lessor's and lessee's places of business as being the determining factor, rather than the supplier, reflects the economic reality of the triangular nature of the leasing transaction. Indeed by referring to a finance lease as a "transaction" rather than a "contract", the drafters were attempting to emphasise that the transaction in question actually consists of two contracts and that:

> ". . . what is involved is not so much two separate contracts as a single complex tripartite transaction setting in motion the interaction of two mutually interdependent agreements."[6]

Only tripartite transactions are covered, namely, where the supply agreement and the leasing agreement are integrally related, that is where the lessee will have chosen the equipment down to the detailed specifications and will have also chosen the supplier. The wide immunity under the UNIDROIT Rules, such as that seen in Article 8, to the lessor for breaches of the supply agreement are premised on the principle that it is the supplier and not the lessor who should be liable to the lessee in such cases. Article 10 of the Convention provides that the duties of the supplier under the supply agreement shall also be owed to the lessee, as if he were a party to that agreement and as if the equipment were to be supplied directly to the lessee. If the lessee's remedies duplicate those of the lessor, leaving the lessor's independent remedies intact might occasion double recovery. It is for this reason that Article 10 recognises that the supplier cannot be liable to two parties for the same loss or damage.

The finance lessor considers itself as a supplier of money rather than a product. This financial role is recognised under the UNIDROIT rules where even "hell or high water" clauses are tolerated. This is where the lessee agrees to pay rentals to the lessor whatever happens and regardless of whether the goods prove to be defective. The crucial point is the time

---

[6.] See *UNIDROIT Preliminary Draft Uniform Rules on International Financial Leasing*, Study LIX Doc. 18 (1985) p. 55.

---

at which the promise to pay becomes enforceable which, in the case of the finance lease, is upon the lessee's acceptance of the goods. Interestingly, under the 1985 UNIDROIT draft Rules, a limited "right to cure" was recognised in the sense that by virtue of Article 10(2) the lessor and supplier were given an additional period of time to substitute a conforming tender. This has been replaced under the Convention, and the lessor's right to cure a failure in performance is now expressed to be exercisable on the same conditions and in the same manner as if the lessee had agreed to buy the equipment from the lessor under the terms of the supply agreement. The balance is still firmly tilted in favour of the lessor as the supplier of the finance, because after acceptance of the goods, the lessee has no right to withhold rentals for non-conforming delivery.

In summary the Leasing Convention is only concerned with *inter partes* rights and obligations of parties to a tripartite international financing leasing transaction. These rules, when adopted, will override the national law otherwise applicable to the transaction. This does not mean that the Convention ignored third-party rights. Indeed, concern of international lessors that the domestic law of lessees' states may not always respect their ownership rights, when unsecured creditors and bankruptcy trustees of lessees make claims to leased equipment, is accommodated in Article 7(1)(a) to (b) which provides that the lessee's "real rights" in the equipment shall be valid against the lessee's trustee in bankruptcy and creditors. The applicable law, in the case of a lease of equipment of a kind normally moved from one state to another, is that of the state where the lessee has its place of business.[7] In the case of a lease of any other type of equipment, it is the law of the state where the equipment is situated,[8] and in the case of a lease of an aircraft, it is the law of the state where the aircraft is registered under the Convention on International Civil Aviation, Chicago, 1944.[9] It would appear therefore that lessors will need to comply with the public notice requirement (if any) of the applicable law if their interests are to be protected. The significance of the Convention is that the choice of law rules do not prescribe the *lex situs* where public notice of a security interest in mobile equipment is involved, that is those jurisdictions which treat finance leases as security agreements. As such, this represents a departure from the conflict of law rules seen in England.

UNIDROIT Progress Towards a Convention on International Interests in Mobile Equipment

UNIDROIT has been working on a proposed Convention on international interests in mobile equipment since April 1989. Discussions are still

---

[7.] Art. 7(3)(c).
[8.] Art. 7 (3)(d). The applicable law in the case of a lease of a registered ship is the law of the state in which the ship is registered in the name of the owner: see Art. 7(3)(a).
[9.] See Art. 7(3)(b).

proceeding, although the shape of a Convention can be seen in the First Draft that it will provide "for the creation and effects of an international interest in mobile equipment".[10] As such the proposed Convention is conceptually different from previous conventions including that on International Finance Leasing. What is being proposed is not a harmonising provision in respect of international contracts but is rather international procedural and substantive law, that is it includes the extinguishment for certain purposes of rights *in rem*. Essentially it involves the creation at an international level of a personal property security regime similar to that seen in certain North American jurisdictions.

The nature of the interests covered by the Draft Convention include: first, conventional security interests arising by way of the granting of a charge; secondly, retention of title clauses and leases of equipment are treated as unconventional security interests. The proposed Convention sets up a priority regime in respect of international interests, and in determining what is an international interest the test is not whether the parties are in different states but rather the nature of the equipment involved. Potentially all mobile equipment could be covered by this expansive approach. So long as there has been a registration of the international interest in the International Registry, by reference to the serial number or other specific identification mark of the equipment, this will ensure priority over "any other interest acquired from the chargor, buyer or lessee at a time when the international interest was registered".[11] Curiously the First Draft provides that an international interest will only be valid against the trustee in bankruptcy if there has been a further registration by reference to the name of the chargor, buyer or lessee.[12]

The location of the Central Registry, in respect of the international interest, will inevitably prove to be problematical. The reasoning here is that priority is strictly accorded to the time of registration, and depending upon the location of the Central Registry certain time-zone jurisdictions will inevitably be prejudiced.[13] This is further compounded by the fact that it is anticipated that there will be different means of registration including writing (delivery) and transmission.[14] Moreover it appears that a registration notice is treated as valid despite an irregularity, unless this is deemed to be seriously misleading.[15] In North America this has proved to be one of the most difficult issues to resolve and has provoked much litigation. On an international level it would appear that the problems

[10] First set of Draft Articles of a Future UNIDROIT Convention on International Interests in Mobile Equipment (1995), Art. 1(1). See Mooney C. "Exporting UCC Article 9 to an International Convention: The Local Law Conundrum" (1996) 27 *Can. Bus. Law* 278.

[11] *Ibid.* Art. 19.3.

[12] *Ibid.* Art. 5.3(b).

[13] *Ibid.* Art. 14.3.

[14] *Ibid.* Art. 14.2.

[15] *Ibid.* Art. 14.5.

associated in determining what is "seriously misleading" and to whom are almost insuperable. It is likely that subsequent drafts will deal with this problem.

The Draft Convention does not solve conflict of law problems because it is proposed that the remedy at issue is dealt with in conformity with the procedural law of the place where exercise of the remedy is sought.[16] The following points emerge: first, what is the applicable law of the contract and should this apply if the asset is elsewhere? secondly, what happens if the place where the exercise of the remedy sought involves slow procedures, thereby preventing expedition? Furthermore, it would appear that the international security interest will fall within the local bankruptcy regime.[17] This would mean that the interest will be vulnerable to super priority interests, such as liens, and also to bankruptcy freezes.

Outside of the proposal for a separate register of aircraft engines, the Draft Convention does not deal with the problem of determining ownership of accessories. At the same time by linking priority to the fact of registration of the main chattel, obvious difficulties will emerge in respect of the liability of the Registrar which, given the scope of the proposed International Register, will have to be limited. Periodical review both of the limits of the liability and also the state of technology and methods of access are self-evident.

Clearly the work of UNIDROIT is valuable and whilst the project is ambitious, there is no doubting that conflict of law rules dealing with security interests in movables are, to say the least, not predictable as between the foreign security interest and domestic interests in mobile equipment. A certain legal environment might stimulate the facilitation of credit where hitherto financing organisations are reluctant to provide financing for high cost mobile equipment moving between international frontiers.

[16.] *Ibid*. Art. 12.1.
[17.] *Ibid*. Art. 19.6.

Part 5

Selected Precedents
and Appendices

Precedent 1

Repudiation of Hire Contract

Actions against Hirers

IN THE COURT OF HIGH JUSTICE   19 . .B, No. . .
QUEEN'S BENCH DIVISION
            DISTRICT REGISTRY

Writ issued the   day of   199 .

BETWEEN   Plaintiff and   Defendant

STATEMENT OF CLAIM

1. By an agreement in writing dated   day of   19 . .
and made between the Plaintiff and the Defendant ("the Agreement") it
was agreed that the Plaintiff should hire to the Defendant [state
equipment] for a period of [state term] commencing
19 . . on payment of the sum of [state amount] payable by [state
monthly instalments or other periods] of [state amount] payable on the
[date] of each [state month or period] commencing 19 . .

2. The Plaintiff will refer to the agreement for its full terms, true
meaning and effects as may be necessary.

3. Pursuant to the said agreement the Plaintiff delivered the said
[equipment] to the Defendant.

4. The Defendant has paid the total sum of £   to the
Plaintiff by way of [state period] instalments. Wrongfully and in breach
of contract the Defendant is in arrears with the said instalments in the
total sum of £   .

PARTICULARS

[State how arrears are made up.]

5. By letter dated the   day of   19 . . the Defendant repudiated the agreement and refused any longer to be bound by it.

6. Further or in the alternative, notwithstanding repeated demands by the Plaintiff, the Defendant has wrongfully and in breach of the agreement failed and refused to pay any further sums.

7. By his conduct as set out in paragraphs 5 and 6 above, the Defendant has evinced an intention no longer to be bound by the said agreement and he has repudiated the same.

8. The Plaintiffs as they were entitled to do, accepted the Defendant's repudiation by letter dated   19 . .

9. By reason of the foregoing the Plaintiffs have lost the benefit of the agreement and lost the revenue they would otherwise have received under it and thereby suffered loss and damage.

PARTICULARS

  (i) Rental for the residue of the term of the said agreement from [state period].
 (ii) The Plaintiff will give credit for the estimated cost of the future maintenance of the [equipment] of £   and for the accelerated payment of the said rent at £   .

10. Further the Plaintiff claims interest upon the said sum pursuant to Section 35A of the Supreme Court Act 1981 at   per cent from   or at such other rate and for such other period as the Court shall consider just.

AND the Plaintiff claims:

  (1) the said sum of £   arrears of instalments;

  (2) damages for repudiation of the said agreement;

  (3) interest.

(signature)

SERVED this   day of   by   & Co. of [address and reference], Solicitors for the Plaintiff.

Failure to Accept Goods

Actions against Hirers

IN THE COURT OF HIGH JUSTICE   19 . .B, No. . .
QUEEN'S BENCH DIVISION
               DISTRICT REGISTRY

Writ issued the   day of   199 .

BETWEEN   Plaintiff and   Defendant

STATEMENT OF CLAIM

1. By an written agreement dated   19 . . made between the Plaintiff and the Defendant, the Defendant agreed to hire from the Plaintiff [specify equipment] in consideration of the payment of [state amount and period].

2. On   19 . . the Plaintiff delivered the said equipment to the Defendant's property at [address].

3. The Defendant wrongfully and in breach of contract refused to accept delivery of the said equipment.

4. By reason of the aforesaid breach the Plaintiff has suffered loss and damage.

PARTICULARS

[State schedule of losses.]

5. Further the Plaintiff claims interest upon the said sum pursuant to Section 35A of the Supreme Court Act 1981 at   per cent from   or at such other rate and for such other period as the Court shall consider just.

AND the Plaintiff claims:

(1) Damages as set out herein;
(2) Interest thereon pursuant to Section 35A of the Supreme Court Act 1981.

(signature)

SERVED this   day of   by   & Co. of [address and reference], Solicitors for the Plaintiff.

Damage to Goods During Hire

Actions against Hirers

IN THE COURT OF HIGH JUSTICE   19 . .B, No. . .
QUEEN'S BENCH DIVISION
        DISTRICT REGISTRY

Writ issued the   day of   199 .

BETWEEN   Plaintiff and   Defendant

STATEMENT OF CLAIM

1. The Plaintiff is and was at all material times the owner of [state equipment].

2. By a written agreement made on   19 . . the Plaintiff agreed to hire [the equipment] for a period of [state terms and amount].

3. It was an express and/or implied term of the said agreement that the Defendant should take reasonable care of [state the equipment] while in his custody.

4. On the said   19 . . the [equipment] was duly delivered to the Defendant pursuant to the said agreement.

5. The Defendant did not take due or proper care of the [state equipment] while it was in his care and custody.

PARTICULARS

[state damage]

6. By reason of the matters aforesaid the Plaintiff has suffered loss and damage.

PARTICULARS

[State schedule of losses.]

7.   Further the Plaintiff claims interest upon the said sum pursuant to Section 35A of the Supreme Court Act 1981 at   per cent from   or at such other rate and for such other period as the Court shall consider just.

AND the Plaintiff claims:

(1)   the said sum of £   arrears of instalments;

(2)   damage for repudiation of the said agreement;

(3)   interest.

(signature)

SERVED this   day of   by   & Co. of [address and reference], Solicitors for the Plaintiff.

Precedent 4

Conversion of Goods

Actions against Hirers

IN THE COURT OF HIGH JUSTICE   19 . .B, No. . .
QUEEN'S BENCH DIVISION
         DISTRICT REGISTRY

Writ issued the   day of   199 .

BETWEEN   Plaintiff and   Defendant

STATEMENT OF CLAIM

1.   The Plaintiff is the owner of [state equipment].

2.   By an agreement in writing dated   19 . . made between the Plaintiff and the Defendant, the Plaintiff agreed to hire the said [equipment] to the Defendant for a [state term and amount].

3.   Further to the said agreement, the Plaintiff delivered the [state equipment] to the Defendant on   19 . .

4.   On or about   19 . . the Defendant [or his agent sold] the [said equipment] thereby wrongfully depriving the Plaintiff of [the said equipment] and wrongfully interfering with the Plaintiff's rights in the [said equipment] by converting it to his own use.

5.   By reason of the matters aforesaid the Plaintiff has suffered loss and damage.

PARTICULARS

[Give details of loss of hire charges and value of equipment.]

---

6. Further the Plaintiff claims interest upon the said sum pursuant to Section 35A of the Supreme Court Act 1981 at   per cent from   or at such other rate and for such other period as the Court shall consider just.

AND the Plaintiff claims:

(1) Damages;
(2) The aforesaid interest thereon pursuant to Section 35A of the Supreme Court Act 1981.

(signature)

SERVED this   day of   by   & Co. of [address and reference], Solicitors for the Plaintiff.

Goods Wrongfully Interfered with by Detention of the Goods After Termination for Non-Payment of Hire

Actions against Hirers

IN THE COURT OF HIGH JUSTICE   19 . .B, No. . .
QUEEN'S BENCH DIVISION
           DISTRICT REGISTRY

Writ issued the   day of   199 .

BETWEEN   Plaintiff and   Defendant

STATEMENT OF CLAIM

1. By an agreement in writing dated   19 . . made between the Plaintiff and the Defendant, the Plaintiff agreed to let and the Defendant agreed to hire the [state equipment].

2. By the said agreement it was provided inter alia as follows:
[Set out material terms including the right of termination].

3. The Plaintiff will refer at the trial to the agreement for its full terms, true meaning and effect.

4. In breach of the said agreement the Defendant failed to pay the sums of [state amount] due on the [state period].

5. By written notice dated   19 . . the Plaintiff determined the agreement and demanded from the Defendant the return of the [said equipment].

6. The Defendant has failed and refused and still fails and refuses to return the [said equipment] to the Plaintiff and has thereby wrongfully

interfered with the Plaintiff's goods by converting the said to his own use.

7. By reason of the matters aforesaid the Plaintiff has suffered loss and damage.

PARTICULARS

[Give details of loss of hire charges and value of equipment.]

8. Further the Plaintiff claims interest upon the said sum pursuant to Section 35A of the Supreme Court Act 1981 at   per cent from   or at such other rate and for such other period as the Court shall consider just.

AND the Plaintiff claims:

(1) The sum of £. . . . [arrears of hire];
(2) An order for delivery up of [the said equipment] or £. . . . its value;
(3) Damages;
(4) Interest pursuant to Section 35A of the Supreme Court Act 1981 on all sums found due and owing to the Plaintiff.

(signature)

SERVED this   day of   by   & Co. of [address and reference], Solicitors for the Plaintiff.

Precedent 6

Injury to Reversionary Interest in Goods

Actions against Hirers

IN THE COURT OF HIGH JUSTICE   19 . .B, No. . .
QUEEN'S BENCH DIVISION
        DISTRICT REGISTRY

Writ issued the   day of   199 .

BETWEEN   Plaintiff and   Defendant

STATEMENT OF CLAIM

1. The Plaintiff is and was at all material times the owner of [state equipment].

2. By a written agreement made the   day of   19. . the Plaintiff let the [said equipment] on hire to X for a period of [state period].

3. At all material times the said X has had possession of the [said equipment] but the reversionary property and interest in it belonged to the Plaintiff.

4. On   , while the [equipment] was being used by the Defendant the Defendant wrongfully damaged the [equipment] by [state nature of damage].

5. By reason of the matters aforesaid the [equipment] has been permanently damaged, threreby damaging the Plaintiff's reversionary interest in the said [equipment] and causing the Plaintiff loss and damage.

367

PARTICULARS

[State the nature and extent of the damages claimed].

6. Further the Plaintiff claims interest upon the said sum pursuant to Section 35A of the Supreme Court Act 1981 at [state amount] per cent from [state date] or at such other rate and for such other period as the Court shall consider just.

AND the Plaintiff claims:

(1) Damages;
(2) Interest pursuant to Section 35A of the Supreme Court Act 1981 on all sums found due and owing to the Plaintiff.

(signature)

SERVED this   day of   by   & Co. of [address and reference], Solicitors for the Plaintiff.

Failure to Deliver Goods Hired

Actions against Owner

IN THE COURT OF HIGH JUSTICE   19 . .B, No. . .
QUEEN'S BENCH DIVISION
          DISTRICT REGISTRY

Writ issued the   day of   199 .

BETWEEN   Plaintiff and   Defendant

STATEMENT OF CLAIM

1.   The Plaintiff is [state nature of business and address].

2.   By an agreement in writing dated   19. . made between the Plaintiff and the Defendant, the Plaintiff agreed to hire from the Defendant a [state nature of equipment] for use in connection with his business for a period [set out period] commencing on   19. . at the hire rent of £   per month.

3.   The Defendant failed to deliver the said [equipment] on time or at all.

4.   By reason of the said non delivery the Plaintiff was deprived of the use of the said [equipment] for a period [set out period] thereby incurring loss.

PARTICULARS

[set out losses]

5.   Further the Plaintiff claims interest upon the said sums pursuant to Section 35A of the Supreme Court Act 1981 at [state amount] per cent from [state date] or at such other rate and for such other period as the Court shall consider just.

AND the Plaintiff claims:

    (1) the said sum of £   arrears of instalments;
    (2) damages for repudiation of the said agreement;
    (3) interest.

[Adapt as appropriate]

(signature)

SERVED this   day of   by   & Co. of
[address and reference], Solicitors for the Plaintiff.

Trespass to Goods

Actions against Owner

IN THE COURT OF HIGH JUSTICE   19 . .B, No. . .
QUEEN'S BENCH DIVISION
          DISTRICT REGISTRY

Writ issued the   day of   199 .

BETWEEN   Plaintiff and   Defendant

STATEMENT OF CLAIM

1.   The Plaintiff is [set out business].

2.   By an agreement in writing dated   19. . made between the Plaintiff and the Defendant, the Plaintiff agreed to hire from the Defendant a [state nature of equipment] for use in connection with his business for a period [set out period and also rentals].

3.   It was an express and/or implied term of the said agreement that the Defendant would give the Plaintiff possession of the [said state equipment] and let the Plaintiff remain in quiet possession of the [equipment] for the period of the hiring.

4.   In breach of the said express and/or implied term on or about   19. . the Defendant retook possession of the [equipment] and wrongfully deprived the Plaintiff of possession thereof.

5.   By reason of the said breach the Plaintiff was put to inconvenience and loss.

PARTICULARS

[Set out schedule.]

6.   Further the Plaintiff claims interest upon the said sum pursuant to Section 35A of the Supreme Court Act 1981 at [state amount] per cent from [state date] or at such other rate and for such other period at the Court shall consider just.

AND the Plaintiff claims:

(1)   the said of £   arrears of instalments;
(2)   damages for repudiation of the said agreement;
(3)   interest.

[Adapt as appropriate.]

(signature)

SERVED this   day of   by   & Co. of [address and reference], Solicitors for the Plaintiff.

Breach of Implied Terms

Actions against Owners

IN THE COURT OF HIGH JUSTICE   19 . .B, No. . .
QUEEN'S BENCH DIVISION
         DISTRICT REGISTRY

Writ issued the   day of   199 .

BETWEEN   Plaintiff and   Defendant

STATEMENT OF CLAIM

1.   At all material times the Defendant has carried on business from [state address].

2.   By an agreement in writing dated   19. . and made between the Plaintiff and the Defendant, the Defendant agreed to hire to the Plaintiff [state equipment] for a period [state period] at the rate of [state amount of rentals and frequency of payment].

3.   There were implied terms of the said agreement that the [equipment] would be of satisfactory quality and would be reasonably fit for the purpose for which it was hired, that is, [state purpose].

4.   The said term as to fitness for purpose was implied from the following circumstances [state the circumstances].

5.   In breach of the aforesaid terms the [state equipment] was not of satisfactory quality nor reasonably fit for the said purposes.

PARTICULARS

6.   By reason of the said breach of warranty the Plaintiff was deprived of the use of the [equipment] and suffered loss and damage.

PARTICULARS

[Set out particulars of damage and loss.]

7. Further the Plaintiff claims interest upon the said sum pursuant to Section 35A of the Supreme Court Act 1981 at   per cent from   or at such other rate and for such other period as the Court shall consider just.

AND the Plaintiff claims:

(1) the said sum of £   arrears of instalments;
(2) damages for repudiation of the said agreement;
(3) interests.

[Adapt and amend as appropriate.]

(signature)

SERVED this   day of   by   & Co. of [address and reference], Solicitors for the Plaintiff.

Precedent 10

Goods Not Fit for Purpose

Hirer's Defences

IN THE COURT OF HIGH JUSTICE   19 . .B, No. . .
QUEEN'S BENCH DIVISION
        DISTRICT REGISTRY

Writ issued the   day of   199 .

BETWEEN   Plaintiff and   Defendant

DEFENCE

1. The Defendant admits that he agreed to hire from the Plaintiff the [said equipment] referred to in the Statement of Claim for the period and at the rent there alleged.

2. Further as to [state paragraph] of the Statement of Claim the said equipment was hired by the Plaintiff to the Defendant in the course of the Plaintiff's business [state nature of business].

3. The Defendant avers that it was an implied condition of the agreement that the [equipment] should be of satisfactory quality and fit and suitable for the purpose for which the Defendant hired the [equipment] namely [state the special purpose as agreed].

4. In breach of such condition the [equipment] was not of satisfactory quality and/or not fit for the said purpose.

PARTICULARS

5. By reason of the matters hereinbefore complained of the Defendant was unable to use the [equipment] and returned it to the Plaintiff on   19. .

375

6.   The Defendant admits that he has paid £   as averred in the Statement of Claim but denies that he is liable to pay the £ claimed or any sum to the Plaintiff.

7.   By reason of the aforesaid facts and matters the Defendant denies that he is liable as alleged or at all.

(signature)

SERVED this   day of   by   & Co. of [address], Solicitors for the Plaintiff.

Precedent 11

Wrongful Use of Goods Denied

Hirer's Defences

IN THE COURT OF HIGH JUSTICE   19 . .B, No. . .
QUEEN'S BENCH DIVISION
         DISTRICT REGISTRY

Writ issued the   day of   199 .

BETWEEN   Plaintiff and   Defendant

DEFENCE

1. The Defendant admits that on   19. . he agreed to hire [the equipment] from the Plaintiff as alleged in [state paragraph] of the Statement of Claim.

2. The Defendant denies that there was any express or implied term as alleged in [state paragraph] of the Statement of Claim.

3. The Defendant admits that he used the [state equipment and use] but denies that it was a breach of any term agreed with the Plaintiff.

4. The Defendant admits [set out the complaint] in the Statement of Claim but denies that he is under any liability to the Plaintiff in respect thereof.

PARTICULARS

5. By reason of the matters hereinbefore complained of the Defendant was unable to use the [equipment] and returned it to the Plaintiff on   19. .

6. The Defendant admits that he has paid £   as averred in the Statement of Claim but denies that he is liable to pay the £ claimed or any sum to the Plaintiff.

377

7.   By reason of the aforesaid facts and matters the Defendant denies that he is liable as alleged or at all.

(signature)

SERVED this   day of   by   & Co. of [address], Solicitors for the Plaintiff.

Impossibility of Returning Hired Goods

Hirer's Defences

IN THE COURT OF HIGH JUSTICE   19 . .B, No. . .
QUEEN'S BENCH DIVISION
           DISTRICT REGISTRY

Writ issued the   day of   199 .

BETWEEN   Plaintiff and   Defendant

DEFENCE

1. The Defendant admits the agreement referred to in [state paragraph] of the Statement of Claim.

2. The Defendant admits that he failed to return the [equipment] referred to in the agreement but avers that the loss of the [equipment] occurred without any default or neglect on the part of the Defendant by reason of the facts and matters hereinafter set out [state facts which refer to the loss].

3. In consequence of the foregoing matters it is averred that the Defandant is absolved from any liability to return the [equipment] to the Plaintiff and it is denied that he is liable to the Plaintiff as alleged or at all.

PARTICULARS

4. The Defendant admits that he has paid £   as averred in the Statement of Claim but denies that he is liable to pay the £
claimed or any sum to the Plaintiff.

5. By reason of the aforesaid facts and matters the Defendant denies that he is liable as alleged or at all.

(signature)

SERVED this   day of   by   & Co. of [address], Solicitors for the Plaintiff.

Defence to Claim for Trespass

Lessor's Defence

IN THE COURT OF HIGH JUSTICE   19 . .B, No. . .
QUEEN'S BENCH DIVISION
_____ DISTRICT REGISTRY

Writ issued the   day of   199 .

BETWEEN _____ Plaintiff and _____ Defendant

DEFENCE

1. The Defendant admits the agreement referred to in [state paragraph] of the Statement of Claim and will refer to the agreement at the trial for its full terms, true meaning and effect.

2. It was an express and/or an implied term of the said agreement that the Defendant would maintain in repair the [equipment] to the Plaintiff under the said agreement.

3. The Defendant admits that he retook possession of the [equipment] on   19. . in order to have the [equipment] inspected and any necessary repairs executed. The Defendant denies that the retaking was in breach with the agreement or was wrongful as alleged or at all.

4. The Defendant denies that the Plaintiff has suffered the loss and damage alleged or that the said or any loss or damages due to the alleged or any breach of the agreement by the Defendant.

(signature)

SERVED this   day of   by   & Co. of
[address], Solicitors for the Plaintiff.

Defence Denying Implied Terms

Lessor's Defence

IN THE COURT OF HIGH JUSTICE   19 . .B, No. . .
QUEEN'S BENCH DIVISION
         DISTRICT REGISTRY

Writ issued the   day of   199 .

BETWEEN   Plaintiff and   Defendant

DEFENCE

1.   The Defendant admits the agreement referred in [state paragraph] of the Statement of Claim but denies that the terms thereof are fully or accurately set out therein. The Defendant will refer at the trial to the agreement for its full contents, true meaning and effect.

2.   The Defendant denies that the alleged terms as to satisfactory quality and to fitness for purpose were to be implied into the said agreement.

3.   The Plaintiff inspected the [said equipment] which did reveal or should have revealed all the defects complained of in the Statement of Claim.

4.   Further or in the alternative the Defendant avers that the Plaintiff did not in all the circumstances rely upon the skill or judgment of the Defendant.

5.   By reason of the matters aforesaid it is denied that the Defendant is liable for the alleged or any fault or defect in the [said equipment].

6.   Save as herein before expressly admitted each and every allegation in the Statement of Claim is denied.

(signature)

SERVED this   day of   by   & Co. of [address], Solicitors for the Plaintiff.

Claim Based on the Contract of Sale between the Owner and the Supplier

Claims by the Creditor or Owner against the Supplier

IN THE COURT OF HIGH JUSTICE   19 . .B, No. . .
QUEEN'S BENCH DIVISION
          DISTRICT REGISTRY

Writ issued the   day of   199 .

BETWEEN   Plaintiff and   Defendant

STATEMENT OF CLAIM

1. By a contract of sale made between the Plaintiff and the Defendant on   19. . , the Defendant sold to the Plaintiff a [state nature of the equipment]. At the time of such sale the Defendant knew that the Plaintiff was purchasing the goods for the purpose of letting them on hire to [state hirer].

2. The following were necessarily implied conditions of the contract:

(a) that the Defendant had the right to sell the goods;
(b) that the goods would be reasonably fit for the purpose for which the Plaintiff required them, namely for letting on hire to [state hirer];
(c) that the goods should be reasonably fit for the purpose for which [the hirer] required them, namely [set out purposes];
(d) that the goods should be of satisfactory quality.

3. In breach of the condition(s) set out in [state condition(s)] hereof, the Defendant did not [state breach].

PARTICULARS

4. By reason of these matters, [the hirer], as he was entitled to do treated the hire agreement as having been repudiated by the Plaintiff, returned the goods to the Plaintiff and claimed:

(a) repayment of all sums paid under the hire agreement, namely:
£   ;
(b) damages for breach and/or repudiation of the hire agreement, namely:

    (i) cost of repairs: £   ;
    (ii) hire of alternative goods: £   ;

5. The Plaintiff as he was obliged to do, accepted the goods back and paid the said sums to [the hirer].

6. In the premises the Defendant repudiated the sale contract and by a letter dated   19. . , the Plaintiff accepted that repudiation.

7. By reason of the Defendant's breach and/or repudiation of the said contract, the Plaintiff has suffered loss and damage.

PARTICULARS

[Set out losses and include credit for the value of the goods and for any accelerated payment.]

And the Plaintiff claims:

(a) Damages for breach and/or repudiation of contract.
(b) Contractual interest, alternatively interest pursuant to Section 35A of the Supreme Court Act 1981 or any damages awarded at such rate and for such period as the court thinks fit.

(signature)

SERVED this   day of   by   & Co. of
[address] Solicitors for the Plaintiff.

Claim for Arrears of Rent, Return of the Goods, Payment Under a Minimum Payment Clause and Damages

Claims by an Owner against a Hirer under the Consumer Credit Act 1974

IN THE COUNTY COURT   19 . .B, No. . .

Writ issued the   day of   199 .

BETWEEN _____ Plaintiff and _____ Defendant

PARTICULARS OF CLAIM

1. By a hire agreement in writing [state date], the Plaintiff let to the Defendant on hire a [specify equipment] for a term [specify period] at a rent of [specify amount and frequency of payment].

2. Clause   of the Agreement provided that the hiring should continue throughout the term and that the Defendant should not be entitled to determine the hiring during the term.

3. Clause   of the Agreement provided, if any instalment of rent remained unpaid for   days [the Plaintiff] should be entitled to serve a Notice of Default and Termination and that, if the Defendant failed to remedy the default within the time stated, upon the expiry of a notice the agreement and the hiring shall determine.

4. Clause   of the Agreement provided that, upon a termination under Clause   , the Defendant should forthwith return the goods and pay [state sums].

5. In breach of the agreement, the Defendant failed to pay the instalment of rent due or any rent due thereunder.

6. By a Default and Termination Notice dated   19 . , the Plaintiff required the Defendant to remedy the breach within   days and gave notice that if the breach were not remedied, the agreement and the hiring would terminate at the expiry of that period. At the date of the Notice the rent was £   in arrear and the value of the goods was £   .

7. The Defendant failed to remedy the breach within the period or at all and on   19. ., the agreement and the hiring duly determined and the Defendant became liable to return the goods to the Plaintiff. The Defendant has failed or refused to return the goods to the Plaintiff.

8. Upon the termination of the agreement the following sums were due:
[state sums]

9. Further or alternatively the Defendant repudiated the agreement and by the Notice of Termination the Plaintiff accepted such repudiation. By reason of such repudiation, the Plaintiff has suffered loss and damage:

PARTICULARS

Balance of rent to the end of the hire term: £

[Less: value of the goods, if recovered: £   ]

Discount for accelerated payment: £

And the Plaintiff claims:

(a) an order for the return of the goods or payment of £   their value;
(b) arrears of rent: £   ;
(c) cost of repairs: £   ;
(d) agreed damages: £   ;
(e) alternatively to (d), damages for breach of contract;
(f) contractual interest, alternatively interest pursuant to Section 69 of the County Courts Act 1984 at the rate of –% per month.

Dated this   day of   199 .

. . . .
[Solicitor's name address and reference.]

Solicitors for the Plaintiff who will
accept service of all proceedings on
his/her behalf at the said address.

To: The District Judge of the
      County Court
      and to the Defendant.

Claim Based on Wrongful Repossession with Reliance on Section 132 of the Consumer Credit Act 1974

Claims by an Owner against a Hirer under the Consumer Credit Act 1974

IN THE COUNTY COURT   19 . .B, No. . .

Writ issued the   day of   199 .

BETWEEN   Plaintiff and   Defendant

PARTICULARS OF CLAIM

1.   By a hire agreement in writing [state date], the Defendant let a [state equipment] to the Plaintiff on hire for a term of [state term] at a monthly rental of £   .

2.   The agreement was a regulated consumer hire agreement under Section 15 of the Consumer Credit Act 1974.

3.   Further to the agreement the Plaintiff paid [state number] instalments of rent totalling £   .

4.   On [state date], wrongfully, without the consent of the Plaintiff and in breach of Section 132 of the Consumer Credit Act, the Defendant repossessed the goods.

5.   Further to Section 132 (1) of the Consumer Credit Act, the Plaintiff seeks an order that:

(a)   the sum of £   be repaid to the Plaintiff; and
(b)   the Plaintiff's obligation to make payments to the Defendant under the agreement do cease forthwith.

And the Plaintiff claims:

(1) an order that the Defendant do pay to the Plaintiff the sum of £   or such sum as the court may think just;
(2) an order that all obligations of the Plaintiff under the hire agreement do cease forthwith;
(3) interest pursuant to Section 69 of the County Courts Act 1984.

Dated this   day of   199 .

. . . .
[Solicitor's name address and reference.]

Solicitors for the Plaintiff who will accept service of all proceedings on his/her behalf at the said address.

To: The District Judge of the
     County Court
     and to the Defendant.

Appendix 1

Memorandum of Understanding between the RMI and HPI

1. The Finance & Leasing Association (FLA) and the Retail Motor Industry Federation (RMI) have agreed to issue this Memorandum of Understanding to members of both Associations.

2. This Memorandum of Understanding shall not in any way whatsoever affect the legal rights and obligations of the FLA, the RMI and the members of both Associations.

3. The FLA and the RMI urge their members to make every effort to ensure that they promptly and accurately register and search with HP Information plc (HPI), particulars of road vehicles in which they have a financial interest through a hire-purchase, conditional sale, leasing or contract hire agreement.

4. The RMI will urge its members to act with diligence in providing details of registration marks and chassis numbers and to take particular care where offered a vehicle with a registration number that could be a cherished number and will remind its members of the existence of insurance against the risk of obtaining a vehicle subject to outstanding finance.

5. In the event that there is a dispute between an FLA member and an RMI member arising out of failure to register promptly or accurately, and the RMI member promptly and accurately searched with HPI, and the matter cannot be resolved between the two parties, RMI members will be urged to refer particulars of the case to the RMI.

6. The RMI will provide the FLA with full particulars of the case.

7. The FLA will refer the matter to senior management within the FLA member company for urgent investigation.

8. If the matter remains unresolved, the Chief Executives of the FLA and the RMI shall investigate.

9. Where appropriate, the Chairman of the FLA's Motor Finance Division and the President of the RMI shall investigate.

10. If the matter still remains unresolved, it is not envisaged that further participation by the Associations shall lead to a solution that is satisfactory to both parties who will then be free to pursue any other action that they consider appropriate.

11. In issuing this Memorandum of Understanding, the FLA and the RMI will encourage their members to use the provisions of the Memorandum of Understanding before resorting to legal proceedings but acknowledge that neither party could be obliged to resolve the dispute and that in the final event both may choose to adhere to what they consider to be their rights at law.

12. This Memorandum of Understanding came into force on June 2, 1992 and supersedes the Memoranda of Understanding between the Finance Houses Association (FHA) and the RMI, effective from August 31, 1990, and the Equipment Leasing Association (ELA) and the RMI, effective from September 25, 1991. The Memorandum of Understanding does not apply retrospectively. The superseded Memoranda of Understanding apply to members of the FHA, ELA and RMI from the dates they came into force until

June 1, 1992. The FHA and the ELA merged on January 2, 1992 to form the FLA.

Appendix 2

UNIDROIT Convention on International Financial Leasing

Preamble

THE STATES PARTIES TO THIS CONVENTION.

RECOGNISING the importance of removing certain legal impediments to the international financial leasing of equipment, while maintaining a fair balance of interests between the different parties to the transaction,

AWARE of the need to make international financial leasing more available,

CONSCIOUS of the fact that the rules of law governing the traditional contract of hire need to be adapted to the distinct triangular relationship created by the financial leasing transaction,

RECOGNISING therefore the desirability of formulating certain uniform rules relating primarily to the civil and commercial law aspects of international financial leasing,

HAVE AGREED as follows:

Chapter I — Sphere of Application and General Provisions

Article 1

1. This Convention governs a financial leasing transaction as described in paragraph 2 in which one party (the lessor),

   (a) on the specifications of another party (the lessee), enters into an agreement (the supply agreement) with a third party (the supplier) under which the lessor acquires plant, capital goods or other equipment (the equipment) on terms approved by the lessee so far at they concern its interests, and
   (b) enters into an agreement (the leasing agreement) with the lessee, granting to the lessee the right to use the equipment in return for the payment of rentals.

2. The financial leasing transaction referred to in the previous paragraph is a transaction which includes the following characteristics:

   (a) the lessee specifies the equipment and selects the supplier without relying primarily on the skill and judgment of the lessor;
   (b) the equipment is acquired by the lessor in connection with a leasing agreement which, to the knowledge of the supplier, either has been made or is to be made between the lessor and the lessee; and

(c) the rentals payable under the leasing agreement are calculated so as to take into account in particular the amortisation of the whole or a substantial part of the cost of the equipment.

3. This Convention applies whether or not the lessee has or subsequently acquires the option to buy the equipment or to hold it on lease for a further period, and whether or not for a nominal price or rental.

4. This Convention applies to financial leasing transactions in relation to all equipment save that which is to be used primarily for the lessee's personal, family or household purposes.

Article 2

In the case of one or more sub-leasing transactions involving the same equipment, this Convention applies to each transaction which is a financial leasing transaction and is otherwise subject to this Convention as if the person from whom the first lessor (as defined in paragraph 1 of the previous article) acquired the equipment were the supplier and as if the agreement under which the equipment was so acquired were the supply agreement.

Article 3

1. This Convention applies when the lessor and the lessee have their places of business in different States and:

(a) those States and the State in which the supplier has its place of business are Contracting States; or

(b) both the supply agreement and the leasing agreement are governed by the law of a Contracting State.

2. A reference in this article to a party's place of business shall, if it has more than one place of business, mean the place of business which has the closest relationship to the relevant agreement and its performance, having regard to the circumstances known to or contemplated by the parties at any time before or at the conclusion of that agreement.

Article 4

1. The provisions of this Convention shall not cease to apply merely because the equipment has become a fixture to or incorporated in land.

2. Any question whether or not the equipment has become a fixture to or incorporated in land, and if so the effect on the rights *inter se* of the lessor and a person having real rights in the land, shall be determined by the law of the State where the land is situated.

Article 5

1. The application of this Convention may be excluded only if each of the parties to the supply agreement and each of the parties to the leasing agreement agree to exclude it.

2. Where the application of this Convention has not been excluded in accordance with the previous paragraph, the parties may, in their relations

with each other, derogate from or vary the effect of any of its provisions except as stated in Articles 8(3) and 13(3)(b) and (4).

Article 6

1. In the interpretation of this Convention, regard is to be had to its object and purpose as set forth in the Preamble, to its international character and to the need to promote uniformity in its application and the observance of good faith in international trade.
2. Questions concerning matters governed by this Convention which are not expressly settled in it are to be settled in conformity with the general principles on which it is based or, in the absence of such principles, in conformity with the law applicable by virtue of the rules of private international law.

Chapter II — Rights and Duties of the Parties

Article 7

1. (a) The lessor's real rights in the equipment shall be valid against the lessee's trustee in bankruptcy and creditors, including creditors who have obtained an attachment or execution.
   (b) For the purposes of this paragraph "trustee in bankruptcy" includes a liquidator, administrator or other person appointed to administer the lessee's estate for the benefit of the general body of creditors.

2. Where by the applicable law the lessor's real rights in the equipment are valid against a person referred to in the previous paragraph only on compliance with rules as to public notice, those rights shall be valid against that person only if there has been compliance with such rules.
3. For the purposes of the previous paragraph the applicable law is the law of the State which, at the time when a person referred to in paragraph 1 becomes entitled to invoke the rules referred to in the previous paragraph, is:

   (a) in the case of a registered ship, the State in which it is registered in the name of the owner (for the purposes of this sub-paragraph a bareboat charterer is deemed not to be the owner);
   (b) in the case of an aircraft which is registered pursuant to the Convention on International Civil Aviation done at Chicago on 7 December 1944, the State in which it is so registered;
   (c) in the case of other equipment of a kind normally moved from one State to another, including an aircraft engine, the State in which the lessee has its principal place of business;
   (d) in the case of all other equipment, the State in which the equipment is situated.

4. Paragraph 2 shall not affect the provisions of any other treaty under which the lessor's real rights in the equipment are required to be recognised.

5. This article shall not affect the priority of any creditor having:

(a) a consensual or non-consensual lien or security interest in the equipment arising otherwise than by virtue of an attachment or execution, or
(b) any right of arrest, detention or disposition conferred specifically in relation to ships or aircraft under the law applicable by virtue of the rules of private international law.

Article 8

1. (a) Except as otherwise provided by this Convention or stated in the leasing agreement, the lessor shall not incur any liability to the lessee in respect of the equipment save to the extent that the lessee has suffered loss as the result of its reliance on the lessor's skill and judgment and of the lessor's intervention in the selection of the supplier or the specifications of the equipment.
   (b) The lessor shall not in its capacity of lessor, be liable to third parties for death, personal injury or damage to property caused by the equipment.
   (c) The above provisions of this paragraph shall not govern any liability of the lessor in any other capacity, for example as owner.

2. The lessor warrants that the lessee's quiet possession will not be disturbed by a person who has a superior title or right, or who claims a superior title or right and acts under the authority of a court, where such title, right or claim is not derived from an act or omission of the lessee.
3. The parties may not derogate from or vary the effect of the provisions of the previous paragraph in so far as the superior title, right or claim is derived from an intentional or grossly negligent act or omission of the lessor.
4. The provisions of paragraphs 2 and 3 shall not affect any broader warranty of quiet possession by the lessor which is mandatory under the law applicable by virtue of the rules of private international law.

Article 9

1. The lessee shall take proper care of the equipment, use it in a reasonable manner and keep it in the condition in which it was delivered, subject to fair wear and tear and to any modification of the equipment agreed by the parties.
2. When the leasing agreement comes to an end the lessee, unless exercising a right to buy the equipment or to hold the equipment on lease for a futher period, shall return the equipment to the lessor in the condition specified in the previous paragraph.

Article 10

1. The duties of the supplier under the supply agreement shall also be owed to the lessee as if it were a party to that agreement and as if the equipment were to be supplied directly to the lessee. However, the supplier shall not be liable to both the lessor and the lessee in respect of the same damage.
2. Nothing in this article shall entitle the lessee to terminate or rescind the supply agreement without the consent of the lessor.

Article 11

The lessee's rights derived from the supply agreement under this Convention shall not be affected by a variation of any term of the supply agreement previously approved by the lessee unless it consented to that variation.

Article 12

1. Where the equipment is not delivered or is delivered late or fails to conform to the supply agreement:

   (a) the lessee has the right as against the lessor to reject the equipment or to terminate the leasing agreement; and
   (b) the lessor has the right to remedy its failure to tender equipment in conformity with the supply agreement,

as if the lessee had agreed to buy the equipment from the lessor under the same terms as those of the supply agreement.

2. A right conferred by the previous paragraph shall be exercisable in the same manner and shall be lost in the same circumstances as if the lessee had agreed to buy the equipment from the lessor under the same terms as those of the supply agreement.

3. The lessee shall be entitled to withhold rentals payable under the leasing agreement until the lessor has remedied its failure to tender equipment in conformity with the supply agreement or the lessee has lost the right to reject the equipment.

4. Where the lessee has exercised a right to terminate the leasing agreement, the lessee shall be entitled to recover any rentals and other sums paid in advance, less a reasonable sum for any benefit the lessee has derived from the equipment.

5. The lessee shall have no other claim against the lessor for non-delivery, delay in delivery or delivery of non-conforming equipment except to the extent to which this results from the act or omission of the lessor.

6. Nothing in this article shall affect the lessee's rights against the supplier under Article 10.

Article 13

1. In the event of default by the lessee, the lessor may recover accrued unpaid rentals, together with interest and damages.

2. Where the lessee's default is substantial, then subject to paragraph 5 the lessor may also require accelerated payment of the value of the future rentals, where the leasing agreement so provides, or may terminate the leasing agreement and after such termination:

   (a) recover possession of the equipment: and
   (b) recover such damages as will place the lessor in the posiiton in which it would have been had the lessee performed the leasing agreement in accordance with its terms.

3. (a) The leasing agreement may provide for the manner in which the damages recoverable under paragraph 2(b) are to be computed.

(b) Such provision shall be enforceable between the parties unless it would result in damages substantially in excess of those provided for under paragraph 2(b). The parties may not derogate from or vary the effect of the provisions of the present sub-paragraph.

4. Where the lessor has terminated the leasing agreement, it shall not be entitled to enforce a term of that agreement providing for acceleration of payment of future rentals, but the value of such rentals may be taken into account in computing damages under paragraphs 2(b) and 3. The parties may not derogate from or vary the effect of the provisions of the present paragraph.

5. The lessor shall not be entitled to exercise its right of acceleration or its right of termination under paragraph 2 unless it has by notice given the lessee a reasonable opportunity of remedying the default so far as the same may be remedied.

6. The lessor shall not be entitled to recover damages to the extent that it has failed to take all reasonable steps to mitigate its loss.

Article 14

1. The lessor may transfer or otherwise deal with all or any of its rights in the equipment or under the leasing agreement. Such a transfer shall not relieve the lessor of any of its duties under the leasing agreement or alter either the nature of the leasing agreement or its legal treatment as provided in this Convention.

2. The lessee may transfer the right to the use of the equipment or any other rights under the leasing agreement only with the consent of the lessor and subject to the rights of third parties.

[Chapter III — Final Provisions]

Article [F]

A Contracting State may declare at the time of signature, ratification, acceptance, approval or accession that it will substitute its domestic law for Article 8(3) if its domestic law does not permit the lessor to exclude its liability for its default or negligence.

Index

All references are to page number